Rethinking Kerouac

Rethinking Kerouac

Afterlives, Continuities, Reappraisals

Edited by
Erik Mortenson and Tomasz Sawczuk

BLOOMSBURY ACADEMIC
NEW YORK · LONDON · OXFORD · NEW DELHI · SYDNEY

BLOOMSBURY ACADEMIC
Bloomsbury Publishing Inc
1385 Broadway, New York, NY 10018, USA
50 Bedford Square, London, WC1B 3DP, UK
29 Earlsfort Terrace, Dublin 2, Ireland

BLOOMSBURY, BLOOMSBURY ACADEMIC and the Diana logo are
trademarks of Bloomsbury Publishing Plc

First published in the United States of America 2025

Copyright © 2025 Lynn Ellen Patyk and Irina Erman

Each chapter © Contributors

For legal purposes the List of Figures on p. vii and Acknowledgments on p. xi
constitute an extension of this copyright page.

Cover design by Daniel Benneworth-Gray
Cover images: Jack Kerouac, reading his work in New York City, 1958
(exact date unknown) © Phillip Harrington / Alamy

All rights reserved. No part of this publication may be reproduced or transmitted
in any form or by any means, electronic or mechanical, including photocopying,
recording, or any information storage or retrieval system, without prior
permission in writing from the publishers.

Bloomsbury Publishing Inc does not have any control over, or responsibility for,
any third-party websites referred to or in this book. All internet addresses given
in this book were correct at the time of going to press. The author and publisher
regret any inconvenience caused if addresses have changed or sites have ceased
to exist, but can accept no responsibility for any such changes.

Library of Congress Cataloging-in-Publication Data
Names: Mortenson, Erik, 1970- editor. | Tomasz, Sawczuk, 1984- editor.
Title: Rethinking Kerouac: afterlives, continuities, reappraisals / edited
by Erik Mortenson and Tomasz Sawczuk.
Description: New York: Bloomsbury Academic, 2025. | Includes bibliographical references
and index. Identifiers: LCCN 2024023550 (print) | LCCN 2024023551 (ebook) |
ISBN 9798765105269 (paperback) | ISBN 9798765105276 (hardback) |
ISBN 9798765105283 (ebook) | ISBN 9798765105290 (pdf)
Subjects: LCSH: Kerouac, Jack, 1922–1969–Criticism and interpretation. |
Beats (Persons) | Authors, American–20th century.
Classification: LCC PS3521.E735 Z855 2025 (print) | LCC PS3521.E735
(ebook) | DDC 813/.54–dc23/eng/20240709
LC record available at https://lccn.loc.gov/2024023550
LC ebook record available at https://lccn.loc.gov/2024023551

ISBN:		
	HB:	979-8-7651-0527-6
	PB:	979-8-7651-0526-9
	ePDF:	979-8-7651-0529-0
	eBook:	979-8-7651-0528-3

Typeset by Integra Software Services Pvt. Ltd.
Printed and bound in the United States of America

To find out more about our authors and books visit www.bloomsbury.com
and sign up for our newsletters.

Contents

List of Figures   vii
Foreword   *A. Robert Lee*   viii
Acknowledgments   xi

Introduction   *Erik Mortenson and Tomasz Sawczuk*   1

Part One   Rethinking the Writing

1. Reading a Copy of *On the Road*   Matt Theado   17
2. Choruses for Kerouac   Aldon Nielsen   31
3. Jack Kerouac's Paintings: Color, Texture, Movement   Frida Forsgren   43
4. A House of Mirrors at Coney Island: Kerouac's Obscure Experiments in Screenwriting   Brett Sigurdson   61
5. *Lonesome Traveler*, Buddhism, and the Fictions of Kerouac's Non-Fiction   Steven Belletto   73
6. "Radical Vulnerability" in Kerouac's *Big Sur*, *Satori in Paris*, and *Vanity of Duluoz*   Deborah R. Geis   87

Part Two   Kerouac and the Social

7. Anti-homosexual Paranoia, Queer Love, and Cold War Poetics in Jack Kerouac's *Visions of Cody*   Pierre-Antoine Pellerin   99
8. Teaching Kerouac in the Time of Trump: An Orwellian Approach to *The Dharma Bums*   John Whalen-Bridge   113
9. Recovering Jack Kerouac's Blackface Novel *Pic*   Kurt Hemmer   129
10. Jack Kerouac and the Language of Populism   Nancy M. Grace   143
11. Kerouac's Fellahin Poetics: Reimagining Global Culture against Nation and Empire   Hassan Melehy   157

Part Three   Kerouac's Influence and Legacy

12. From Beat Generation to Hacker Generation: The Experimental Road Narratives *On the Road* and *1 the Road*   Peggy Pacini   173

13	Kerouac's Enduring Influence on Anglo-American Popular Music Composers and Performers *Simon Warner*	187
14	Jack Kerouac American Avatar *Ronna C. Johnson*	199
15	The Futures of Kerouac's Past: Public Humanities and the Kerouac Archive at 100 *Michael Millner*	213
16	Kerouac in Translation: A Conversation with Farid Ghadami, Minami Aoyama, and Maciej Świerkocki *Erik Mortenson and Tomasz Sawczuk*	227

Afterword *Tim Hunt*	240
Notes on Contributors	244
Index	249

Figures

1.1	Jack Kerouac, the first completed *On the Road* typescript (April 1951)	20
3.1	Jack Kerouac, *Heart and Handgun*, n.d., oil on paper, 23 × 30.5 cm. Used by permission of Jim Sampas, Literary Executor of the Estate of Jack Kerouac	43
3.2	Jack Kerouac, *Truman Capote*, 1959, oil on canvas, 51 × 40.3 cm. Used by permission of Jim Sampas, Literary Executor of the Estate of Jack Kerouac	45
3.3	Jay DeFeo, *The Eyes*, 1958. © 2023 The Jay DeFeo Trust / BONO, Oslo	46
3.4	Michael McCracken, *Portrait*, undated, oil on canvass, 105 × 107 cm. Kristiansand Katedralskole Gimle	47
3.5	Jack Kerouac, *The Slouch Hat*, 1960s., oil and charcoal on paper, 43 × 35.2 cm. Used by permission of Jim Sampas, Literary Executor of the Estate of Jack Kerouac	48
3.6	Jack Kerouac, *Woman (Joan Rawshanks) in Blue with Black Hat*, n.d., oil on canvas, 40.6 × 30.5 cm. Used by permission of Jim Sampas, Literary Executor of the Estate of Jack Kerouac	50
3.7	Jack Kerouac, *Blonde in the Grass*, n.d., oil on canvas, 30 × 22 cm. Used by permission of Jim Sampas, Literary Executor of the Estate of Jack Kerouac	51
3.8	Jack Kerouac, *The Gary Buddha*, oil, 35.56 × 43.18 cm. Used by permission of Jim Sampas, Literary Executor of the Estate of Jack Kerouac	53
3.9	Michael Bowen, *Dream–Figure Moves Outside Cave*, undatert, Oljeskisse på papir, montert på papp, 107 × 96 cm. Kristiansand Katedralskole Gimle	54

Foreword
A. Robert Lee

Remember Kerouac in *Desolation Angels* (1965)? "To be *and* not to be, that's what we are."[1] It isn't the one or final summary, but it captures something of the life appetite that has gone on winning him attention—for both followers and detractors.

To take on the Kerouac we now inherit, as this collection does with alacrity and breadth, is indeed to rethink the man and the writing. A century on from his birth has it been anything like enough to see him only as Beat figure, easily designated counterculture spirit with Ginsberg, Burroughs, Corso, and Cassady, and in their different weights and measures, Diane di Prima, Michael McClure, Herbert Huncke, John Clellon Holmes, Lawrence Ferlinghetti, Gary Snyder, Joyce Johnson, ruth weiss, and the early LeRoi Jones/Baraka? Is *On the Road* always to preside as his only true banner, the iconic postwar American road text with all else in his output a kind of ambient extra?

Not if you read the essays gathered here.

Rethinking Kerouac does necessary service in contesting any one-dimensional version. Turn to the poetry, *Mexico City Blues* with its Charlie Parker–inspired jazz measure or his haiku and further verse with his capacity for inspirational flow or image.[2] Be sure, in reading *On the Road*, that the text carries Kerouac's own editorial best intent. Look to his artwork, the drawings and paintings that confirm his taste for spontaneity, figurations in paint or ink of a kind with his famous writing mantra of first thought, best thought. Give due heed to his Buddhism, the complex spiritual thread to be met not only in the fiction but a meditative composition like *The Scripture of the Golden Eternity*.[3] There is, too, the Kerouac who once dubbed himself a running Proust and which he saw himself reflecting in the "true life" narratives that make up the Duluoz legend—most expressly *Vanity of Duluoz* (1968)—each with its interaction of self-venture and vulnerability.[4]

In the emergence of the cultural and gender politics of LGBTQ+ where, exactly, do we situate Kerouac, the bromance with Cassady, his own sexual self-queries, the novels from *The Subterraneans* (1958) with its zen inflections and cross-racial love affair across to *The Dharma Bums* (1958) and *Visions of Cody* (1972)?[5] In the transition from the white consensual Eisenhower 1950s into the Civil Rights and Black Power era of the 1960s, how best to read Kerouac and race, especially a text like *Pic* (1971)?[6] If Kerouac, at best, holds sway through his propulsive dynamics of style, then should we not especially alight on his ear for vernacular American pitch or rhythm? These dimensions again open into a writer well beyond Beat-only holograph, the single flourish.

The Kerouac legacy, in these respects, has been notably wide, at times near global whether Anglophone, European, or beyond into Pacific reaches and Asia. He himself drew eclectically on other writers—Melville and Thomas Wolfe from American literary tradition; James Joyce, Rimbaud, and Tolstoy along with T.S. Eliot, Indian sutra, and Japanese haiku; and of prime importance the French and French Canadian writing for which his bilingual Massachusetts childhood of English and *joual* uniquely prepared him. That he had also interest in Nietzsche and reworking the concept of the *fellahin* in relation to his own literary generation's pathfinders should not surprise.

Latterly the footfalls have taken yet other points of direction. How do we rate the qualities of experimentalism in his work, voice, measure, pattern, down a timeline that has now fully entered the age of internet with its apps and hacking? Whether *Mexico City Blues*, or his famous piano and text reading with Steve Allen for *The Tonight Show* in 1959, or the plethora of jazz allusions and echoes in his fiction, or friendship and performances with David Amram, Kerouac belongs in the collective history of American music as he does in its fiction. Here, too, he has assumed his role as avatar, literary bluesman, Canada-shirted roadster, ardent jazznik, and for all his vaunted shyness, toper, and on occasion rowdie.

There remains a vast and still to be fully extracted archive, that held by the Kerouac estate and in the New York Public Library and elsewhere. Much has been done as to the drafts of the novels, his letters, his multifarious notebooks, but there remains yet more. Equally there is Kerouac in translation, be it into Farsi, Polish, Japanese among different languages, or from his own endeavors into English from the Québec-colloquial French of his parents and upbringing.

The full attentive map, in kind with that of any consequential writer, has yet to be completed. Maybe it cannot. But a centennial essay-collection like that gathered here supplies guiding and greatly enlightening latitudes and longitudes. These essays are written from both within and beyond the penumbra that has gathered around Kerouac.

It was Ginsberg who spoke early of Kerouac's "beat genius," Corso of "a Beat Christ-boy," Joyce Johnson of "a Zen pilgrim in Salvation Army clothes."[7] The accounts available in *Rethinking Kerouac: Afterlives, Continuities, Reappraisals*, even so, tread well beyond mere encomium. To borrow from Kerouac's own enduring image they reach for new roadways, an ongoing traffic of exploration for a writer inextricable from America's modern literary fashioning.

Notes

1   Jack Kerouac, *Desolation Angels* (1965) (New York: Penguin Classics, 2012), 5.
2   Jack Kerouac, *Mexico City Blues* (New York: Grove Press, 1959).
3   Jack Kerouac, *The Scripture of the Golden Eternity* (Chevy Chase: Totem Press/Corinth, 1960).
4   Jack Kerouac, *Vanity of Duluoz: An Adventurous Education, 1935–1946* (New York: Coward-McCann, 1968).
5   Jack Kerouac, *The Subterraneans* (New York: Grove Press, 1958); *The Dharma Bums* (New York: Viking, 1958); and *Visions of Cody* (New York: McGraw-Hill, 1972).
6   Jack Kerouac, *Pic* (New York: Grove Press, 1971).

7   Allen Ginsberg, "Dream Record: June 8, 1953," in *Reality Sandwiches, 1953–60* (San Francisco: City Lights Books, 1963); Gregory Corso, "Elegaic Feelings American," in *Elegaic Feelings American* (New York: New Directions, 1970); Joyce Johnson, *Minor Characters: A Young Woman's Coming of Age in the Beat Orbit of Jack Kerouac* (1983) (New York: Penguin Books, 1999).

Acknowledgments

The editors' deepest gratitude goes out to a number of people for their ongoing encouragement throughout the process of bringing this book to life.

Foremost are two great editors from Bloomsbury—Amy Martin, acquisitions editor, who put her trust in the project and was generous with assistance all along the way, and Hali Han, assistant editor, who was always ready with advice whenever it was needed. With her unflagging support and understanding, Amy made the process of publishing with Bloomsbury a pleasure. The entire editorial staff at Bloomsbury was a delight to work with and we would like to thank them here.

We would also like to thank Jim Sampas, literary executor of the Kerouac Estate, for his willingness to support the book as well as Hassan Melehy for his aid. Steven Belletto offered valuable advice and always made time to chat.

Erik Mortenson would like to thank his wife Lia McCoskey who has always been there for him, as well as his daughter Zelda for the love and meaning she brings to his life.

Finally, Tomasz Sawczuk is forever thankful to his wife, Monika, his daughter, Oliwka, his parents, and brother, Piotr, whose continued faith and support mean a world to him.

Introduction

Erik Mortenson and Tomasz Sawczuk

Jack Kerouac is a difficult writer to pin down. To borrow a word from his beloved influence Herman Melville, Kerouac is protean, offering readers a variety of positions and personas to choose from. Depending on inclination, he is the famous jazz-loving hipster of *On the Road* fame, the Zen Buddhist lunatic scrambling up the mountainside, the poet, the spontaneous bop prosodist, the flaunter of convention, or the arch conservative later in life. He was a womanizer, but also maybe gay, or perhaps bisexual. Kerouac is the all-American football-playing boy, but at the same time the son of French-Canadian immigrants who spoke nothing but a dialect of French until he was six years old. His various opinions on race, gender, sex, and class may or may not be a problem, depending on the audience and the moment. As anyone who has seen or heard his interviews knows, Kerouac could also be purposefully contrarian, disavowing or amending previous viewpoints. Best not to speak of Kerouac, then, but of *Kerouacs*. The plural is important. The truth, of course, is simply that he is all these things, but at the same time, much more than the sum of these myriad parts.

This collection of essays by esteemed Beat commentators provides a long-overdue re-evaluation of one of the twentieth century's most emblematic but often misunderstood American writers. Despite amassing a substantial body of influential work and becoming a recognizable figure globally, Kerouac has often suffered critical neglect and misunderstanding, and this volume seeks to offer a range of fresh perspectives on Kerouac's unique literary output, his vexed relation to social issues, as well as his continuing cultural afterlife, thus providing an indispensable account of the relevance of both Kerouac the writer and Kerouac the cultural icon. *Rethinking Kerouac* is as eclectic as its subject. Through an examination of classic works like *On the Road* to more obscure ones like *Pic*, from early pieces to later less-discussed novels, these essays excavate new facets of Kerouac's writerly investments. They also recalibrate our understanding of Kerouac by placing his work in dialogue with current cultural issues and theoretical angles, providing a re-evaluation of how important issues such as race, gender relations, populist rhetoric, and queerness inform his work and its contemporary reception. Given Kerouac's continued visibility in both the United States and abroad, these essays also examine how the peculiarities of global circulation and social media influence the ongoing cultural appropriation of Kerouac in popular music, film, and literature. A century after his birth, Kerouac remains an important figure, and this volume hopes to understand not only the reasons for his success but the possibilities for his work going forward.

A Problematic Reception

Delving into Kerouac's life and work reveals a world of paradox and contradiction. Take, for example, the writing itself. Kerouac's early work and first novel, *The Town and the City* (1950), are written in a more straightforward style. Kerouac would go on to abandon this approach in favor of his now-famous spontaneous prose, which the author envisioned as his unique contribution to not just American but indeed World Letters. The ambition of this young novelist was breathtaking. In a December 1950 letter to his friend Neal Cassady, where he compares his work to Melville, young Tolstoy, and Faulkner, Kerouac complains to his soulmate that *The Town and the City* was missing from the end-of-the-year book lists.[1] In another letter Kerouac compared the manuscript of what is now known as *Visions of Cody* (then titled *On the Road*) with James Joyce's *Ulysses* (1922) and demanded that it "should be treated with the same gravity."[2] Kerouac clearly saw himself entering the pantheon of the "great" writers of history.

But at the same time Kerouac wanted to be famous, at least early in his career. While the young writer came of age during the golden years of radio, by the time Kerouac started publishing, mass media as we know it today was on the rise. Television was reaching into more and more homes, and magazines like *Life* and *Time* garnered nationwide circulation. The idea of a writer becoming a household name was a distinct possibility. The pursuit of this seemingly impossible task of earning mass audiences' attention while being recognized by critics for remarkable literary accomplishments is captured in Kerouac's December 1952 correspondence to Stella Sampas. In part an outcry against the sneers of the New York literary establishment, the letter voices the writer's twofold ambition for the years following the completion of *On the Road* and *Doctor Sax*: "But what they don't know is that I am going to be famous, and the greatest writer of my generation, like Dostoevsky."[3] Kerouac's desired nothing less than to bridge the gap between "highbrow" and popular audiences. Kerouac, in sum, wanted it all.

Another irony is that Kerouac achieved one but not the other, at least initially. *On the Road* brought Kerouac instant celebrity, if not critical recognition. Kerouac believed that his spontaneous method had the ability to reach everyone, since, as he explains it in his "Essentials of Spontaneous Prose," everyone has the "same laws operating in his own human mind."[4] But not everyone reacted to his work in the same manner. *On the Road* was a best seller but, for the most part, was lambasted by critics. While some like Gilbert Millstein saw Kerouac as a stylistic innovator whose now-famous spontaneous prose method captures the exuberance of life lived in the moment, for most contemporary reviewers he represented an undisciplined author whose work was not only unformed and inchoate, but an affront to mainstream American values.

David Dempsey's review of *On the Road* in the *New York Times* disapproved of the Beats, calling them a "sideshow [of] freaks" and expressed serious concerns about the abundance of crimes and misdemeanors presented to the reader.[5] In a similar vein, Herbert Gold's review of the book in *The Nation* elaborated the idea that *On the Road* was "proof of an illness rather than creation of art, a novel."[6] While he initially relished the fame, money, and the women that his celebrity garnered, he was vexed that the literary establishment did not immediately recognize his contributions.

Kerouac's novel was often read into a sociological register rather than a literary one. Even supporters like Norman Mailer in "The White Negro" and John Clellon Holmes in "The Philosophy of the Beat Generation," while acknowledging his literary accomplishments, were enamored with his portrayal of a new set of social values founded on an image of a Beat hipster outlaw in unresolvable conflict with the white, middle-class world. Kerouac himself entered this fray, appearing on numerous television programs and publishing pieces like "Origins of the Beat Generation" in magazines like *Playboy* in an attempt to set the record straight. In the end, the idea of Kerouac as promoter of social rebellion, sexual licentiousness, and drug experimentation won out over Kerouac the innovative literary stylist. Although Kerouac attempted to countermand these images in public discourse and would continue to explore his fame in his own writings (perhaps most notably in *Big Sur*), by the time of his death, he had clearly lost the battle to control his image.

This schism between the writing and the lifestyle still reverberates today. Kerouac continues to enjoy a popular reception that is often at odds with the scholarly attempt to validate his work within the academy. Fans of the author, many of whom arrive at Kerouac through musical tribute, film versions of his novels, or social media, celebrate not just his style but his social rebellion and the challenge his work poses to received customs, norms, and institutions. For many of these enthusiasts, academic attention undermines the marginal, "Beat" aspects of Kerouac. The result is often as ridiculous as it is paradoxical: Beat scholars and Beat enthusiasts both reacting positively to the work but nevertheless arguing vehemently over the reasons why.

Kerouac Studies often responds by "doubling down" on Kerouac's writing in a bid to earn institutional validation for his work. Once the phenomenon of Beat social rebellion began to subside, attention turned toward the work itself. The academic field can be said to have begun with Ann Charters's *Kerouac: A Biography* (1973) which was followed by Gerald Nicosia's biography *Memory Babe* (1983). Ground breaking studies such as Tim Hunt's *Kerouac's Crooked Road: Development of a Fiction* (1981) and *The Textuality of Soulwork: Jack Kerouac's Quest for Spontaneous Prose* (2014), as well as Regina Weinreich's *Kerouac's Spontaneous Poetics: A Study of the Fiction* (1987) sought to emphasize the innovative nature of Kerouac's prose in part as a counterbalance to earlier notions of Kerouac as a social phenomenon. A steady stream of scholarship has followed, too numerous to name in its entirety. Some studies like Matt Theado's *Understanding Jack Kerouac* (2000) or Nancy Grace's *Jack Kerouac and the Literary Imagination* (2007) seek to provide the wider context and framework necessary to fully appreciating his oeuvre. Others like James T. Jones's Kerouac's *Duluoz Legend: The Mythic Form of an Autobiographical Fiction* (1999) or Tomasz Sawczuk's *On the*

Road to Lost Fathers: Jack Kerouac in a Lacanian Perspective (2019) use a particular lens for understanding Kerouac's life and work. And studies like John Tytell's early *Naked Angels: The Lives and Literature of the Beat Generation* (1976), Erik Mortenson's *Capturing the Beat Moment: Cultural Politics and the Poetics of Presence* (2010), and Steven Belletto's *The Beats: A Literary History* (2020) track Kerouac's relationship to other Beat writers to make larger points. The recent centenary of Kerouac's birth in 2022 signaled a renewed interest in his work and led to important conferences such as the Beat Studies Association's "Jack Kerouac Centenary Conference" and City Lights's "Still Outside: Kerouac@100," further solidifying Kerouac's status. Belletto's recent *The Cambridge Companion to Jack Kerouac* (2024) demonstrates the acceptance of Kerouac as a legitimate object of scholarly inquiry.

Yet Kerouac remains polarizing within the academy. Many critics outside Beat Studies still dismiss his work as rudimentary and thus unworthy of critical study. Others simply consign it to a postwar cultural moment. But by far the strongest critique comes from those who see Kerouac as an anachronistic relic of an era best forgotten. In an age of trigger warnings and cancel culture, detractors point to his work as evidence of misogyny and naïve racism, and not unjustly. Kerouac's vision can well be perceived as hindered by the trappings of his white heterosexual male privilege.[7] This has undoubtedly taken its toll in the popular and critical reception of the writer's output. Alongside idealizing his past, Kerouac romanticized and reinforced misrepresentations of the non-white racial and ethnic "other," which, at best, has been translated as "romantic naïveté"[8] and, at worst, has earned him a reputation of a "bohemian racist."[9] A classic example occurs in *On the Road*, when the narrator laments, "I wished I were a Denver Mexican, or even a poor overworked Jap, anything but what I was so drearily, a 'white man' disillusioned."[10] Critics have struggled with such passages, with some, like Amor Kohli in his contribution to *The Cambridge Companion to Jack Kerouac* and Manuel Luis Martinez in *Countering the Counterculture: Rereading Postwar American Dissent from Jack Kerouac to Tomás Rivera* (2003) taking Kerouac to task for such depictions while others, like Hassan Melehy in his important work *Kerouac: Language, Poetics, and Territory* (2016), arguing that as a French-Canadian, Kerouac's sense of his own whiteness was conflicted. What should we make of a writer who celebrates non-white life, but for the wrong reasons? This important question has been at the heart of criticism of Kerouac from his initial emergence and is explored in several chapters of this work.

No less problematic is his objectification of female characters. Pointing to the demeaning depictions of women, Elle Hunt observes in a recent *Guardian* piece that "sixty-five years since publication, the misogyny of *On the Road* looks overt, even gleeful."[11] Is Kerouac just another "dead white male" to be replaced in the university curricula by authors who have taken much greater strides in portraying women, people of color, and non-Westerners in a more sensitive and nuanced manner? Holly George-Warren asks the question "Can a Feminist Still Love Jack Kerouac?," summoning a roster of female scholars, writers, and performers to establish a much-needed dialogue between this major Beat writer and current feminist readers.[12] There is a general consensus among George-Warren's interviewees that their adolescent and young adult selves were enamored with and formed by the emancipatory and frenetic charge of Kerouac's works, which in time gave way to the awareness that the typically hypermasculine characters that populate Kerouac's fictions have dire implications for underprivileged groups. There is, of course, no correct answer to the question of how to deal with Kerouac's problems. Every reader must decide for themselves what to do (if anything) with these problematic moments in Kerouac's work. This is no easy task, even for supporters; both the editors of this volume are fathers of young daughters who wonder how best to introduce their beloved author, if at all.

Yet even with Kerouac's obvious misogyny and romanticized depictions of race, complications emerge to make things less than clear. Kerouac, along with other Beats like his friend Allen Ginsberg, was part of a larger mid-century trend of confessional writing. How should we handle a writer who expresses all facets of his thinking, even the less-than-pleasant ones? Is it better to simply keep quiet when you know that a feeling might be negatively received, or is it better to bring troubling thoughts into the light of day for analysis and perhaps even extirpation? The derogatory overtones of Kerouac's writing have been redeemed by some critics, if only partially, by the writer's sincerity and his very own awareness of his flawed and biased views on gender and race. According to Beat scholar Fiona Paton, Kerouac "lays out all of his own prejudices against women and people of color," but, significantly, "he confesses them and says, 'Yeah, I'm an asshole,'" which Paton finds "a redemptive quality in Kerouac."[13] Kerouac is a writer who forces his readers to take a position.

Despite these valid concerns, Kerouac's popularity endures. After the initial sensation of *On the Road*, Kerouac continued to publish, with his work becoming a touchstone for a number of subsequent artists, most notably Bob Dylan. Documentaries like *Kerouac, The Movie* (1984) and *What Happened to Kerouac?* (1985) appeared in the 1980s, along with other representations in various media. By the 1990s, Kerouac and the Beats were again "discovered" by artists and influential outlets like MTV, and Kerouac's posthumous appearance (along with Ginsberg and William S. Burroughs) in a 1994 Gap Khaki ad caused renewed controversy. This media presence continues into our century. A recent spate of films like *On the Road* (2012) and *Big Sur* (2013; among others that deal with the Beats more broadly) has kept Kerouac in the public eye. Kerouac's official Facebook, Instagram, X (formerly Twitter), and YouTube accounts enjoy a strong online following with, respectively, half million, thirty-one thousand, two and a half thousand, and almost eight hundred followers so far. Alongside these authorized channels are a dozen of unofficial fan pages, fan groups, profiles, and podcasts, all of which foster interaction between fans and, at the same time, further disseminate memes and other representations. While Kerouac struggled with his media image early on (then grew frustrated with his neglect), his subsequent media presence has remained. Given Kerouac's media penetration, it remains likely that his image and his work will be in circulation for some time to come, even if he and his fellow Beats must compete with an ever-widening array of images and icons in our digital age.

The Future of Kerouac

Kerouac's legacy continues, in large part because the paradoxes and complexities of his life and work push thinking in new and exciting directions. Take, for example, Kerouac's penchant for travel and his love of the vagabond tradition of the American hobo. We tend to see the author as peripatetic, a self-proclaimed member of the "rucksack revolution" that he helped to propagate. But another seeming incongruity of Kerouac's life is that he was very much a homebody as well. Not only did he enjoy spending time at home recuperating and recovering from his travels (and from his drinking), but he needed this domestic space to store the extensive archives he amassed. This desire for documentary stability is an interesting counterpoint to a writer generally celebrated for his love of spontaneous action in the ever-unfolding present. Kerouac's archival investments speak to another Kerouac worthy of investigation. Given the recent "turn" toward examining the concept of the archive inaugurated by Jacques Derrida's influential *Archive Fever: A Freudian Impression* (1995), Kerouac provides another "take" on Derrida's concept, explored by scholars who examine how the idea of archive helps us to better understand the "Great Rememberer," as Kerouac was often called.

Other seeming disparities in Kerouac's corpus offer opportunities to rethink not just his life and work, but important concepts with implications for us all. Another common conception of Kerouac is that of the all-American writer. With his celebration of life in cities and towns across the United States as well as the rugged landscapes separating them, Kerouac himself was instrumental in fashioning this conceit. But as the recent work in Kerouac Studies by scholars like Melehy and Jean-Christophe Cloutier demonstrates, Kerouac was very much influenced by his French-Canadian roots. Not only that, but Kerouac was thinking (and acting) globally in much of his work: Kerouac was himself an international traveler, and on the instigation of his friends Sebastian Sampas and William Burroughs, was very much influenced by the theories of Oswald Spengler. Kerouac's novel *Doctor Sax* is subtitled "Faust Part Three," a nod to the German writer whose popularization of world culture is still an important touchstone for debates in Comparative Literature. The recent interest in transnational theories helps us to better understand Kerouac. But Kerouac, in turn, provides interesting material for thinking through what it means to negotiate multiple cultures, a trend in the scholarship extremely relevant to our globalized world.[14]

Another productive irony of Kerouac's corpus is that it has proven highly amenable to the digital. Kerouac is often envisioned as the champion of authenticity. His work seeks to "capture" the moment in a bid to save it from the ravages of time. This notion of the present as a poignantly fleeting experience of time drives many Beat writers to view their work in what Ginsberg calls a "sacramental" sense. But that has not stopped artists in various media from employing an author known for spontaneity in projects that question the supposed authenticity of life in the present. The tension between the authentic and the digital has been well thematized by Erin Zwaska, a designer and a book artist, who in 2012 conceptualized and published *On the Open Road*, a reinterpretation which restricts Kerouac's novel to a compilation of book passages amassed by tracking the fragments with the greatest mass appeal among Kindle users.[15] And Ross Goodwin's *1 the Road* (2018), a work discussed extensively in this volume, seeks to recreate Kerouac's road trip with a camera and computer as recording devices rather than a human being. Putting Kerouac's work into dialogue with the digital reveals interesting possibilities that beg for further exploration.[16] On the one hand, being an author who embraced the intersubjective spontaneity of the jazz club, Kerouac may very well have embraced the participatory creative practices seen on dedicated digital platforms. Likewise, the transmedial and transcultural character of Beat artistic endeavors, which posed challenges to the then-prevailing understanding of temporality and spatiality, finds its continuity in the group effort of committed online collectives, whose global character alters the meaning of space, time, and distance and whose many-to-many model of interaction remains very much in the democratic spirit of Beat sociality. Yet, on the other hand, we can ask whether Kerouac's notion of intersubjective collectivity, based as it is on embodied presence, the "being there" with others, is in consonance with a digital world that has tended to distance us from each other. Reinterpreting Kerouac's work helps us to ask such relevant questions.

Kerouac's recent centennial witnessed numerous attempts to find a key to his legacy in order to pin down this complicated and multifaceted writer. In the end, however, it seems impossible to reduce Kerouac to just one manifestation.[17] Ultimately, it is up to each reader to choose their Kerouac. Douglas Kennedy speculates on the relevance of Kerouac and his work against the backdrop of our current sociopolitical moment:

> Generation Z is dealing with a world in which the majority of all major cities are unaffordable to those not working in finance or tech; where hipsterism is now signaled by wearing edgy spectacles and sipping a flat white while Zoom-conferencing on a MacBook. As such, some 65 years on from its initial publication, *On the Road* has almost become a remembrance of things past, a throwback to more fluid times.[18]

Is Kerouac a mid-century anachronism? Or might his writing still have something to teach us a half-century after his death? The relevancy of Kerouac resides in the fact that we keep asking those very questions. That critics keep returning to his work and view it through so many registers demonstrates the range, malleability, and persistence of thinking Kerouac's work fosters. The tensions and paradoxes of his life and work, rather than being a problem for Kerouac scholarship, should be seen as an opportunity to question and explore. Understanding which Kerouac we choose and why we choose it is really, in the end, about self-understanding. Kerouac functions as a cipher, and the ways we read him not only reveal our assumptions and beliefs but allow us to redirect our thinking in useful ways.

Kerouac's work has not only stayed in print but has indeed flourished. New work keeps coming out, to critical and popular success. His name and face are instantly recognizable to many, thanks to his presence on social media and the silver screen alike. Artists in various media attest to his influence and the number of places where his name pops up is surprising. But despite this market penetration, Kerouac and his work are still the subject of debate. What do we make of these disparate and at times contradictory responses to Kerouac and his work? The goal is not to redeem Kerouac, defending him like a lawyer against the charges leveled against him. He is indeed a controversial figure and will likely remain one. But the debates that swirl around him afford an opportunity to question not only his place in the literary canon but the role(s) he might have to play in United States and even global culture going forward. Kerouac's ability to evoke heated response is an asset to his legacy, forcing readers to make sense of an author incapable and unwilling to fit into neat boxes and tidy categories. The study of Kerouac will always be the study of an author who raises more questions than he answers. This volume seeks to present Kerouac in all his complexity so readers can make up their own mind as to what to make of the writer, his work, and his legacy going forward.

Rethinking Kerouac is divided into three sections. Section One delves into Kerouac's writing. Attention has generally fixated on Kerouac's development of "spontaneous prose," outlining how the author came up with the method and tracking its progression across his texts. While the important consideration of Kerouac's signature style is indeed addressed in several of the essays, the focus in these essays is considerably wider. Matt Theado begins the volume by examining Kerouac's most famous and influential work, *On the Road*. Every reader of Kerouac probably knows Kerouac's masterpiece, but as Theado argues, the actual book the title references is not as stable as we might think. Tracking the various writerly and editorial processes that *On the Road* underwent reveals that there is not really a final, definitive version of the novel. Rather, there are numerous *On the Road*s, just as there are numerous Kerouacs. Theado's work not only provides a revealing look at the production process "behind" Kerouac's novel; it also calls into question the supposed stability of *any* literary production. While the book we hold in our hands might seem the final word of the author, Theado usefully reminds us that things are never so simple.

Aldon Nielsen continues this reevaluation with a discussion of Kerouac's poetry. While Kerouac himself wanted to erase generic distinctions, his extensive poetic output has generally received less attention than his prose despite the Library of America's *Collected Poems* (2012), which runs to over 700 pages. With verve, humor, and much musical knowledge, Nielsen ranges across Kerouac's poetic output offering insight into Kerouac's method and intentions along the way. Nielsen finds an incessant desire in Kerouac's poetry to continue, to keep going, to add "alluvials" as Kerouac himself states so that while forms may mutate they nevertheless never end. Kerouac, in this reading, is seeking salvation, and if the line ever does end, it ends in heaven. Nielsen reads this jazz-inspired aesthetic into a necessarily racial register. Like many modernists before him, Nielsen argues that Kerouac's poetry is seeking something in (black) jazz that is absent in (white) culture. Nielsen's piece traces that arc productively in a lyrical essay that implicitly argues that this never-ending desire to find a meaning in the American jazz tradition is a fraught but, for that very reason, necessary endeavor whose accomplishments must inevitably give way to periodic failures.

The next chapter continues the "Reappraisal" in this book's title. Frida Forsgren, an expert on mid-century American visual culture, takes a look at Kerouac's painting in order to reveal its importance for understanding Kerouac's poetic practice. Few readers realize that Kerouac was quite fond of drawing and painting, and while primarily a writer, he nevertheless produced enough visual work to warrant two volumes of his artistic output: *Kerouac: Beat Painting* (2018) and *Departed Angels: The Lost Paintings* (2004). Forsgren helps us to understand not just Kerouac's artistic practice, but how this practice sheds light on his writing strategies. Just as his keystrokes are informed by a bodily connection to the spoken word, his brushstrokes seek to capture an embodied moment of space and time. Forsgren usefully reminds us that Kerouac's painting and writing did not occur in a vacuum. Kerouac was very much conversant with and influenced by the abstract expressionist artists he mingled with in New York and to a lesser extent San Francisco. Thus, his aesthetic practice, both written and visual, was informed by a larger cultural context which is crucial to fully appreciating what he was attempting to accomplish in mid-twentieth-century American arts.

Just as Forsgren examines Kerouac's painting to better understand his approach to his artistic practices, Brett Sigurdson looks at another under-discussed genre that Kerouac explored—the art of screenwriting. Kerouac was an avid film lover throughout his life, so it is perhaps no surprise that he turned his attention to writing film scripts and treatments, including ones that deal with his own novels. Though none of these saw publication or production, Sigurdson argues that Kerouac's attempts to write for the silver screen reveal a fascinating binary in Kerouac's corpus. Sigurdson draws on a trove of archived materials to effectively demonstrate that Kerouac oscillated between a desire to explore his own avant-garde interests and a wish to achieve commercial success by playing to conventions meant to satisfy audience expectations. While Kerouac was unsuccessful in his attempts to reconcile these two tendencies, his unpublished film works nevertheless pushed his writing in interesting new directions and deserve further inquiry not just for their own sake, but for what they might have to tell us about Kerouac's relationship to both film specifically and the visual image more broadly.

If Kerouac's poetry has received short shrift, his non-fiction prose is even more neglected. Steven Belletto's piece remedies that lack. Focusing mainly on the less-discussed collection *Lonesome Traveler*, Belletto examines how Kerouac's interest in Buddhism informs his thinking on genre. Kerouac was drawn to the Buddhist concept of the world as illusion. If the world is really non-existent, a fabrication of our own minds, then distinctions between fiction and non-fiction are equally spurious—an insight that has vast ramifications for how we understand Kerouac's "Duluoz Legend." Belletto draws on an insightful series of readings of Kerouac's Buddhist work to effectively demonstrate how the author's concept of "vision" helps us to understand Kerouac's rejection of generic difference. He then proceeds to compare similar passages that appear in multiple versions of Kerouac's texts, and looks at how the author reworked an earlier non-fiction essay for its eventual publication in *Lonesome Traveler*. The result is not only a revealing look into Kerouac's writerly process, but likewise a meditation on Kerouac's idea that everything is a "dream," including genre distinctions.

A large part of what makes Kerouac's work so compelling to readers, as well as so problematic at times, is his desire to confess his innermost thoughts and feelings.

This section ends with Deborah Geis's exploration of this desire to bare own's soul to the reader. Geis argues that Kerouac, along with other Beats like Ginsberg, is usually discussed through the concept of the "confession." However, the notion of confession is usually accompanied by the idea of guilt and absolution—one confesses so that they may "get something off their chest" and be forgiven their sins. Geis argues, however, that Beats like Kerouac are not writing to be absolved. Rather, they are striving to write their full selves onto the page without fear of "failure or criticism." In contrast to the confessional mode, Geis instead offers Gayatri Spivak's concept of "radical vulnerability" as a means of understanding Kerouac's attempts to explain himself to the reader. This premise allows us to rethink Kerouac's writing as a co-mingling with the feelings and thoughts of the Other, rather than an admonition of guilt. Whether this display of vulnerability is enough to redeem moments of racism and misogyny in Kerouac's work is up to readers to decide, but Geis's work offers a compelling new way of making sense of Kerouac's attempts to bridge the gap between himself and his readers.

Section Two continues this reappraisal, focusing on the vexed social issues of race, gender, class, and sexuality that continue to haunt our understanding of Kerouac's corpus. To claim that Kerouac's work is "problematic" is a gross understatement. Kerouac's treatment of gender is notoriously misogynistic at times, and even his positive celebration of African American life is troubling in its naivete. Kerouac managed to move from an interest in class struggle in his early years to an uncomfortable support of the Vietnam War later in life. His treatment of sexuality is equally fluid and mercurial. Given these excesses, Kerouac and his work have rightly come under attack, especially in today's world of trigger warnings and cancel culture. But matters are never so simple. Through careful re-readings of Kerouac's life as well as his works, the authors in this section take on these issues, providing a thoughtful rethinking of Kerouac's relationship to difficult social issues and how we might address his work in today's cultural and political climate.

The section begins with Pierre-Antoine Pellerin's discussion of the importance of sexuality in Kerouac. Looking specifically at a text Kerouac considered his masterpiece, *Visions of Cody*, Pellerin deftly reveals how male-to-male desire is inscribed in the text. Embedding Kerouac's experimental novel within a Cold War political and cultural framework, Pellerin argues that the novel unwittingly discloses the gender anxiety and agency panic that informed Cold War poetics. His reading reveals a peculiar dynamics of eroticism in Kerouac, describing writing that shifts between heterosexual desire to a homoerotic desire that is further abandoned by the narrator when the stable gender identity of the "archetypical" American male is threatened. Pellerin's historically nuanced account is crucial for understanding the complicated sexual dynamics at play in Kerouac's work.

Kerouac has enjoyed a strong media presence from the publication of *On the Road* to the present day. But his legacy is bolstered through other channels as well. While Kerouac never himself taught in the classroom, his works continue to appear there. Beat Studies is only now beginning to explore this important aspect of their legacy. Nancy Grace's *The Beats: A Teaching Companion* (2021) and more recently Erik Mortenson and Tony Trigilio's *The Beats and the Academy: A Renegotiation* (2023) both seek to train a scholarly eye on how Beat writers like Kerouac "work" in the classroom setting. John Whalen-Bridge's chapter examines his approach to teaching Kerouac's *The Dharma Bums* at the National University of Singapore. Using George Orwell's essay "Why I Write" as a lens, Whalen-Bridge argues for the need to separate the historical accuracy of Kerouac's text from its rhetorical strategies. Much of Kerouac's work is based on life experience, but that does not mean that the entire novel should be read as autobiography. On the contrary, Whalen-Bridge stresses the difference between the two to develop a syntax for students to usefully differentiate biography, historical context, stylistic approach, and political orientation. The result is not only useful for students, but for anyone reading Kerouac, as there is always the danger of reducing his texts to a single category that misses out on the fecund multiplicities that Kerouac's work offers—a concern even more salient given today's highly polarized world.

From issues of sexuality we turn to another vexed social issue in Kerouac's work, that of race. Kurt Hemmer explores Kerouac's naïve primitivism and understanding of Black life through a reading of the much-neglected last novel *Pic*. Through a series of insightful readings of both the novel itself and African-American writers' responses to it, Hemmer demonstrates how Kerouac's often problematic depictions of race are, at the same time, a struggle to understand his own whiteness and his relationship to his French-Canadian upbringing. The result is a useful essay that does a good job of not simply absolving Kerouac for his racial difficulties, but one that nuances them through a productive discussion of how racial issues get refracted and reframed through Kerouac's particular personal history and social investments.

Kerouac's vexed political commitments likewise provide a productive site for thinking through the new social landscape inaugurated by Donald Trump. While Kerouac's relation to race, gender, and sexuality has been extensively debated, less discussed are his thoughts on class. Nancy Grace remedies this lack in her piece. Drawing a distinction between an "inclusive" and "exclusive" populism, Grace argues that Kerouac is an example of the former. In comparison with his father Leo (an example of the latter), Kerouac's populism seeks to build something like a coalition between the downtrodden and oppressed in order to envision a freer, more open America. Through an appeal to Kerouac's less-discussed works, Grace does a fine job tracking Kerouac's difficult feat of attempting to reconcile these two populist tendencies in a way that helps to explain his often-tortured political commitments. This essay concludes that while Kerouac never really "solves" his struggles and in the end was more interested in artistic freedom than social amelioration, nevertheless the way Kerouac deals (or fails to deal) with class issues has vast implications for how we understand our own era of Trumpian populism.

This section ends with a discussion of another difficult concept in Kerouac's work—his celebration of the non-US "fellaheen" culture that he found in Mexico and other parts of the world. While often seen as the embodiment of the "American" writer, Melehy cogently argues for a more global Kerouac. While Melehy acknowledges a primitivist strain in Kerouac's depiction of non-European Others, ultimately Kerouac's stereotypes are only the starting point, giving way to "greater cultural realities" worthy of investigation. Through insightful readings of not just Kerouac but the influential

Spengler and Goethe, Melehy sees Kerouac's conception of the "fellaheen" as not simply a negation of Western culture but as a positive force for critiquing Western rational imperialism, including an assault on the natural world that has come into sharper focus with climate change and the ecological problems it has wrought.

Kerouac might have passed over fifty years ago, but his writing and the legend that surrounds it continue to live on into today. Section Three examines the afterlife of Kerouac and his prodigious output. Given Kerouac's influence over the years, it is surprising how little academic work has focused on this cultural legacy. Perhaps in a bid to secure his place in the pantheon of American letters, critics have tended to focus on Kerouac's writing over his iconic image. But Kerouac's influence can be felt in a myriad of places. Peggy Pacini begins with a discussion of Ross Goodwin's *1 the Road*, an AI-generated text produced by an assemblage of camera, GPS, microphone, and clock all mounted to a car in order to record the vehicle's experience rather than that of its human passengers. The result is a chronicle of a road trip that throws Kerouac's *On the Road* into sharp relief. Goodwin's work raises important questions, not the least of which deal with issues of how technology, speed, and today's important buzzword, Artificial Intelligence, help us to rethink the road trip genre that Kerouac himself helped popularize almost a century ago.

Kerouac's work has had an influence on a number of literary artists since its inception. But he has also been extremely important for popular music. Simon Warner, a noted cultural musicologist who has specialized in the intersection between Beat, counterculture, and musical scenes, brings his expertise to bear on Kerouac's influence on rock music. Drawing on his own work as well as that of other critics, Warner demonstrates the outsize influence Kerouac has exerted on a range of musicians from his own era and into our own. The result reminds us that Kerouac is by no means fixed nor static—while his views might be problematic to some, nevertheless his work inspires not only writers but artists in other media and will undoubtedly continue to do so for some time to come.

Ronna C. Johnson continues this exploration of Kerouac's afterlife. Kerouac ranges over numerous themes in his work, but certainly one of the most prominent concepts he explores is that of America and what it might mean. Kerouac's work explores both city and country, chronicling the people and places that make up a nation that both fascinates and frustrates him. Arguing that Kerouac should be seen as an "American avatar," Johnson presents a case for highlighting the "Americanness" of the author. Johnson stresses the distinctly American nature of Kerouac and his work, even when his influences seem to lie outside the country. According to Johnson, Kerouac's absorption of the various strains and hybridizations of US discourse and his postmodern embrace of a wide range of influences is very much in the American vein. Kerouac, as Johnson claims, can be therefore explicated through his performance of the white male postwar subject, an avatar of the American myth of expansion, both in geographical and in cultural terms. Kerouac thus offers a fresh view on a country continually trying to (re)define itself.

What is Kerouac's future? How will we continue to think about this writer? For Michael Millner, the future of Kerouac resides in the archive. Kerouac himself kept copious notes of his childhood games, writings, publications, and correspondence. In addition, he thankfully left us with a wealth of documents that have inaugurated a new "turn" in Kerouac studies since John Sampas left over 7,000 items to the University of Massachusetts Lowell's Archive upon his death in 2017. Millner draws on his own work as curator of this vast archive and his role as director of the Kerouac Center to argue that Kerouac is the perfect figure for a publicly engaged humanities. Given Kerouac's appeal to both scholarly and popular audiences, his archive can become a site for a participatory "scene" with Kerouac and his work that allows patrons to engage Kerouac in meaningfully disparate ways. Millner shares both the fun and frustration of managing such events, providing us with a sense of how Kerouac's archive might continue as not just a site for scholarly exploration but as a place where everyone can find out what Kerouac might mean for themselves.

From the very start, Kerouac has been a global presence. Not only did Kerouac travel extensively, but the Beat phenomenon which he was a part quickly turned into an international movement. While he did not promote the Beat Generation abroad as Ginsberg did, Kerouac's works were disseminated, translated, and discussed in a number of countries. And that influence has only increased with time. The final chapter of *Rethinking Kerouac* is an interview conducted by the editors with three translators of Kerouac's work: Farid Ghadami of Iran, Minami Aoyama of Japan, and Maciej Świerkocki of Poland. Bringing together translators from several disparate language groups across the globe allows us to investigate not only how linguistic difference and cultural specificity influence the choices made in translating Kerouac, but likewise how Kerouac and his fellow Beats are received in various countries in both print and popular cultures. Reception has often been given short shrift in Beat Studies, but it is crucial in understanding how the Beat message, especially Kerouac's, has been appropriated and recontextualized in order to be delivered to a new set of readers globally.

Notes

1 Jack Kerouac, *Selected Letters: 1940–1956*, ed. Ann Charters (New York: Penguin, 1996), 239.
2 Ibid., 355. Also, see Tim Hunt's "Afterword" in this book.
3 Ibid., 390. Later in the letter Kerouac compares himself to Ezra Pound, a writer of important influence but who ended up "in the madhouse" (390).
4 Jack Kerouac, "Essentials of Spontaneous Prose," in *The Portable Beat Reader*, ed. Ann Charters (London: Penguin Group, 1992), 57.
5 David Dempsey, "In Pursuit of 'Kicks,'" *New York Times*, September 8, 1957, 3.
6 Herbert Gold, "Hip, Cool, Beat—and Frantic," *The Nation*, November 16, 1957, 349.
7 Hilary Holladay, in her preface to the volume *What's Your Road, Man?: Critical Essays on Jack Kerouac's* On the Road (Carbondale: Southern Illinois University Press, 2009), which she edited with Robert Holton, remarks apropos of *On the Road*'s fiftieth anniversary in 2007, "Now more than ever, it seems, reading Paradise's tale brings out the questing wanderer in many a reader, no matter one's age, gender, nationality, or

predilection for all things Beat" (x). Looking back from the vantage point of 2024, this assessment seems downright halcyon.

8 Omar Swartz, *A View from* On the Road: *A Rhetorical Vision of Jack Kerouac* (Carbondale: Southern Illinois UP, 1999), 86.
9 Jerry Watts, *Amiri Baraka: The Politics and Art of a Black Intellectual* (New York: New York University Press, 2001), 488n59.
10 Jack Kerouac, *On the Road* (1957) (New York: Viking Press, 1959), 180.
11 Elle Hunt, "The Road Well Travelled: 100 Years of Jack Kerouac," *The Guardian*, March 12, 2022, accessed January 16, 2024, https://www.theguardian.com/books/2022/mar/12/road-well-travelled-100-years-of-jack-kerouac.
12 Holly George-Warren, "Can a Feminist Still Love Jack Kerouac?," *OprahDaily.com*, March 16, 2022, accessed January 17, 2024, https://www.oprahdaily.com/entertainment/books/a39327744/jack-kerouac-holly-george-warren.
13 Ibid.
14 See also Nancy Grace and Jennie Skerl's *The Transnational Beat Generation*, Jimmy Fazzino's *World Beats: Beat Generation Writing and the Worlding of U.S. Literature*, and Erik Mortenson's *Translating the Counterculture: The Reception of the Beats in Turkey* for further examples of this transnational impulse.
15 Erin Zwaska and Jack Kerouac, *On the Open Road* (Providence, RI: Erin Zwaska, 2012).
16 The last decades have also witnessed a growing interest among video game developers deploying Beat references in the design of their narratives. Two such examples are the critically acclaimed *Life Is Strange*, an adventure/mystery video game narrative released by Square Enix, as well as *Fallout 4*, an action/role-playing game from Bethesda and a winner of Game of the Year award. See Tomasz Sawczuk, "Digging the Digital: Beat Modalities and the Representation of the Beats in Video Games," *European Journal of American Studies* [Online], 17-2 (2022), accessed January 20, 2024, http://journals.openedition.org/ejas/18309, doi:10.4000/ejas.18309.
17 Kerouac has also been picked up by more conservative thinkers, further adding to the number of his manifestations. See Paul G. Kengor, "Remembering Jack Kerouac: Novelist, Beat, Conservative, Catholic," *The Institute for Faith & Freedom*, January 9, 2020, accessed January 16, 2024, https://www.faithandfreedom.com/remembering-jack-kerouac-novelist-beat-conservative-catholic. Kengor surveys a host of newspaper articles and essays on Kerouac's worldview that insist on his faith and religiosity as central in navigating his writing, speaking to the multiple uses his legacy can be put to.
18 Douglas Kennedy, "Jack Kerouac's Contested Legacy," *The New Statesman*, March 9, 2022, accessed January 16, 2024, https://www.newstatesman.com/culture/books/2023/03/jack-kerouac-contested-legacy.

Part One

Rethinking the Writing

1

Reading a Copy of *On the Road*

Matt Theado

Have you read *On the Road* by Jack Kerouac? You probably have the book on your shelf right now. But what did you read, and what do you have on your shelf? We take it on faith that *On the Road* is a fixed text. We assume that we're reading the same classic American novel others have read for decades, but in fact the text of *On the Road* has been shifting fluidly since the moment of its inception. Early in the composition process, Kerouac wrote drafts he intended as his road novel that are hardly recognizable as the book you might read today. Later in the process, both Kerouac and publishing house editors made changes that affected the text right up to the moment of publication. Even *after* publication of the first edition by Viking Press in 1957, the text has continued to change, and although these changes may be subtler than the prepublication changes, they are nonetheless significant to the work's ongoing reputation. We can understand the nature of these changes by tracing how Kerouac put the text together, how Viking Press editors revised the text, and how the published text continues to change over time.

Let's start with the present situation of the novel. Today is September 15, 2024; I type the words "Jack Kerouac On the Road" into the search bar at Amazon. The first item in the results list is *On the Road: The Original Scroll* by Jack Kerouac, edited by Howard Cunnell. This book presents an edited version of the famous 120-foot-long typescript Kerouac typed in 1951. The second item is *On the Road: 50th Anniversary Edition* by Jack Kerouac that turns out to be an Audible audiobook. The cover proclaims the work is NOW A MAJOR MOTION PICTURE and shows images from the 2012 movie. The third item is *Jack Kerouac: Road Novels 1957–1960: On the Road / The Dharma Bums / The Subterraneans / Tristessa / Lonesome Traveler / Journal Selections*. Finally, we get to a book titled *On the Road* by Jack Kerouac. This paperback book has a photograph of Neal Cassady and Jack Kerouac on its cover. Published by Pearson Education, the book has eighty pages and sells for $75.34. As I scan these results, I notice a link integrated with the audiobook description for "On the Road Paperback— Deckle Edge, June 1, 1999." Clicking this link displays another version of *On the Road*, this one with comic book-style illustrations on the cover.

All these items are versions of *On the Road* by Jack Kerouac, but none of them is what I was looking for. What I wanted was a definite, standard, agreed-upon edition of a work written by Jack Kerouac titled *On the Road*. I'm not surprised I didn't find it. Such a book does not exist.

This situation is not unique to *On the Road*. If you want to read Mark Twain's classic novel about Huckleberry Finn, you'll find dozens of various editions, some titled *Adventures of Huckleberry Finn* and others titled *The Adventures of Huckleberry Finn*, some with passages that are not in others, some illustrated and others not, and so on. Some classic American works of literature including *Adventures of Huckleberry Finn* have been published in authoritative or critical editions. For example, the Cambridge Edition of *The Great Gatsby* is intended to present F. Scott Fitzgerald's novel exactly as he wrote it, before his editor Maxwell Perkins altered the text. Yet that version of *The Great Gatsby* is just that: another version. It stands on bookstore and library shelves among alternative *Gatsby*s. Which of them is the real *Gatsby*? To put the matter bluntly, there is no one true *Gatsby*.

To understand why we don't find a single, definitive book titled *The Great Gatsby* or *On the Road*, it may be helpful to reconsider what we mean when we say *book*. In its most basic function, a book is a device that stores text. So, what exactly is *text*? Basically, *text* is letters that make words that make meaningful compositions like stories and novels. The editors of *An Introduction to Bibliographical & Textual Studies* provide a useful description: the physical embodiment of a text may appear as "letters written, impressed, or transferred onto a surface or encoded in digital form, that is, in a manuscript, book, computer file, and so on." Without a text, we have nothing to read. These editors make a delightful claim: "Texts have lives."[1] We like to think of a story coming to life before our eyes, which is the magic of reading, but the texts themselves also change through time, revealing that they, like the trees the pages are made of, have lives. They grow, they shrink, they morph. Since texts are living things that change through time, conscientious readers shouldn't just pick up the first copy of *On the Road* they happen to find. Nor should they do that with any title.

A literary work is not the same thing as a book that stores its text. A literary work begins when the concept of a story springs into the author's mind; a work takes form in the notes they jot down on coffee shop napkins; the work may continue as a draft they leave unfinished, a draft they complete, a typewritten version, an edited typewritten version, the first published edition; these are all forms of the work. *On the Road* is a literary work whose text began to appear in the late 1940s. On August 23, 1948, Kerouac pondered a book to be titled *On the Road*: "I have another novel in mind—'On the Road'—which I keep thinking about;—about two guys hitch-hiking to California in search of something they don't really find, and losing themselves on the road, and coming all the way back hopeful of something else."[2] This is Kerouac's first mention of a work he titled *On the Road*.

For the purposes of this essay, we can think of a work as all the ideas that a writer might have about a story. The work can go through many textual forms before and after the publication of the first edition. The concept of *On the Road* remained in Kerouac's mind for years as he tried various approaches to writing it. Each time he sketched out ideas or jotted down notes, he was creating *On the Road*. Kerouac composed a series of drafts that he failed to bring to completion but nonetheless are versions of the work.

In some cases, these drafts contain sentences and ideas that would appear in his first successfully completed draft composed in April 1951.

Readers tend to divide the process of making a book into two distinct stages. The first stage comprises all the steps that the author takes while they are working in their study or bent over their notebook, hashing out ideas of their imagined work. Gradually, they are turning their imagined work into a visible text of the work. We tend to prioritize this stage of composition because it derives from the author's hard work, inspiration, and genius. We value it over the stages that will occur after the author hands the text over to other agents of change, such as friends, advisers, editors, and printers, to say nothing of those who will enact changes in reprints, translations, and scholarly or critical editions. We prioritize the first stage because we tend to value the creative impulses of the author over the revisions, emendations, libel-proofing, censoring, and proofreading done by editors. This was the rationale for publishing the Cambridge Edition of *The Great Gatsby*.

Let's focus on that initial stage as the writer is transmitting the work from their mind into text. First of all, writers have ideas, or if these ideas remain insufficiently formed, they have inspiration. To share the inspiration with an audience, whether in a chat with a friend or in a letter to their literary advisor, they must put their ideas into words. They work within the constraints of the language in which they compose—the sounds of words and shapes of letters, as well as the rules that govern the semantic and grammatical contours of language. The reduction of the imagined work into text represents the first and most profound transmission of the work. That first text is possibly a handwritten text, or in the case of writers working after the development of affordable typewriters, a typescript. For many centuries, handwriting was the only available method of composition; Elizabethan writers, for example, typically composed with pen and ink. The later development of the pencil relied first on lead, then graphite, and made erasures possible. Composing by pen-and-ink and pencils resulted in handwritten drafts called manuscripts (the prefix *manu* means *hand*). The first reliable typewriters were mass-produced in the late 1800s and early 1900s; their emergence revolutionized record-keeping, correspondence, and dictation in business offices. By the middle 1900s, portable typewriters were popularized for home use and were widely adopted by writers. Typewritten drafts are typically called *typescripts*, although the term *manuscript* carried over to refer to any form of an author's draft.

In any case, writers must contend with physical aspects of the composition process. Handwriting, as we all know, can cause the writer's hand to grow tired or cramped, or perhaps the handwriting is nearly illegible, which can lead to misinterpretation. Composing text requires physical material that must be acquired and maintained, such as paper. Writers face meddling questions of technique: when the writer fills the page with text, do they turn the paper over to write on the back or flip the page over as in the case of a legal pad? Do they number the pages as they go? All of these are physical considerations in the transmission of the work into textual form. Famously, Kerouac surmounted some of these physical hurdles because he was a fantastic typist. Although he handwrote some early drafts of "On the Road," he could type quickly, with very few errors, for long periods. In the case of his composition of the first completed *On the*

Road typescript in April 1951, he used sheets of paper varying in length from 11 to 16½ feet that he rolled into his typewriter so that he could type without interruption for longer periods than if he had been limited to regular size typing paper. Imagine the ways the work is differently conveyed into text because Kerouac could type smoothly without having to interrupt his thoughts every minute or two to number and place a text-filled sheet into the stack of growing pages then roll a fresh sheet into his typewriter.

In short, the work is converted to text, and that text resides on some physical artifact. In the case of *On the Road*, the document of the text is the series of long sheets of paper that Kerouac typed on. We can think of those long strips of paper as "hosting" the text that he produced. This typescript is not an example of Kerouac's spontaneous prose, which he would develop later that year, a method that more effectively, he believed, conveyed his work into text. Nonetheless, he saw this scroll typescript as a breakthrough in modern literature because he was freely transmitting his concept of the work—his inspiration, his imagination, and his memory, buoyed by and merging with his notes, journals, letters, and earlier drafts—into text.

This original scroll typescript is a testament to Kerouac's focus, discipline, and fervent belief in his destiny as writer. It is the first completed draft of his long-dreamed-of road novel. However, it is not a finale; it is part of a process. The process was fluid and continuous. Kerouac edited some of the lines immediately after he typed them. The most direct method he used was to bang the x key of his typewriter over portions of the text that he wanted to delete. In several cases, he squeezed some typewritten words in the margin or above a line to indicate an insertion. The second major form of emendation of his typescript comes with pencil editing. This editing likely occurred after he completed the typescript and was reading it over. Kerouac used pencil throughout the scroll typescript to draw lines through text and large Xs over entire passages of text he apparently wanted to delete. He also penciled in words and phrases.

The scroll typescript as first typed might be a breakthrough in the process of composition, but Kerouac's initial editing makes clear that it was not a completion. Contrary to the legendary notion of Kerouac's refusal to edit his texts once he'd written them, we see that he was not only willing to consider revisions, but he was the first to undertake them. That's not all. Within days of completing the original scroll typescript, Kerouac began retyping the entire story on separate sheets of paper. When he did this

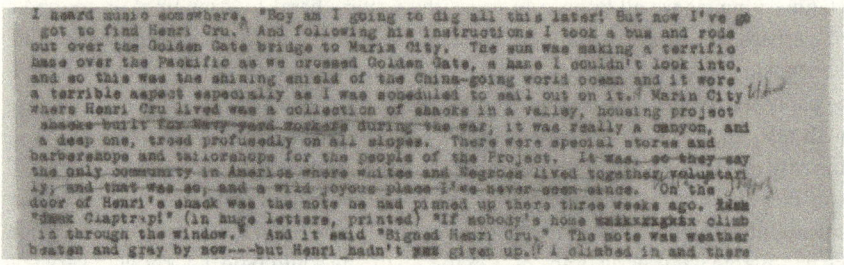

Figure 1.1 Jack Kerouac, the first completed *On the Road* typescript (April 1951).

retyping stint, he made numerous changes to the text; he changed the names of the characters, emended descriptions, toned down some of the sexual language, added romanticized and sentimentalized phrases, and inserted whole new sections of his story. I mention Kerouac's initial acts of editing for two reasons. First, they complicate a commonly asserted notion that the original scroll typescript is superior to the published versions that we read. Allen Ginsberg was among the first to make this claim, writing in the *Village Voice* in 1958 of the sadness that *On the Road* "was never published in its most exciting form ... The original mad version is greater than the published version, the manuscript still exists and someday when everybody's dead will be published as it is."[3] Rather than lamenting the loss of the "original mad version," we can also see the original scroll as a version of the work on the road toward its publication. Kerouac's edits justify at least in concept the processes of editing that this text will go through at the hands of Viking editors. Sure, we can say that the first changes made in the text by Kerouac were justified by authorial intention; he's the author, he knows what he wants. Yet, as is also likely, he was willing to change the text to satisfy what he thought others might want. He was undoubtedly thinking of Robert Giroux, his editor at Harcourt, Brace who had guided his first novel, *The Town and the City* (1950) to publication. Kerouac relied on his editors and the editing process to convey his story in book form. The relationship of the original scroll to Viking's first edition is not as clear-cut as Ginsberg makes it out to be.

To get an idea of how Kerouac changed the original scroll typescript of *On the Road*, let's track the development of the novel's closing passages from the time Sal meets Laura, the girl he "had always searched for and for so long."[4] We'll look at how these passages developed in Kerouac's journals and typescripts, and how Kerouac revised them, and how Viking editors emended them before publication.

As noted above, Kerouac began working in the late 1940s on versions of *On the Road*. Even though Kerouac was not writing about characters named Sal and Dean, a passage in one of these drafts would appear in a different form in *On the Road*. In January 1951, Kerouac wrote a passage that he identified as "AN EXAMPLE OF HOW TO BEGIN A GREAT NOVEL":

> One night in America when the sun went down—beginning in the East at dusk of the day by shedding a lovely gold in the air that made dirty old buildings look like Rembrandt's temples of golden darkness, then outflying its own shades as it raced three thousand miles over the raw bulge of the continent to the West Coast before sloping down the Pacific, leaving the great rearguard shroud of night to creep upon our earth, to darken all of the rivers, cup the peaks and fold the final shore in, as little lights twinkled & everybody mused—[5]

This passage appears in a set of handwritten notebook pages that Kerouac titled "Ben Boncoeur excerpt (written January Jan. 1951 in Richmond Hill)." According to New York Public Library archivist Isaac Gewirtz, Kerouac soon modified this prose in a subsequent short draft, shifting the verbs from past to present tense: "But in America when the sun goes down ...."[6]

Three months later, Kerouac would recast this passage not as the beginning but as the ending of the scroll typescript of *On the Road*. We don't know precisely how Kerouac concluded his text of the original scroll because, according to Kerouac's handwritten note at the end of the scroll, a dog chewed up the final portion. The entire second typescript is intact, however. Possibly Kerouac typed the second typescript before the dog-chewing incident, in which case he would have been looking at the original scroll as he typed; but it's also possible the dog had already done the deed and Kerouac had to recreate the conclusion from memory and imagination. In any case, the second typescript moves seamlessly from the extant portion of the original scroll into its final section. Dean, Sal, and Stan roll into the vibrance and confusion of Mexico City, and Sal gets sick with fever. Dean leaves Sal in Stan's care and sets off to drive back to New York.

Immediately after this, the second typescript's fifth and final section titled "BOOK FIVE: 'CAN'T TALK NO MORE ... '" begins with these words: "A week later the Korean War began."[7] Sal returns from Mexico and meets Laura. On the first night of their meeting, Sal proposes marriage, Laura accepts, and five days later they marry. The narrative jumps to winter, with Sal and Laura planning to move to San Francisco; Dean volunteers to come from San Francisco to New York to help them, with the understanding that Sal and Laura need five weeks to save money. Dean arrives early, justifying his appearance by saying he wants to meet Sal's "sweet wife." He also needs to make arrangements with his New York girlfriend, Inez; Kerouac typed the word "pregnant" above her name to emphasize their urgent situation: "With <pregnant> Inez he spent one night fighting and she threw him out." Sal's friend Remi Boncoeur refuses to give Dean a ride to Penn Station. Sal repeatedly refers to Laura as his wife in this section. As he watches Dean walk around the corner to start his return journey to San Francisco, Sal muses that if he hadn't been married, he would have gone with him.

After this admission and without a paragraph break, Sal narrates the melancholic closing passage by redrafting the version that originally appeared in the Ben Boncoeur draft above:

> So in America when the sun goes down and I sit on the old brokendown river pier watching the long, long skies over New Jersey and sense all that raw land that rolls in one unbelievable huge bulge over to the West Coast, all that road going, all the people dreaming in the immensity of it, and in Iowa I know by now the evening-star must be drooping and shedding her sparkler dims on the prairie, which is just before the coming of complete night that blesses the earth, darkens all rivers, cups the peaks to the west and folds the last and final shore in, and nobody, just nobody knows what's going to happen to anybody besides the forlorn rags of growing old, I think of Dean Pomeray, I even think of Old Dean Pomeray the father we never found, I think of Dean Pomeray, I think of Dean Pomeray.

After completing this passage, Kerouac edited it, just as he edited every single page of the second typescript. He started by crossing out the first three words with black crayon and capitalizing the W of *when*, so the edited passage begins "When the sun goes down ...." After the phrase "and in Iowa I know by now" he penciled in a passage: *children must be crying in that land where they let the children cry, + tonight the stars'll be out.* With a darker pencil, perhaps indicating a later addition, he added an asterisk after that passage. The corresponding asterisk at the bottom of the page indicates this passage to be inserted: *and dont you know that God is Poo Bear?*

Kerouac extended the last sentence by penciling in a phrase: "I think of Dean Pomeray *in the sad American night.*" Apparently unsatisfied with this, he emended it again: "I think of Dean Pomeray *that hero of the* ~~Hip~~ *Beat Generation in the idealistic sad American night.*" Erasures indicate that he tried out other variations of the closing sentence as well.

It is likely that this is the version of the text that Kerouac submitted to Alfred Knopf publishing company in October 1954. Knopf senior editor Joseph M. Fox returned the typescript with the stipulation that it be retyped. The heavy editing that Kerouac had done on every page may have been a factor in Fox's request for a fresh typescript. If Knopf had accepted the second typescript for publication, we might be reading a version of it as the novel we know as *On the Road*. Sal and Laura would be married, Sal would blame that marriage for preventing him from going on the road with Dean again, Dean's last name would be "Pomeray" (and his wife in San Francisco would be "Dorothy"), and the novel might have ended with a paean to Dean Pomeray as the hero of the Beat Generation in the sad American night. As fate would have it, Knopf refused to read that second typescript and insisted on a freshly typed draft of the text, which gave Kerouac another shot not only at ending his novel, but at refashioning sentences all the way through.

In November 1954, Kerouac typed the novel for the third time and submitted this typescript to Knopf, who subsequently rejected it. This third typescript is vitally important, though. Viking Press had maintained interest in the novel since their reading of it the previous year and asked Kerouac to resubmit it to them. When he did, Kerouac submitted this third typescript. This is the typescript that Viking accepted and used as their setting copy for editing, house styling, proofreading, and printer's copy.

A close examination of this third typescript shows that Kerouac had continued to edit the novel. First, this is a different form of the text from both the original scroll and the second typescript. In fact, rather than constituting a continuing development from the first typescript, to second, to third, this third typescript more closely adheres to the original scroll than it does to the second typescript. That is, it seems that, after having the second typescript rejected by a series of publishers over the course of three years, Kerouac went back to the original scroll to which he more closely adhered when he produced the third typescript. But that doesn't mean that he ignored the second typescript; numerous changes that he made for the second typescript were brought over into the third typescript. In all three cases—original scroll, second typescript, third typescript—Kerouac continually made changes via retyping and by using handwritten changes and deletions.

In the third typescript, Dean's last name is Moriarty, and his wife in San Francisco is Camille. As the third typescript concludes, there is no mention of the Korean War. Sal meets Laura, proposes to her, and marries her five days later. Dean arrives in New

York earlier than expected, eager to meet Sal's new wife. Dean again walks off around the corner, but this time Sal does not say that he would go with him if he weren't married. And this time, after the sentimental closing paragraph the novel concludes with these words:

> I think of Dean Moriarty, I even think of Old Dean Moriarty the father we never found, I think of Dean Moriarty, I think of Dean Moriarty ...[8]

Viking accepted the novel for publication, and Kerouac cooperated in making many changes in the text of the typescript. These include excisions of some long passages and alterations of characters' names and circumstances to avoid libel. Kerouac did not participate in the line-by-line copy editing, though, nor did he participate in other significant cuts that Viking made. In addition to the hundreds of changes in the text to bring the grammar, punctuation, and spelling into line with their house styling, Viking editors went beyond house styling in other changes. Let's look again at the closing section of the novel.

When Kerouac submitted the third typescript to Viking, Sal returns from Mexico and meets "the girl with the pure and innocent dear eyes that I had always searched for and for so long. That night I asked her to marry me and she accepted and agreed. Five days later we were married." With a series of deft deletions and edits, Viking editors removed all references to their marriage. In the Viking version, Sal meets "the girl with the pure and innocent dear eyes that I had always searched for and for so long. We agreed to love each madly." After Sal's walk in the neighborhood, he reports that he "came back to my wife." After Viking's edits, Sal says that he "came back to my girl." Viking took other steps in an apparent attempt to make the scene less middle-class domestic and more hip. Where Kerouac had typed "She stood in the dark parlor," Viking substituted "She stood in the dark little pad." Sal mentions their "television set," which Viking changed to "radio." Dean tiptoes in "from the dark kitchen"; after Viking's editing he comes in "from the dark hall." Dean says he "wanted to see your sweet wife and you—gone and done it, old man," while in Viking's edited version he says he simply "wanted to see your sweet girl and you." When Dean goes off alone, Sal comments on the reaction of "Poor little Laura, my wife"; Viking changed this to "Poor little Laura, my baby."

Despite Kerouac's clear intention, Sal does not marry Laura at the end of Viking's novel, and the story loses a degree of symmetry. The opening line of the third typescript, "I first met Dean not long after my wife and I split up," is no longer balanced by Sal remarrying at the end of the novel. Viking's change may have been an attempt to avoid libel. Kerouac had married Joan Haverty when he returned from Mexico, just as Sal married Laura. By 1956, though, when Viking was preparing the novel for publication, they were no longer together. Haverty, who was seeking child support payments, may have had grounds to sue for libel if she were a recognizable character in the novel; it's possible that Viking sought to distance the character Laura from Haverty.

The original scroll does not begin with the narrator saying he first met Neal shortly after he and his wife split up, but instead "not long after my father died." That beginning foreshadows one of Kerouac's themes in the novel, the search for lost fathers. In fact, that theme reverberates in the closing mention of "Old Dean Moriarty, the father we never found." Kerouac had included references to Sal's deceased father which Viking cut, unaware of Kerouac's intention to have the novel resonate with the theme of lost fathers.

Good literary critics read closely, attentively, insightfully. They rely on the authority of the text as they craft interpretations and judgments. Yet they can read more effectively if they have a sense of the evolution of the work through various textual forms. For example, insightful readers would understand how that missing father creates a bit of confusion at one point. In Viking's published novel, Sal is alone in Denver at the beginning of Part Three when he muses, "Either you find someone who looks like your father in places like Montana or you look for a friend's father where he is no more" (180). Why would Sal mention Montana in this context, especially since he has never been there? In the preceding section, Sal says goodbye to Dean and Marylou in San Francisco and sets out to cross the country by bus. Sal mentions that his sandwiches would turn bad before he "got to Dakota," but this is the extent of his reference to the return trip. Viking editors deleted the subsequent section in the typescript where Sal recounts his return trip via the Northern route. In this deleted section Sal describes how in Butte, Montana, he saw "an old card dealer who looked exactly like W.C. Fields and made me cry thinking of my father." This is what Sal is referring to when he's alone in Denver, but readers would never know this, since editors deleted the antecedent. Viking editors wished to remove some of Sal's solo adventures to shorten the novel and focus on Sal and Dean's time together. In this instance, the deletion dilutes Kerouac's theme of lost fathers and adds confusion to Sal's statement. My point is that after the third typescript was out of Kerouac's hands, Viking made changes to the text that Kerouac didn't see until he held the published book. These changes affected at least two themes in the novel, the significance of marriage and the centrality of the lost father. On the other hand, Viking's changes may have intensified the friendship between Sal and Dean by bringing greater focus on that theme.

Among other house styling changes in that closing passage, a Viking editor deleted the repetition of the last phrase and changed the ellipsis to a single period. Here's the text as Kerouac submitted it:

> I think of Dean Moriarty, I even think of Old Dean Moriarty the father we never found, I think of Dean Moriarty, I think of Dean Moriarty ...

And here's the text as Viking published it:

> I think of Dean Moriarty, I even think of Old Dean Moriarty the father we never found, I think of Dean Moriarty.

Maybe we ought not quibble with Viking's editing decisions; after all, *On the Road* climbed the *New York Times* best seller list, got attention from coast to coast, and was successfully sold for paperback and overseas reprints. But you may have seen the video of Kerouac reading on Steve Allen's television program in 1959. When he read from the copy of On the Road that he held in his hand, he spoke the closing lines the way he had submitted them in the third typescript, with the repetition of "I think of Dean Moriarty," and maybe in the way he stretched out the pronunciation of the name he was conveying the effect of the ellipsis. This is one version of the work in which the final lines match the third typescript. The version of the work we read (or listen to) may lead us to different conclusions about how significantly Kerouac emphasized the themes of lost fathers or the domesticating effects of marriage. We may also receive varying emotional effects based on the rhythms of the sentences and the repetition of words and names. After all, why do we read novels if not for these thematic and emotional outcomes?

I'd like to bring up a rather mysterious editing change that might have occurred after Viking finished their editing job and sent the typescript to the printing company. In the third typescript, Sal reports that Dean drove a car so mercilessly that "the rods were busted." Even though there is no correction on that page of the typescript, the Viking first edition doesn't say that the rods were busted but rather "the bearings were beat" (112). At another point later in the typescript: "No sooner were we snoring than he gunned the car up to eighty, bad rods and all." Here again, although there's no emendation in the typescript, the Viking publication has "bearings" instead of rods (135). "Rods" might refer to the connecting rods or tie rods, and it's impossible to drive a car if these parts are broken. For that reason, the changes to *bearings* are warranted. But if these words weren't marked in the typescript, who made these late changes? I have a pet theory that a Linotypist in the printing factory who knew more about cars than Kerouac or the Viking editors made this change. If this is the case, and I have absolutely no evidence to back it up, then this print shop worker contributed to the text of one of America's greatest novels, joining the community of people responsible for putting the text together.

The Viking Press book came out on September 5, 1957. A *New York Times* reviewer proclaimed its publication as a "historic occasion" and Kerouac's novel as "an authentic work of art."[9] It's possible but unlikely that many of us have read or even held in our hands a first printing of Viking's first edition of On the Road. It's not exactly a rarity, but copies of the first edition in good condition go for thousands of dollars and are stored in special collections. Lest we think that a first-edition, first-printing of On the Road would bring us closer to Kerouac's original work, textual scholar Peter Shillingsburg has some news for us: "no one ever read the original of any work," he tells us, since "each is a copy or a copy of a copy. None, not even the first copy, is the original. We work at an unbridgeable distance from the object of our attention."[10] I hope that by tracing the stages of the composition of the text up to the publication of the first edition we can see the process as both cumulative and ongoing. Scrutiny of different copies of the novel reveals distinctions in the text. That is a fact of reproduction. We assume stability of the text at our peril.

In 1958, Signet published the first paperback version and sold many thousands of copies, enjoying far greater sales than the Viking hardcover edition. Was the novel experienced differently by those who read it wrapped in Viking Press's serious-looking black first-edition covers than by those who beheld Signet's celebratory and sensational pocket-size paperback, with its cover trumpeting the novel as the "bible of the 'beat generation'—the explosive best seller that tells all about today's wild youth and their frenetic search for Experience and Sensation"? And it's not just the book's size and colors and blurbs that affect the presentation of the work; Signet's publication is a resetting of the type from the Viking edition. Did intentional or inadvertent changes occur in the text with the resetting of type? Although you can pick up these Signet paperbacks today for a fraction of the cost of the first hardcover edition, most of today's readers have not read that version, either. Check your own copy of *On the Road*. Look on the reverse of the title page to identify the publisher, year of publication, number of reprints of that version, and more. What year was your copy made? Don't despair if a great span of time and textual transfers separate your copy from the first edition. Textual scholar G. Thomas Tanselle points to the value of later printings and editions, for they allow us to see "what wording was being furnished to readers at particular times."[11] It's not just that these books contain texts that may be at variance with the earlier publications—it's also the fact that the later editions are much more widely read than the earlier ones. As Tanselle points out, "Some later editions have exerted a far greater influence than the original editions."[12] Which are the editions today that are exerting that influence? What is their birthright, and from which previous editions did they come? How does one version of the work differ from another?

Throughout the third typescript, Kerouac wrote the everyday phrase people say when they part ways; he spelled it "goodbye." He based his spelling on his belief that the word comes from "God be with ye," a resonance he felt to be lost in the "machinelike" spelling "good-by."[13] In the third typescript Kerouac submitted to Viking, he invariably used "goodbye," and in each case an editor had changed it to "good-by." The word appears as "good-by" in Viking's first edition published in 1957 and in Signet's 1958 paperback reprint. I happen to have a copy of the British Pan 2nd printing (1963) which spells the word as "goodbye." The Penguin Modern Classics edition (1972) blends these two versions of the word as "good-bye." Does it matter which version of the word you have in the text you read? Would you catch the suggestion of "God be with ye" in "goodbye"? I mentioned in the introduction to this essay that Amazon lists an Audible audiobook version. If you listen to the audiobook version of *On the Road* even with high-fidelity earbuds, it's unlikely you'll detect a difference in pronunciation between "goodbye," "good-by," and "good-bye." In fact, listeners can't know which version of that word appears in the text the voice actor is using.

Where the book is published also matters: the Penguin Modern Classics 1972 edition uses the British spelling "tyre" where Kerouac had written "tire." Again, this won't have any effect in an audiobook edition (would the voice actor have a British accent? If so, would that matter?), but it might affect the reader whose eye scans the term in the text. For American readers, the word "tyre" might give the story a British flavor. For British readers, the word might make the story feel more local. Should the story feel more local to British readers, or should they read the word "tire" so the story feels more American? Undoubtedly you would detect many more changes in the text if you were to compare multiple editions of the work word by word.

Today, plenty of people access the text of literature via digital readers, and this form of access results from yet another transmission of the text. Digitized versions of *On the Road* are available for Kindle and other readers. How were these texts prepared? From what source were they made? What kinds of textual degradations occurred as the paper text was scanned and converted to digital text and then presented on the screen? The answer is, we don't know, just as we don't know the nature and number of variations that exist among the many printed editions of *On the Road*. In his essay "Reproducing the Texts of Documents," Thomas Tanselle makes the case:

> There can be no identical copies of printed books, just as there can be no identical copies of manuscripts or of any other objects; but the differences in some cases may be such that one will consider them insignificant for the purpose at hand. (They may not, however, seem insignificant to another person, with other interests or greater perceptiveness.)[14]

To extrapolate from Tanselle's point: no two copies of *On the Road* are identical. We're confronted with numerous variations of the text presented in numerous formats that are all shifting through time. The work resides in these texts, and understanding the road of *On the Road* helps us see the story more clearly. Kerouac traveled, mused, noted, sketched, wrote, typed, revised ... all before sending the story on its road to editors, lawyers, printers, translators, movie makers, audiobook voice actors, text digitizers, and more.

So in America when the sun goes down and we sit in our old broken-down reading chairs leafing through the long, long text of *On the Road* and sense all that raw prose that Kerouac typed on one unbelievably huge page, and all that road going, all the readers dreaming in the immensity of it, and nobody, nobody knows what's going to happen to the work besides the long future of republication in new editions and innovative formats, we think of *On the Road*, we even think of the handwritten and typed versions that preceded the first publication, all the changes and emendations to the text and the various covers, colors, and themes that have since adorned and affected it, we think of *On the Road*, we think of *On the Road* ...

Notes

1. William Proctor Williams and Craig S. Abbott, *An Introduction to Bibliographical & Textual Studies* 4th edn. (New York: MLA, 2009), 5 and 6.
2. Isaac Gewirtz, *Beatific Soul: Jack Kerouac on the Road* (New York: New York Public Library, 2007), 74.
3. Allen Ginsberg, "The Dharma Bums," *The Village Voice*, November 12, 1958, https://news.google.com/newspapers?nid=KEtq3P1Vf8oC&dat=19581112&printsec=frontpage&hl=en.
4. Jack Kerouac, *On the Road* (New York: Viking Press, 1957), 306. Subsequent page references will appear in parentheses in the text.

5   Gewirtz, *Beatific Soul*, 99.
6   Ibid., 100.
7   Jack Kerouac, *On the Road* Typescript, revised. The Second Draft of the novel. 297 leaves, Jack Kerouac Papers, Berg Collection, New York Public Library, b. 25 f. 1. Subsequent references to this source will be stated in the text, not in endnotes.
8   Jack Kerouac, *On the Road* Typescript, revised. The Third Draft of the novel. 340 leaves, Jack Kerouac Papers, Berg Collection, New York Public Library, b. 26 f. 1.
9   Gilbert Millstein, "Books of the Times," *New York Times*, September 5, 1957, 27.
10 Peter Shillingsburg, *Textuality and Knowledge* (University Park: Pennsylvania University Press, 2017), vii.
11 G. Thomas Tanselle, *A Rationale of Textual Criticism* (1989) (Philadelphia: University of Penn Press, 1992), 51.
12 Ibid., 53.
13 Jack Kerouac, *Selected Letters: 1957–1969*, ed. Ann Charters (New York: Viking, 1999), 130. Kerouac expressed his ideas regarding the use of "goodbye" in a letter to Viking editor Helen Taylor during the editing of *The Dharma Bums*.
14 Tanselle, *A Rationale of Textual Criticism*, 51.

2

Choruses for Kerouac

Aldon Nielsen

Add alluvials to the end of your line when all is exhausted but something has to be said ...

—Jack Kerouac

CHORUS I

This geographical metaphor, Kerouac's trope for the *always more* of his writing, stands as his own take on the concepts of seriality common among his crew in the "New American Writing" of the post-Second World War era. Not to be confused with the serialism of musical composition, the approach of Webern, Schoenberg, Stockhausen, Berg, and so on (which might aptly be seen as close kin to seriality in poetics), this concept augured against the view of the poem as verbal icon championed by the New Critical establishment and descended from the experiments with the poetic sequence of Pound and Williams. Then, too, there was the seriality of mass narrative entertainments. Like Amiri Baraka, Kerouac had grown up on a diet of radio and movie house serials. So had novelist John Edgar Wideman. In *Writing to Save a Life: The Louis Till File*, a work that itself springs from passages in that ur-modern serial, Pound's *Cantos*, Wideman writes: "Serials don't worry about last time, just this time, just keep on running ... Serials remember only what they want to remember ..."[1] The something more of Kerouac's metaphor is something that is already in the stream, carried along from its source, carried by the force of the writing till it comes to its seeming emptying out, to be deposited as some sort of delta formation, perhaps delta blues. When he reaches the end of the line under hand, "something has to be said for some specified irrational reasons."[2] And for those of us who pause wondering what it means to be a *specified* irrational reason, Kerouac insists, perhaps contra structuralism, "poetry is NOT a science." This is the opening of his brief statement for Donald Allen's anthology *The New American Poetry 1945–1960*, but his far better-known statement of his compositional approaches is his "Essentials of Spontaneous Prose," first published in *Black Mountain Review* and then restated in *The Moderns,* edited by his friend LeRoi Jones (Amiri Baraka). In that essay, Kerouac sets out a bit more fully the, as he puts it, essentials of what will be termed "Bop Prosody," and what he says here is, if anything, more applicable to his work in verse than his better-known prose compositions. Musical improvising and the "sketch" are presented as his primary analogues to the modes of writing he pursues. In "Essentials" he advises holding the object in mind and sketching in language as "an undisturbed flow."[3] But since he also advises against selectivity of expression, that flow will gather up associations for that later alluvial deposit. What he is hoping for is a stream "from the mind of personal secret idea-words," but just here is where the analogy gets a bit rough around the edges. The "*blowing* (as per jazz musician) on subject of image" is not quite, in the case of actual jazz musicians, the production "without consciousness"[4] that he also proposes. Miles Davis used to joke that to be a jazz musician you had to know a lot of cliches. What he was getting at was the vast catalogue of possible figures any great improviser masters in years of woodshedding so that they can achieve that "blowing" that Kerouac so admires. But it is not Kerouac's knowledge of actual musical practice that is crucial here; rather, the example the musician offers to his attention.

Illinois Jacquet often told the tale of his invention of his memorable solo on "Flying Home" with the Lionel Hampton band in 1942. As Jacquet has retold the story many times, when his turn to solo came around, the musician sitting next to him said "go for yourself," the result being an improvisation of epic length and invention. But even that couldn't compete for marathon blowing with what took place on the stage of the 1956 Newport Festival during a performance by the Duke Ellington Orchestra, when Ellington told saxophonist Paul Gonsalves to take as long as he wanted, resulting in the famous twenty-seven choruses inserted between "Diminuendo in Blue" and "Crescendo in Blue" that had the festival audience on their feet dancing and shouting encouragement. On another night, with the Count Basie Band playing Birdland, what the audience likely thought was the ending of a Wild Bill Davis arrangement of "April in Paris" turned into one of those alluvial continuations. The audience heard Basie shout out "one more time" in the time-honored tradition of dramatic endings, but then he shouted it again, and again, till coming to an actual (sort of) ending, Basie shouted "one more—once." Each of these moments instantiates the aesthetic that Kerouac was going for, though there was presumably less involvement of the subconscious than he was hoping for in his own improvisations. Still, the concept of potentially unending choruses, one following hard on the heels of another, became a fertile model for his work in poetry. There are 242 choruses of "Mexico City Blues," 80 choruses of "San Francisco Blues," 71 choruses of "Orizawa 210 Blues," 51 choruses of "Orlando Blues," and "Cerrada Medellin" Blues is divided into two solos, one of 12 and the other of 10 choruses. On his 1958 recording with Steve Allen, *Poetry for the Beat Generation,* Kerouac intones numerous choruses from *Mexico City Blues* among the many selections, three of them identified on the release simply as "Charlie Parker." Parker Kerouac recognizes as "A great musician and a great / creator of forms."[5] "Charlie Parker" comprises choruses 239–41 of *Mexico City Blues,* and each chorus is paradigmatically an unclosed form. Chorus 239's last words are "what have you"; 240 ends "one after one, in time,"[6] and 241, the antepenultimate chorus of *Mexico City*

Blues, blends into the final chorus with the prayer: "–Charlie Parker, lay the bane, / off me, and everybody." There is no period at the end of that not quite final sentence. Each chorus seems to give promise of that alluvial furtherance that the poet advises in his "Statement" for the Donald Allen anthology, and that sentence is, of course, immediately followed by one more chorus, which is in its turn followed, in Kerouac's *Collected Poems* by an alluvial 521 pages of more poetry.

CHORUS II

Charlie Parker, forgive me

Apostrophe: What are the terms of address of Kerouac's choruses? Is his writing of them like the musician woodshedding, playing to an imagined future audience? It does seem that the improvisation is in the writing itself. On the evidence of the commercially released recordings of his poetry, Kerouac was not particularly given to improvisation in the reading of his poems. "Mexico City Blues 239–241," identified on the album *Poetry for the Beat Generation* simply as "Charlie Parker," only registers two small alterations from the published text: the dropping of a definite article in 239, and the repetition of the word "talking" in 240. For the rest, the poet sticks to his text. To the extent that there is improvisation here, it is in his voicings of the lyrics.

When Kerouac appeared on Steve Allen's nighttime television show, he appeared to be reading directly from a copy of *On The Road*, though readers of that novel recognized at once that the introductory notes he was reading are not to be found in the novel his host has just asked him to read from. As he arrives at his final passage, he stretches out the repetition of the name "Dean Moriarty," shaking his head slowly in rhythm with the concluding lines of the Blues Steve Allen has been playing on the piano, to the soft accompaniment of guitar, bass, and drums. It's an effective performance, particularly following on the awkward brief interview that introduces it. By then, Steve Allen and Jack Kerouac had reached at least a modicum level of comfort working together in the music studio, as *Poetry for the Beat Generation* had already been recorded, following a spur of the moment pairing during Kerouac's set at the Village Vanguard. David Perry, in his liner notes to *The Jack Kerouac Collection,* quotes Steve Allen as having remarked "It seemed appropriate for Kerouac. He did not give a dramatic reading at all. I was the performer, he wasn't. He simply read. No dramatics, no histrionics."[7] It is the case that listeners will hear none of the performative inflections familiar to generations of Slam and Spoken Word poetry aficionados, still, his characteristically low-key performance (in contrast, say, to reports of his shouting "Go, Go, Go," as Ginsberg read "Howl" at the Six Gallery debut), was none-the-less a mode of performance, one well suited to those earlier days of the stereo long playing record, itself a tremendous advance over those 78s on which the Beats had first listened to Charlie Parker.

But could any listener, let alone reader, ever hear these poems as overheard speech? When the poet is right in front of us looking into our eyes, it's hard enough to think of the work as an overheard monologue (not to mention those frequent narrative introductions so common among today's poets), but even listening to a recording or reading to ourselves it seems difficult to abide that one particular theory of lyric verse. Kerouac's eyes, as he read on Steve Allen's show, went from the novel to his host to the assembled audience to the uncounted and unaccounted for watching over their televisions in those early days of late-night entertainment. Those multiplied audiences shared an experience of the living, somewhat awkward and nervous, author speaking to Allen and to them, more directly than they perhaps had ever witnessed an author before. In the introductory conversation, Kerouac makes an uneasy distinction between his narrative novels, as he terms them, and his symbolistic serious impressionistic novels, which he writes in pencil. Allen remarks that he's set eyes on his guest's poetry written in pencil, likely referring to their then recent session in the studio that resulted in *Poetry for the Beat Generation*. Do we feel any more or less directly addressed when listening to these recordings than when reading the poetry off the page to ourselves?

In the 239th chorus of *Mexico City Blues*, Kerouac narrates the end of Charlie Parker, sitting and watching TV as so many were to watch Kerouac himself on *The Tonight Show*. The poet imagines the musician as a beatific "Perfect Musician,"[8] a veritable Buddha with "lidded eyes." Parker had the habit of looking out over his alto saxophone directly at his audience while playing, at times, as he leaned back in midstream improvisation, his eyelids would *almost* close, a sign Kerouac took to signify that all is well. "A great musician and a great / creator of forms / That ultimately find expression / In mores."[9] An intriguing suggestion—not only that the great innovator of a revolution in harmonics was continually spinning out new forms, but that he was leading listeners somehow to an ethics, a suggestion the poet tosses off with a casual "and what have you." And yet, that dismissive final clause is, if anything, a prompt for another chorus. The 240th opens with praise and a complaint. Kerouac sees Parker as being every bit as important as Beethoven, but not equally regarded. This founding figure of Bebop is certainly ranked in the pantheon of musical artists today, but is still a name heard infrequently in association with the classics. Parker had an ear for strings, however, and Kerouac's poem invokes a then unusual entry in the Bebop catalogue, recognizing Parker as "A genteel conductor of string / orchestras."[10] In 1949 and 1950, Parker had recorded two albums worth of music adding string quartets to his jazz rhythm section. (There are some intriguing surprises in these sessions. Appearing on oboe in the first set is none other than Mitch Miller, later to become famous for his television program "Sing Along With Mitch" in addition to his long career producing and arranging at Columbia Records.) Jazz names that would have been familiar to the poet included Ray Brown on bass and Buddy Rich on drums. Also in 1950, Parker took to the stage of Carnegie Hall, with its impeccable classical credentials. He appeared with the Neal Hefti Orchestra, and the number "Repetition" was released as a limited edition 78. Though *Charlie Parker With Strings* was reputedly the alto saxophonist's own favorite among his recording projects, it was not met with universal approval. It was commercially successful and spawned a large number of other albums of jazz in orchestral settings but was seen in some quarters (perhaps mostly among jazz fans who didn't know of Parker's intense interest in "modern classical" composers) as a sort of sell out. On the evidence of *Mexico City Blues*, however, Kerouac was among the more avid listeners to this experiment. His chorus transitions to a view of a rocking jazz club where Parker's "patootle stick," his alto sax, is compared to Saint Patrick whistling the masses into eternity.

It is in the 241st chorus that we encounter Kerouac's lyric apostrophe, his direct address and plea for forgiveness summoning Parker himself. Here the poet breaks into rhyme:

> Forgive me for not answering your eyes–
> For not having made an indication
> Of that which you can devise–
> Charlie Parker, pray for me–
> Pray for me and everybody[11]

The power of prayer might strike some as unexpected in this context, had it not been for the earlier insistence that Parker's playing itself might provide the mores for mid-century mankind. And then there was that widespread graffiti following Parker's demise: "Bird Lives." The chorus concludes, to the extent that any chorus can be seen as a conclusion, with a plea for Parker to "lay the bane" off Kerouac and "every body"— There is no final punctuation here, suggesting an opening onto the "whatever" that might follow. (The following chorus, the 242nd, again ends with no period. The 240th does conclude "in time" with a full stop.) And the emphasis of the body in "every body" implies a mode of miraculous curative for the distress in the world. Earlier in the same chorus, in the cited passage, the word is typed in the more usual manner, "everybody." But at this stage, Charlie Parker is no longer Charlie Parker, rather the bearer of a "secret unsayable name" in nirvana, complicated by the assertion that this nirvana is "of your brain / Where you hide." In some ways, it seems this chorus is a kind of atonement. The poet begs forgiveness for not answering Parker's eyes with an indication, so perhaps we should read this poem as the indication that had been lacking. Kerouac asks forgiveness "For not having made" something on the order of what he here, and now, makes.

But just who is this "Charlie Parker"?

[BRIDGE]

In my mid-century childhood, every drug, dime, and grocery store featured an entire wall holding racks of magazines and books. The variety on offer then easily challenges the plenty of today's World Wide Web. I dawdled over everything from *Rodeo News* to *Amateur Rocketeer* and such favorites as *Alfred Hitchcock's Mystery Magazine* and *Tropical Fish Hobbyist*. The book racks carried their share of overheated romance, lurid murder mysteries and priced-to-sell reprints of classic literature, and I could catch first glimpses of what was new in American fiction. (No poetry to speak of, sad to say.) And it was there, on a drugstore book rack, that I first saw that fifty cents Signet edition, "complete and unabridged," that promised to be "the bible of the 'Beat Generation,'" an explosive best seller "that tells all about today's wild youth and their frenetic search for Experience and Sensation." I didn't have fifty cents, was pretty sure I didn't qualify as wild youth, had no idea what "frenetic" meant, and had been in grade school long enough to find puzzling the capitalization of "Experience and Sensation." The cover certainly promised a lot. In the center was a young, dark-haired man wearing a striped shirt (which I was too young then to recognize as the mainstream's way of signaling Beatness—sharp contrast to the vertical stripes of more wholesome folk singers' shirts), while around him were smaller scenes of love making, violence, and a woman dancing suggestively in front of a group of men.

But I had already seen the author on our recently acquired television. My family had moved West to Denver, which meant that Steve Allen's *Tonight Show* aired much earlier for us than for folks in time zones to our East, and I was able to look in at the goings on. My family subscribed to *Newsweek* magazine, and so when I was twelve years old, though I had not yet read Kerouac, I did read the review of a book of his that termed it the work of "a tin-ear Canuck." I had to look up *Canuck* in my dictionary (another drugstore purchase) but still didn't really get the criticism. A few years on, finally reading *On the Road*, I could understand why *The New York Times Book Review* termed his writing "garrulous hipster yawping." But by then I had started to read Whitman, and I wasn't sure why hipster yawping might be a bad thing.

By the time I actually purchased and read *On the Road*, all traces of Beatery, of any people at all, had vanished from the cover. Instead, there was just a burning bright sun against an orange background. Though I had no such term as "reception theory" in my young brain, it occurred to me that the relationship between that book and, at least, the marketing department had changed substantively. By the time I had gone through college and grad school and begun teaching, the current cover featured a photograph of the author himself, in the company of the man I'd known as Dean Moriarty.

Over time, I was mentally charting the evolution of our reading of Kerouac by way of these ever-changing paperback covers. An early Avon edition of *The Subterraneans* (just thirty-five cents!) was introduced by Henry Miller, and advertised itself, much as had that early *On the Road*, as "a magnificent and bitter novel of the Beat generation." Bitter? The first copy I owned was fronted by a photo of a couple, the man wearing a leather jacket, the woman, clearly of mixed race, wearing, well, nothing. The two were looking away from one another. What was that all about? (Just as I had not known Neal Cassady shared my childhood Denver streets, I had no clue that the "young novelist looking like Leslie Howard" in *The Subterraneans* was William Gaddis, whose *Recognitions* I read around the same time.) By the time that I first taught the novel, the hipster had returned in triumph (only later to bear the brunt of so many jokes) and the book cover had adapted accordingly, now showing a dimly lit scene of bohemian rhapsody, a central figure playing an acoustic guitar while various Beats looked on in deepest thought. But across the course of my life and career, Kerouac had gone from literary bad boy to canonical, and when I teach the book today, my students have an edition with just a photo of Kerouac himself, doubled.

Nothing like this seems to have been happening with the marketing of Kerouac's poetry. That first copy of *Mexico City Blues* bore an abstract black-and-white drawing suggesting a human figure. The cover promised (or warned) that there were 242 choruses inside. *Scattered Poems* simply presented a photo of the poet wearing a jaunty cap. The Penguin edition of *Book of Blues*, with an introduction by Robert Creeley, featured two photos of San Francisco, one a city scape centered on Coit Tower, the other a period street scene of North Beach cafes and clubs. These poetry volumes were not marketing themselves so much as keys to the bohemian underground, but then the sort of reader likely to buy a book of Kerouac's poetry almost certainly already knew of his novels and the Beat realms depicted therein. And they just as likely knew from their reading that Kerouac, and everybody, might have more reason to ask forgiveness.

CHORUS III

Poems for the Beat Generation opens with Steve Allen improvising around a standard and Kerouac reading "October in the Railroad Earth," composed about a year-and-a-half after *On the Road* and first published in 1957 in *Evergreen Review*. Often referred to as a prose poem, it is not included in the author's *Collected Poems*, but here it is serving as the entryway to *Poems for the Beat Generation*. It is a veritable textbook example of Kerouac's "spontaneous bop prosody," composed of a fluid presentation of San Francisco observations. We're in an alley back of the Southern Pacific station, which should recall Ginsberg's "In Back of the Real," set a bit to the south in San Jose and written not long after Kerouac's piece. The poet watches businessmen rushing by with their copies of the *San Francisco Chronicle*, he remembers the scene of an accident spotted as he returned from a run down to Hollister and San Jose, a good-looking girl who approached him, a fight he almost got into, all presented in a rush of rhythmic remembrance. There, too, we hear of "even Negros so hopeless." Kerouac has "insane conversations with Negros in second-story windows above," and hearing Ruth Brown's classic "(Mama) He Treats Your Daughter Mean" he feels

> all wondrous
> knowing about the Negro the essential American out there
> always finding his solace his meaning in the fellaheen street
> and not in abstract morality and even when he has a church
> you see the pastor out front bowing to the ladies on the make
> you hear his great vibrant voice on the sunny Sunday afternoon
> sidewalk full of sexual vibratos saying "Why yes
> Mam but de gospel do say that man was born of woman's
> womb-"

And just here we have to pause in wonder ourselves. These notes are so common among the Beat writers, and among their non-Beat contemporaries and predecessors, that they all too often go all together unremarked. When the "best minds" of the Beat generation are found dragging themselves through "the negro streets" looking for a fix, yes, we may remind ourselves that the Columbia University of Kerouac and Ginsberg is located in Harlem, but that is not the real weight of these metaphors. Even our most antiessentialist critics may pause at the assertion that the "Negro" is "the essential American," though American culture would be unrecognizable, unimaginable, without its African American heart. But it's more than a little worrisome that the Beats' Blacks are nearly always presented in such a sexualized context, nearly always bearing the burdens of White America's unease and bad conscience.

Kerouac and most of the other Beats were continuing a project of Western modernism, one accurately characterized by Achille Mbembe:

> From the 1920s on … discourse on aesthetics, notably among the avant-garde, viewed Africa as a land of difference, a reservoir of mysteries, and the ultimate kingdom of catharsis and the magico-religious.[12]

Readers of *On the Road, The Subterraneans*, and the other Kerouac novels will recognize in this an apt description of a familiar phenomenon; Kerouac regarded Indians, Mexicans, African Americans, nearly anybody he saw as a racial other, as being in some mystical way beyond the damaging shade of American puritanism. While the term wouldn't be coined till long after Kerouac's death, something of *the magical Negro* shrouds many of the characters we encounter in his works. Why else would he expect Charlie Parker to be not only a creator of forms, but a veritable Buddha?

Another of the poems performed on *Poetry for the Beat Generation* is the 221st chorus of *Mexico City Blues*, listed on the album as "Deadbelly." It opens with Steve Allen beating out a standard blues pattern on the piano. Kerouac begins by invoking "Old Man Mose / Early American Jazz pianist"[13] "Mose" was a not uncommon name. Among Kerouac's contemporaries, pianist, singer and songwriter Mose Allison was a popular figure. But in jazz history, perhaps the earliest "Old Man Mose" was the figure in a song created in 1935 by Louis Armstrong and Zilner Randolph. It was quickly covered by other artists. Eddie Duchin recorded his version in 1938 (a version supposedly banned in Britain due to a mishearing of the word "bucket"). The following year, Betty Hutton, advertised as America's number one jitterbug, recorded the song and performed it on film. In one release the song is paired with "Swinging with the Goon" and played by Vincent Lopez and his Orchestra. There are other covers by Nat King Cole, Teresa Brewer, Manhattan Transfer, and many more. In none of these versions is Old Man Mose a piano player. What they all have in common, and share with Kerouac's poem, is that Mose is dead, or at least, as the lyrics have "(We believe) he kicked the bucket / (We believe) that Old Man Mose is dead."

Kerouac's 221st Chorus will put many in mind of poems like William Carlos Williams's "Ol' Bunk's Band," written after the poet and his wife had attended a club appearance by Bunk Johnson and his group. The Williams poem is very much in the same mode as Kerouac's, though the latter introduces a sort of Blues genealogy into the mix, with the appearance of Mose's grandson, one "Deadbelly." Mose here is like something out of Willa Cather, "walloping" his "wildhouse Piany / with monkeys in his hair / drooling spaghetti, beer / and beans," a "furtive madman." Something approaching an idiot savant. Deadbelly is contrasted to Leadbelly, the real-life Huddie Ledbetter, known to music lovers simply as Leadbelly. Reputed, perhaps incorrectly, to have sung his way out of a prison sentence, Leadbelly had become a feature on the folk club scene by the time Kerouac appeared in the Village. Along the way, he had stopped off at a meeting of the Modern Language Association in 1934, accompanying folklorist John Lomax, an early bridge between the worlds of the Blues and of poetry scholars. In the poem there seems little if any connection between Leadbelly and Old Man Mose's grandson, other than the play between their names. "Lead killed Leadbelly," the poet tells us, though in fact he had been diagnosed with ALS, Lou Gehrig's Disease. Kerouac gives him a yet more tragic, if romantic, ending, and it's not at all clear in the end what he's doing in this chorus, other than drawing together allusions to the blues with Kerouac's verbal play. "Deadbelly modern cat" as the poem has it. Leadbelly would seem a fitting representative of the modern already, but Kerouac's invention is a sort of grandson of the modernists. "Cool–Deadbelly, Man." In the end: "Old Man Mose is Dead / But Deadbelly get Ahead."[14] (Despite footnoting everything from Hoot Gibson and Gore Vidal to King Sariputra, the *Collected Poems* volume gives precious little information regarding these figures who were so important to the poet.)

What's going on here is pretty much a continuation of the ways that jazz had figured in the works of American modernists. Hart Crane, e.e. cummings, Williams, even Eliot with his rag time, all came to Black jazz and Blues seeking something they felt lacking in themselves and in their culture. As Mbembe describes the history of this tendency: "jazz ... appeared as a celestial path to return to one's origins, a kind of grace by which sleeping powers could be awakened, myths and rituals reinvented, tradition rerouted and undermined, and time reversed."[15] "Most primitive thing we know / About man is music ...."[16] So avers Kerouac in Chorus 53. The exoticism and primitivism that marked so much Modernist art clearly extended into the Beat era, even as Charles Olson, and along with him Amiri Baraka, argued for the primitive as first things. Not a primitivism of reclamation, but an archeology of beginnings. But Kerouac, as much as beginnings, was seeking otherness. In the 54th chorus, he recalls a 1941 bus ride to the South, where all he "saw on the long / Avenue were Negroes."[17]

There is on the one hand a heartening celebration of Americana in these choruses. The 116th begins "The Jews Wrote American Music,"[18] which is followed by shout outs to Mexican children and to the poet's own "Canucks." At poem's end, he almost rescues us from the sort of racial masquerade so prominent in American culture: "The Great Jazz Singer / was Jolson the Vaudeville Singer?" Many would join Kerouac in answering, "No." But then he adds, "and not Miles, me." Clearly this is a bit of amused braggadocio, and yet, there is much unsettling about the joke, from vaudeville singer Jolson being touted as *the* jazz singer, to Kerouac's all too clever displacement of Miles Davis.

But there is more than hubris to be forgiven. Among the poems in the "uncollected" section of Kerouac's *Collected Poems* is a lengthy work titled simply "Heaven." As the title would suggest, this work is a lyric imagining of what it may be like to arrive in heaven, "a wise angel of the dead / among the blind unborn angels."[19] As the poem proceeds, the poet catalogues the angelic inhabitants of the beyond. There is his brother Gerard sharing a stanza with Chirico and Buddha and Christ himself. In this future vision of visitation, Kerouac sees Allen Ginsberg, Peter Orlovsky, and hero of *On the Road*, Neal Cassady, as well as Cassady's "prim" wife Carolyn. Lucien Carr and friend Leroi Jones share a stanza, but they share it with Hitler, for, as the poem is to explain:

> Heaven is big enough
> (It's all empty space
> endless) to take in
> unnumerable non-numbers
> of anything & everything[20]

At the close of one stanza Kerouac suggests he is going to "shut up," but, as with the choruses of *Mexico City Blues*, he does not, instead continuing to catalogue the inhabitants of the beyond and imagining coming face-to-face with God himself. It's when he comes to a contemporary event, a tragedy in Chicago, that the race card plays itself. His reference is to the deaths of ninety-two students and three nuns in the 1958 blaze that struck Our Lady of the Angels School. (Here again the annotations fail us. While the Library of America makes sure we know who each of the enumerated Beat inhabitants of heaven is, as well as sports figures such as Roy Campanella, there is no mention in the notes of the event Kerouac is responding to.) But when Kerouac imagines the terror of the burnt children in heaven, he sees them:

> like little black
>   niggers in the Virgin Mary's
>   beautiful blue & white
>   golden yard
>   Forever[21]

To the extent that Charlie Parker's music is to give us mores, Kerouac seems here not to have learned the lessons. "Charlie Parker, forgive me—"

CHORUS IV

And here, too, is a tension that animates nearly all of Kerouac's writings. At their heart Kerouac's poems sing from a soul yearning after freedom, and project a utopian ideal. But that utopia is warped at birth by the legacies of Western modern ideologies which the poet never completely overcomes. In some ways, he sees our jazz and blues as the very epicenters of those tensions:

> Improvise, black saxist, improvise!
> Tell them with your black soul

That America is blue,
That America is the blues[22]

And so it is an American blue heaven that he sees in prospect. "Let's Go–to heaven–," he invites in his long prose poem "Old Angel Midnight." "Bob Kaufman wants to come too–all aboard–"[23] Kaufman was, of course, co-founder of the publication *Beatitude*, whose issues offer a veritable mapping of the Beat literary landscape. Heaven also opens up to us in the 12th chorus of "Cerrada Medellin Blues," where it is again a multiracial afterlife bringing fugitive Beats together in paradise:

Move my hand Lord
    move my hand
  Tell Ray Bremser
    something calm him
      down
  Tell Leroi Jones
    & Diane di Prima
      tooo[24]

(Note how Kerouac generally spells Baraka's early authorial signature with a small "r," thus typographically demoting his friend's more regal self-fashioning of the time. The annotations spell it as Baraka did, "LeRoi.") Bremser was a poet who shared Kerouac's love of jazz, and his friendship with Baraka. He was later to publish a book titled *Black Is Black Blues*. When he was released from one stint in jail, it was Baraka who signed on to be his supposed sponsor in liberty. Baraka and di Prima together produced the crucial mimeo zine *Floating Bear* (as well as daughter Dominique). This short lyric begins with its own sort of appeal to the muses, but it's a Gospel-tinged appeal. Kerouac has no doubt heard that song composed by the former blues pianist Thomas Dorsey that begins "Precious Lord, take my hand." This section is in turn a part of the *Book of Blues*. Like the Blues, these poems are endlessly expansive. Kerouac's *Book of Blues* opens with an authorial note explaining that the form of the poems is determined by the size of the small notebook in which they were first written. "As in jazz," he offers, "the form is determined by time,"[25] and he promises to keep to the technique of non-stop ad libbing, like the improvised fills of the blues, hence the spontaneity of his bop prosody. Over time, most folk blues, like poetic magnets (or the epics of the past) attracted additional stanzas as they passed through time and successive musicians. Not only do we have the ever-growing stream of Kerouac's choruses, late in the *Collected Poems* we encounter the epic prose poem "Old Angel Midnight," which, like *On the Road*, was patently not constrained by the size of a notebook page. In retrospect, this wild thing must be seen clearly as a predecessor of such phenomena as L=A=N=G=U=A=G=E poet Ron Silliman's *Ketjak* and *Tjanting* and second-generation New York School poet Clark Coolidge's *Book Beginning What and Ending Away*. "You're a good enuf old boy but my God you write too much," Kerouac is told, only to reply: "But I'm only reporting the sounds out the window."[26]

It is this possibility of never ending, or of only ending in some Beat afterlife with Buddha and everybody in empty space, that comprises Kerouac's utopian ideal and form. Jack Kerouac was forever seeking some sort of salvation. He had heard hints of a hereafter in the unrolling strophes of the blues, and pursued them in the continuous, spontaneous generation of forms. Whether by feeding one end of a teletype roll into his typewriter, or by filling pocket notebook after pocket notebook, his was the constant rebeginning of the blues chorus, "the form of emptiness / which is emptiness having taken the form of form."[27]

Notes

1. John Edgar Wideman, *Writing to Save a Life: The Louis Till File* (New York: Scribner, 2016), 180.
2. Jack Kerouac, "Statement," in *The New American Poetry*, ed. Donald Allen (New York: Grove Press, 1960), 414.
3. Jack Kerouac, "Essentials of Spontaneous Prose," in *The Moderns*, ed. LeRoi Jones (New York: Corinth Books, 1963), 343.
4. Ibid., 344.
5. Jack Kerouac, *Collected Poems*, ed. Marilène Phipps-Kettlewell (New York: Library of America, 2012), 171.
6. Ibid., 172.
7. David Perry, "The Jack Kerouac Collection," in *The Jack Kerouac Collection*. Audio recordings (Los Angeles, CA: Rhino Word Beat, 1990), 7.
8. Kerouac, *Collected Poems*, 170.
9. Ibid., 171.
10. Ibid.
11. Ibid., 172.
12. Achille Mbembe, *Critique of Black Reason* (Durham, NC: Duke University Press, 2017), 40.
13. Ibid., 156.
14. Kerouac, *Collected Poems*, 157.
15. Mbembe, *Critique of Black Reason*, 41.
16. Kerouac, *Collected Poems*, 41.
17. Ibid., 42.
18. Ibid., 85.
19. Ibid., 603.
20. Ibid., 605.
21. Ibid., 608.
22. Ibid., 575.
23. Ibid., 494.
24. Ibid., 368.
25. Ibid., 195.
26. Ibid., 502.
27. Ibid., 179.

3

Jack Kerouac's Paintings: Color, Texture, Movement

Frida Forsgren

A juicy blotch of heart-shaped red paint smeared on a soft pink backdrop. A shining blue hand emerging from a black surface. A red-mouthed smoking woman dressed in blue. A swirling ocean of paint forming circular movements. Pages of sketchbooks filled with people, Buddhas, crucifixes, and cats made with expressive, gnarled lines on paper.

Figure 3.1 Jack Kerouac, *Heart and Handgun*. With a shining red heart emerging from the background, Kerouac's *Heart and Handgun* shows a bold use of colors.

Jack Kerouac painted, just like his fellow Beat writers ruth weiss, William Burroughs and Lawrence Ferlinghetti. In addition, he wrote about art, he made covers for his books, and he was friends with seminal artists like Willem de Kooning, Franz Kline, and Robert Motherwell. Art was an inextricable part of who he was and of what he made. This is why we should continue to readdress and revisit his art; it says something fundamental about his aesthetics.

Previous studies have focused attention on aesthetic and thematic similarities between Kerouac's art and his writing, with a stress on the written works.[1] My essay, however, sees Kerouac's art from an art historical perspective, using the collection of Beat art at the University of Agder (Norway) as a point of comparison. The collection was assembled in San Francisco in the 1950s and 1960s by Reidar Wennesland, who visited artist's studios, saw exhibits, went to poetry readings, and attended plays. The collection is a unique timepiece of US Beat culture. Although Jack Kerouac's art is not included in the Wennesland collection, his aesthetics resonate with the wider cultural and material context: particularly with the Bay Area Figurative Movement and with Beat art.[2]

Jack Kerouac's Artistic Background

Even though Jack Kerouac is predominantly known as the writer of important Beat literary works such as *The Subterraneans*, *On the Road*, and *The Dharma Bums*, he was also a painter with an acute visual perception. According to his childhood friend John Sampas, Kerouac dreamed of becoming a painter long before he became a writer.[3] He had studied art history with renowned art history professor Meyer Schapiro while at Columbia University (1940–2), and was especially enthralled with pre-classical, Byzantine, and medieval art.[4] Among the Modernists he had a predilection for Paul Cezanne, Vincent Van Gogh, and Pablo Picasso, but older artists as Rembrandt, William Blake, and James Whistler also appealed to him. In letters to friends, he writes with enthusiasm about these artists in a lush, vibrant, painterly vocabulary.[5] In 1958 he was introduced to the New York School painters Willem de Kooning, Franz Kline, Robert Motherwell, and Stanley Twardowicz by his friend and lover, the painter Dody Muller. He frequented the Cedar Tavern in Greenwich Village, where many of the second-generation abstract expressionists hung out, painted at Muller's studio, and probably took painting lessons from Willem de Kooning.[6] These encounters resulted in experiments with pure abstract works between 1958 and 1960 as we see in the oil painting *Truman Capote* (1959). Here the idea of Capote is rendered as a fast-pacing whirlwind of colors. There are no facial features, just color and movement.

All these diverse artistic impulses sharpened and shaped his writing, but more importantly also resulted in an independent artistic production and a manifesto on painting titled "Use Only Brush."[7] In the short manifesto Kerouac admonishes the painter to use only brush, to paint spontaneously, and to paint what you see in front of you. No fiction. The variety of his techniques—pen and ink, oil on canvas, acrylic on wood, mixed media—make clear that his artistic influences were wide-ranging.

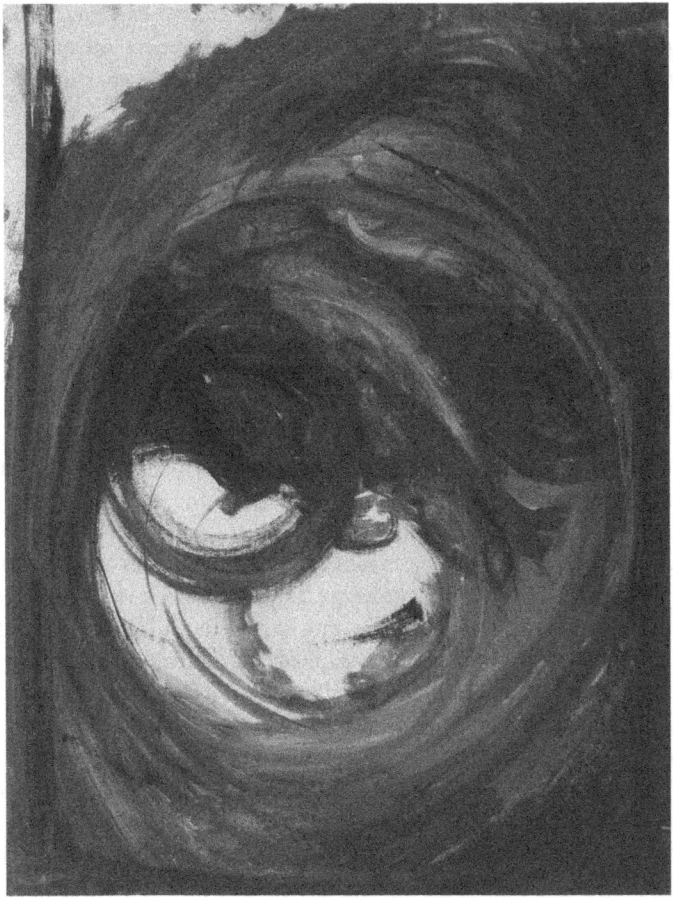

Figure 3.2 Jack Kerouac, *Truman Capote*. In Kerouac's oil painting *Truman Capote* his portrait is rendered in swirls of color.

In the vast literature on Jack Kerouac, the bibliography for his visual art is extremely limited. In fact, there are only two essential sources: Ed Adler's *Departed Angels: The Lost Paintings* (2004) and Sandrina Bandera's *Kerouac Beat Painting* (2018). But by only studying Jack Kerouac the writer, we risk losing his work's interdisciplinary nature. Indeed, Jack Kerouac's visual art deserves particular attention. In his sketches and paintings, we see works that transcend words, appealing to the body, to the sense of touch and to the eyes. We see the trajectory of movement, lines, pace, and energy jotted down in ink, pencil, and paint. According to philosopher John Dewey in his seminal work *Art as Experience* (1934) the process of art making has a particular existential dimension: "making art was the most successful effort to have an experience."[8] By experience he meant a total involvement of mind and spirit resulting in the deepest meaning and fulfillment of the human condition.[9] Dewey did not draw distinctions between high art, craft, and low art but saw all artistic experiences as equally meaningful to the maker. By looking at Kerouac's artistic practice, we may come closer to understanding his aesthetics as a place where he found meaning and fulfillment. And where he could be at ease, play and experience creative flow.

Beat Art

I see Kerouac's art as Beat art, and the concept needs a closer definition. Beat art is visual art that has aesthetic and thematic similarities with Beat literature.[10] Beat art was made in the bohemian subcultural communities in Los Angeles's Venice West, San Francisco's North Beach, and New York City's Greenwich Village in the 1950s.[11] Like Beat literature, Beat art is often direct and visceral; it is critical, anti-materialist, and anti-establishment. It includes a diverse set of styles such as Abstract Expressionism, Bay Area Figuration, and Funk. Artists such as Joan Brown, Jay DeFeo, and Bruce Conner made collages and assemblages from junk and left-over materials, quite like the literary cutups of William Burroughs. Painters like Leo Valledor made paintings such as "Miles," "Sonny's Side," and "That's the Spirit" inspired by jazz music blowing the strokes onto the canvas like the jazz poetry of ruth weiss and Jack Kerouac. And sketching was a way to get your thoughts down fast and unfiltered in painting and writing alike. Like Beat literature, Beat art was often interdisciplinary. Poets painted, artists wrote, poetry was performed to music, and art was exhibited at poetry readings. It was a fully visual, audible, material, and bodily entangled artistic culture. The relationship between poets and painters was particularly close as the humanities program at the California School of Fine Arts attests.[12] Here poet Jack Spicer had an important role in the teaching of art students. Another well-known example of how Beat poetry inspired art is Jay DeFeo's painting *The Eyes* (1958) made after a stanza from a poem by Beat poet Philip Lamantia.[13]

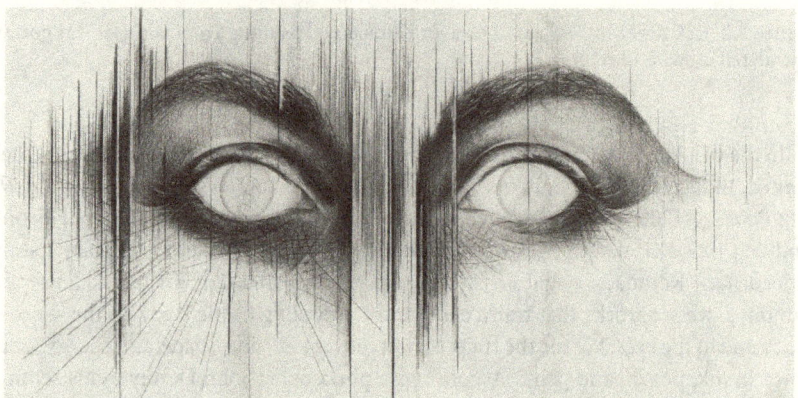

Figure 3.3 Jay DeFeo, *The Eyes*. Jay DeFeo's *The Eyes*, which draws on a stanza from Philip Lamantia, is an example of the close relationship between poets and painters in the San Francisco Beat Era.

Moreover, the visual Beats and the literary Beats shared common social and cultural spaces. Venues such as The Six Gallery and The Dilexi Gallery were spaces for art exhibits, for jazz concerts, and for public poetry readings.[14] The Six Gallery reading on October 7th, 1955, is the best-known example of this fusion between art, jazz music, and literature in the Beat canon.

In Norway, the concept *beat art* has been used extensively to contextualize the Reidar Wennesland Collection by several authors.[15] The Wennesland Collection comprises approximately 800 works of art by artists that were affiliated with Beat culture through the collector Reidar Wennesland. He was friends with several of the Beat writers and artists, supported them economically, and collected their works. Wennesland moved in diverse artistic circles and had a holistic understanding of Beat culture. Today, the collection exhibited at the University of Agder and the Kristiansand Cathedral School Gimle is a fruitful place to study visual Beat culture. On the walls, students and staff are faced with sketches by such artists as Jay DeFeo, George Herms, Arthur Monroe, Michael Bowen, and Michael McCracken showing angels, portrait heads, and oil canvases with non-figurative color fields from the 1950s and 1960s. A poignant example from the collection is Michael McCracken's portrait of his wife Carol McCracken.

Figure 3.4 Michael McCracken, *Portrait*. Michael McCracken's *Portrait* is an example of the Bay Area Figurative Movement which favored a return to figuration in the 1950s and 1960s.

The Figurative Turn

A striking feature of Jack Kerouac's sketches, drawings, and paintings is how concrete and to-the-point they are. They show close-ups of portrait heads, they show groups of people relaxing, and people in landscapes on the move. They are rendered in a fast-paced figurative sketch-like style, as if he were in haste when producing his work. Some sketches are jotted down with a pencil on pages in notebooks, some are accompanied with texts, others are painted directly in oil on canvases. A fine example is *The Slouch Hat* (oil and charcoal on paper, *c.* 1960) which evokes the people in the famed Cedar Tavern in the Village in New York.

In the art collection at the University of Agder we may observe a similar sketchy, hasty, yet concrete set of motives that aligns with Kerouac's spontaneous bop prosody. The collection is dominated by sketches of the trio Michael Bowen, Michael McCracken,

Figure 3.5 Jack Kerouac, *The Slouch Hat*. Kerouac's sketch *The Slouch Hat* shows people in the famed Cedar Tavern in New York's Greenwich Village.

and Arthur Monroe who shared a loft in 72 Commercial Street in San Francisco in the late 1950s. Their studio at Commercial Street is lively described in Jerry Kamstra's *The Frisco Kid* as a creative place sprinkled with sketches, people, and their pet chicken.[16] A large part of the University of Agder's collection consists of portraits from this studio space. They are large-scale, close-up portraits executed in a spontaneous style. Some are attributed self-portraits or portraits like the ones of Arthur Monroe or Carole, Michael McCracken's wife, but most portraits are unattributed. We assume they were people they met on the streets, or friends who were in their group. Arthur Monroe reminisces about this period:

> Everybody was always drawing everybody else, at readings and at parties, even though it might not be exhibited, the activity served its purpose just the same. It was a widely accepted notion among painters that it did not matter what one paints as long as it is well painted.[17]

This constant sketching has several similarities with Jack Kerouac's writing method described in his "Essentials of Spontaneous Prose."[18] In the initial part of his text called "SET-UP," Kerouac recommends starting with what you have right in front of your eyes: "Set [the object] before the mind, either in reality, as in sketching (before a landscape or teacup or old face)." Kerouac advises us to start with what you know, what you see, with what you have around you. In his painting manifesto written in 1959, Kerouac admonishes a similar concrete approach: "Paint what you have in front of you. No 'fiction.'"[19] This is quite like Monroe, who drew people at readings and at parties, the people he was friends with and had before his eyes.[20] In Kerouac's visual sketches we see the same approach. He draws portraits of his family and his friends Robert Frank, William S. Burroughs, Larry Rivers, and Dody Muller, among others. He draws cats and random people on the streets. This concrete, matter-of-fact sketching of your world and what you have right in front of your eyes might seem to be what artists always do and have always done. But the technique is also part of the art movement called Bay Area Figuration, termed "the most salient postwar development on the West Coast" by Caroline A. Jones.[21]

The Bay Area Figurative movement was initiated in the late 1940s and early 1950s by David Park who was tired of the art establishment's favoring of newness and intellectual pursuits. Park states: "I believe that we are living at a time that overemphasizes the need of newness, of furthering concepts."[22] Park further states on the topic of his abstract canvases: "What the paintings told me was that I was a hard-working guy who was trying to be important … I have found that in accepting and immersing myself in subject matter I paint with more intensity and that the 'hows' of painting are more inevitably determined by the 'whats.'"[23] Instead, he wished for his compositions to have the kind of "sting" that a fixed subject could make.[24] So instead of non-figurative work, David Park in 1948 returned to the figure, producing paintings of people and landscapes. He went back to basics, so to speak.

Stylistically, Bay Area Figuration has two main characteristics: a figurative subject matter, combined with broad and vigorous brushwork inspired by the abstract

Figure 3.6 Jack Kerouac, *Woman (Joan Rawshanks) in Blue with Black Hat*. Kerouac's painting *Woman (Joan Rawshanks)* is an example of how familiar people became his painted subjects.

expressionists. The paint is fleshy, it is applied on the canvas in large, spontaneous strokes and has bold, bright colors, much like we may observe in Jack Kerouac's painting of Joan Rawshanks with its short brushstrokes, strong colors, and dense paint application or in the oil study *Blonde in the Grass*, where the woman lying in the grass is painted with fresh oil paint directly on paper.

Several of the artists in the Bay Area Figurative movement, like Richard Diebenkorn, David Park, and Elmer Bischoff, belonged to the academic milieu around the California School of Fine Arts. And several of them frequented the Beat milieu, as for instance Joan Brown. Brown made a figurative series of her dog, her son, the food she ate, and the people she knew in a fleshy painterly style.[25] This highly concrete registering of

Figure 3.7 Jack Kerouac, *Blonde in the Grass*. With its figurative subject matter, combined with broad and vigorous brushwork inspired by the abstract expressionists, Kerouac's painting displays affinities with Bay Area Figuration.

the world and its objects is a defining part of Beat culture. It has a concrete, hands-on quality where "the landscape or a teacup or old face" occupies a fundamental place as a bridge between the world and your emotions.[26] It is a culture which is centered around the relational processes between people, rather than on intellectual ideas. An emphasis is placed on *how* you paint, not *what* you paint. In Arthur Monroe's words, "art is not an intellectual way of Thinking," rather it is occupied with the here and with the now.[27] Whether Jack Kerouac had knowledge of the Bay Area Figurative movement when he stayed in San Francisco in 1948–50, and later when he attended the Six Gallery poetry reading in 1955, is unknown. But according to Bay Area artist Dean Fleming, "everybody was doing Bay Area Figurative work" at the time, so it was part of the scene.[28] And that Kerouac's visual sketching and the turn to the figure shared a common ground is clear. In time, this return to the figure corresponds with Kerouac starting to elaborate on his writing method of "sketching" and when he begins to rewrite *On the Road*.[29]

Sketching as Method

Besides their concrete, figurative, hands-on subject matter, Kerouac's figurative sketches, moreover, raise interesting methodological issues. His sketches are executed in a swift, hasty, and spontaneous style that relates to Kerouac's recommendations in his "Essentials of Spontaneous Prose." When describing a writer's procedure, Kerouac admonishes: "sketching language is undisturbed flow from the mind of personal secret idea-words, blowing (as per jazz musician) on subject of image." And when it comes to one's mental state, one should write "'without consciousness' in a semi-trance (as Yeats' later 'trance writing') allowing subconscious to admit in own uninhibited interesting necessary."[30] Again in 1959, he also makes similar recommendations in his painting manifesto: "USE BRUSH SPONTANEOUSLY. i.e. Without drawing, without long pause or delay, without erasing … pile it on."[31] As pointed out by several scholars, the spontaneous prose of Kerouac has a precedent in surrealist automatic writing and drawing championed by André Breton and André Masson.[32] Based on Sigmund Freud's ideas, the Surrealists believed that if you let go of your conscious self, you would move into the subconscious field where your dreams, fears, and true self were stored. In this natural, uninhibited, unfiltered state you could "come from within, out-to relaxed and said" as Jack Kerouac says, inspired by the writing of psychiatrist Wilhelm Reich. This body-mind holism, as Daniel Belgrad calls it, has similar parallels in painting at the time.[33] Upon painting his large-scale non-objective canvases American abstract expressionist painter Jackson Pollock uses his body's intuitive dance-like movements to inflict paint on the canvas. To express the connections between his subconscious, his movements, and the traces on the canvas he describes how he is in a trance-like state, and that he feels as if he "is nature."[34] In a similar vein, artist Fred Martin would make sketches as he was driving. The steering wheel would support his canvas as he would register what went on around him, literally painting spontaneously "on the road."[35] And Arthur Monroe from the visual Beat milieu talks about a constant chain of expressions made by painters in a state of urgency: "Today and the experience of painting were the most important things. People poured everything they had into it. They wanted to discover what painting could mean for them with a tremendous feeling of urgency."[36]

The method allows access to the subconscious by letting your mind roam free. For Kerouac, his written automatism and visual sketching are tied to his need for truth and for authenticity.[37] And perhaps this is why his artwork seems so raw and unfiltered, alive, and breathing. Immediate and true. Because they are a result of Jack Kerouac's "now" in Arthur Monroe's terminology. "NOW was the most important thing."[38]

Beat, Beatific, Beatitude

The feeling of NOW, and the "in-the-moment-ness" that we experience in Jack Kerouac's art, has close affinities with the place religion played in his life. He was raised Catholic but developed a syncretic religious belief merging Catholicism with Hinduism and Buddhism during his life span. This syncretistic religious view was something he shared with other Beat writers. The Beats studied "gnosticism, mysticism, native American lore, Aztec and Myan mythology" in the same breath as Protestantism, Judaism, and Catholicism.[39] Kerouac says that he prayed to Buddha, to Jesus Christ, and to the Virgin Mary.[40] Importantly, Kerouac stressed that Beat to him did not signify to be "beat down," but to be beatific, to be on a holy search toward a higher spiritual enlightenment.[41] Kerouac says, "I want to speak for things, for the crucifix I speak out, for Lao-tse and Chuang-tse I speak out." His books *The Dharma Bums* and *Mexico City Blues* are perhaps the most significant examples of his religious beliefs, but his visual art also provides answers to the place religion played in his life.

Figure 3.8 Jack Kerouac, *The Gary Buddha*. *The Gary Buddha* shows Kerouac's fusion of Buddhist and Christian themes.

His sketches show innumerable examples of Catholic religious imagery such as the sketched body of a grieving Madonna, Mary Magdalena, Angelic Visions, Crucifixes, a depiction of Cardinale Montini (copied multiple times from a photograph found in *Time* magazine), and a painting of Pope John Paul II. There are also several examples of his syncretistic religious belief with sketches showing Buddhist meditation and his so-called "holy fool" persona.

Again, we might draw a parallel to the Wennesland Collection to understand how Jack Kerouac's art connects to a wider material culture. In addition to the portraits commented on above, the religious imagery is the most prominent part of the Wennesland collection. And as is the case with Jack Kerouac's sketches, also here the body of work is syncretistic. We see paintings of prophets, swirling mandalas, Buddhist monks, and temples, as well as Zen-inspired calligraphy. Michael Bowen's *Dream—Figure Moves Outside Cave* is a striking example from the Wennesland collection, as are the mandalas by Keith Sanzenbach.

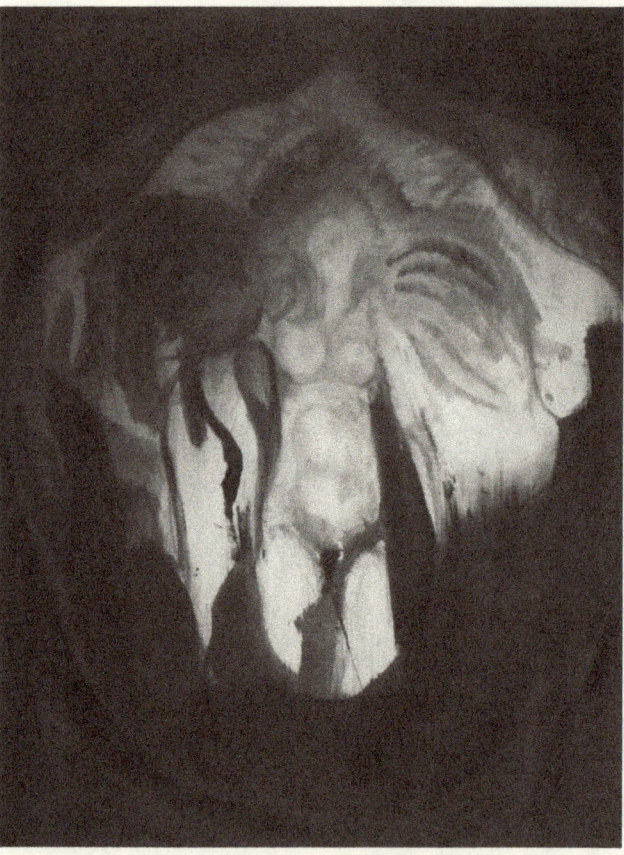

Figure 3.9 Michael Bowen, *Dream–Figure Moves Outside Cave*. The naked angel inscribed in the mandala expresses the syncretistic religious view in the Beat milieu.

Beat artist Jay DeFeo explored religious imagery in her *Wise and Foolish Virgins* based on the parable in St. Matthew, and painted devotional scenes such as *The Annunciation*, *The Veronica*, and a series of Crucifixes during her time in Florence.[42] In her monumental painting *The Rose* she created a syncretistic work that combines Medieval Catholic symbolism of the Virgin Mary with the Buddhist Mandala.

These religious works were painted at a time when religious painting was strong in the United States. Mark Rothko's monumental monochromatic paintings were made to evoke "basic human emotions—tragedy, ecstasy, doom and so on" and were deeply connected to his religious experience.[43] They made, and still make, people weep because people are having the same religious experience as Rothko had when he painted them. As Herman Roodenburg argues, "Rothko's affective rhetoric, his striving for *energeia*, and his viewer's tearful engagement find their origin in an affective handling of color, tonal gradation, light, and shadow or *impasto*, already developed by Titian, Rembrandt, and other 'non-classical' painters versed in the period's sacred rhetoric."[44] They belong to a sacred practice. In a similar vein, Jackson Pollock's drip paintings also channeled a deeper religious meaning inspired by Navajo Indian ritual sand painting. Sand painting was originally part of a religious healing ritual designed to vanquish illness or evil as the tribe's medicine man would pour colored sand and minerals on the floor. When Pollock was involved in his gestural paintings, he experienced a healing "flow" and was free from the ghosts that haunted him.[45] These descriptions of artistic practices echo the thoughts of John Dewey referred to above, where the artistic experience is seen as the place where one could experience completion and meaning. It is a place where you are at ease and where you experience unity. This experience of wholeness and completion can be likened to a religious experience. Jack Kerouac's religious art may thus not only be seen as figurative and representative imagery, but part of his devotional practice. As Mark Rothko's paintings attest, colors have an immense power to create emotions. Experiencing a color is different from reading or writing about a color. And tracing a line on a paper or a swirling brushstroke is different from reading about movement. The study of lines, traces, and textures is an effective and affective way to access the movements of the body. Kerouac's religious painting may thus be seen as a way to communicate and activate the emotive and affective apparatus through art and by art. In this respect, Kerouac is part of a larger set of ideas that sees the body as the center of people's world of cognition and experience. Philosophers, such as the French phenomenologist Maurice Merleau-Ponty, believed that all experiences are primarily shaped by and in the body.[46] And psychoanalysts such as Sigmund Freud and Wilhelm Reich focused on the close ties between the body, sexuality, and the psyche. Kerouac's painting and sketching were different ways to access the feeling of NOW, and the "in-the-moment-ness" that he and his generation sought.

Discussion: But Is This Art?

An inevitable question when discussing Jack Kerouac's artistic production is whether his art is art in its own terms. Would his visual work have been interesting without *On the Road* and Kerouac's other novels? Some critics argue that Kerouac's skill as an artist is questionable,[47] and some argue that his paintings cannot be evaluated independently from his writing.[48] Others, like Ed Adler, do see Kerouac as an "insider" in the world of art, but still read his art in connection to his writing, thus maintaining and strengthening the close links between art and poetry.[49] In this text I treat Jack Kerouac's art as art. And I have used the Beat art collection at Agder as a point of comparison to point to the wider material and visual culture that his art may be contextualized within. And the chosen thematic areas—figures, sketching, religion—do show affinities with the overall production of the Beat artists in themes and in artistic temperament. I suggest that his paintings should not be reduced to an expansion of his written practice and that they are independent artistic expressions. *Affordance* is a useful concept to fully comprehend the impact of Kerouac's art. Affordance denotes "a feature of an object that promotes a specific use or interaction" and was coined by visual psychologist James J. Gibson in 1979.[50] Gibson directed our attention to the diverse properties that pertain to objects and to environments. Adapted to visual theory, an object's affordance is what characterizes its individual visual properties. The affordances of painting and drawing are different from the written words on a page. So, when actively sketching and painting with a pencil or a paint brush on paper or canvas Kerouac deliberately made use of a different set of visual affordances. And he does so in a competent and engaging way. His gnarled, expressionistic, and energetic lines and strokes show deep commitment. His way of handling and applying the colors shows an understanding of colors and how they balance and play against each other. And his works show skill for visual composition. They balance, they are off-balance, and they boast rhythm and movement. They are fundamentally something different from his texts. Texts too, of course, have a visual quality. But the visual affordances of a work of art have a particular ability to create affect and compassion. John Dewey emphasizes how art making is the place and the space where we might "have an experience" and thus find the deepest meaning and fulfillment of the human condition. Art making and creation is a place where we might find meaning without using our intellectual capacities, but simply exist in a state of flow while engaging with the material. The immediacy is transmitted through visual affordances as texture, color, and movement. It is in this capacity that Kerouac's art captures his flow of life in a deeply moving and engaging manner.

Also on a less existential note, Kerouac's art connects to the artistic theories and tendencies of his times. A comparison with artists such as Arthur Monroe, Michael Bowen, and Michael McCracken in the Beat collection at Agder and the movement Bay Area Figurative art shows that "turning to the figure" and "sketching" were concrete, hands-on means to engage with the concrete subject of the world around you. David Park saw the non-figurative visual language as alienating and consciously made figurative imagery that anyone might relate to. This has affinities with Kerouac's sketching. Whereas Ed Adler suggests we understand Jack Kerouac's sketches in the light of Early European Modernism,[51] I find it more pertinent to see his work in connection to a painterly school such as the American Bay Area Figurative Movement. His figurative subject matter combined with the vigorous brushwork of the American Abstract Expressionist does resonate with this movement. Kerouac's non-figurative works are easier to place firmly in the context of New York School expressionism through his direct contact with Willem de Kooning, Franz Kline, and Dody Miller as several scholars have argued.[52] The ease, the energy, and the color-play of his non-figurative works belong to the American Abstract Expressive style.

Moreover, the large body of devotional and religious works made by Jack Kerouac resonates well with the large body of religious works made by diverse painters such as Mark Rothko, Jackson Pollock, Jay DeFeo, and Michael Bowen in the postwar period. They illustrate that religious and devotional art was as dominant in the underground post-war US culture as in the established art world. By exploring the visual affordances of painting, Jack Kerouac could explore and deepen his devotional art. Recent studies in art history have pointed to the emotive character of art, to thinking about artworks as something "beyond representation" and beyond theory.[53] Artworks do not just represent something, but they act on us and deeply affect us in a sensory and bodily manner. In this capacity, Jack Kerouac's art does not simply illustrate his literary works, but they work as independent material agents on us and affect us.

Notes

1   See studies by Ed Adler, *Departed Angels. Jack Kerouac. The Lost Paintings* (New York: Thunder's Mouth, 2004); Michael Hrebeniak, *Action Writing: Jack Kerouac's Wild Form* (Carbondale: Southern Illinois University Press, 2006); Daniel Belgrad, *The Culture of Spontaneity. Improvisation and the Arts in Postwar America* (Chicago: The University of Chicago, 1998); and Sandrina Bandera, Alessandro Castigioni, and Emma Zanella, eds., *Kerouac Beat Painting* (Milano: Skira, 2018).
2   I have decided to not go into detail about Kerouac's affinities with American Abstract Expressionism since this is a well-researched topic in Daniel Belgrad, *The Culture of Spontaneity. Improvisation and the Arts in Postwar America* (Chicago: The University of Chicago, 1998), Michael Hrebeniak, *Action Writing: Jack Kerouac's Wild Form* (Carbondale: Southern Illinois University Press, 2006) and Sandrina Bandera, Alessandro Castigioni, and Emma Zanella, eds., *Kerouac Beat Painting* (Milano: Skira, 2018).
3   Adler, *Departed Angels. Jack Kerouac. The Lost Paintings*, 142.
4   Ibid., 37.
5   Ibid., 274–5.
6   Adler states that Helen Elliot, a close friend of Jack Kerouac from 1949 to 1969, told of the probability of painting lessons to Jack Kerouac by Willem de Kooning. See Adler, *Departed Angels. Jack Kerouac. The Lost Paintings*, 229. This is further elaborated in Irving Sandler, *The New York School: The Painters and Sculptors of the Fifties* (New York: Harper & Row 1978), 32–3.
7   Adler, *Departed Angels. Jack Kerouac. The Lost Paintings*, 148.
8   According to Thomas M. Alexander, art was for Dewey "the most successful effort to have an experience." See Thomas M. Alexander, *John Dewey's Theory of Art, Experience and Nature: The Horizons of Feeling* (Albany: State University of New York Press, 1987), 191. An experience, then, means a total involvement of mind and spirit resulting in the deepest meaning and fulfillment of the human condition.

9. Maurice R. Berube, "John Dewey and the Abstract Expressionists," *Educational Theory* 48 (2) (1998): 212.
10. The first writer to connect the Beat writers with the visual artists was Bay Area art critic Thomas Albright in his chapter "The Beat Era: Bay Area 'Funk.'" Here he looked at cross-connections between funk painting and Beat poetry with a particular focus on the Bay Area. See Thomas Albright, *Art in the San Francisco Bay Area: An Illustrated History* (Berkeley: University of California Press, 1985). The first visual venue that compared Beat art and poetry was the 1996 Whitney Museum exhibition *Beat Culture and the New America 1950–1965*, where poets such as Jack Kerouac were exhibited with artists such as Bruce Conner, Wally Hedrick, and Robert Rauschenberg, among others. See Lisa Philips, *The Beat Generation and the New America* (New York: Whitney Museum of American Art, 1995). Other influential texts are Rebecca Solnit's *Secret Exhibition: Six Artists of the Cold War Era* (San Francisco: City Lights Bookstore, 1990) which examines the work of the subcultural or underground artists working in California during the 1950s, and Richard Candida-Smith's book *Utopia and Dissent: Art, Poetry and Politics in California* (Berkeley: University of California Press, 1996). The relationship between Beat writers and artists is also featured in Rebecca Kelley Young Schoenthal's "North Beach to Haight-Ashbury: Underground artists and community" (PhD dissertation, University of Virginia, 2005).
11. Rebecca Solnit, *Secret Exhibition: Six Artists of the Cold War Era* (San Francisco: City Lights Bookstore, 1990); Lisa Philips, *The Beat Generation and the New America* (New York: Whitney Museum of American Art, 1995); Stephen Freedman, *Semina Culture: Wallace Berman & His Circle* (Santa Monica: Santa Monica Museum of Art, 2005).
12. The humanities program and the role of poet Jack Spicer at the California School of Fine Arts is referred to in the interview between JoAnn Low and Kevin Killian: https://openspace.sfmoma.org/2018/12/openings-in-the-veil-joann-low-and-kevin-killian-in-conversation/.
13. "Tell him I have eyes only for Heaven as I look to you Queen Mirror of the Heavenly Court."
14. John Natsoulas, *Lyrical Vision: The 6 Gallery 1954–1957* (Davis: Natsoulas Novelzo Gallery Press, 1990).
15. Gerd Hennum, *På sporet av beatbohemen* (Oslo: Ascheoug, 1995); Thor Myhre, *Kunst og kolera. Dr. Reidar Wennesland og kunstsamlingen i Kristiansand* (Kristiansand: HøyskoleForlaget, 1996); Frida Forsgren, *San Francisco Beat Art in Norway* (Oslo: Press Pub., 2008); Mette-Line Pedersen and Cecilie Nissen, *Art Is Not an Intellectual Way of Thinking. Undiscovered Drawings from the Beat Era in San Francisco* (Kristiansand: Kristiansand Kunsthall, 2014).
16. Jerry Kamstra, *The Frisco Kid* (New York: Harper & Row, 1975), 55–5.
17. Arthur Monroe, "The Decade of Bebop, Beatniks and Painting," Somarts Cultural Center, 1998, 4.
18. Jack Kerouac, "Essentials of Spontaneous Prose," in *The Portable Beat Reader*, ed. Ann Charters (London: Penguin Books, 1992), 58.
19. Adler, *Departed Angels. Jack Kerouac. The Lost Paintings*, 66.
20. Monroe, "The Decade of Bebop, Beatniks and Painting," 4.
21. Caroline A. Jones, *Bay Area Figurative Art 1950–1965* (Berkeley, CA: University of California Press, 1989), 1. According to Bay Area artist Dean Fleming who studied at the California School of Fine Arts in the 50s "everybody was doing Bay Area

22 Jones, *Bay Area Figurative Art 1950–1965*, 1.
23 Ibid.
24 "However, I often miss the sting that I believe a more descriptive reference to some fixed subject can make." Jones, *Bay Area Figurative Art 1950–1965*, 1.
25 Karen Tsujimoto, *The Art of Joan Brown* (Berkeley: University of California Press, 1998).
26 Jack Kerouac, "Essentials of Spontaneous Prose," in *The Portable Beat Reader*, ed. Ann Charters (London: Penguin Books, 1992), 58.
27 Pedersen and Nissen, *Art Is Not an Intellectual Way of Thinking. Undiscovered Drawings from the Beat Era in San Francisco*.
28 Oral history interview with Dean Fleming, August 6 and 7, 2013. Archives of American Art, Smithsonian Institution.
29 Kerouac was in SF in 1948–50, and he was there for the first HOWL reading in 1955—he would have been acquainted with the art and with the painters. Fred Martin's sketches and funk sculptures were exhibited in the Six Gallery.
30 Jack Kerouac, "Essentials of Spontaneous Prose," 58.
31 Adler, *Departed Angels. Jack Kerouac. The Lost Paintings*, 66.
32 Ibid., 248; Sandrina Bandera, "Jack Kerouac: Surprising Cultural Interactions," in *Kerouac Beat Painting*, 34.
33 Belgrad, *The Culture of Spontaneity. Improvisation and the Arts in Postwar America*, 110.
34 Claude Cernuschi, *Jackson Pollock: Meaning and Significance* (New York: HarperCollins, 1992).
35 Personal communications from Fred Martin.
36 Monroe, "The Decade of Bebop, Beatniks and Painting."
37 Jack Kerouac, "Essentials of Spontaneous Prose."
38 Monroe, "The Decade of Bebop, Beatniks and Painting."
39 Stephen Prothero, "On the Holy Road: The Beat Movement as Spiritual Protest," *The Harvard Theological Review* 84 (2) (1991): 216.
40 Ibid.
41 Ibid., 207.
42 Frida Forsgren, "Jay De Feo's Forgotten Roses: The Wise and Foolish Virgins," *Konsthistorisk Tidsskrift* 78 (3) (2009): 131–41.
43 In a 1956 interview with critic Selden Rodman, Mark Rothko explained the deeply emotional nature of his lager multiform paintings. Mark Rothko in M. López-Remiro, ed., *Writings on Art* (New Haven, CT: Yale University Press, 2006), 119–20.
44 Herman Roodenburg, "Rooted in the Sacred? On Mark Rothko, Tears Flowing, and Enargeia," in *The Secular Sacred: Emotions of Belonging and the Perils of Nation and Religion*, ed. Markus Balkenhol, Ernst van den Hemel, and Irene Stengs (Cham: Springer International Publishing, 2020), 217–34. doi.org/10.1007/978-3-030-38050-2_11.
45 Evelyn Toynton, *Jackson Pollock* (New Haven & London: Yale University Press, 2012), 55.
46 The book *Phenomenology of Perception* from 1945 discusses how our understanding of the world is rooted in our bodies' understanding of its surroundings and its situation. Maurice Merleau-Ponty, *Kroppens Fenomenologi* (Oslo: Pax Forlag A/S, 1994).

47 See Thea Hawlin's review "Jack Kerouac's paintings remind us that his real talent was for words" in *Apollo Magazine*, February 27, 2018. Here she states: "Although many of the artworks themselves—somewhat half-hearted." https://www.apollo-magazine.com/jack-kerouacs-art-reminds-us-that-his-real-talent-was-for-words/.
48 Others like Bandera feel that "the works should not be approached using an art critic's traditional methods … After all, Kerouac felt the need to convey his ideas and feelings through an array of tools and visions, seeing artistic expression in its totality" (32).
49 Adler, *Departed Angels. Jack Kerouac. The Lost Paintings*, 142.
50 Jen Jack Gieseking and William Mangold, *The People, Place, and Space Reader* (New York: Routledge, 2014), 56–60.
51 Adler, *Departed Angels. Jack Kerouac. The Lost Paintings*, 238.
52 Belgrad, *The Culture of Spontaneity. Improvisation and the Arts in Postwar America* and Hrebeniak, *Action Writing*.
53 Erica Doss, "Makes Me Laugh, Makes Me Cry: Feelings and American Art," *American Art* 25 (3) (2011): 2–8. doi.org/10.1086/663948.

4

A House of Mirrors at Coney Island: Kerouac's Obscure Experiments in Screenwriting

Brett Sigurdson

One day in 1943, Jack Kerouac slipped a blank piece of US Army stationary into a typewriter and entered the movie business. He typed promotional copy for a fictional movie premiering at Radio City Music Hall, *America*, "from the pen of the great new writer, Jack Kerouac."[1] The film would tell the epic story of a Harvard student "who discovers the real America," Kerouac writes.[2] The film's cast was as large as it was eccentric, featuring actors that ranged from Hollywood heavyweights (Gary Cooper, Burgess Meredith) to middlebrow performers (Veronica Lake, Tyrone Power) to B-movie mavens (Brenda Marshall, Brenda Joyce). If America was conceptually a melting pot, then Kerouac imagined his film about it containing multitudes—even if the picture was to be helmed by the auteur John Ford and produced by the director's adversary Daryl Zanuck.

While he never actually attempted a treatment of *America*, Kerouac's expansive concept suggests a confused interplay between popular movies and auteur-driven cinema—between low and high art—that would mark Kerouac's unsuccessful attempts at writing for the screen throughout his career. As some of the unpublished, unproduced screenplays in his archives illustrate, Kerouac could never successfully reconcile his paradoxical love of film as art and entertainment, as if his cinematic sensibility was cut from the same complaint one Hollywood producer, Jerry Wald, leveled at him:

> The characters in Mr. Kerouac's novel act like youngsters running around in the House of Mirrors at Coney Island. They are trying to get out but they keep bumping into their own reflections and become failures.[3]

"I Only Wanted to Be a Movie Maker"

Wald was the first to attempt a film adaptation of Kerouac's *On the Road*, a novel whose impact was still rippling through American culture months after its September 1957 publication. But he quickly encountered problems assimilating the narrative with Hollywood conventions. In a memo he shared with Kerouac in early 1958, Wald admits that Kerouac doesn't have a "dramatic structural mind." "He unfortunately failed to provide us with the workings of a good plot," Wald writes.[4] Wald felt the novel was too sprawling. It needed a "dramatic fury" grounded in a central conflict and a dynamic resolution at the climax to make a mark at the box office.

While Kerouac balked at some of Wald's suggestions to adapt the narrative for the screen—among them, that Dean Moriarty would die in a fiery car crash in the denouement—he also reveled in the notion of going Hollywood, with all the glamour, wealth, and new narrative possibilities an *On the Road* film would engender for him. It would be the culmination of his celluloid dreams, for as he once told his literary agent, Sterling Lord, "I only always wanted to be a movie maker, among other things."[5]

Kerouac had envisioned himself in movies at a young age. In parochial school, for instance, Kerouac imagined his life as the subject of a film recorded by "drooling Heaven with their Chaplin handcrank cameras."[6] The most prosaic moments of his life would be documented—everything from eating his morning oatmeal to playing games in his room at night—for posterity. Such fantasies were also fed by his father, who, legend had it, played cards with the likes of W.C. Fields when his print shop produced advertisements for theaters in Kerouac's hometown of Lowell, Massachusetts. In high school, Kerouac was legendary for the number of times he skipped school to read books at the Lowell Public Library and catch movies at the Rialto Theatre. He continued the movie house habit after settling in New York City in the early 1940s, first as a Columbia University student and later as a burgeoning Beat writer. And in the mid-1940s, Kerouac's Hollywood dreams were realized—however tangentially—when he landed a job providing script synopses for 20th Century Fox, a job he would return to when he needed money through the early 1950s.[7]

Like the scent of popcorn lingering in a movie theater, thoughts of Hollywood fame nagged Kerouac as he gained literary notoriety following the publication of *On the Road*. When producers like Wald and actors like Marlon Brando pitched adaptations of the novel, Kerouac momentarily presumed himself a new silver screen player, going so far as to write Brando to pitch his services as the actor to play Sal Paradise.[8] "Have to figure out a movie for Robert Frank, have to write big 5000 word letters to Hollywood producer giving ideas, etc.," Kerouac wrote to his fellow Beat, Allen Ginsberg. "[I]t's getting out of hand."[9] The movie he created with the photographer Robert Frank was *Pull My Daisy* (1959), an avant-garde short film based on Kerouac's play, *The Beat Generation* (1957), that featured Kerouac's extemporaneous narration. It became something of an underground classic and remains a fascinating glimpse into the years of Beatdom's brief reign.

Pull My Daisy also hinted at Kerouac's dalliance with the underground film scene, whose rise paralleled the cresting fame of the Beats in the late 1950s. As film scholar David Sterritt notes, Beat writers and avant-garde filmmakers "veered away from the rationality-bound ambitions of mainstream fiction and cinema, with their logical narratives, carefully coded conventions, and heavy investments in temporality, sequentially, and linearity."[10] For a time, Kerouac imagined he might contribute to the movement through a production company, G-String Films, which he created with Frank and Alfred Leslie, the producer of *Pull My Daisy*. Perhaps he'd write a movie in which his friends Peter and Lafcadio Orlovsky played the brothers they were in real life, with Ginsberg and William S. Burroughs their evil father and uncle.[11] By late 1960, Kerouac had enough credibility to receive an invitation from the proprietors of the New Yorker Theater, a revival house favored among cinephiles like Peter Bogdanovich and Jonas Mekas, to review a retrospective for their program. Among the films was W.C. Fields's *The Dentist* (1932).[12]

Fields was just one of the many Hollywood allusions to appear in his oeuvre. Aside from how Fields evoked his father, Kerouac liked the actor's sympathetic, bumbling everyman persona.[13] This accords with Kerouac's embrace of sentimentality in flicks like *Union Pacific* (1939) and *Le Quai des Brumes* (1938), which, as he writes in *Vanity of Duluoz*, features "that bitter lemon smile of Michele Morgan in the seaside bedroom."[14] As Sterritt notes, Kerouac's cinematic taste "smacks more of eager entertainment-hunting than of refined cinematic taste."[15] Indeed, Kerouac's "kitschy proclivities," as Sterritt calls them, separate him from writers and directors who sought a more inspired, demanding form of narrative filmmaking. Especially as he aged, Kerouac didn't appreciate the high-art concept of "drab" prestige films like *Who's Afraid of Virginia Woolf*, the Academy Award winner for Best Picture in 1966, which he decried in a journal entry.[16] By the late 1960s, he preferred to watch movies on television, where viewers increasingly encountered lowbrow fare, and where he could catch Bert Lahr's campy-cultured performances in Lay's potato chips commercials—high art masquerading as lowbrow (or vice versa).[17]

From a life steeped in movies that spanned relative critical and commercial successes, it's little wonder that Kerouac's efforts to write original screenplays led to chaotic results that were at times lowbrow and at times high-art—a paradox that no doubt frustrated his attempts to complete the scripts. "Jack loved films, had perceptive taste about them," his friend John Clellon Holmes recalled, "but he never understood script-writing as a separate genre. His was, after all, a narrative and lyrical gift, not an intensely dramatic one, and he loved films without thinking overmuch about the techniques of cinema."[18]

Still, his efforts at writing for the silver screen are worth considering for their revelations into Kerouac's attempts to reconcile his outré narrative predilections within the staid confines of popular film that Wald telegraphed in his letter to Kerouac.

Claude and Sam

In the spring of 1946, Kerouac wrote a ten-page screen treatment that described the murder of an older man by a younger poet. The crime of passion Kerouac describes in the untitled scenario almost certainly takes its inspiration from the real-life events of August 14, 1944, when his friend Lucien Carr stabbed David Kammerer, an older man who'd stalked Carr since his youth in St. Louis and deposited his body in the Hudson River. (Kerouac was charged as an accessory to the crime for his disposal of the Boy Scout knife Carr used.) The events are considered the consecrating moment of the Beat Generation because it was the first story the core members—Kerouac, William

S. Burroughs, and Allen Ginsberg—attempted to chronicle. Soon after, Ginsberg attempted a novel he titled "The Bloodsong," though he soon abandoned it.[19] Kerouac collaborated with Burroughs on a novella about the murder, *And the Hippos Were Boiled in Their Tanks*, in 1945.[20]

In the spring of 1946, Kerouac also seemed to draw on these events in his story about a penniless poet named Claude—a pseudonym Kerouac often used for Carr among his friends and in his work—who pushes his older roommate, Sam, off their apartment roof in a gratuitous crime of passion: Sam had just won $1,600 playing dice, and Claude was desperate for money so he could spend a year writing in Mexico. After Claude covers up his crime by refashioning Sam's unfinished letter to resemble a suicide note, events begin to spiral out of control as a police officer—a secret poet who becomes obsessed with Claude for his resemblance to his deceased son—and a beautiful neighbor begin to discover the reality of Sam's death. By the conclusion of Kerouac's treatment, nearly every character has died because of the lies they've lived.

As film scholars have noted, the late 1940s saw the rising popularity of film noir, whose crime-centered plots, antiheroes, and general air of danger embodied pessimism about postwar American life.[21] In his violent tale of Claude and Sam, Kerouac captures the hopelessness of the postwar bohemians in his circle with a grittiness reminiscent of Raoul Walsh's *White Heat* (1949) and Jacques Tourneur's *Out of the Past* (1947). But Kerouac also makes choices that subvert film noir, drawing upon, it seems, the easy moralizing of crowd-pleasing films like *It's a Wonderful Life* (1946). For instance, the honest cop, Jeb, who has doubts about Claude's story, wrestles with his feelings for Claude, who resembles his son, a good man who was put to death for a similar crime of passion a decade before. When Jeb realizes Claude staged Sam's suicide, he confronts Claude with a melodramatic monologue about the cruelty of humanity and the grace of forgiveness.

The archival record indicates Kerouac never attempted a full-length script based on his scenario about Claude and Sam. But Kerouac seemed to draw on it as he began writing his first published novel, *The Town and The City*, in 1946. In one of the penultimate scenes, a character named Waldo Meister falls from the window of Kenneth Wood's apartment, an apparent suicide that the police immediately doubt.[22] In contrast to Kerouac's film treatment—which mines guilt and iniquity to foster a decidedly film-noirish atmosphere—*The Town and The City* broods on the consciousness that follows catastrophic events, awakening Peter Martin to the sordidness of his new life in the city and setting up the emotional punch of George Martin's eventual death in the subsequent chapters.

Christmas in New York

Jerry Wald's *On the Road* film adaptation would have featured Dean Moriarty perishing in a police chase on Christmas Eve. Such a harsh, unsympathetic demise frustrated Kerouac.[23] In a letter to Wald, Kerouac extolled Sal and Dean's tenderness, their desperation in the face of societal circumstances. But Kerouac would come to know anger and anguish over the portrayal of the Beat Generation, especially in "beatsploitation" films, which similarly attributed violence to the people associated with Kerouac's supposed movement[24]. Like the failed adaption of his novel *The Subterraneans* (1960), Kerouac felt Wald missed the point of his book.[25]

And yet, in 1947, while Kerouac was staying with Henri Cru in Marin City, California, and working there as a security guard at a construction barracks, he penned a screen treatment of a violent caper film he called *Christmas in New York*. The plot centers on Mike Fitzgerald, a deckhand who lives with his parents and son, Gerard, in a run-down New York tenement. On a brief shore leave, Mike arrives home on Christmas Eve to find the sweet, sickly Gerard—cut from the same persona as Tiny Tim in Charles Dickens's *A Christmas Carol*—eagerly waiting for him. Nine-year-old Gerard suffers from an unnamed disease that could be addressed with expensive surgery—if only Mike could afford it.[26]

As Mike walks into the tenement, he crosses paths with Tom Seward—a wealthy, Harvard-educated man with a criminal streak—who gives him an offer he can't pass up.[27] Tom and his partner need a third person to help rob $30,000 from a warehouse safe that night. Mike's cut would be enough to pay for Gerard's surgery. But in the early morning darkness of Christmas Day, just as he's about to enter the warehouse with Tom and his partner Romano, Mike has a sudden vision of moral clarity and rushes home to Gerard. Moments later, the police appear, and Tom is wounded in the ensuing shootout. As Mike arrives home, he finds his parents crying. Just after midnight, Gerard began to hemorrhage, and he died at the hospital.

That Kerouac labeled this screen story a "potboiler" in his notes indicates he drafted the story for popular consumption. The narrative is ideologically conservative, shaped by Kerouac's sentimental religiosity and French-Canadian family values—the kind of inoffensive message films that would become the Hollywood norm in the wake of the House Un-American Activities Commission and the cautious narrative hegemony engendered by anti-communism.[28]

Yet, for all the emotional schlock at the heart of *Christmas in New York*, Kerouac was also drawn to neorealism for his attention to the postwar social conditions that frame the Fitzgerald family's economic woes. Kerouac's descriptions of the story's *mise-en-scene*—a poor Jewish neighborhood where other down-and-out immigrant communities live, Italians and French-Canadians among them—show he was hyper-aware of his characters' lives as ethnic outsiders. Scenes that jump between settings in tenement apartments and wealthy enclaves populated by merchant mariners, multigenerational households, and well-to-do Park Avenue denizens show an awareness of class divisions reminiscent of 1930s Hollywood films and novels.[29] But, like *The Town and the City*, Kerouac fills the script with glimpses into the lives of so many characters—Mike's shipmates Big Slim and Old Glory, Romano's Italian parents, and Gerard's doctor, among them—that the scenario ultimately craters from the breadth of Kerouac's ambitions.

Still, after completing *Christmas in New York*, Kerouac confidently proclaimed the story was "highly saleable." Several movie studios rejected his treatment, perhaps put off by the tonal inconsistencies created by Kerouac's competing characters and unfocused narrativity.

Obbligatos to the Narrative

Kerouac's attempts at screenwriting would continue a confused path, though his narrative untidiness became much more deliberate.

In 1950, he pitched a Western, *The Wild Galoots*, to 20th Century Fox. The story centers on an anachronistic outlaw, Smiley Jessup, who struggles to find himself when he returns to his Old West hometown to find it suburbanized. When Smiley discovers corruption among the owners of the town's powerful water supply company, he organizes a group of citizens—whom he dubs the wild galoots—to chase the officials away, reconnecting the townspeople to the charms of their outlaw heritage. But Bertram Bloch, a story editor for 20th Century Fox, advised Kerouac the concept wasn't worth pursuing. The characters were underdeveloped, and the plot was too unbelievable. "If a writer can't work out a story for pictures with reasonable dispatch, he shouldn't keep hammering away at it," Bloch wrote to Kerouac. "The odds are too much against him."[30]

Kerouac would put the Western movie idea away, but he didn't give up on a dream to write for the movies. He decided to lean into the unconventional. If Kerouac's earliest attempts at writing for the screen were torn between lowbrow and highbrow visions, his later screen ideas were decidedly more avant-garde. In 1954, he developed the concept of bookmovies, or mindmovies, which he described as "camera-eye visions of a definite movie of the mind."[31] Kerouac compared the style to his childhood tendency to watch a film's celluloid blips and scratches. When he realized that others in the theater were paying attention to a show, he got the idea that he was only aware of a small part of a larger whole, that film imperfections were a small part of a movie story the same way a story is a small part of an entire life. He wanted to translate the depth of a whole life to the reader through prose using parallel techniques like fade-ins, pans, and close-ups.[32]

Sometime later in 1954, Kerouac put his bookmovie concept into practice with a brief film treatment called *The French Night*. Writing in the style of a traditional script, Kerouac nonetheless spends most of the short scenario describing in detail the physical features of a French man and his lover as they stand in a doorway of a foggy evening.[33] Like Kerouac's "vertical, metaphysical descriptions" of Cody Pomeray in *Visions of Cody* (1972),[34] narrative conventions fall away as Kerouac builds what Beat scholar Tim Hunt calls "subjective elaborations, even digressions, that would function as obbligatos to the narrative."[35] Given its brief length, *The French Night* is more a writing exercise than a serious screenplay attempt, but Kerouac would attempt a much longer script based on the bookmovie form when he adapted his novel, *Doctor Sax* (1959), into a full-length screenplay.

Written in 1966, shortly after Grove reverted the novel's publishing rights to Kerouac, the script is sequenced as 314 short scenes of Kerouac's impressionistic, camera-eye action lines and occasional dialogue. For instance, scene 127 consists of an action line that describes a portentous rainy evening that Kerouac compares to foreboding storms he would see in old airplane films.[36] That Kerouac considered *Doctor Sax* adaptable for the screen is no surprise given the bookmovie form is, as Nancy M. Grace notes, premised on using "screenplay cues to ... locate the construction of the scenes in a distinctly remote point in time."[37] As with the novel, in which Kerouac destabilizes narrativity by vacillating between melodrama and fantasy, Kerouac's screenplay amplifies the carnivalesque dream world of Jackie's imagination—one populated by a vampire, wizard, gnomes, and a 100-foot-long snake—that imbricates his life in Lowell. In sum, the genre-bending bookmovie form unsettles the boundaries between author and viewer, the past and the present, reality and myth—the kind of nonrational discourse trumpeted by avant-garde filmmakers like Stan Brakhage.[38]

In light of the experimental aspects of the *Doctor Sax* screenplay, the moments of conventional narrative appear more distinctive—especially when Kerouac expands on brief scenes from the novel, amplifying moments of humor and pathos he embraced in his earliest screenplay efforts. For instance, Kerouac constructs a more extended scene from the boys' attempts to trap the Moon Man in a hole along the sandbank, only to find out the mysterious figure was their friend Gene Plouffe—a much more ribald scene than the novel. Duluoz's recollection of Jesus, the Virgin Mary, and Santa Claus pushing the foot of his bed comes off as much more surreal and horrifying in the script than in the novel. At the script's denouement, the camera focuses on the two women praying atop the Grotto in Lowell. They look askance at Jackie—roses in his hair, as in the novel—who warns them about the giant snake. More than any in the novel, this scene communicates how much of the story takes place in Jackie's vivid imagination.[39]

On the one hand, it's possible to write off Kerouac's attempt to write a screen treatment of *Doctor Sax* as a foolish, desperate exercise intended to make a quick buck, a factor in many of Kerouac's late-career publications. On the other, taking Kerouac's desire for a *Doctor Sax* film adaptation at face value reveals Kerouac's sense of the possibility of the film genre reflecting the heteroglossia of the novel's eclectic narrative elements. Kerouac saw his *Doctor Sax* screenplay as emblematic of Marshall McLuhan's notion of the "mosaic": short scenes capable of being read in any order, similar in respect to avant-garde filmmaker Stan Brakhage's conception of montage. The narrative element "has the effect of involving the film viewer in the process of the author's mind," Kerouac told Sterling Lord.[40] Such dialogism puts the *Dr. Sax* screenplay in the realm of the avant-garde "by deploying unfamiliar codes of communication," writes Sterritt, "and thus demanding that the reader/spectator play an active role in perceiving and responding to it."[41]

In the spring of 1967, Kerouac expressed frustration that directors and producers weren't responding to his film treatment.[42] In a letter to Sterling Lord, he called his *Doctor Sax* script a "cinematographic classic" that deserves a full-length movie. Filmmakers disagreed. Kerouac was out of style, and his style was too far out, even for the New American Cinema movement then establishing itself in Hollywood. Without further interest in the script, Kerouac took Bertram Bloch's advice and stopped trying to pitch it. With only a few years left to live, it would be his last attempt at writing for the big screen.

Where Are Your Trenches?

In terms of film, Kerouac's most lasting contribution might be the very myth of his image. Stars from Keanu Reeves to James Belushi to Jean-Marc Barr have played Kerouac in the roughly sixteen depictions of Kerouac between 1959 and 2013.[43] These portrayals of Kerouac have distinct similarities: he's often characterized as a holy truth-teller who opens other characters to new insights and revelations. For instance, in the episode of *Quantum Leap* titled "Rebel Without a Clue" (1990), Kerouac represents the wisdom of travel and the necessity of art. "The road is not made of asphalt," intones this Kerouac, bathed in sunlight like an angel, "but of the people we meet." Similarly, the premise of the film *Beat Angel* (2017) centers on the thirtieth anniversary of Kerouac's death, in which his spirit descends from Heaven and transforms the lives of three people he encounters. And in *Kill Your Darlings* (2013), Kerouac, played by Jack Huston, dispenses wisdom to a tyro Allen Ginsberg. "Writers, a real writer, has got to be … in the trenches, in all the broken places. Where are your trenches, Allen?"

In the still-unfolding arc of Kerouac's legacy, such casual poetic pronouncements inform the intensely romantic image of Kerouac that endures—an image reinforced by portrayals of Kerouac-like protagonists in *On the Road* and subverted in *Big Sur*—that will surely cast a shadow over the trenches where Kerouac worked intensely to articulate his vision of Hollywood success.[44] Kerouac's attempts were primarily informed by an inability to harmonize his eclectic taste and limited understanding of cinematic narrative. A cynic might view these attempts, like Truman Capote, as evidence Kerouac couldn't write a compelling story. But it's also true that his periodic attempts at scriptwriting were like writing exercises that provided space to explore stories, characters, and concepts for his novels and poems. If he couldn't—or wouldn't—reconcile the high and low art of the movies he loved on the scripted page, at least he—and perhaps we—could appreciate them as playful experiments, perhaps like the characters Jerry Wald chides for running into their reflections aimlessly at Coney Island's House of Mirrors.

As Kerouac tells Wald, at least they're giggling and having fun along the way. It's the path to something like wisdom.[45]

Notes

1. Jack Kerouac, Typescript notes. "Beginning Monday at the Radio City Music Hall/ 'America.'" (Fictional promo for a movie "From the pen of the great new writer Jack Kerouac." Written on U.S. Army notepaper.) Jack Kerouac Papers, New York Public Library. 7.68.
2. Ibid.
3. "Photocopied correspondence between Jack Kerouac and Jerry Wald, concerning a motion picture based on *On the Road*," Jack Kerouac Papers, New York Public Library. 20.66.
4. Ibid.

5   Jack Kerouac, "Letter to Sterling Lord (November 1959)," Kerouac Letters Dated 1959 (Jan–June). Visions of Kerouac: The John Sampas Collection. University of Massachusetts-Lowell. Cabinet 3. Drawer 1. Series 1. Box 3.
6   Jack Kerouac, "Memory Babe," in *The Unknown Kerouac: Rare, Unpublished and Newly Translated Writings*, ed. Todd Tietchen and Jean-Christophe Cloutier (Ann Arbor, MI: Library of America, 2016), 250–304.
7   See Matt Theado, "'This Was My Hollywood Career': Jack Kerouac's *On the Road* and 1950s Hollywood," in *Beat Drama: Playwrights and Performances of the "Howl" Generation*, ed. Deborah Geis (New York: Bloomsbury Publishing, 2016), 293–307.
8   See Ibid.
9   Jack Kerouac and Allen Ginsberg, *Jack Kerouac and Allen Ginsberg: The Letters*, ed. Bill Morgan and David Stanford (New York: Penguin, 2010), 389.
10 David Sterritt, *Mad to Be Saved: The Beats, the '50s, and Film* (Carbondale: Southern Illinois University Press, 1998), 45.
11 Kerouac and Ginsberg, *Jack Kerouac and Allen Ginsberg*, 389.
12 Kerouac writes about the screening and keeps notes for an eventual review of *Nosferatu* (1922) in Jack Kerouac, Diary #25. Holograph diary "Later 1960." November 9, 1960–New Year's Eve December 31, 1960 (58 leaves), Jack Kerouac Papers. New York Public Library. 57.8.
13 Of course, W.C. Fields also evokes the characters Kerouac based on Neal Cassady, such as Dean Moriarty and Cody Pomeroy. For a discussion of Fields in Kerouac's work, see Fiona Paton, *Style and Subversion: Kerouac and the Cultural Cold War* (Dissertation, The Pennsylvania State University, 1999), 159–65.
14 Jack Kerouac, *Vanity of Duluoz: An Adventurous Education, 1935–1946* (New York: Penguin, 1994), 76.
15 Sterritt, *Mad to Be Saved*, 12.
16 Jack Kerouac, "Letter to Sterling Lord (April 11, 1967)," Kerouac Letters dated 1967. Visions of Kerouac: The John Sampas Collection. University of Massachusetts-Lowell. Cabinet 3. Box 3.
17 For more on Kerouac's preference for television, see Jack Kerouac, "Typescript article 'Are movie television ratings as accurate as they should be? or I watch movies on television / that's better shithead' [sic] 1966," Jack Kerouac Papers. New York Public Library. 13.17.
18 John Clellon Holmes, "Untitled Letter," *Moody Street Irregulars* 22–3 (March 1983): 3.
19 Steven Belletto, *The Beats: A Literary History* (Cambridge: Cambridge University Press, 2020), 4–5.
20 The novella was published in 2008. Kerouac wrote about the event in *The Town and The City* and *Vanity of Duluoz*. For a deeper discussion of *Kill Your Darlings* and its source material, see Fiona Paton, "Angel Tendencies and Gratuitous Acts: Kill Your Darlings and the Legacy of Lucien Carr," in *Beat Drama: Playwrights and Performances of the "Howl" Generation*, ed. Deborah Geis (New York: Bloomsbury Publishing, 2016), 327–43.
21 Mike Chopra-Gant, *Hollywood Genres and Postwar America: Masculinity, Family and Nation in Popular Movies and Film Noir* (New York: Bloomsbury Publishing, 2005), 3.
22 Another parallel: a character named in Judie in *The Town and the City* is a mirror of the character Julie in his untitled film treatment.
23 For more about Kerouac's response to Wald's ideas, see Matt Theado, "'This Was My Hollywood Career': Jack Kerouac's *On the Road* and 1950s Hollywood," in *Beat*

Drama: Playwrights and Performances of the "Howl" Generation, ed. Deborah Geis (London: Bloomsbury Publishing, 2016), 293–307.
24 A selection of these films includes *High School Confidential* (1958), *The Bloody Brood* (1959), *The Rebel Set* (1959), *A Bucket of Blood* (1959), and *Wild for Kicks* (1960).
25 Kerouac called the film "mediocre" in a 1960 journal entry after attending its premiere in New York.
26 This plot point contains a sizeable hole that Kerouac never reconciles. Nina Faust, Mike's estranged wife and mother to Gerard, appears in several scenes as a wealthy Hollywood actress who longs to reconnect with her young son. Based on the backstory Kerouac provides, it seems inconceivable she wouldn't have the means to pay for Gerard's surgery.
27 The description of Tom Seward indicates the character is clearly based on William Seward Burroughs. His character names evoke F. Scott Fitzgerald's *The Great Gatsby*, perhaps intentionally considering the worlds of wealth and poverty that collide in the treatment.
28 For more on this point, see Sterritt, *Mad to Be Saved*, 110–12.
29 In fact, Kerouac's original version of *Christmas in New York*, which he describes in a brief typescript, indicates he planned to have Mike Fitzgerald, destitute and disillusioned after the war, reduced to robbing a bank with a corner gang to make ends meet. See Jack Kerouac, "Typescript, revised. 'Christmas (Love) in the City' Screen-story idea, 20th Century Fox. (1950–)." Jack Kerouac Papers. New York Public Library. 1.29.
30 Jack Kerouac. "Typed letter, signed. From Jack Kerouac to William Hogan. Description of '*On the Road*'. Notes on background, goal, destiny. With holograph notes on verso August 24, 1957 (1 leaf)." Jack Kerouac Papers. New York Public Library. 19.18.
31 Jack Kerouac, *Some of the Dharma* (New York: Penguin Books, 1999), 342.
32 John Clellon Holmes, "Doing Literary Work: An Interview with Jack Kerouac," in *The Unknown Kerouac: Rare, Unpublished and Newly Translated Writings*, ed. Todd Tietchen and Jean-Christophe Cloutier (Ann Arbor, MI: Library of America, 2016), 306–24.
33 Jack Kerouac, "Holograph and typescript, revised. 'First book movie', 'The French Night', 'Paris by Night, TV Play', and six untitled items 1954 (7 leaves)." Jack Kerouac Papers. New York Public Library. 3.35.
34 Jack Kerouac, *Visions of Cody* (New York: Penguin, 1993), np.
35 Timothy Hunt, *The Textuality of Soulwork: Jack Kerouac's Quest for Spontaneous Prose* (Ann Arbor: University of Michigan Press, 2014), 100.
36 Jack Kerouac, Typescript screenplay, revised. "Sax." Jack Kerouac Papers. New York Public Library. 37.4.
37 Nancy M. Grace, *Jack Kerouac and the Literary Imagination* (New York: Palgrave, 2007), 118.
38 See Ibid., 117–20 and Sterritt, *Mad to Be Saved*, 28.
39 Jack Kerouac, Typescript screenplay, revised. "Sax." Jack Kerouac Papers.
40 Jack Kerouac, "Letter to Sterling Lord (April 11, 1967)," Kerouac Letters dated 1967. Visions of Kerouac: The John Sampas Collection. University of Massachusetts-Lowell. Cabinet 3. Box 3.
41 Sterritt, *Mad to Be Saved*, 50.

42 Jack Kerouac, "Letter to Sterling Lord (April 14, 1967)," Kerouac Letters dated 1967. Visions of Kerouac: The John Sampas Collection. University of Massachusetts-Lowell. Cabinet 3. Box 3.

43 These were illustrated by Brian Hassett in a presentation titled "Kerouac at the Movies, Take 2," at Lowell Celebrates Kerouac! in Lowell, Massachusetts, in October 2023. It can be seen at https://www.youtube.com/@BrianHassettVideos.

44 In the film adaptation of *On the Road* (2012), Sal Paradise is played with smoldering earnestness by Sam Riley. A year later, an adaptation of *Big Sur* (2013) featured Jean-Marc Barr as a puffy, bedraggled Jack Kerouac (the film discards the author's pseudonyms). While both films have merits, neither was successful in financial or critical terms, according to budget and rating data from IMDB and Rotten Tomatoes, with several critics pointing to each film as evidence of the limits of adapting Kerouac for the screen.

45 Photocopied correspondence, Jack Kerouac Collection, 20.66.

5

Lonesome Traveler, Buddhism, and the Fictions of Kerouac's Non-Fiction

Steven Belletto

Jack Kerouac's book *Lonesome Traveler* (1960) is made up, as he writes in the Author's Introduction, of "published and unpublished pieces connected together because they have a common theme: Traveling."[1] The published pieces are autobiographical non-fiction essays that had first appeared in venues such as *Holiday*, a travel magazine; *Escapade*, a high circulation men's magazine where Kerouac had a brief run as a monthly columnist; and *Jubilee*, a Catholic interest magazine to which he donated his work, he said, "as a contribution to the Church."[2] Portions of one chapter, "The Railroad Earth," written in spontaneous prose, had appeared in the avant-garde journals *Black Mountain Review* and *Evergreen Review*. Given that much of the material was drawn from already published articles, *Lonesome Traveler* was advertised as "the first non-fiction book by the author of *On the Road*, *The Subterraneans*, and *The Dharma Bums*," and Kerouac told Allen Ginsberg at the time that it was "not a bad book and [was] to be on non-fiction list."[3] And yet in later years, critics have pointed out that *Lonesome Traveler* "began as a novel called 'Beat Traveler,'" and have even sometimes referred to the book as a novel, as in James T. Jones' *Jack Kerouac's Duluoz Legend* (1999)—and in at least one edition of the book, the 1988 Grove Weidenfeld edition, the subtitle "a novel" appears on the cover.[4]

That it's possible to see *Lonesome Traveler* sometimes as a collection of non-fiction essays and sometimes as a novel points to the way Kerouac stretched notions of genre to the breaking point, fond as he was of using seemingly paradoxical terms like "true-story novels" to describe his work (the *New York Times* reviewer split the difference, claiming *Lonesome Traveler* "is not quite a travel book, nor is it quite fiction").[5] Another term, "vision," was a form or perhaps genre of its own, naming something that Kerouac saw as distinct from fiction, a "Deep Form" intended to capture what he actually saw: "The Duluoz Legend is made up of Visions, not Novels—Visions are something that you see, not something you made up—The form of Visions is a deep form, a visionary form, and has nothing to do with the Novel form IT IS NOT SO MUCH A STORY AS THE VISION OF A STORY."[6] The emphasis on seeing gives primacy to Kerouac's own subjective empirical experience, and his art comes from how he shapes this experience with his critical and aesthetic intelligence. While, broadly speaking, this is true of any writer or artist, when Kerouac was thinking through the Duluoz Legend and the form this legend would take, he was also wrestling with Buddhist ideas about form and emptiness, and he drew on the word "vision" to articulate the Buddhist notion that what we perceive of as the "real world" is in fact illusory.

Consider, for example, how Kerouac put this idea in *The Scripture of the Golden Eternity*:

> all things and all truth
> laws are no-things [...]
> AS THINGS OF MIND they dont exist, because
> the mind that conceives and makes them out does
> so by seeing, hearing, touching, smelling, tasting,
> and mentally-noticing and without this mind they
> would not be seen or heard or felt or smelled or
> tasted or mentally-noticed, they are discriminated
> from that which they're not necessarily by imaginary
> judgments of the mind, they are actually dependent
> on the mind that makes them out, by themselves
> they are no-things, they are really mental, seen only
> of the mind, they are really empty visions of the
> mind, heaven is a vision, everything is a vision.[7]

Although these statements occur in a religious document, in this case "vision" does not necessarily name a divine encounter, something akin to a transcendent hallucination of an angel's visitation, but rather its opposite.[8] To invoke the term "vision" in this sense is to emphasize the poverty and limitations of sense perceptions—but it is also, however paradoxically, to name the most clear-eyed understanding of the "real world," that it ought to remain in scare quotes, that this world is "really" how we perceive it, "empty visions of the mind." If this is true, then the "vision" as a genre or form can be both fiction and non-fiction at the same time, just as our perceptions are, from a Buddhist point of view, both real and unreal at the same time.

In *Some of the Dharma*, Kerouac's most extended engagement with Buddhist thought, he returns again and again to the idea that "nothing is real," wrestling with a fundament of Buddhist doctrine, that "form is emptiness, emptiness is form," as the Prajñaparamita Sutra has it.[9] In *Some of the Dharma* Kerouac often uses the term "Mind Essence"—a particular translation he borrowed from Dwight Goddard's *A Buddhist Bible*—to underscore the way one's sensory perceptions create discriminations that appear to deliver the real to us, but are in fact as illusory and evanescent as a dream: "When you feel depressed and you wanta go here, wanta go there, remember Mind Essence; the world, like dreams, will never come true .... IT'S ALL IN YOUR HEAD WHAT HAPPENS SO YOU MIGHT AS WELL THINK HAPPINESS."[10] The realization that "everything is a vision" or "IT'S ALL IN YOUR HEAD" cannot help but to impact how Kerouac began to understand the form (and purpose) of his own literary work: if the real world was something "made up" by our sense perceptions, our Mind

Essence, then making up stories, writing fiction, starts to seem somewhat redundant and pointless: "The Duluoz Legend is made up of Visions, not Novels—Visions are something that you see, not something you made up." During the mid-fifties, when he was both deep in the Buddhist canon and deep in thought about the form of the Duluoz Legend, Kerouac saw the world, including his own sense perceptions, as "made up," and so there is, accordingly, no logical contradiction in a phrase like "true-story novels," since life itself is a kind of fiction, a delusion, a dream. The Deep Form of the vision was one way to articulate—or perform—the idea that Mind Essence creates "the real," a truth that Kerouac recognized was "not even discussable, groupable into / words; it is not even endless, in fact it is not / even mysterious or inscrutably inexplicable; it is / what is; it is that; it is this."[11]

During this period of intense Buddhist study, Kerouac would often use the notion of the "unreal" to describe the world: in *Wake Up: A Life of the Buddha*, for example, he describes Buddha's moment of enlightenment under the Bodhi tree like this: "Came to Buddha in those hours the realization that all things come from a cause and go to dissolution, and therefore all things are impermanent, all things are unhappy, and thereby and most mysterious, all things are unreal."[12] In Kerouac's telling, Buddha's ultimate conclusion, the substance of his enlightenment, is that "all things are unreal," an insight characterized in *Wake Up* as "mysterious" (an adjective found also in this context in *The Scripture of the Golden Eternity* and perhaps routed for him through the Catholic concept of mystery). Tellingly, as he writes in *Some of the Dharma*, "Deep Form" is likewise "unmentionable, mysterious as snow."[13] If "the form of Visions is a deep form, a visionary form," then this "mysterious" form functions to access the unreal world via Kerouac's sense perceptions: the real in the unreal, and vice versa, captured in visions, which are both fiction and non-fiction. Precisely because this deep form is mysterious, understanding it is not so simple as saying Kerouac centers his subjectivity and brings novelistic techniques into otherwise "non-fiction" accounts, as in the roughly coterminous movement of New Journalism; nor does it seem quite correct to say he was merely an early practitioner of that post-postmodern genre we now call auto-fiction, because Kerouac's technique requires us to read across his corpus, to apprehend those mysterious echoes and associations among various kinds of his work—from ostensible fiction to ostensible non-fiction—that taken together represent his vision of a reality fundamentally illusory and fiction-like.

Consider, further, how figures of visions are associated with the "mysterious" in *The Dharma Bums*, when narrator Ray Smith writes: "It was a river wonderland, the emptiness of the golden eternity, odors of moss and bark and twigs and mud, all ululating mysterious visionstuff before my eyes, tranquil and everlasting nevertheless, the hillhairing trees, the dancing sunlight."[14] Such a sentence contains allusions to Kerouac's other work, both obvious ("golden eternity") and not-so-obvious ("mysterious visionstuff") that suggests the way in which all his books are interconnected, and finally meant to be one grand vision read in light of one another—"an enormous paean," as he puts it in his famous introduction to *Visions of Cody*, "which would unite my vision of America with words spilled out in the modern spontaneous method."[15]

Just as "the emptiness of the golden eternity" in the novel *The Dharma Bums* is fleshed out in the non-fiction *The Scripture of the Golden Eternity*, so too does the novel offer texture to the scripture. In the novel, for example, we learn that the "first genuine Dharma Bum" Ray Smith meets would meditate not on Buddhist mantras but on "a tiny slip of paper which contained a prayer by Saint Teresa announcing that after her death she will return to the earth by showering it with roses from heaven, forever, for all living creatures."[16] The syncretism here is apparent in the fact that this "genuine Dharma Bum"—a literal bum Ray meets in a train yard—meditates on a Catholic saint, and that Kerouac uses a Buddhist phrase, "all living creatures" to describe that saint's importance.[17] We further see this fictionalized Dharma Bum behind a moment in *The Scripture of the Golden Eternity*, when Kerouac describes "Sainte Thérèse, choosing / Love for her vocation and pouring out her / happiness, from her garden by the gate, with / a gentle smile, pouring roses on the earth, / so that the beggar in the thunderbolt received / of the endless offering of her dark void."[18] Readers of Kerouac's broader corpus cannot but help to see the Saint Teresa-loving bum from *The Dharma Bums* behind the archetypal "beggar" in *The Scripture of the Golden Eternity*, fiction and non-fiction feeding off and enriching each other, and beginning to erase generic distinctions between them as they form part of Kerouac's "vision."

Indeed, the more one looks in Kerouac's oeuvre, the more one sees echoes and associations bouncing around from work to work: from novels to essays to visions to poetry—so, for instance, a memorable phrase from *On the Road*, "the Earth is an Indian thing," appears again in *Lonesome Traveler*, inviting us to think about how he returns to and reworks not only that sentence, but the larger themes that sentence represents.[19] In *On the Road*, Sal Paradise rhapsodizes about the "Fellahin Indians of the world, the essential strain of the basic primitive, wailing humanity that stretches in a belt around the equatorial belly of the world," and goes on to make the since-famous remark that "the Earth is an Indian thing."[20] Kerouac's interest in the Fellaheen is of course well known, as he and other Beats often wrote about the Fellaheen, a term borrowed from Oswald Spengler's *The Decline of the West*, and referring to indigenous or native peoples who were perceived to be somehow outside the decadent traps of Western civilization and therefore living a better, truer, or more authentic life. The image quoted above from *On the Road*, that the Fellaheen stretch in a "belt" around the world, was reworked from Kerouac's sketchbooks, in which he wrote "the Indian is one with / the Fellaheen World Belt / thru Mexico, Africa, Aramea."[21] This image is taken up once again in the "Mexico Fellaheen" chapter of *Lonesome Traveler*, where the line about the earth being an "Indian thing" appears again, and the Fellaheen "belt" is imagined as "Spine-ribbed mountains all the way from Calexico and Shasta and Modoc and Columbia River."[22]

A subtle but crucial difference in the way this image appears in *On the Road* and *Lonesome Traveler* is that in the latter book, Kerouac prefaces these observations—and his entering into Fellaheen lands—with the statement, "It's a great feeling of entering the Pure Land ... [and] you can find it, this feeling, this fellaheen feeling about life, that timeless gayety of people not involved in great cultural and civilization issues."[23] The key addition here is "Pure Land," a reference to a Buddhist school that sees the Pure Land as "a buddha-field purified of transgressions and suffering by a buddha and thus deemed an auspicious place in which to take rebirth."[24] *The Princeton Dictionary of Buddhism* notes that there are "several denotations" of the term Pure Land in English, and the most famous of the purified buddha-fields mentioned above is associated with Amitābha, a widely worshipped buddha in the Mahayana tradition. This is the sense that Kerouac had in mind when he associated the Pure Land with the "fellaheen feeling about life," an association he made explicit in *Some of the Dharma* when he juxtaposed "Amitabha Buddha" with the phrase "The Apocalypse of the Fellaheen."[25] For Kerouac, "Pure Land" also denoted a place where one could be freed from perceptions that appear to be absolute reality, as he noted that a Bodhisattva is "free to enter the illimitable void of Mind Essence ... This Bodhisattva must truly cast off his chains himself, then the Buddha shall come and lead him to the Pure Land."[26] He put it more straightforwardly in a poem included in *Some of the Dharma*:

> So listen to me
> And I'll try to tell all
> As I heard it long ago
> In the Pure Land Hall.
>
> Life is like a dream,
> You only think it's real[27]

"Life is like a dream," and in the Pure Land one enters a place, a buddha-field, that is either literal, metaphorical, both, or neither, where the Mind Essence is recognized for what it is, and not confused with Absolute Reality or the world as it is. In asserting that the fellaheen land *is* the Pure Land, an actual, enterable buddha-field, Kerouac is not merely rejecting the distinction between metaphorical and literal conceptions of the world in his representations, but in the real world itself, suggesting again how those representations are striving to capture this vision of the real: "When you feel depressed and you wanta go here, wanta go there, remember Mind Essence; the world, like dreams, will never come true .... IT'S ALL IN YOUR HEAD."[28]

The association of the Spenglarian Fellaheen with the Buddhist Pure Land also suggests another point of connection between Kerouac's ostensible fiction and non-fiction visible in a revision he made to the original scroll version of *On the Road*. In that first version, written before Kerouac's Buddhist studies, the image of the Fellaheen "belt around the world" does occur, but it is significantly elaborated in the published version, written sometime after those studies.[29] In the published version, Kerouac has added the phrase "the earth is an Indian thing," and also enriched the imagery of the Fellaheen belt. In the original scroll version, the narrator explains that driving through Fellaheen lands is

> like driving across the world and into the places where we would finally learn ourselves among the worldwide fellaheen people of the world, the Indians that

stretch in a belt around the world from Malaya to India to Arabia to Morocco to Mexico and over to Polynesia[30]

In the published version of *On the Road*, this sentence is embroidered so that driving through Fellaheen lands is

> like driving across the world and into the places where we would finally learn ourselves among the Fellahin Indians of the world, the essential strain of the basic primitive, wailing humanity that stretches in a belt around the equatorial belly of the world from Malaya (the long fingernail of China) to India the great subcontinent to Arabia to Morocco to the selfsame deserts and jungles of Mexico and over the waves to Polynesia to mystic Siam of the Yellow Robe and on around, on around, so that you can hear the same mournful wail by the rotted wall of Cádiz, Spain, that you hear 12,000 miles around in the depths of Benares the Capital of the World.[31]

In addition to defining his terms for readers unfamiliar with the concept of the Fellaheen (hence the insertion of "essential strain of the basic primitive"), Kerouac elaborates on the geography of this "belt," adding in evocative images ("the long fingernail of China"), but also explicitly associating the Fellaheen with Buddhism with the mention of the saffron robes worn by Buddhist monks in Thailand—in *Some of the Dharma*, he refers to the "Yellow Robe, the Eastern, true idea of a priesthood"—and most clearly, in ending the around-the-world tour through the Fellaheen belt in "Benares the Capital of the World."[32] In Kerouac's radically re-imagined global geography, the capital of the world is not London or Paris or New York or any other Western city, but the ancient Indian city of Benares, the holy city on the banks of the Ganges.

And just as the "earth is an Indian thing" line is reused from *On the Road* in *Lonesome Traveler*, so too has Kerouac repurposed the line about Benares from his non-fiction life of the Buddha, *Wake Up*. In that book, after Buddha comes to the mysterious realization that "all things are unreal," thereby achieving enlightenment, immediately "he headed for Benares, the capital of the world. On the road he ran into a former acquaintance ... who [was] struck by the majestical and joyful appearance of the human being who had just singlehandedly remembered the origin of the world."[33] In *Wake Up*, Benares is the "capital of the world" because it is from there that Buddha's word first flowed into the world, inaugurating a new understanding of that world. By inserting this specific characterization of Benares into *On the Road*, Kerouac is strengthening the association between the Fellaheen and Buddhism introduced with the collapse of the Fellaheen lands with the Buddhist Pure Land; the repurposing of this line also implies the fluidity between Kerouac's fiction and non-fiction, the idea that they inform and augment one another, leading finally to the possibility that the generic distinctions among them are not all that meaningful: "Benares the capital of the world" flickers in and out of fiction and non-fiction: it is neither and both, Kerouac's Buddhist learning on display in *Wake Up* hiding behind Sal's romantic descriptions of the Fellaheen in *On the Road*.

Another way to illustrate how Kerouac was playing with notions of the real in his work, often allowing events or episodes to stand between fiction and non-fiction, is to look at how the same events appear in different ways in his work. One of the more well-known two months of Kerouac's life was when, in the summer of 1956, he served as a fire lookout on Desolation Peak in the Cascades in Washington state. This period is so well-known because Kerouac published four different accounts of it in his lifetime. The first account appeared in *The Dharma Bums*, when Kerouac's fictional alter ego, Ray Smith, becomes a fire lookout, and this experience serves as a conclusion to Ray's spiritual journey in the novel: "At night I put on my poncho over my rain jacket and warm clothing and went out to meditate on the foggy top of the world. Here indeed was the Great Truth Cloud, Dharmamega, the ultimate goal."[34] *The Dharma Bums* was published on October 2, 1958, and that same month, a non-fiction travel essay, "Alone on a Mountaintop," appeared in *Holiday* magazine, describing Kerouac's experience as a fire lookout in more detail—thus in the same month, one could read about Ray Smith's fictional experiences on Desolation Peak, and the real experience of Jack Kerouac, "the spokesman of the Beat Generation," as the *Holiday* advertising copy announced, who would probe "the obvious beauty and the hidden meanings of a solitary summer in the High Cascades."[35]

Two years later, Kerouac included the text of "Alone on a Mountaintop"—with minor but important changes—in *Lonesome Traveler*, where it became a chapter with the same title. Finally in *Desolation Angels*, Kerouac's fictional alter ego, Jack Duluoz, again recounts the fire lookout experience in even more detail, reworking some material in *The Dharma Bums* and *Lonesome Traveler*, and framing the experience differently, not as a culmination of the Buddhist wisdom Ray Smith learns from Japhy Ryder in *The Dharma Bums*, but as a last summer of solitude and anonymity before the fame attached to *On the Road* would change Kerouac's life. These four narratives published in Kerouac's life, two "true-story novels," a travel essay, and a chapter in his "first non-fiction book," were supplemented in 2022 with *Desolation Peak*, a book collecting the journals and other material he wrote while on the peak. As *Desolation Peak*'s editor, Charles Shuttleworth, points out, this material adds another layer of understanding to this period in Kerouac's life and helps us see how he framed and fictionalized this period in those narratives he wrote about it.[36] If nothing else, *Desolation Peak* underscores the sense one gets from reading *Some of the Dharma* of the close and complex connection between Kerouac's understanding of Buddhism and his developing vision for the Duluoz Legend.

Looking at the difference between the *Holiday* version of "Alone on a Mountaintop" and the *Lonesome Traveler* version allows us to see how Kerouac was conceptualizing the real as unreal, non-fiction as describing the fiction of existence. That *Holiday* version describes Kerouac's time as a fire lookout on Desolation Peak, and focuses largely on the startling natural beauty of the Cascades: "Dazzles of light to the north show where Ross Lake sweeps all the way to Canada, opening a view of the Mt. Baker National Forest as spectacular as any vista in the Colorado Rockies"; "I was amazed and overjoyed to see a clear blue sunny sky and down below, like a radiant pure snow sea, the clouds making a marshmallow cover for all the world and all the lake while

I abided in warm sunshine among hundreds of miles of snow-white peaks."[37] These are the sort of over-the-top, romanticized descriptions that characterize much of the article, what James Jones calls "the language of tourist brochures," descriptions fitting for a travel magazine, and as such they smooth over the realities of living alone on a remote mountain: "Hot, miserable," Kerouac writes in his journal, "locusts of plagues of insects, heat, no air, no clouds, for the fuck of me I'd like to get the fuck out of here!"[38]

If we compare the *Holiday* version with the one in *Lonesome Traveler*, we can see that Kerouac has added a few sentences that link it to the other chapters. In the book, "Alone on a Mountaintop" comes after the chapter "New York Scenes," a version of another *Holiday* article, "The Roaming Beatniks," consisting of sketches which Kerouac had written with Gregory Corso and Allen Ginsberg describing various "beatnik haunts" in New York.[39] In *Lonesome Traveler*, Kerouac includes a new linking section: "After all this kind of fanfare, and even more, I came to a point where I needed solitude and just stop the machine of 'thinking' and 'enjoying' what they call 'living,' I just wanted to lie in the grass and look at the clouds."[40] In this way, Kerouac creates a kind of plot: rather than two unconnected essays juxtaposed next to each other, this new material suggests a psychological need for the solitude on the mountain, a contrast to the frenetic literary and cultural scene, a basic structure that he also uses in *Desolation Angels* and *Big Sur* (even though, in real life, the media-fueled "beatnik" scene did not develop until *after* Kerouac had spent the summer on Desolation Peak).

But beyond these short connecting passages, there is one major difference between the *Holiday* and *Lonesome Traveler* versions of "Alone on a Mountaintop": toward the end of the latter version, Kerouac inserts two new pages which reflect the intense Buddhist study that he was also doing while on Desolation Peak. Jones is right that on balance the *Holiday* version reads like "the language of tourist brochures," but there is one odd moment in it when Kerouac discovers a bear has raided his food stores overnight, and he names this bear "Avalokitesvara the Bear"—a reference to the Buddhist Bodhisattva of compassion.[41] In *The Dharma Bums*, Ray Smith explains that he and Japhy Ryder had "the same favorite Buddhist saint, too: Avalokitesvara, or, in Japanese, Kwannon the Eleven-Headed."[42] While Avalokitesvara the Bear makes a brief, one-sentence appearance in *The Dharma Bums*,[43] Kerouac had first recorded the story of the bear in his journals:

> Went down to the garbage pit down the trail in a half-foggy morning to salvage an old pound square of hardened sugar I remembered, so as to make syrup for my pancakes, & what do I find but big bear marks & bear shit and cans of hardened milk squeezed & bit into, insanely powerful hands & teeth—felt the mystery of the unseen Behemoth.[44]

In his first impressions, the bear has not yet transformed into "Avalokitesvara the Bear," but still Kerouac saw it as a "mystery"—a word which, as we know, he associated with the insight that "all things are unreal."

In the *Holiday* article, the bear's importance is emphasized insofar as it comes to represent an emblem of the "lesson" Kerouac learns on the mountain. In both the magazine version and in *Lonesome Traveler*, Kerouac ends "Alone on a Mountaintop" with this line: "I turned and blessed Desolation Peak and the little pagoda on top and thanked them for the shelter and the lesson I'd been taught."[45] In the *Holiday* version, this "lesson" is stated, but remains teasingly underdeveloped and elliptical: "I realize that no matter where I am, whether in a little room full of thought, or in this endless universe of stars and mountains, it's all in my mind. There's no need for solitude. So love life for what it is, and form no preconceptions whatever in your mind."[46] The key phrase here is "it's all in my mind," a reference to Kerouac's Buddhist understanding of the real, and underscored by naming the bear "Avalokitesvara"—as we learn in his journals, about a month before he found evidence of the bear's visit, he had been praying to Avalokitesvara, whom he called "(a name, a word as good as any other for That Which Everything Is) asking: 'What is the significance of phenomena?' / 'Nothingness.' / 'What shall I do?' / 'Do what you want, it's the Golden Eternity, the Enlightened Buddha.'"[47]

But one wouldn't know this from the *Holiday* version of "Alone on a Mountaintop," which sketches the "lesson" in just those few lines. In that piece, it is easy to read the lesson as pertaining to the transformative, redemptive power of nature, with the bear representing the mysteries of untamed wilderness. In *Lonesome Traveler*, by contrast, those two additional pages elaborate on this lesson, drawing a direct line back to the fundamental Buddhist idea that "form is emptiness, emptiness is form": "know constantly that this is only you, God, empty and awake and eternally free as the unnumerable [sic] atoms of emptiness everywhere."[48] These new pages come immediately following the line about forming "no preconceptions whatever in your mind":

> I realized I didnt have to hide myself in desolation but could accept society for better or for worse, like a wife—I saw that if it wasnt for the six senses, of seeing, hearing, smelling, touching, tasting and thinking, the self of that, which is non-existent, there would be no phenomena to perceive at all, in fact no six senses of self.[49]

Here again we see an abiding theme of *Lonesome Traveler*, and of the Duluoz Legend in general, that the world is "non-existent," unreal, a product of our human perceptions, and so to write about this world is to produce simultaneously fiction and non-fiction. And again, Kerouac links the term "vision" to this idea: "to know that all is empty and awake, a Vision and a Movie in God's Universal Mind (*Alaya-Vijnana*) and to stay more or less wisely in that ... 'T's only the Golden Eternity of God's Mind."[50] The Sanskrit term *ālayavijñāna*, which Kerouac glosses here as "God's Universal Mind," is generally translated as "storehouse consciousness," and names "a foundational form of consciousness, itself ethically neutral, where all the seeds of all deeds done in the past reside, and from which they fructify in the form of experience."[51] In the terms that Kerouac is working with, *ālayavijñāna* is ultimate or absolute reality, not "phenomena to perceive," as he puts it in *Lonesome Traveler*.

With this in mind, "Avalokitesvara the Bear" takes on a new meaning. In "Alone on the Mountaintop," as I've said, the bear seems a symbol for the mysteries of the natural world and its ability to nourish us. In *Lonesome Traveler*, the carnage left by the bear causes Kerouac to think about his own existence in the sensory world, and to declare that all is a "Vision" inside *ālayavijñāna,* the unreal within the real. When Kerouac revisited the incident of the bear yet again, in *Desolation Angels*, he again associated him with Avalokitesvara, but only after characterizing the animal as being as ephemeral as "Zen Mystery Fog": he is "the Bear, the Primordial Bear ... King Bear with his big mysterious black horseshit by my garbage pit."[52] Duluoz muses on the bear, seeing him as a kind of manifestation of Buddhist approaches to the world: "He continually hears the reassuring rapturous rush of silence, except near creeks, he continually is aware of the light material the world is made of, and never discourses, nor makes signs for meaning, nor complains a breath, but nibbles and paws, and lumbers along snags paying no attention to inanimate things or animate."[53] It is only after this characterization of the bear as a being not caught up in discriminations, "signs of meaning," that the passage culminates in the naming of him: "He is Avalokitesvara the Bear."

Earlier in *Desolation Angels*, we discover that Duluoz has prayed to Avalokitesvara for "immortal understanding"—just as Kerouac often prayed to him, as recorded in both the *Desolation Peak* journals, and throughout *Some of the Dharma*.[54] This understanding Avalokitesvara delivers when he appears in the form of a bear, a ghostly presence that neither Kerouac nor Duluoz ever encountered directly: there but not there, real but not real. In fact, in reading *Some of the Dharma*, we learn that Kerouac thought of Avalokitesvara as an instantiation of *ālayavijñāna*, as the cosmos and everything in it:

Why did Avalokitesvara make himself
into Picasso, pictures, light bulbs?—
Exuberantly he even manifested Whys,
Wherefores, and I-Dont-Cares, all the
attitudes in this great 10-Dimensional movie
in Crystal Reality—
He invented the words real and unreal—neither of which
means anything—[55]

In the *Holiday* magazine travel essay "Alone on a Mountaintop" and the non-fiction book *Lonesome Traveler* and the true-story novel *Desolation Angels*, Avalokitesvara has made himself into a bear, a literal manifestation in the real world, as he is a literal manifestation of everything, including our perceptive discriminations between "the words real and unreal"—neither of which, Kerouac of course notes, "means anything."

If this is the case, then when it comes to Kerouac's writing, we may find no meaningful distinction between fiction and non-fiction. The Duluoz Legend is both and neither, just as the world is—the Legend is evidence of Kerouac's sense perceptions and, at times, a gesture toward *ālayavijñāna*, a most "real" thing that cannot be apprehended via the senses. In *Some of the Dharma*, Kerouac declares that the Duluoz Legend is the "story of Jack Duluoz's discriminating brain-mind, his Visions, ripples on an endless sea," and that the Legend must reveal "details of a great teaching—as if Buddha had written the GAUTAMA LEGEND."[56] He continues: "Naturally it will contain admissions damaging to the Vanity of Duluoz—that isnt an issue any more, who's Duluoz? Who's Kerouac? He is equally to be loved, equally empty, and equally a coming Buddha."[57] In such a vision, ideas of fiction and non-fiction simply don't pertain, since Jack Kerouac is as much of a fictional character, as much of a dream, as Jack Duluoz. To be good readers of Kerouac, we have to accept this view of the real, that, as he put it in *Lonesome Traveler*, "happiness consists in realizing that it is all a great strange dream," and that, with the Duluoz Legend, he was trying, probably in vain, to catch that dream on paper: "the Legend properly done contains all creation."[58] As the "story of Jack Duluoz's discriminating brain-mind, his Visions," the Duluoz Legend is fiction and non-fiction at the same time, the bear *is* Avalokitesvara and a metaphor, the historical Jack Kerouac is a fictional Jack Duluoz, and the generic slippages across the Legend approximate the unreality of our own worldly existence.

Notes

1. Jack Kerouac, *Lonesome Traveler* (1960) (New York: Grove Weidenfeld, 1988), vi.
2. "I Simply Plan a Completely Written Lifetime," in *Conversations with Jack Kerouac*, ed. Kevin J. Hayes (Jackson: University Press of Mississippi, 2005), 43.
3. Advertisement for *Lonesome Traveler*, New York Times, November 3, 1960, 37; Kerouac to Ginsberg (June 20, 1960), Kerouac, *Selected Letters, Vol. II*, ed. Ann Charters (New York: Viking, 1999), 257.
4. Rob Johnson, "Lonesome Traveler," in *Encyclopedia of Beat Literature*, ed. Kurt Hemmer (New York: Facts on File, 2007), 192; James T. Jones, *Jack Kerouac's Duluoz Legend: The Mythic Form of an Autobiographical Fiction* (Carbondale: Southern Illinois University Press, 1999), 181. A typescript fragment of "Beat Traveler" is in the Jack Kerouac Papers at the Berg Collection of the New York Public Library, box 19, folder 41.
5. Kerouac, *Lonesome Traveler*, vi; Daniel Talbot, "On the Road Again," *New York Times* (November 27, 1960), BR38.
6. Jack Kerouac, *Desolation Peak: Collected Writings*, ed. Charles Shuttleworth (Lowell, MA: Sal Paradise, 2022), 88.
7. Jack Kerouac, *The Scripture of the Golden Eternity* (1960) (San Francisco: City Lights, 1994), 46–7.
8. For a discussion of how Kerouac also understood "vision" as related to what Mortenson calls "the Buddhist stillpoint," see Erik Mortenson, "Keeping Vision Alive: The Buddhist Stillpoint in the World of Jack Kerouac and Allen Ginsberg," in *The Emergence of Buddhist American Literature*, ed. John Whalen-Bridge and Gary Storhoff (Albany: SUNY Press, 2009), 123–37. Mortenson argues that "Kerouac's golden eternity is the state beyond mind where everything becomes One, where there is no need to think in terms of carrying gains across from one moment to another since any one moment contains all moments, past and future. The Buddhist stillpoint thus offers Kerouac … a means of jettisoning [his] smaller, more ego-driven [self] in exchange for a conception of self that expands [his] connection to the universe" (128).

9   Jack Kerouac, *Some of the Dharma* (New York: Viking, 1997), 40–1.
10 Ibid., 41; see, for instance, Dwight Goddard, ed., *A Buddhist Bible* (1938) (Boston: Beacon Press, 1966), 159. James Najarian, glossing Kerouac's stated "primary sources" for *Some of the Dharma*, notes that these sources themselves could be viewed as delivering a particular sense of Buddhism—or even "Eastern thought" more broadly—palatable to Western readers. Kerouac had especially lauded Goddard's *Buddhist Bible* and Paul Carus's *The Gospel of Buddha* (1894); Najarian writes: "Carus's *Gospel* (widely panned by Buddhist scholars at the time) takes passages of different Buddhist scriptures and organizes them into a gospel narrative, with chapters and verse, in service of a universal religion. Goddard's *Buddhist Bible* contains translations of *The Diamond*, *Śūrangama*, and *Laṅkāvatāra Sūtras*, but also includes the Tao Te Ching, which is not a Buddhist document, and Goddard's own essay on meditation, written in a pleasant imitation of the repetitive style of Theravadan sutras," in Najarian, "The 'Problem' of Buddhism for Western Literature: Edwin Arnold to Jack Kerouac," in *The Routledge Companion to Literature and Religion*, ed. Mark Knight (New York: Routledge, 2016), 310–19; quotation 314. Najarian's point is to show that Kerouac's readings in Buddhism had already been interpreted through various kinds of Western lenses, and included a strong "universalizing" tendency. Najarian's essay offers a helpful, pithy explanation of American Buddhism, and he is critical of Kerouac both for his dilettantish relationship to Buddhism, and for an over-emphasis on "states of ecstatic experience" (316). Although I find Najarian's explanation of mid-century American Buddhism to be useful, I disagree, as this essay makes clear, that Kerouac's interest in Buddhism was primarily about his search for blissful or ecstatic states, but rather about coming to terms with the notion that "nothing is real."
11 Kerouac, *The Scripture of the Golden Eternity*, 27–8.
12 Jack Kerouac, *Wake Up: A Life of the Buddha* (New York: Viking, 2008), 22.
13 Kerouac, *Some of the Dharma*, 48.
14 Jack Kerouac, *The Dharma Bums* (1958) (New York: Penguin, 1986), 225.
15 Jack Kerouac, *Visions of Cody* (1972) (New York: Penguin, 1993), n.p.
16 Kerouac, *The Dharma Bums*, 9, 5.
17 For more on how Kerouac synthesized Buddhist and Catholic thought, see Bent Sørensen, "Buddhism, Madness and Movement: Triangulating Jack Kerouac's Belief System," in *Encountering Buddhism in Twentieth-Century British and American Literature*, ed. Lawrence Normand and Alison Winch (New York: Bloomsbury, 2013), 105–22.
18 Kerouac, *The Scripture of the Golden Eternity*, 38.
19 Jack Kerouac, *On the Road* (1957) (New York: Penguin, 1991), 281; Kerouac, *Lonesome Traveler*, 22.
20 Kerouac, *On the Road*, 280–1.
21 Jack Kerouac, *Book of Sketches* (New York: Penguin, 2006), 173.
22 Kerouac, *Lonesome Traveler*, 22–3.
23 Ibid., 22.
24 Robert E. Buswell Jr. and Donald S. Lopez Jr., *The Princeton Dictionary of Buddhism* (Princeton: Princeton University Press, 2014), 683.
25 Kerouac, *Some*, 156.
26 Ibid., 185.
27 Ibid., 131.

28 Ibid., 41.
29 Jack Kerouac, *On the Road: The Original Scroll* (New York: Viking, 2007), 381.
30 Kerouac, *Original Scroll*, 381.
31 Kerouac, *On the Road*, 280.
32 Kerouac, *Some of the Dharma*, 276.
33 Kerouac, *Wake Up*, 36.
34 Kerouac, *The Dharma Bums,* 233.
35 See Jack Kerouac, "Alone on a Mountaintop," *Holiday*, October 1958, 68.
36 See Charles Shuttleworth, "Desolation Adventure: the Deeper Story of Jack Kerouac's Mountaintop Experience," in *Desolation Peak*, 8–32.
37 Kerouac, "Alone on a Mountaintop," 121, 126.
38 Jones, *Jack Kerouac's Duluoz Legend*, 177; Kerouac, *Desolation Peak*, 71.
39 Johnson, "Lonesome," 192.
40 Kerouac, *Lonesome Traveler*, 118.
41 Kerouac, "Alone," 81.
42 Kerouac, *Dharma Bums*, 12.
43 Ibid., 242.
44 Kerouac, *Desolation Peak*, 104.
45 Kerouac, "Alone," 81; Kerouac, *Lonesome Traveler*, 134.
46 Kerouac, "Alone," 81.
47 Kerouac, *Desolation Peak*, 84.
48 Kerouac, *Lonesome Traveler*, 133.
49 Ibid., 132.
50 Ibid., 133.
51 Buswell and Lopez, *Princeton Dictionary of Buddhism*, 31.
52 Jack Kerouac, *Desolation Angels* (1965) (New York: Perigee Books, 1980), 56.
53 Ibid., 56.
54 Ibid., 27.
55 Kerouac, *Some of the Dharma*, 353.
56 Ibid., 278.
57 Ibid., 279.
58 Kerouac, *Lonesome Traveler*, 36; Kerouac, *Desolation Peak*, 71.

6

"Radical Vulnerability" in Kerouac's *Big Sur*, *Satori in Paris*, and *Vanity of Duluoz*

Deborah R. Geis

"I keep saying 'ah poetic' because I didn't intend this to be a poetic paean of a book," Jack Kerouac writes in *Vanity of Duluoz* in 1967, perhaps punning a bit on "paean" and "pain."[1] At moments like this, the time frame of the narrative (his account of his alter ego's years from 1935 to 1946) breaks open to reveal the self-consciousness of the present. His lamentation for what he deems an America of "broken convictions"[2] spills backward into an admission that whenever he seems to be approaching a point of "catastrophe" in his life, he is assailed by depression.[3] This is just one example of what, for reasons I will explain, could be described as Kerouac's "radical vulnerability."

It would be easy to define Kerouac's techniques of self-disclosure as belonging to the genre of "confessional" narrative, especially given his Catholic upbringing. However, the idea of the confessional presupposes (1) guilt; (2) the hierarchical sense of the listener being an authority figure; and (3) the desire for absolution. I will argue that the confessional model might usefully be replaced by the more salient and more contemporary "radical vulnerability."

"Radical vulnerability" is a contemporary critical term coming from, but not quite coined by, Gayatri Spivak. Spivak's answer to the question of whether deconstruction was a "declaration of war" was that she preferred to think of it as a "radical acceptance of vulnerability."[4] The elided phrase "radical vulnerability" has been extended beyond postcolonial theory and has become especially important in art and art history criticism; it has also been significant in the fields of cultural theory and translation and in disability studies.[5] Put most simply, the term means, to quote Trevor Mukholi's description of the works of Black feminist artist Stacy Gillian, "the ability for the artists to put all their feeling and being into an artwork or practice without fear of failure or criticism."[6] Or as art critic Jerry Saltz describes it:

> [I]t means trying to deliver up as much as my real opinion about something as possible—even when I am thinking things I don't want to think. It means trying to be conscious of the multiple sub-strata of the experience and knowledge of others. It means being alert to things that jar me so much that they alter my reality.[7]

This consciousness of others' experience is, for theorist Richa Nagar, central to the very definition of radical vulnerability, which she sees as happening when "the individual ego must surrender to a politics of co-traveling and co-authorship."[8] She adds that radical vulnerability "demands that we learn to let go of thinking of ourselves as autonomous or sovereign social beings and internalise that *our* self is intensely co-constituted and entangled with the other."[9] For Kerouac, the idea of radical vulnerability seems to come not only from the alertness to others that Saltz and Nagar mention, but also from an encounter with an othered or reflected self that breaks open his hyperawareness of audience and takes him in the direction of the fearlessness that Gillian describes.

When we think about "new directions" in Kerouac Studies, it's therefore fascinating to see whether the idea of radical vulnerability, often used to describe the work of artists from marginalized communities, can be applied to Kerouac's work throughout his writing life, especially as shown in the fourteen-book "Duluoz Legend." Kerouac is highly self-revelatory, yet hides for the most part behind the genre of fiction. Applying even the word "radical" to Kerouac is complicated, as he was radical in his writing, but increasingly less so in his politics; he was always distrustful of fame and hated being courted as a famous writer. Moreover, it's important to point out that Kerouac always claimed to be writing fiction, even when the largely autobiographical nature of his work was evident. In Kerouac's late works, some of the fictional devices such as speaking "through" a protagonist (as he did, for example, with Sal Paradise in *On the Road*) are stripped away. More so than in earlier novels such as *The Subterraneans*, these later installments in the Duluoz Legend—notably *Big Sur* (1961/1962), *Satori in Paris* (1966), and *Vanity of Duluoz* (1967/1968)—reveal a narrator who has less of the nostalgia of, say, *Maggie Cassidy* or *Visions of Gerard*, and more ambivalence about his own abilities. In this essay, I would like to explore how the idea of "radical vulnerability" both does and doesn't fit these three works. Ultimately, "radical vulnerability" is useful in its very imperfection as a conflicted concept to apply to Kerouac's late writing.

Big Sur

Of all of Kerouac's novels, *Big Sur* most overtly and often painfully marks a struggle for self-recognition and an acknowledgment of failure. The narrator's attempts to find solace at his friend Lorenzo Monsanto (Lawrence Ferlinghetti)'s remote cabin on the California coast are repeatedly derailed by his booze-infused paranoia. At the beginning of the novel, he describes the feeling of being besieged by autograph seekers and wannabe beatniks at his mother's house ever since the publication of *On the Road* made him a celebrity; he says that he has been "driven mad" by "endless telegrams, phonecalls, requests, mail, visitors, reporters, snoopers," even a reporter who runs into his bedroom, teenagers yelling at him to come and party with them, a woman who says "I want a real beatnik at my annual Shindig party," "[d]runken visitors puking in my study, stealing books and even pencils—Uninvited acquaintances staying for days because of the clean beds and good food my mother provided."[10] What prevents all of this from being amusing is that it has sent him into a desperate state: "Me drunk practically all the time to put on a jovial cap to keep up with all this but finally realizing I was surrounded and outnumbered and had to get away to solitude again or die."[11] In other words, he has become increasingly unable to reconcile the attention he once longed for with the realization that fame comes at a cost to his autonomy, privacy, and creativity.

His "radical vulnerability" comes in his admission right after this that the past three years for him have been filled with a "drunken hopelessness which is a physical and spiritual and metaphysical hopelessness."[12] The key image he uses here is one of contemplating his own reflection: he describes "[t]he face of yourself you see in the mirror with its expression of unbearable anguish so hagged and awful with sorrow you cant even cry for a thing so ugly, so lost."[13] The moment works both literally and figuratively: he sees his own lost youth, his lost physical beauty, but he also is aware of how he's using the mirror to reflect upon himself, to give him a hard-truth message about loss and desperation. Throughout the narrative that follows, he continually flashes forward to his eventual breakdown, again emphasizing the image of terrifying transformations when he points out that early on in his sojourn, he happens to be reading a copy of *Doctor Jekyll and Mister Hyde*; he comments, "Small wonder that I myself turned from serene Jekyll to hysterical Hyde in the short space of six weeks, losing absolute control of the peace mechanisms of my mind for the first time in my life."[14] The Jekyll/Hyde comparison resonates when he describes how simple things in his retreat that gave him joy at first—the fog, the stars, the moon—later had "all changed and become sinister ... my eyes and my stomach nauseous and my soul screaming a thousand babbling words."[15] Again using the imagery of the reflection, he begins to "see myself as just doomed, pitiful" and fears that he is "just a sick clown" who has been fooling himself.[16]

When the young wannabe Beatnik poet whom he calls Ron Blake tries to befriend him, he feels resistant, saying that he's "sick and tired of all the endless enthusiasms of new young kids trying to know me."[17] After they spend a night drinking and yelling songs, he wakes up feeling tortured, and describes it in ways we haven't really seen him do in previous works, as he admits to feeling "sick in the greatest sense of the word,"[18] and his attention to the physical effects (tongue, teeth, hair, eyes) again renders his sensations in a visceral way, leading to an image in which this time, the mirror is the sky and the world itself: "he looks up at the blue sky and there's nothing there but empty space making a face at him—He looks at the world, it's sticking its tongue out at him."[19] Things get even worse for him when he comes back to the cabin a week or so later with Cody Pomeray (Neal Cassady)'s mistress Billie Dabney (Jackie Gibson Mercer), with whom he has been having an affair sanctioned by Cody, her little boy Elliot (Eric Gibson), his friend Dave Wain (the poet Lew Welch), and his girlfriend Romana Swartz (the poet Lenore Kandel). He compulsively visits and revisits the creek, "but it's all an insane revolving automatic directionless circle of anxiety"[20]—in other words, he feels caught in a kind of vortex or whirlpool. In her biography of Kerouac, Ann Charters describes this by saying that "he had caught up with the grim reality of how little his life was offering him anymore, always passing through."[21] He can't sleep, and likens his state to "the time in the movie Humphrey Bogart who's just killed his partner [is] trying to sleep by the fire and you see his eyes staring into the fire rigid and insane."[22] It's only by fixating on an image of the cross from his Catholic childhood that he's able to quiet the voices in his head. Throughout these sections, Kerouac's narrator deploys the same kind of stream-of-consciousness prose we have seen him use in earlier works, but somehow the tone here is different: it is more desperate, more naked, more deeply wounded. Robert Genter goes so far as to speculate that the novel marks Kerouac's descent into a deeper distrust of words as informed by Cold War paranoia and by his growing wariness about the confessional mode insofar as confession, as mentioned earlier, is informed by the assumption of guilt and absolution. "Words," Genter says, "which had once flowed so freely from Kerouac's typewriter, were now seen as futile attempts to communicate truths that were inexpressible."[23] Kerouac's attention to his own failures—social, psychological, creative—can be seen as radical vulnerability in his admission that writing, or language itself, fails to be its usually reliable means of deflecting his emotional upheaval.

If conversational language has betrayed him, then Kerouac's narrator attempts to find solace in the onomatopoetic sounds and nonsense syllables evoked by the ocean. What became the final section of the published novel, his epic poem "Sea," uses sound, repetition, and allusions to invoke the mysticism and buried narratives suggested by his contemplation of the ocean. "These gentle tree pulp pages," he writes, have "nothing to do/with yr crash roar, /liar sea."[24] He admits to his fear of the sea's power: "these waves scare me–/I am going to die/in full despair–/Wake up where?"[25] He says that "[e]ven the sea cant stop me from/writing something to read in my old age,"[26] lines that are doubly poignant in our knowledge that Kerouac in fact never made it to old age. He evokes John Keats and Percy Bysshe Shelley in the Romantic idea of apostrophizing the sea as a way of attempting to chart his own turbulent emotional state. By the end of the poem, the sounds that he imitates echo the sounds of his own name: "Kerm—Kurn—Cow—Kow—/Cash—Cac'h—-Cluck-/Clock" and he concludes by saying he'll "see you/ … soon anarf/in Old Brittany,"[27] alluding to the search for his name and ancestry in France that he'll pursue later in *Satori in Paris*.

Satori in Paris

In *Big Sur*, the narrative of failures breaks open something raw in Kerouac's authorial voice; in *Satori in Paris*, while he sets up his story like an absurdist travelogue, we see that here, too, he is driven by the need for a form of self-exposure at whatever cost to his pride or inhibitions. The oft-repeated mirror imagery in *Big Sur* occurs as well near the beginning of *Satori in Paris*, when the narrator says that "made-up stories and romances about what would happen IF" are for kids or idiotic grownups "who are afraid to read themselves in a book just as they might be afraid to look in the mirror when they're sick or injured or hungover or *insane*."[28] And indeed, as he holds a literal or figurative mirror up to himself, what we realize in this book is that the "radical vulnerability" lies in what ensues from making mistakes. In his article on the novel,

Hassan Melehy calls it "a demonstration of the failure of rootedness and a valorization of the new configurations of identity that result from the extravagance of the quest."[29] I appreciate Melehy's description of this novel's narrative as "cultural vagabondage ... a story of error and misdirection, both cartographic and epistemological."[30]

Kerouac's mistakes and dead ends as a traveler are almost always the source of improvisatory joy in his earlier works such as *On the Road*. In that novel as well as in others like *Dharma Bums* and *Desolation Angels*, time spent in isolation finds a reprieve when a train or a car (or a friend in a bar) derails the narrator's plans and takes him somewhere unexpected. These diversions take on a different tone by the time he writes *Satori in Paris*: the moments of ecstasy are fewer, more qualified, more difficult to obtain. Yet the dead ends and errors, and his efforts to deal with the resulting frustration, become the core of the narrative. "This book," he continues at the beginning of the third chapter, will "say, in effect, have pity on us all, and dont get mad at me for writing at all."[31] He regrets the loneliness he feels in Paris after deciding not to look up an old flame; when he leaves a whorehouse, he cuts himself on the Swiss army knife he was trying to use as protection from muggers; a gendarme misdirects him to the secured area around de Gaulle's buildings when he's looking for the National Library; the librarian there can't find the files he's searching for; he can't get the waiter's attention in a crowded restaurant; the secretary at his French publisher's doesn't believe he's an author and won't let him see his editor; his plane to Brest leaves without him with his suitcase onboard; once he arrives there, he can't find a hotel room and has to go to a police station to ask for help; a mailman doesn't know (or won't tell him) where the airline office is so that he can retrieve his suitcase; he misses his train back to Paris by three minutes; when he gets his suitcase back, he can't unlock it. As Ann Charters says, "His estimate of himself was never tougher, almost as if in his pride with his Breton ancestry he found it unbearable to face the reality of his life as he confronted his origins on French soil."[32] Although Charters' point about his ancestral pride being wounded is well-taken, I would argue that underneath this is a fear of incompetence, and the gradual revelation of that fear is key to understanding what makes his narrative voice different here.

His openness both to making mistakes and to admitting when he makes them is part of the "radical vulnerability" even if there is also a kind of slapstick comedy aspect to his misadventures. His mistakes compete with the possible moments that he describes as "satori: the Japanese word for 'sudden illumination', 'sudden awakening', or 'simply kick in the eye.'"[33] Several such moments occur, beginning and ending with the magic skills of the cabdriver who brings him back to Orly airport, but also including his conversation with a "quiet soup gentleman" at a Parisian restaurant,[34] the sidelong look of approval he thinks he gets from a priest after his outburst about God,[35] or the hotel proprietor in Brest who gives him a little butter bucket to bring back to his mother.[36] His misadventures on this trip bring him nowhere close to achieving his original goal of tracing his French ancestors (though Melehy points out that he also withheld some information for the sake of his intentional use of "misdirection").[37] That is, we could always say that even "radical vulnerability" has a performative element. On the other hand, underlying issues such as his depression and his alcoholism might bolster the argument that even if Kerouac is indeed "performing" vulnerability, his enactments themselves are more than surface behaviors. On some level, his constant thirst for a cognac or a beer simultaneously gives him a kind of social bravado even as it contributes to the missteps that he takes. The book is ultimately a puzzling and somewhat dissatisfying one if we try to read it as an actual travelogue, but more to the point, Kerouac's narrative style here mimics his voyage itself: it's a series of false starts, sudden stops, ironic self-aggrandizements, detours, in-jokes, asides, language games. Yet the narration reveals an essential level of loneliness, fear, and misdirection that stays with the reader in spite of the forays into glibness, in part because the very brevity of the book forces us into a sudden and unexpected intimacy with the storyteller.

Ann Douglas sees this intimacy as key to understanding Kerouac's narrative stance in these late works. Her description calls to mind the "fellow-traveler" aspect of radical vulnerability invoked in Richa Nagar's definition of the term cited earlier. Douglas describes Kerouac as taking the reader "into areas which the world sometimes seems to prohibit us from sharing with anyone—our feelings about our bodies, our self-imagings, the moods that inspire and afflict our need to believe."[38] She responds to critiques of the apparent despair and self-indulgence of both *Satori in Paris* and *Vanity of Duluoz* by saying that "though Kerouac claims to place no hopes in me, his reader, I as his reader am still part of the story ... [W]hat other writer has told his reader what it feels like to fail without trying to convert artistic bankruptcy into narcissistic gold ... ?"[39]

Vanity of Duluoz

Kerouac wrote *Vanity of Duluoz* in 1967, two years before his death. For the purposes of this discussion, I want to focus on the narrative interjections that occur mostly near the beginnings of chapters, the moments in which he steps out of his story about his years from the late part of high school to his time in the mid-1940s at Columbia University and with the Merchant Marine. Kerouac uses the device of addressing the narration to "wifey" (Stella Sampas), therefore directing it both toward her in a personal way, as Kerouac was close friends with her brother who was killed in the Second World War, but also as a means of creating a sense of conversational intimacy with the reader, who by default also becomes the "wifey" upon hearing the story (interestingly, regardless of the reader's gender). He refers from the very first chapter to what he calls his "particular form of anguish," saying that it comes from feeling that "people have changed so much" in the past three decades that "I don't recognize them as people any more or recognize myself as a real member of something called the human race."[40] In other words, his immediate stance is to distance himself from present-day society, to imply that he is at a breaking point because he is still writing what is considered fiction, yet is dismayed by the idea that everyone around him seems to be creating lies: "everybody's begun to lie and because they lie they assume that I lie too."[41] The mirror imagery, which we saw in both *Big Sur* and *Satori in Paris* as markers of moments of radical vulnerability, resurfaces in *Vanity of Duluoz* as well. He continues by saying that lying is omnipresent to the point that "when a man tells the truth, everybody, looking in the mirror and seeing a liar, assumes that the truth-teller is lying, too."[42] In a sense, here, the "radical vulnerability" comes about because he is trapped in a hall of mirrors, of infinite reflection: the self-imposed room from which he can't find an escape is the genre of fiction itself, but the reflective, mimetic "reality" he finds within it is increasingly distorted and more difficult to recognize in its endless and increasingly meaningless replications. It may even aid in our overall understanding of Kerouac's trajectory if we imagine him as being like a mirror: reflective, divided, and eventually shattered.

Later, in the same passage that I cited at the beginning of this essay ("I keep saying 'ah poetic' because I didn't intend this to be a poetic paean of a book"), he rails against an America that has become "such a potboiler of broken convictions."[43] The book as a whole includes the return to some murky areas of his past, including why he stopped playing football, what it was really like in the Merchant Marine, and of course, infamously, his potential complicity in the murder of David Kammerer by his friend Lucien Carr. Again, these revelations are not simply confessional ones because he does not seem to be either admitting guilt or seeking absolution. One could argue that the apparently confessional mode is, rather, part of his "radical vulnerability," but I would add a caveat here. The paradox, of course, is that this is still a fictionalized narrative, with aliases given to all of the characters. In these jumps into the present, though, he questions his own status as a writer, asking, for example, at the beginning of Book Ten, when he mourns what he calls "the stupid 'literary' dead end I find myself trapped in now" and asks rhetorically, "Does it matter to five thousand sneering college writing instructors that I wrote seventeen novels after a youth of solitary practice amounting to over two million words,"[44] in this case replacing images of mirrors with images of the various windows from which he has conducted this practice over time, beginning with his adolescent bedroom window and ending with the window of a prison cell. That prison is briefly a literal one, when he is thrown into jail over the Kammerer case, but it also represents his feelings of entrapment by fame, by expectations of "beatnik" behavior, and by his increasingly conflicted religious and political beliefs. It is also a figurative prison in the sense that having started the "Duluoz Saga" as a fictional endeavor, he now is bound to stay more or less within his own self-invented genre. In his earlier works, Kerouac simply did not have to negotiate the effects of becoming a celebrity; of the eventual labeling and commodification associated with being a member of the "Beat" movement; or even, to some extent, his belief structure (such as his childhood Catholicism vs. his later interest in Buddhism). *Vanity of Duluoz*, like these other later works, illustrates how these newer challenges to his self-representation created extreme pressures.

Ronna Johnson makes a strong case for the way the novel "appropriates a celebrity Kerouac as a constitutive part of a Kerouac story," describing how it can be seen as "both implicit and explicit testament to the continuing depredations of celebrity."[45]

She notes how the recursion to Kerouac's own earlier coming-of-age stories "suggests a fatigue of invention whose cause, we are invited to conclude, is the occasion for the novel."[46] Describing what she calls the "anti-narrative uncertainty of subjectivity,"[47] Johnson convincingly portrays Kerouac's narrative persona in the novel as "a facsimile self estranged from his own physicality and secreted in an appropriated, alien corps."[48] That "alien corps" is the aging, alcoholic physical body that becomes clownish as in *Satori in Paris*, for example, when he can't open the locks on his suitcase. But it is also something more metaphysical: the narrator who increasingly feels dissociated from his own apparent authenticity.

Feelings of anger and despair, and the vulnerability involved in admitting they exist, permeate the last part of the book. He even remarks that as he is narrating it, he somewhat understands the rage behind the behavior of an especially abusive first mate when he was in the Merchant Marine at age twenty-one in 1943, "now that I'm forty-five years old and in a continual rage myself."[49] After he returns to New York City following his brief time in jail and another stint with the Merchant Marine, he spends a year trying to write but also passing an increasing amount of time with Old Bull Hubbard (William Burroughs) and being drawn further into taking more drugs and meeting what he calls "characters of the underworld."[50] Here, the mirror image manifests itself in a photo he sees of himself at the time: "It was a year when I completely gave up trying to keep my body in condition and a photo of myself on the beach at the time shows soft and flabby body. My hair had begun to recede from the sides. I wandered in Benzedrine depression hallucinations."[51] He contrasts this to his dying father's adherence to the idea that "people should make the best of it" and seems to be addressing both the narratee of the book, i.e., "wifey," and the reader when he uses "you" to continue, "I myself, as you can see from this while insane tirade of prose called a book, had been thru so much junk anyway you can hardly blame me for joining in with the despairists of my time."[52] Hospitalized with thrombophlebitis and therefore physically confined, he rails against what he calls the "overlaid mental garbage of 'existentialism' and 'hipsterism'" and says that he "began to get a new vision of my own of a truer darkness."[53]

As he did near the end of *Big Sur*, despite disavowals of religious "redemption,"[54] he claims to have a vision of the cross: "I cant escape its mysterious penetration into all this brutality."[55] The chalice that he figuratively offers at the very end of the novel is perhaps a tongue-in-cheek version of communion, but his closing words, "be sure there's wine in it,"[56] mark both a nod to his own past bacchanalia associated with drinking and a sort of passing of the cup, to "wifey" and to readers, leaving them with the responsibility of being the ones to make sure it stays full. In Kerouac's later works, especially *Vanity of Duluoz*, his increased feelings of melancholy self-abnegation that seem to have followed upon his late-career fame (and its accompanying pressures) pose a challenge for readers who prefer to linger in the wild exuberance and optimism of his earlier writings. What this essay has attempted to show, however, is that looking at his later texts through the prism of "radical vulnerability" (as opposed to simply "confessional" writing) allows for a degree of empathy that perhaps Kerouac, for all of his defiance, would have found both slightly amusing and secretly validating.

Notes

1. Jack Kerouac, *Vanity of Duluoz* (1967/1968) (New York: Penguin USA, 1994), 103.
2. Ibid.
3. Ibid., 104.
4. Gayatri Chakravorty Spivak, *The Post-Colonial Critic: Interviews, Strategies, Dialogues*, ed. Sarah Harasym (London: Routledge, 1990), 18.
5. See Simone Drichel, "Towards a 'radical acceptance of vulnerability': Postcolonialism and Deconstruction," *Sub Stance* 42 (3) (2013): 46–66 and Michelle Jarman, "Resisting 'Good Imperialism': Reading Disability as Radical Vulnerability," *Atenea* 25 (1) (2005): 107–16.
6. Trevor Mukholi, "'Radical Vulnerability' in Stacey Gillian's Work," *FormFora*, March 8, 2022, accessed October 29, 2022, www.formfora.com, 1.
7. Jerry Saltz, "Radical Vulnerability," *The Brooklyn Rail*, October 13, 2013, accessed October 29, 2022, www.brooklynrail.org, 1.
8. Richa Nagar, "Hungry Translations: The World through Radical Vulnerability," *Antipode* 51 (2015): 6.
9. Ibid., 21.
10. Jack Kerouac, *Big Sur* (1961/1962) (Eastford, CT: Martino Fine Books, 2019), 4–5.
11. Ibid., 5.
12. Ibid., 7.
13. Ibid., 8.
14. Ibid., 18.
15. Ibid., 29.
16. Ibid., 41.
17. Ibid., 109.
18. Ibid., 111.
19. Ibid., 112.
20. Ibid., 199.
21. Ann Charters, *Kerouac: A Biography* (1974) (New York: St. Martin's Press, 1994), 334.
22. Kerouac, *Big Sur*, 202.
23. Robert Genter, "'Mad to Talk, Mad to Be Saved': Jack Kerouac, Soviet Psychology, and the Cold War Confessional Self," *Studies in American Fiction* 40 (2013): 27.
24. Kerouac, *Big Sur*, 220.
25. Ibid., 233.
26. Ibid., 234.
27. Ibid., 241.
28. Jack Kerouac, *Satori in Paris* (1966) (London: Penguin, 2020), 3.
29. Hassan Melehy, "Kerouac's Quest for Identity: *Satori in Paris*," *Studies in American Fiction* 41 (2014): 51.
30. Ibid., 62.
31. Kerouac, *Satori in Paris*, 4.
32. Charters, *Kerouac*, 348.
33. Kerouac, *Satori in Paris*, 1.
34. Ibid., 32–4.
35. Ibid., 52.
36. Ibid., 70.

37 Melehy, "Kerouac's Quest for Identity," 64.
38 Ann Douglas, "'Telepathic Shock and Meaning Excitement': Kerouac's Poetics of Intimacy," *College Literature* 27 (2000): 9.
39 Ibid., 19.
40 Kerouac, *Vanity of Duluoz*, 9.
41 Ibid., 13.
42 Ibid.
43 Ibid., 103.
44 Ibid., 167.
45 Ronna C. Johnson, "'You're Putting Me On': Jack Kerouac and the Postmodern Emergence," *College Literature* 27 (2000): 33.
46 Ibid.
47 Ibid.
48 Ibid., 34.
49 Kerouac, *Vanity of Duluoz*, 179.
50 Ibid., 259.
51 Ibid., 260.
52 Ibid., 261.
53 Ibid., 262.
54 Ibid., 264.
55 Ibid., 265.
56 Ibid., 268.

Part Two

Kerouac and the Social

7

Anti-homosexual Paranoia, Queer Love, and Cold War Poetics in Jack Kerouac's *Visions of Cody*

Pierre-Antoine Pellerin

Looking at a man in the eye is now queer.
Why else should you be looking a m. in the e.[1]

Written in the heydays of McCarthyism—yet published in its entirety some twenty years later—*Visions of Cody* (1972) is arguably Jack Kerouac's most unusual novel, if only because of its experimental form that overlaps various literary genres, suspends linear time, and evades narrative closure. The book presents abstract drawings and sketches, includes transcripts of taped conversations, resorts to collage and parody, incorporates self-translation from Joual to English as well as a passage in mirror writing, plays on the limit between reality and fiction, and blurs the distinction between prose and poetry. Those formal innovations have led some critics to consider it as "a species of late modernist fiction that ... anticipates the impatience of postmodernism with grand narratives,"[2] as an exemplar of "proto-postmodernism" or of "terminal American Joyceanism"[3] or else, from the perspective of Gerald Nicosia in the latest version of his seminal biography of Kerouac, "the first postmodern novel."[4] The avant-gardist nature of the work is also one of the reasons why Kerouac's critics have hailed the novel as the author's most accomplished book, the one that best exemplifies his "sketching" technique which he later theorized in "Essentials of Spontaneous Prose" (1957): "sketching language is undisturbed flow from the mind of personal secret idea-words, *blowing* (as per jazz musician) on subject image."[5] As Regina Weinreich has argued, *Visions of Cody* marks "the renunciation of a linear prose in favor of a more sprawling, impressionistic writing that takes 'free prose' to the outermost definition."[6] It also accounts for Allen Ginsberg's harsh dismissal of the novel which, he thought, was unpublishable. In response to a May 15, 1952, letter in which Kerouac referred to *Visions of Cody* as a historic literary achievement—"it is like *Ulysses* and should be treated with the same gravity"—Ginsberg replied that it sounded "like you were just blowing and tacking things together, ... juss crappin around thoughtlessly with that trickstyle *often*, and it's not so good."[7] In the introductory note which he wrote for the 1960 edition (which only contains selected excerpts), Kerouac himself describes *Visions of Cody* as "a 600-page character study of the hero of *On the Road*,

'Dean Moriarty,' whose name now is 'Cody Pomeray,' ... with words spilled out in the modern spontaneous method,"[8] thereby making it the epitome of his artistic ethos of spontaneity—"spilling words" on the page just as others were dripping paint on canvases at the same period. "[W]hat I am beginning to discover now," he wrote to John Clellon Holmes on June 5, 1952, "is something beyond the novel and beyond the arbitrary confines of the story," something he called the "wild form": "Wild form's the only form [that can] hold what I have to say."[9]

However true these various characterizations may be, *Visions of Cody* cannot simply be confined to a formal exercise in literary experimentation. Instead, its literary aesthetics—its stylistic idiosyncrasies and formal innovations—should be read in the political and cultural context of the immediate postwar period during which Kerouac wrote and published most of his works. The early Cold War years with the Soviet Union had domestic implications, one of which was the rise of an agency panic which historians of masculinity have analyzed in detail.[10] In particular, the publication of the Kinsey report on male sexuality in 1947 (for which Kerouac was interviewed) led to the idea that the United States faced what was described as a growing epidemic of homosexuality. The Red Scare expanded into a Lavender Scare and containing communism now meant containing homosexuality and effeminacy.[11] Those concerns, however, were not limited to the political sphere and the popular media. Instead, they quickly contaminated literary productions, most notably that of Beat Generation writers. In *Guys Like Us: Masculinity in Cold War Poetics* (2003), Michael Davidson examined how male poets then developed "a 'homo-textual' discourse of male bonding" and articulated an "ideal of heroic masculinity"[12] which, according to him, are symptomatic of the rampant homophobia and misogyny of the period. In that regard, Kerouac is no exception. In a letter written to his agent Sterling Lord in 1957, Kerouac explicitly referred to his books as Cold War weapons aiming to celebrate the vigor and strength of American men: "[Allen Ginsberg] says the Soviet are looking for raw stories about the real America. The claim that we are softies certainly wouldn't stand up in the sufferings and endurances of Dean Moriarty."[13] Most of the novels that compose Kerouac's autobiographical cycle seem imbued with similar preoccupations surrounding masculinity and male authorial identity. In *Vanity of Duluoz* (1968) for instance, Kerouac fictionalized the notorious 1944 murder of David Kammerer in which he was an indirect participant and transformed a homophobic crime into an "honor slaying."[14] Borrowing the codes of noir fiction, the police investigation that ensued is depicted as revolving around the sexual practices of the individuals involved, thereby giving Kerouac's narrator and alter ego the opportunity to reassert his heterosexuality several times during the interrogations. Likewise in *Desolation Angels* (1965), while outing Allen Ginsberg's alter ego and participating in the anti-homosexual paranoia that characterized the period—"60% or 70% of our best writers (if not 90%) are queers, for man sex"[15]—Kerouac asked for the preface written by Seymour Krim to be rewritten in order to clear himself of suspicions of homosexuality: "I never was, or wanted to be, a homosexual, so I inserted the truth: our hero 'compassionately include(d) non-participant acceptance of the homosexuality of his literary confreres.'"[16] Yet, while *Visions of Cody* does voice the anxiety surrounding male (homo)sexuality, often resorting to the strategies and techniques of Cold War surveillance, it gives unprecedented visibility to male intimacy, homoerotic desire, and sex between men at a time when homosocial relationships were the object of close scrutiny.

"I Love You, Man": *Visions of Cody* as a Love Letter to the Male Muse

In the short preface he wrote for the 1960 publication of excerpts of *Visions of Cody*, Kerouac explained how he conceived of the book as "a vertical, metaphysical study of Cody's character and its relationship to the general 'America'" rather than "just a horizontal account of travels on the road."[17] Indeed, the novel goes beyond the genre of the American travelogue to which *On the Road* belongs and only marginally recounts the cross-continental adventures already narrated in Kerouac's most popular novel. Instead, it takes the form of a hagiographic praise of Cody, illuminating "his position as an archetypal American Man."[18] In other words, Kerouac elevates the protagonist of his novel to the rank of specimen, making him the epitome of American masculinity, if not the last representative of a vanishing species of men. The book is explicitly described as a scripture, a Gospel-like report of the words and deeds of Saint Cody ("THE SAINT, THE GOOF")[19] which God himself urged him to write:

> At the junction of the state line of Colorado, its arid western one, and the state line of poor Utah I saw in the clouds huge and massed above the fiery golden desert of eveningfall the great image of God with forefinger pointed straight at me through halos and rolls and gold folds that were like the existence of the gleaming spear in His right hand, and sayeth, Go thou across the ground; go moan for man; go moan, go groan, go groan alone, go roll your bones, alones; go thou and be little beneath my sight; go thou, and be minute and as seed in the pod, but the pod the pit, world a Pod, universe a Pit; go thou, go thou, die hence; and of Cody report you well and truly.[20]

In a speech that is dramatized in a way that is reminiscent of biblical style—with its alliterations in /g/ and assonances in /əʊn/, the anaphoric repetition of "go" and the syntactic amplification of the prose—Kerouac's narrator and alter ego presents the art of writing as the result of a religious calling, the writer as an apostle or a disciple, and the protagonist as the embodiment of perfection ("I saw him as ... a god").[21] In unequivocal terms, he expresses his boundless admiration for this man whom he places above all others ("the King of all my friends")[22] and draws an exalted portrait underpinned by multiple superlatives, worshipping Cody and chanting (or "moaning") his glory: "Cody was so great, so good, that I couldn't believe—he was by far the greatest man I had ever known."[23]

Yet, Cody is not simply the central character of the novel but, to some extent, the addressee of the entire work which therefore reads as a letter to his friend and muse. Though the novel contains several letters, the epistolary genre is not just one intertext among others, but stands as the novel's central architext. Since it provides a space of shared intimacy hidden from the gaze of others, the letter is the privileged locus and vehicle for expressing feelings and desires which most often remain unvoiced in Kerouac's novels. The genre of the letter is therefore paradigmatic of a poetics that takes place between men, a man-to-man communication in which the female subject is secondary, if not entirely absent. The narrator and Cody have even invented a cypher so as to avoid being understood in case women (and wives in particular) should intrude on this homosocial space: "last summer he'd worked out an elaborate code for talking about Josephine [Cody's mistress], it was at the head of the letter *Dear Cody* (she was coming) or just *Cody* (she wasn't)."[24] At the same time, the letter is here offered to the gaze of the reader, paradoxically exhibiting to the public eye what is supposed to remain hidden and private, such as love affairs and homoerotic longings.

Toward the beginning of the novel, Kerouac inserts a letter to Cody—"my last remaining complete great pal—I don't think I'll ever have another like you"—which contains a compelling declaration of love:

> I can't think of ... anybody who knows the sum and substance of what I know and feel and cry about in my secret self all the time when I don't feel strong, the sorrows of time and personality, and can therefore on all levels make it all the way with me—who knows and loves even jazz as I do, and digs it as I do, who's been AROUND and then some. I'm completely your friend, your "lover," he who loves you and digs your greatness completely—haunted in the mind by you ... I dig Joyce and Proust above Melville and Céline, like you; and I dig *you* as we together dig the lostness and the fact that of course nothing's ever to be gained but death; I only wanted to tell you how great I think you are (after all). So hear my plea—*write*—let me know if that attic's still open, for the three, four weeks I be there; hip me to anything you can think of. Don't give me up, I'm lost—especially since her[25]

In a passage that is reminiscent of Michel de Montaigne's description of his friendship with La Boétie, Kerouac establishes a relationship of identity and reciprocity between the sender ("I") and the recipient ("you") of the letter: "because he was he, because I was I," the narrator seems to imply. This letter to the male protagonist of the novel follows the codes of a love letter and the structure of a lover's discourse. Though the sender starts by voicing out his friendship with Cody, the terms he uses soon evoke a passionate love affair which he describes as a source of suffering, and the letter ends with a plea for reciprocity. Cody is not just a character in the book, but a specter that haunts the narrator, an absent recipient whom he seeks to conjure up in order to make up for his painful absence and unbearable silence.

This letter—and the novel as a whole—resembles a hyperbolic eulogy of "the archetypal American Man" which, through multiple markers of emphasis, magnifies not only the object of desire, but desire itself. The final request ("is the attic still free?") is strangely reminiscent of "the madwoman in the attic" and of the homosexual's closet. At the same time, the narrator confesses that Cody can "make it all the way with [him]," a statement whose ambiguity is the very hallmark of homoeroticism. Yet, love between men threatens masculine camaraderie and must therefore be confined to the intimacy of the letter, which closes with an interesting postscript addressed to Cody's wife who is presented as an obstacle to the relationship between the two men: "anyway Evelyn, I hope I'm still wanted; I'm Cody's friend, not his devil. Ain't you by the way about to run out of names for the kiddies? We never know where we're going. Love Jack D."[26] The narrator pleads his case with his best friend's wife, while mocking her fertility and the family life which Cody seems to have become a prisoner of.

It is only three hundred pages later that Cody admits to a reciprocal feeling: "But it was only yesterday that Cody said to me and nobody's said such a thing in over a year, 'I love you, man, you've got to dig that; boy, you've got to know.'"[27] It is this declaration of love from man to man (marked by the gendered apostrophes "boy" and "man") that the entire narrative seeks to articulate through so many detours and abortive attempts. Immediately afterwards, however, the narrator struggles to conceal his embarrassment and suddenly reaffirms his heterosexuality by evoking his longing for a woman's love: "And I suddenly realized that women, those flesh embodiments of perfume, would love me too, a thing I had forgotten.... 'Okay Cody' I said 'I heard you, I sure do know it now.'"[28] This declaration, however, does not leave him indifferent, since he comes back to it soon after: "But the fact that any man has to say 'I love you' when obviously he doesn't have to (and also the fact he said it to me) makes me feel good; I will say it too, I will say it to the women I love and to the men (like Cody) I love."[29] However, love for a man is harder to confess and cannot be articulated as such without threatening the physical integrity of the narrator, who transforms homoerotic desire into a murderous impulse: "I'd be on my toes for a killing. Yes, we could kill each other, me kill him or him kill me, whichever way the breaks went."[30] Male love is transformed into a fight to the death, as if to make the reader forget the romance that binds the two characters together.

The end of the novel itself takes the form of a lyrical farewell to the male muse, as if the narrator were finishing a 400-page letter to his muse and lover, a passage whose obvious tenderness Allen Ginsberg can only emphasize ("how tender—a compassionate farewell to Love & the Companion"):

> Goodbye Cody—your lips in your moments of self-possessed thought and new found responsible goodness are as silent, make as least a noise, and mystify with sense in nature, like the light of an automobile reflecting from the shiny silverpaint of a sidewalk tank this very instant, as silent and all this, as a bird crossing the dawn in search of the mountain cross and the sea beyond the city at the end of the land.
> Adios, you who watched the sun go down, at the rail, by my side, smiling—
> Adios, King.[31]

The narrator once again uses the direct address to evoke the distance that now separates the two characters in elegiac fashion. Cody, now a father and married man, has not lost his power of attraction and beauty. The nostalgic evocation of his lips, compared to the sunlight and the flight of a bird at dawn in a long rising cadence, prepares the final image of the two friends standing side by side against a railing, smiling blissfully and contemplating the sunset on the horizon.[32] Whereas *On the Road* ends with the narrator meeting a new lover as Dean/Cody returns to his wife, *Visions of Cody* closes with the romantic image of the two male friends frozen for eternity.

"Olympian Perversities": Homosexuality through the Keyhole

It is therefore particularly revealing that this very letter, whose homoerotic content has just been outlined, is preceded by a passage in which the narrator denies any homosexual inclination, distancing himself from those he calls the "sensualists"—"I say sensualists because one of them was that unspeakably sensual fag."[33] The narrator tries to clear himself of any suspicion of homosexuality and repeats this denial in more explicit terms in the letter: "I'm fundamentally opposed on principle and because I don't like it."[34] At the same time, the letter offers one of the most sensual descriptions of the male body in Kerouac's cycle of novels, with a barely contained homoerotic content. Indeed, the narrator recounts a conversation (on a revealing theme, writer Jean Genet) with Swenson, a friend whose knowledge of the Parisian milieu of transvestites he emphasizes: "he even knew in detail the characters of the books, the names of the great mythological French queers of the underworld Paris, Froufrou, Mimi, Ange Divine and the lot."[35] The narrator then describes the lustful expression in Swenson's eyes, and the thinly veiled sensual, if not sexual, tension that develops between them:

> [A]fter a whole minute of his eyes struggling from their demure downward cast to turn over to me, his face suffusing with a sudden blush that seems to advertise his glances, writhing with his body one way while his gorgeous enormous eyelids unfurled the other way, in my direction, to reveal eyeballs in the act of rolling with indescribably veiled languor, mixed with shy shames and raptures of all kinds, as if from premeditated evil depths, from long private preparations no man could ever dream was possible to the mind, mincing deliciously all ever like this big lovely child that reads the Apocalypse, wrapping himself around doors, melting[36]

Kerouac's portrait of Swenson is enlivened by the "-ing" forms that set the male body into motion, emphasizing its languorous contortions and striking arabesques. The structure of the striptease, which usually links a male subject and a female object, is here applied to the male body. Adopting the dialectics of veiling and unveiling, the text lays bare the male body as it exposes and stages itself, a rehearsed spectacle ("premeditated," "long private preparations") whose active spectator is the narrator himself ("in my direction"). Their eyes meet at length, in an exchange whose innocence and feverishness evoke the romantic *topoi* of love at first sight, and the gaze becomes the silent vehicle for the feelings shared by the two characters. The combination of excitement and shame, pleasure and embarrassment ("a sudden blush," "languor, mixed with shy shames and raptures") is reinforced by the strangeness of queer desire.

The narrator can only admire the beauty of the male body before him ("gorgeous," "deliciously," "lovely"), while at the same time linking it to moral corruption ("evil depths") and damnation ("the Apocalypse").

The eye here conveys a whole range of affects in allusive fashion, thereby becoming the privileged vehicle for the expression of an unspeakable love. Yet, the almost haptic quality of the gaze is also what makes it threatening, as if eye contact between men was so fraught with ambiguity that it had become impossible:

> What is it now, that a well-dressed man who is a plumber in the Plumber's Union by day, and a beat-dressed man who is a retired barber meet on the street and think of each other wrong, as the law, or panhandler, or some such cubbyhole identification, worse than that, things like homosexual, or dopefiend, or dope pusher, or mugger, or even Communist and look away from each other's eyes with great tense movements of their neck muscles at the moment when their eyes are about to meet in the normal way that eyes meet on the street, and sometimes with their arm muscles all tense too from the feeling that there might have been contact, which arises from the vague abstract mental suspicion that there's going to be a sudden fistfight or assault with deadly weapon intent, followed by the same old excuses when the moment of meeting is past and both parties realize it was just two fears meeting on the street, not two sacrifices, really, to coin a ph—or explain it that way. Looking at a man in the eye is now queer. Why else should you be looking a m. in the e.[37]

There's no better way to sum up the paranoia running through American society (and homosocial relations in particular) at the time, a paranoia for which the gaze is the privileged vehicle. Through this chance encounter between a plumber and a barber, Kerouac's narrator describes a society under surveillance in which suspicions of homosexuality condition men's relationships with one another and enforce compulsory heterosexuality. What is particularly striking is the way the fear of being the object of homosexual desire is reinforced by the even more pernicious fear of being identified as the subject of that desire. This fear is so intense that the narrator can only refer to such a gaze in the coded form of initials ("a m. in the e."), as if it were something obscene that therefore had to be censored. Anti-homosexual paranoia is not simply enforced through panoptic surveillance but proliferates along a multiplicity of reciprocal gazes which police male behavior and make other men a threat. The net result is a performance of masculinity that relies on virility ("with great movement of their neck muscles," "with their arm muscles all tense"). Not surprisingly, in his commentary on the novel, Allen Ginsberg underlined the homophobic overtones of the passage: "'looking at a man in the eye is now queer'. A perfect expression, in Whitmanic terms, of what went wrong when two American males muscles biceps tensely meet on the street: Low panhandler homosexual dopefiend mugger communist, Paranoia."[38] In the age of the Lavender Scare, the narrator can only lament the disappearance of innocent camaraderie between men, a simple exchange of glances having become a threat of penetration.

Queer desire resurfaces several pages later in a passage already narrated in the third section of *On the Road*. In the spring of 1949, the narrator and Cody travel together from San Francisco to New York after they both end up being thrown out by Cody's wife. In Sacramento, they get a ride from a man who propositions them, and Cody tries to hustle some money from him. Yet, while the man simply turns down the offer in *On the Road*, *Visions of Cody* offers a very different account of the scene:

> The grave automobile, and the sensible pervert, carried us over the green hills of Vallejo to old Sacramento. That night the gangbelly broke loose between Cody and the skinny skeleton, sick: Cody thrashed him on rugs in the dark, monstrous huge fuck, Olympian perversities, slambanging big sodomies that made me sick, subsided with him for money; the money never came. He'd treated the boy like a girl! ... I sat in the castrated toiled listening and peeking, at one point it appeared Cody had thrown him over legs in the air like a dead hen: it swallowed me back, gad I was horrified, it was murder, I have my good reasons now for not succumbing to any of these Arabian pleasures ... —But enough, it wasn't characteristic of Cody as he is now in his workingman's life and marriage.[39]

As Kerouac seeks to develop the spontaneity of his prose and free himself of any form of control, he comes to reveal the actual outcome of the negotiation. The terms are crude, and the narrator gives free rein to the disgust this scene inspires in him, othering homosexuality as abject through the metaphor of mental illness ("pervert," "sick" twice, "perversities"). The Gothic atmosphere of the scene is highlighted through the semantic field of death ("grave," "night," "skeleton," "dark," "monstrous," "dead," "horrified," "murder"), thereby conveying the repulsion he feels as a witness to the scene, as well as its physical violence ("broke loose," "slambanging," "thrown in the air"). Yet, the "archetypal American Man" is placed in the position of the dominant, active male ("he'd treated the boy like a girl"), once again encoding homosexuality in heteronormative terms to salvage his masculinity. The narrator thereby assures the reader that the event is merely an accident, an exception that should not taint the protagonist's heterosexuality and respectability ("his workingman's life and marriage"). The confined space in which he finds himself serves the function of a closet which separates him from sexual practices which he describes in terms which imply their radical un-Americanness through periphrases like "Arabian pleasure" and "Olympian perversities." Yet, he is not simply a passive spectator here, but an active voyeur: he listens and peeks (rather than simply hears or sees). The metaphor of swallowing ("it swallowed me back"), in addition to its revealing sexual connotations, conveys his fear that he too may be indulging in a crime (he speaks of "murder") that threatens to castrate him, a condition which he metonymically displaces onto the toilet. The metaphor of the keyhole used by Kerouac in the preface—"the world of raging action and folly and also of gentle sweetness seen through the keyhole of his eye"[40]—could not be more fitting.

"Dirty Old Voyeurs": The Pornographic Brotherhood

The male body, however, cannot remain the object of the narrator's gaze for long, and the abomination to which Cody indulged in the eyes of the narrator is compensated for by an ideal, seraphic vision of the hero elsewhere in the novel. A few pages earlier, he had already expressed a clear-cut distinction between his not-so-platonic relationship to the angel-man, Cody, and his exclusively libidinal attraction to Cody's first wife:

> I walked beside him on tiptoe, I didn't want to disturb the delicate balance that existed between *this angel and me;* as for Joanna, because she was a woman, I had designs on her, I kept looking at her breasts and thinking of her lips and her legs spread revealing her cunt and me there bending over her naked heart with my hair falling over my eyes like moronic French actors or the pimpish characters in Parisian postcards and dirtybooks.... *My feeling for Cody was ethereal, like for a character in a book, for Joanna, earthy—that's to say, sexy, malevolent, manlike;*[41]

This passage draws a clear-cut distinction between, on the one hand, physical desire for women who are reduced to a series of erogenous zones and, on the other, chaste love for men described as a form of spiritual ecstasy. Whereas the female body is described in crude language ("breasts," "cunt"), the materiality of the male body is transcended into a virginal abstraction that language should not violate or desecrate. When the narrator declares that he feels for Cody as he would for a character in a novel ("like a character in a book"), his pious admiration once again evokes the devotion that believers feel for saints in biblical stories. Women, by contrast, can only be evoked through the genre of erotica ("dirtybooks"). In the process, Kerouac's narrator can present himself as a hyperactive champion of heterosexuality ("manlike," "sexy") and dispel suspicions of homosexuality ("ethereal"). At the same time, it reinforces relationships between men as it is shown to circulate from man to man—and between Cody and the narrator in particular: "Cody used to say 'have this picture, I've used it.'"[42] What's more, it is often consumed by men in homosocial settings like adult bookstores, and therefore participates once again in male socialization: "Cody and I are continually interested in the pictures of women's legs—little black and white books nudged among many in a Times Square or Curtis Street bookstore window."[43] The gaze is thus constantly redirected toward the female body in order to "straighten" the perception of the narrator, reinforce male bonding, and tone down homoeroticism. As the narrator remarks himself, "the dirty magazines of boyhood become the religious publications of manhood."[44] In that perspective, pornography is a vital part of men's identity and serves to confirm their masculinity.

As a consumer of pornography and a regular visitor of vice districts across the country, the narrator introduces his reader to the rituals of the homosocial community organized around pornography. His description of Times Square—then one of the hotspots of New York's nightlife where all manner of misfits consorted with small-time drug dealers and prostitutes—maps out an urban geography of vice that lays particular emphasis on the way those homosocial spaces are structured by the libidinal gaze of men:

> DIRTY OLD VOYEURS. On Times Square all these dirty old men we all hate some of whom try to make boys as well as girls and are the ugliest old lechers, make you think of the Arabian proverb "A young woman flees an old man"—they wears hats, why all the time wears hats!—hang around subway entrances, little bookstores, library parks, chess arcades—prowl up and down—some so innocuous you don't notice what they are till they stop in front of you (say as you lean against a building) trying to look casual but somehow with their dirty old hardpants pointed straight at you like a hex, a hoodoo pointed at the man goin down Dauphine Street to die—Nevertheless Cody and I have the same soul and we know what they do, we stood with them at dirty-pictures window from coast to coast—So here it goes, all this was just defensive preamble.[45]

This "defensive preamble," however, appears to miss the mark. It is quite paradoxical that the narrator should seek to legitimize his attraction to pornographic material by comparing himself to the perverts and deviants of Times Square whom he describes through the semantic field of abjection ("hate," "dirty," "ugliest," "lechers"). Though he appears to want to distance himself from them, he eventually admits to a sense of affinity and of affiliation that binds Cody and him to this brotherhood of vice. The distinction between "them" ("Dirty old voyeurs") and "us" ("Cody and I") is blurred, and the narrator is forced to acknowledge that they share a common identity ("the same soul"). The novel's two heroes know the codes and rituals that structure this homosocial space ("we know what they do," "we stood with them"), and it is thus from the mouth of an expert in pornography that the reader receives a lesson in voyeurism.[46]

Indeed, Kerouac's narrator then devotes two entire pages to the description of a photograph showing Nora Eddington and Rita Hayworth at the latter's 28th birthday party on Errol Flynn's boat in Acapulco in 1948. Written in the present tense as if the fantasy were acted out in the moment of its expression, this moment of erotic contemplation suspends narrative progression and invites the reader to participate in the narrator's voyeuristic pleasure. His gaze objectifies and dislocates the female body, thereby reduced to body parts that cannot function as anything other than a means of masculine wish-fulfillment. The litanic repetition of terms like "breast" and "knee" conveys the obsessive and impulsive nature of scopophilia as well as the relentless *jouissance* experienced by the narrator. He strips off a shoulder, covers a hip, scrutinizes a mole, sketches the outline of a breast, hides a nipple, glimpses at a thigh, and leers at a crotch as if he were attending a striptease show. He even comes to admit that he could well dispense with the entire body and simply keep "a nameless but revealing nipple which would tell us everything we need to know, ... the exact nipple will tell us more than Ruth's entire life story."[47] The narrator's gaze is even presented as an epistemological tool—a carnal knowledge of sorts—that offers a much deeper understanding of life and self than biographical and historical narratives. What it does, however, is inscribe the semiotics of male desire into the text, and the reader's gaze is led to follow that of the narrator as the text progressively unveils one erogenous zone after another, bit by bit, one word at a time. The violence of the male gaze is ultimately equated to that of a rape ("we lechers by now really raping the poor girl ... in cowardly revenge"), but the responsibility and guilt, though it reinforces the insidious pleasure experienced by the narrator—"its secret girlish shame, which is best of all what we want"—are immediately transferred onto the female subject: "I didn't ask her to have three-fifths of her living breast that I want to nudge between my photographed lips, she offered it herself and I'm sure God will reward her for doing it."[48] Quite literally here, the narrator can, in the words of film critic Laura Mulvey, "live out his phantasies and obsessions through linguistic command by imposing them on the image of woman still tied in her place as bearer of meaning, not maker of meaning."[49] In other words, the female body is reduced to a silent fetish that obeys heteronormative fantasies of masculinity ("we know it'll never happen, it's only a picture, but IF IT DID!")[50] and serves to dispel gender anxiety and the agency panic of the period.

If, as Eric Mottram has stated, "*Visions of Cody* is history since it recreates and records, as fiction, love between two men,"[51] this love can only take shape under the controlling gaze of the narrator, and the history it conveys is that of the anti-homosexual paranoia that proliferated in the late 1940s and early 1950s. Rather than just a formal experiment in spontaneous poetics, it stands as an ambivalent literary archive of Cold War masculinity that maps out the complex textual relationships between homosociality, homoeroticism, homosexuality, and homophobia. Though several critics have analyzed the representation of sexuality in Kerouac's novels, they have often done so by confronting his autobiographical writings with biographical data, thereby exposing the author's (open) secret—i.e., his several homosexual experiences and his supposed closetedness.[52] Such readings appear to place the author on a psychoanalyst's couch, thereby limiting our understanding of his works to the dynamics of the Oedipal triangle (namely, father absence, maternal attachment, and castration anxiety).[53] As this paper hopes to have shown, our understanding of Kerouac—and of what is queer about Kerouac—is greatly improved when his works are read from a perspective that relies on close reading practices and recent historiography on gender and sexuality, for it allows us to attend to the dynamics of male desire where it is materially inscribed, that is, in the mechanics of the text itself.

Notes

1   Jack Kerouac, *Visions of Cody* (1972) (New York: Penguin, 1993), 262.
2   R. J. Ellis, "'Dedicated to America, Whatever That Is': Kerouac Versions of *On the Road*," in *What's Your Road, Man? Critical Essays on Jack Kerouac's* On the Road, ed. Hillary Holladay and Robert Holton (Carbondale: Southern Illinois University Press, 2009), 134.
3   Kathryn Winner, "*Visions of Cody* and Media: Jack Kerouac as Late Modernist," *Journal of Modern Literature* 43 (1) (Fall 2019): 146. doi.org/10.2979/jmodelite.43.1.08.

4   Gerald Nicosia, *Memory Babe: A Critical Biography of Jack Kerouac. Centennial Edition* (San Francisco: Noodlebrain Press, 2023), 22.
5   Jack Kerouac, "Essentials of Spontaneous Prose," in *Good Blonde and Others* (San Francisco: City Lights, 1993), 69.
6   Regina Weinreich, *The Spontaneous Poetics of Jack Kerouac: A Study of the Fiction* (New York: Paragon House, 1990), 58.
7   Jack Kerouac and Allen Ginsberg, *Jack Kerouac and Allen Ginsberg: The Letters*, ed. Bill Morgan and David Stanford (New York: Viking, 2010), 173, 177.
8   Kerouac, *Visions of Cody*, np.
9   Jack Kerouac, *Selected Letters I: 1940–1956*, ed. Ann Charters (New York: Penguin, 1996), 371.
10 See for instance Robert J. Corber, *Homosexuality in Cold War America: Resistance and the Crisis of Masculinity* (Durham: Duke University Press, 1997) and K. A. Cuordileone, *Manhood and Political Culture in the Cold War* (New York: Routledge, 2005).
11 See David K. Johnson, *The Lavender Scare: The Cold War Persecution of Gays and Lesbians in the State Department* (Chicago: The University of Chicago Press, 2004).
12 Michael Davidson, *Guys Like Us: Citing Masculinity in Cold War Poetics* (Chicago: University of Chicago Press, 2003), 14, 20.
13 Jack Kerouac, *Selected Letters II: 1957–1969*, ed. Ann Charters (New York: Penguin, 2000), 103.
14 Jack Kerouac, *Vanity of Duluoz. An Adventurous Education, 1935–46* (1968) (New York: Penguin, 1994), 228.
15 Jack Kerouac, *Desolation Angels* (1965) (London: Flamingo Modern Classics, 1995), 259.
16 Kerouac, *Selected Letters II*, 445.
17 Kerouac, *Visions of Cody*, np.
18 Ibid.
19 Ibid., 356.
20 Ibid., 295.
21 Ibid., 298.
22 Ibid., 387.
23 Ibid., 298. It should be added that, in that regard, Kerouac is no exception, and his appraisal will later be echoed by novelist Ken Kesey whose comic eulogy of the protagonist of *On the Road* was titled "The Day After Superman Died" (Northridge: Lord John Press, 1980).
24 Ibid., 92.
25 Ibid., 39–41.
26 Ibid., 43.
27 Ibid., 328.
28 Ibid.
29 Ibid., 330.
30 Ibid., 331.
31 Ibid., 398.
32 For a Lacanian analysis of nostalgia and the role of the gaze in *Visions of Cody*, see Tomasz Sawczuk, "Longing for What (Never) Was: Jack Kerouac and the Nostalgic Subject from a Lacanian Perspective," in *Dwelling in Days Foregone: Nostalgia in American Literature and Culture*, ed. Weronika Łaszkiewicz, Zbigniew Maszewski, and Jacek Partyka (Newcastle: Cambridge Scholars, 2016), 174–83.

33 Kerouac, *Visions of Cody*, 36.
34 Ibid., 39.
35 Ibid., 40.
36 Ibid.
37 Ibid., 261–2.
38 Allen Ginsberg, "Visions of the Great Rememberer," postface to Kerouac, *Visions of Cody*, 415.
39 Kerouac, *Visions of Cody*, 358.
40 Ibid., np.
41 Ibid., 340; italics ours.
42 Ibid., 76.
43 Ibid.
44 Ibid.
45 Ibid., 75.
46 Cody himself is presented as an avid consumer of pornography and a regular practitioner of masturbation: "He [Cody] masturbates five or six times a day when his wife is sick (in fact all the time), has private secret rags all over the house (that I have seen)." Ibid., 299.
47 Ibid., 76.
48 Ibid., 76–7.
49 Laura Mulvey, "Visual Pleasure and Narrative Cinema," *Screen* 16 (3) (Fall 1975): 6.
50 Kerouac, *Visions of Cody*, 76.
51 Eric Mottram, "A Preface to Visions of Cody," *Review of Contemporary Fiction* 3 (2) (1983): 59.
52 For more on this topic, see Ellis Amburn, *Subterranean Kerouac: The Hidden Life of Jack Kerouac* (New York: St. Martin's Griffin, 1999).
53 For instance, James T. Jones detects an Oedipus complex in Kerouac's novels and explains how "Jack's guilt about his father parallels the way his dependence on his mother carries over into his writing." James T. Jones, *Jack Kerouac's Duluoz Legend: The Mythic Form of an Autobiographical Fiction* (Carbondale: Southern Illinois UP, 1999), 14. He even goes as far as presenting Sigmund Freud as Kerouac's "literary father" and the Oedipus myth as the "foundation of his fictional autobiography." Ibid., 244.

8

Teaching Kerouac in the Time of Trump: An Orwellian Approach to *The Dharma Bums*

John Whalen-Bridge

Just a few pages into Jack Kerouac's 1958 roman à clef *The Dharma Bums*, several of the characters, in the midst of a party that follows what seems to be a representation of the actual Six Gallery Reading in San Francisco, engage in group sex. My students at the National University of Singapore have questions:

- Is tantric sex really practiced in this way?
- Do American readers find this shocking?
- Did Kerouac, Ginsberg, Snyder, and "Princess" really do such a thing?
- Is this description offered as celebration, or is it critique?

What I wish to focus on is the problem of autofiction, the situation in which we cannot always tell novel from made-up story. Since one of the benefits of teaching a novel like *The Dharma Bums* is that it provides a kind of Beat origin story (at least regarding the West Coast history), it is important to allow for the distinction between biographical, aesthetic, and political information, even though these motivations behind the literary expression are anything but mutually exclusive.

Anyone paying attention to American and European culture in the last ten years knows that the liberal-progressive values we often take for granted in the literature classroom are currently up for grabs. Just as US academics and actors with Leftist sympathies were targeted during the McCarthy Period, politicians in several Right-leaning states have been attacking campus progressivism. I teach in Singapore, and people often assume I cannot talk about things that I discuss every semester because it is a relatively conservative culture, so in this piece I want to discuss ways to approach literary texts when the audience might feel shy about hyperbolic topics such as transgressive sex, illegal drugs, or music and art associated with social transgression. My approach in Singapore might be useful to people teaching the Beats, especially in "red" states. Relative to the United States and Europe, the Republic of Singapore is a conservative place when it comes to how we talk about sex, drugs, and rock-and-roll, but things like liberal-progressive values and the status of LGBTQ expression are constantly undergoing negotiation, so it is very interesting to teach Beat writing as the way to begin my postwar American literature seminar precisely because literature and art are the expressive zones in which my students have the most opportunity to practice voicing opinions. Singapore's relative cultural conservatism may also be useful for classroom teachers in the United States and elsewhere who find that students are not all on the same page, politically.[1] Educators around the world may be finding it more difficult to discuss controversial matters because our discourses are increasingly subject to political polarization, so in this essay I offer ways to conceptually distinguish political and aesthetic elements of a text.

When it comes to the more transgressive elements of counterculture like those regularly encountered in *The Dharma Bums* (1958), I feel the need to prepare the way carefully. In my American Literature survey course, we start with *The Dharma Bums* and also read selections from William S. Burroughs (e.g., "The Man Who Taught His Asshole to Talk")[2] and Diane di Prima (e.g., the first three or four poems of *Revolutionary Letters*).[3] During the class on Ginsberg's "Howl," we had a detailed discussion about the angel with a sword in the Turkish bath—spoiler alert: it is not a biblical reference calling for deliverance from sin from an angry God (which one genuinely thoughtful student, being innocent about the nature of bath-houses, initially assumed).[4] My students are not prudes, but as a class they do not tend to start from the reflexive wish to transgress bourgeois mores.

The bohemian critique of bourgeois culture espoused by fictional characters like Japhy Ryder may or may not compute to students in Singapore, and class discussion will go better if I open with the possibility that Beat values have both costs and benefits. Given the widespread critical habit of picking up *The Dharma Bums* by either the biographical or countercultural handles, it is often the case that students have trouble seeing it as a work of art.

Part One
Kerouacian Confusions

To many students and a few scholars, there is no difference between author Jack Kerouac and character Ray Smith, which leads to less compelling understandings of the text, even though it is clearly the case that the latter is based on the former.[5] It is a serious if understandable problem when a representation in a novel is taken as literary history when there is no corroborating evidence whatsoever.[6] Regarding this situation and its related consequences, I want to give extended voice to John Osborne's complaint.[7] In a rich and precise bit of critical invective, Osborne calls into question the widespread and effective rhetoric of Beat writing and criticism in which one goes "on the offensive against society, a policy of bugging the squares—or, as it would become known in the 1960s, 'freaking the straights' (a revival of the time-honoured avant-garde tactic of *épater les bourgeois*)."[8] Osborne points to what I am calling polarization within both the primary literature and the secondary criticism, which he relates to the ways in which Kerouac's novels blur the lines between historical reality and fiction:

That many Beat authors not only adopted this lifestyle, but also used it as the subject matter of their art is indisputable. Kerouac's novels are heavily fictionalized chronicles of the antics of him and his pals, Allen Ginsberg becoming the Alvah Goldbook of *The Dharma Bums*, Lawrence Ferlinghetti becoming the Lorenzo Monsanto of *Big Sur*, William Burroughs being pseudonymized as Old Bull Lee in *On the Road*, Gregory Corso appearing as Raphael Urso in *Desolation Angels*, and so on, thereby creating the misleading impression that the reader might pierce the text in order to grasp an originatory autobiographical "truth."[9]

The blurred line is one problem, but the partisan approach to literary criticism—in which the critic participates rather uncritically in the fantasies celebrated in the text—is even more problematic. A large body of commentary on Beat writing shares too many qualities with fan-fiction:[10]

> Another problem is that many non-writers adopted the lifestyle, with the result that even the more useful studies of the Beats are apt to be gossipy, sociological tours of one or another of their bohemian haunts with no attempt being made to discriminate the literary praxis from the general behavioural code.[11]

The last point quoted above is critical: *The Dharma Bums* is biographically interesting, but it is not in itself a basis for factual assertion. We know Kerouac changed some details, but we do not have hard facts about some of the most controversial representations. Kerouac presents a version of himself as opposed to the objective truth that one might suppose from consulting multiple witnesses. For example, one would never suspect from *The Dharma Bums* that Kerouac ever had sexual contact with another man.[12]

The problem in the classroom is also a problem for critics. Osborne argues that the confusion of history and biography has blurred distinctions between major and minor figures in the Beat movement in ways that make some Beat historiography more than a little questionable:

> [M]ajor Beat writers have themselves sought to include amongst their number certain friends whose lifestyles they admired, but whose literary talents are irredeemably minor (Herbert Huncke, Carl Solomon, Peter Orlovsky and Neal Cassady are but the most conspicuous instances).[13]

Commenting on a half-century of literary history before it, Osborne's argument is twenty years old, and yet the problem remains.[14] To Osborne's call for corrections, I would add a wish for depolarization, meaning really a clearer sense of the differences between the political expression in the text, views we may share about the current world situation, and judgments about how the writer has attempted to please readers with words. Political affiliation and aesthetic evaluation cannot be neatly separated, but if we are to appreciate the synchronic and diachronic ways in which a text exists, in its time and through our present reading, it can be helpful to distinguish these not-always-harmonic possibilities or responsibilities.[15] The wish to assert self, to represent history, to create beauty, and to change the world are siblings in a family, but they do not always get along. They must be understood both relationally and individually, as best we are able to.

Part Two
Melville, Magnetism, and Depolarization

Please allow a momentary Melvillian digression: just once in my life I spent a little more money on a wristwatch. As I have a terrible sense of direction, I was excited about a watch with a built-in compass, even though this watch cost three times what I had previously paid. The compass on this fancy watch kept failing, and at a certain point the shop refused to attempt further repairs. In my frustration, I decided to distract myself by cleaning the glass of my six-foot marine aquarium, and it was then that I realized the strong magnets on my aquarium glass scrubbing brush were ruining my fancy watch. It continued to tell the correct time, but the watch had become polarized, so the compass function was spoiled. Could the watch be depolarized?

In *Moby-Dick*'s famous 124th chapter "The Needle," a lightning strike reverses the polarity of the ship's compass, which Ishmael describes using some rather surprising words:

> Instances where the lightning has actually struck the vessel, so as to smite down some of the spars and rigging, the effect upon the needle has at times been still more fatal; all its loathsome virtue being annihilated, so that the before magnetic steel was of no more use than an old wife's knitting needle.[16]

Why should a mariner's compass be described as having a "loathsome virtue"? We must remember that Ishmael, as lone survivor of the Pequod, knows where Ahab will take that crew (except for Ishmael the survivor), if he can repolarize a bit of steel and make a functioning compass.

Thus, the random lightning strike *might* have saved the crew of the Pequod from the destruction shaped by Ahab's monomaniacal orientation, except that Ahab uses a whaling lance and manages to magnetically polarize the steel by hammering it. My undergraduate teacher Milton R. Stern's first book was entitled *The Fine Hammered Steel of Melville*, and it was mainly concerned with a New Critical connoisseur's attention to aesthetic achievement, but as George Orwell tells us in "Why I Write" there is no brick wall separating the exclusive properties of politics and aesthetics.[17] Orwell picks a line from Milton with the word "labour" to illustrate his apparently purely aesthetic joy in sounds and odd spelling: "So hee with difficulty and labour hard/ Moved on: with difficulty and labour hee ...."[18] Dropping in "labour" in this way is Orwell's wit: mixing the (supposedly) pure aesthetic enthusiasm of enjoying antiquated spelling with a double reference to "labour," and thus class conflict in *Paradise Lost*, shows his awareness that the motivations propelling a text are not mutually exclusive. We can and should expect overlap, and that fact in no way means we must collapse one motivation into another, as we do when we lazily say, "everything is political."[19]

Part Three
Kerouac and the Four Causes

I use Orwell's "Why I Write" to help teach Kerouac because the essay lays out a procedure for depolarizing our reading of a text—Orwell, in my reading, is the anti-Ahab. In highly polarized times, we need the skills of the anti-demogogue. If we look for a demogogue we favor to displace one we fear, that is akin to Ahab's correction of the Pequod's compass (which leads to disaster). The biggest problem with Ahab is that he allows one motivation (his personal revenge) to override all other causes of action (e.g., simple profit motive). We must have our own political motivations to resist the Ahabs of our world, but if we lose balance and nuance, the Ahabs will have won.

Something similar to the magnetization/polarization I have been describing happens with inexperienced readers but also with many literary scholars when reading Kerouac's *The Dharma Bums*. In proposing an "Orwellian" reading of Kerouac's novel, I do not mean to project my very present concerns about totalitarianism onto a text which is not at all shaped by fears of a fascist takeover. Rather, it is the other Orwell I want to channel, the happy rationalist who planted roses and might have been "a happy vicar" if he had not been born into a world of political upheaval.[20] Orwell famously politicized the apparently apolitical, such as when he (approvingly, one could even say lovingly) contextualized, in "Outside the Whale," the anarchic assertions of sexual joy in Henry Miller's writings. For Orwell, Miller was a kind of Jonah-figure, swallowed up by the womb-whale of sensual joy as a way to avoid the political tides that rise up in every book Orwell ever wrote. The thing about *this* Orwell was that he was always concerned with balance—always attentive to the ways in which one kind of motive for the writer or concern on the part of reader-interpreters could plow under everything in its path. To organize his thinking, he wrote "Why I Write," an essay in which he could strongly assert the importance of political assertion without losing sight of other reasons for writing.

Orwell begins by complaining about the kind of information pollution (my phrase, not Orwell's) that is one of his most famous themes. In what might be a moment of playful faux-nostalgia, Orwell says he'd have been a happy vicar in a previous century precisely because the political demands were less in those times. The real meat of the essay for me is in the four-part declaration of motives, which is actually based on Aristotle's four causes. I'll lay out the Orwell/Aristotle alignment in a table before going on to the Kerouac application. The first column lists the terms Orwell used in his essay, the second column lists the corresponding cause identified by Aristotle, and the third column works out two analogies that I use to make the analytic schema concrete for my students.

We can suppose the need for (a) a human being to make it, (b) knowledge of chair-making, (c) building materials, and (d) the wish to have a chair, perhaps merely to sit

Table 1 Multiple Motivation in the Literary Text[21]

Orwell's Reasons	Aristotle's Causes	Chair Analogy	Kerouac Application
Sheer Egotism	Efficient Cause	A *maker* is needed, in this case a carpenter	Kerouac as maker: relates to biographical information in and outside the text
Aesthetic Enthusiasm	Formal Cause	*Craft, art*: knowledge of carpentry is needed	Formalist and stylistic elements: relates to elements such as lyrical prose, haiku and spontaneous poetics, *roman à clef*, and contrapuntal silliness and sadness
Historical Impulse	Material Cause	*Material* is needed, e.g., wood, screws, glue, stain	Referential aspects of the novel: relates especially to postwar bohemianism, e.g., challenges to religious and sexual mores; representation of Bay Area and northern Californian lifestyles; and mountaineering practices
Political Purpose	Final Cause	An overall *purpose* is posited	Primarily, for Kerouac, a vision of retreat from mainstream American life encapsulated in the "rucksack revolution" passage

on it or maybe use it as a throne—depending on what purpose we construe. Lacking any of these—no chair. An essay by George Orwell requires (a) George Orwell (ego, and all), (b) the topical material (which Orwell designates "historical purpose"), (c) the artistic choices or dictates that condition the written result, and (d) the writer's (stated? inferred?) purpose—his wish to "push the world in a certain direction," as Orwell wrote in "Why I Write."[22] Orwell's phrasing of the efficient cause as "sheer egotism" is especially interesting. Orwell is fending off the attacks on a writer in which the value of a book is diminished through an ad hominem attack, e.g., he only did it for the money, or the writer just wanted attention. Orwell's rhetorical strategy in this case is one of concession rather than refutation: yes, the writer is a crying baby who craves attention—so what? Now let us discuss the art, historical accuracy, and political vision. Orwell admits that politics (namely democratic Socialism) is very important to himself, but the first three motives together might outweigh that final cause. The most important work of this essay-machine is to avoid the reductivism in which calling attention to one motivation (e.g., the cancellation move of attacking details about the life) blocks attention to the other important elements in the field of meaning.

The Dharma Bums has been treated as if it were a flat-out memoir by several biographers and top-flight scholars (e.g., Charters). Much of the text is biographically verifiable, and some points are disputed, but my concern is not so much with individual details (e.g., was there an open-view orgy to celebrate the Six Gallery reading). Rather, the danger, especially for inexperienced readers such as my students at the National University of Singapore, is that questions of historical accuracy and aesthetic appreciation can interfere with each other.

The utility of this text in a course on Beat and postwar writings has quite a bit to do with the polarities of the novel, but I submit that, in this increasingly polarized age, it will be good to avoid submitting entirely to the ways in which the text may be polarized. What do I mean by "polarized?" The text is an excellent introduction to the ways in which a group of actual writers (Gary Snyder, Jack Kerouac, Allen Ginsberg, with glimpses of several others) saw themselves in relation to the mainstream. My students in Singapore, some of whom come from Buddhist traditions of a less bohemian sort than Kerouac or Snyder or Ginsberg embraced, need to understand the motives within countercultural movements and their expressive texts, and putting *The Dharma Bums* at the beginning of the course makes it easy to connect biographical details with the interested self-construction of "Beat" literature in the infancy and adolescence of that movement. This self-construction has everything to do with a rather polemical construction of the American 1950s, with our literary heroes (and their fictional avatars) entirely on the side of the "rucksack revolution" that the novel's Ray Smith prophesizes. The alignments that my students and we scholars recognize in the text are not wrong, but they can (in my classroom experience, at least) occlude recognition of the artistic achievements of the text. Anyone who has researched writing with strong political valence(s) will have noticed the tendency of reviewers and many scholarly critics to assume an "either/or" attitude about the balance of political and aesthetic motivations that bring a literary text into existence. One solution to this polarization of literary experience is to say all literature (and other symbolic expression) is political because it is social—but that way trivializes political action. The other wrong way to go is of course the supposition of a zero-sum relationship between political significance and the other causes of art—this fallacious approach being a primary engine of "cancel culture."[23]

The teacher who is wary of polarities steers a course between rocks and hard places, and the other extreme is to construe the *political* and the *aesthetic* as immiscible substances. The purpose of a chair may be to sit—which is pretty neutral—or one can be fashioning a throne—which is of course, in Orwell's words for the political, "pushing the world in a certain direction." Both of these extremes are clearly wrong and are not what any of us do, but I mark the abstract possibilities to better notice the tendency we have to polarize a text like *The Dharma Bums*, first because it is clearly based in Kerouac's historical and autobiographical observations, and also because it was produced in the Cold War bipolarity that continues to this day—we all find ourselves in this culture war if we choose a channel to receive our news. When we present *The Dharma Bums* to our students, we will often locate the political valence of the text—the rucksack revolution, the celebration of "Oriental" culture less than a decade after the war with Japan and five years after the cessation of war in Korea, and the linking of poetry with ecstatic states—in relation to the reverberations of the politics of Kerouac's time within our own. Books are now being banned in American libraries not because they are anti-American, but because they are perceived as left of center.[24] Our heartfelt convictions are such that we may want to support banned books because they are, in a partisan way I cannot disown, the enemy of my enemy. The danger is that we lose the ability to discern literariness when our language, pedagogy, and tastes are polarized.[25]

Late in life, Kerouac became disgusted with these polarities, and perhaps he was disgusted with life generally,[26] but we have a kind of tipping point between cynicism and sentimental idealism in this novel—a wish to push the world in a certain direction, and a wish to transcend the dualities and polarities that divide people in the world. These two wishes often exist in contradiction, but we can see the signs of political activism in the rucksack revolution passage, and we can see the wish to transcend political difference in the passage in which Ray Smith, unlike Japhy Ryder, feels affection for the Chinese "Chamber of Commerce" Buddhists. Japhy's Buddhism is an ideologically committed expression of progressive activism in a way Ray's is not, and Ray faults Japhy somewhat for a dualistic feeling of superiority.

In my classroom in Singapore, confusion around these contradictions may be heightened for cultural and historical reasons, but the problem of mixing up motivations is something that attaches to many texts during a time when belief in objective news reporting is constantly under attack: the border between fiction and non-fiction isn't what it used to be. In purely literary contexts, readers are often teased with autofictions that generate curiosity but sometimes doubt and confusion. Which parts of a non-fiction novel like *The Executioner's Song* were fictional? Which parts of Maxine Hong Kingston's "memoir" *The Woman Warrior* were not accounts of her real life, and which parts are mythic fantasy? Too many critics have referred to a character named "Maxine" when the five chapters that make up the book contain no mention of "Maxine"—the primary speaker is a No Name Woman. We may want to ask, Why does it matter? We do not always have to settle questions of biographical accuracy to enjoy a book, but we do need to sort out different kinds of writerly motivation in a non-reductive way. I begin my course on the Beats with *The Dharma Bums* because it brings together biography, history, style, and politics, but I want students to have a language for sorting these matters without excluding any of the information, hence the choice to have them read Orwell's "Why I Write."

Part Four
Kerouac and History

The four analytic categories Orwell proposes are not mutually exclusive. It would be a fool's errand to try to distinguish between the biographical, historical, and formal elements of a *roman à clef*. It is precisely because elements common to these categories slosh together that the differences, in principle, must be established in class: biographical detail and autobiographical self-reference in a work of fiction are not the same thing. To work out such matters in advance of our developed discussion of the novel itself, I (1) assign the Orwell essay, (2) have them read Ann Douglas's premier bio-critical introduction to the 2006 Penguin Classics edition of *The Dharma Bums*, and (3) I circulate a PDF of the novel's first chapter in which will be found signs and traces of all four sometimes-overlapping motivations.

Biography can be baggage and our buddy, all at once. Suppose for example that one or more students, unfamiliar with mid-Fifties American culture, googles "Jack Kerouac" to learn about our author of the week; suppose she or he comes across "Jack Kerouac, Misogynist Creep: Inside His Ugly Infatuation with Marilyn Monroe," a 2015 article in *Salon* by David J. Krajicek. My readers get three guesses about the general thrust of this article, which draws on some insensitive comments in letters from Kerouac to Herbert Huncke written days after Marilyn Monroe's suicide. In short, Kerouac wrote that "She was fucked to death."[27] There are many unfortunate facts about Kerouac's life, and some of them resonate with moments from *The Dharma Bums*. It is dishonest to rule out the biographical particulars, but we must also avoid collapsing biographical contexts and artistic texts. To negotiate dilemmas such as this, we must allow for conceptual distinctions that we will have to apply in situations in which the variously claimed details of one overlap quite confusingly with published expression of the other.

When Kerouac sat down at his typewriter to begin *The Dharma Bums*, he most certainly intended to promote himself and his friends, to represent a developing intellectual ecology centered in the Bay Area, to promote the growth of what he called the "rucksack revolution," and he very much wanted to write some beautiful sentences. We can infer his socio-political purpose from the famous rucksack revolution speech that Japhy Ryder makes in Chapter 13:

> I see a vision of a great rucksack revolution thousands or even millions of young Americans wandering around with rucksacks, going up to mountains to pray, making children laugh and old men glad, making young girls happy and old girls happier, all of 'em Zen Lunatics who go about writing poems that happen to appear in their heads for no reason and also by being kind and also by strange unexpected acts keep giving visions of eternal freedom to everybody and to all living creatures, that's what I like about you Goldbook and Smith ....[28]

The rucksack, which we now tend to call a "backpack" on a university campus, is the imagistic condensation of the Buddhist and bohemian ideals enunciated by Japhy Ryder in the novel, and, often, by Gary Snyder in his talks, essays, and poetry.[29]

We can correlate Ray Smith's Buddhist boosterism with exchanges between author Jack Kerouac and his subject, Gary Snyder by reviewing the *New Yorker* profile by Dana Goodyear, which explains how the novel made Gary Snyder famous and why he was not particularly grateful due to the reputational effects of the *roman à clef*. While we can find a few instances in Snyder's writing that celebrate saturnalian rebellion against bourgeois sexual mores, I do not think there are any witnesses to a group sex party after the Six Gallery reading on October 7, 1955. The point I want to make with my students is that the text purports to be fiction, although the author clearly prides himself on accuracy. There is no record of Snyder complaining about accuracy when Kerouac asked him to sign a release form before the publication of *The Dharma Bums*: "Kerouac wrote to Snyder about signing a release form. 'As you see, I've got you down pretty accurate but I made some changes in your personal life, girlfriends, etc. ... to throw off the scent.'"[30] What were the changes? We can easily align Japhy Ryder with Gary Snyder, Alvah Goldbook with Allen Ginsberg, and so forth. The identities of female sexual partners such as Princess remain obscure in Kerouac's published text.[31]

We do not usually think of the texts of Kerouac as "culturally dense," at least compared to more allusive or even encyclopedic authors such as Thomas Pynchon or

Don DeLillo or A.S. Byatt, but one aspect of the novel that is not properly appreciated is the granularity with which Kerouac represented the cultural encounter between Asia and the United States, as it occurred within the minds of several only-apparently ne'er-do-well literati. To develop an understanding of this encounter in the novel, I have students make a close study of this extended passage from Maria Damon's essay, "Beat Poetry: HeavenHell USA, 1946–1965," in which she gives us a sense of how complex a phenomenon Kerouac was managing within his fictional representation of the so-called dharma bums:

> A third strain of philosophical influence from abroad was that of Buddhism, particularly Zen, which entered the United States from the West Coast, via Chinese and Japanese immigrants in the early part of the twentieth century, but also from U.S. war veterans returning from duty in the East after WWII. Figures such as Gary Snyder, Philip Whalen (who became a Zen priest and abbot), Lew Welch, Ginsberg, and, less seriously but with more popular impact, Kerouac studied and helped to popularize the meditation practices, the philosophy of spontaneous insight (and hence spontaneous writing, epitomized by the axiom "first thought best thought"), and interdependence of phenomena of East Asian Buddhism.[32]

The cultural collision (or hybridization, or creative interplay) has political, psychological, spiritual, and aesthetic aspects that are variously given voice in the novel, even though some critics impatiently dismiss Kerouac as a faker who did not understand genuine Buddhism.[33] The main point is that we must separate the transmission of complex philosophical ideas in Kerouac's life and the representation of cultural transmission in the novel—Kerouac and Smith are similar, but they are not the same.

Conclusion
Beautiful Sentences

Alright, now that we have all that settled, let us have a look at just the first chapter of *The Dharma Bums*. All four of the Orwellian/Aristotelian motivations can be found in any chapter of the book and perhaps on every page, but it is good to use just one chapter to demonstrate how the sorting of motives can work, and, of course, how we can find multiple motivations in many sentences along the way: we are to consider overdetermination and not fall into the error of either/or. Was Jack Kerouac an alcoholic? Yes, he was. This fact can be related to sentences such as "and I figured I needed a poorboy of Tokay wine to complete the cold dusk run to Santa Barbara," but if we *stop* with the self-congratulatory schadenfreude of noticing someone else's addiction, we might miss the resounding assonance of "poorboy" with "Tokay," and if we miss that we will certainly miss how the spondee of "*cóld dúsk*" resolves upward and lightly in the dactyl at the end of the line, "Santa *Bárbara.*"[34] Jack Kerouac may, by 1969, have destroyed himself with alcohol out of a kind of negative egotism, but "egotism" does not account for the poetry of his lyrical sentences. History lesson: class will please note that Kerouac was not the first American to celebrate the huge opportunity of geographical freedom, as we see in the instance of Ray Smith riding the rails. Huck Finn headed out for the territory (Oklahoma, not then a state) to avoid the corruption and contradictions of conventional society, and Ishmael, when he found himself at the rear of every funeral, went to the sea. Upton Sinclair's *The Jungle* (1906) also includes hoboing as social critique, and it was very positively reviewed by another rail-rider, Jack London.[35] Kerouac's recollection of railroad life has an historical dimension, clues to his biographical specificity as a writer, and of course there is the politics of turning one's back on suburban and urban life to work and even hobo in in-between places like railway yards.[36]

Kerouac, in constructing blandly named Ray Smith as a character infatuated with the luminous Japhy Ryder, reports in this chapter that he had not yet met Ryder but that he already considered himself a "Dharma Bum" and a religious wanderer. The writer (Kerouac) is certainly "pushing the world in a certain direction" with his critique of mainstream values and the imagination (and/or description) of alternative values and practices. Kerouac, like Ginsberg and others, writes in a way so as to avoid separations between his life (e.g., alcohol) and his ideals (e.g., mashing up elements of Buddhism with prayers to Saint Teresa):

> The little bum in the gondola solidified all my beliefs by warming up to the wine and talking and finally whipping out a tiny slip of paper which contained a prayer to Saint Teresa announcing that after her death she will return to the earth by showering it with roses from heaven, forever, for all living creatures.[37]

This passage may have seemed absurd to some readers over the decades, and some students may object to the mixture of alcoholism and evangelical surrender, but it would be hard to argue that the thinking and the writing are anything but innovative, and many would call it beautiful.

There has been a shelf of books and articles about "The Intentional Fallacy" as described by Wimsatt and Beardsley. Here is their opening salvo, in their defense of the aesthetic approach to the literary text: "The Intentional Fallacy is a confusion between the poem and its origins, a special case of what is known to philosophers as the Genetic Fallacy. It begins by trying to derive the standard of criticism from the psychological causes of the poem and ends in biography and relativism."[38] Biography, psychology, and relativism: Oh my! The main problem with this defense, which divides readers into classically Cold War binaries that are on the right and wrong side, is that the tool—the designated fallacy—has been used to cudgel any and all contextual information that the cudgeling critic wishes to diminish as extratextual. The New Critical defense against (political) reductiveness can and often has resulted in an aesthetic or apolitical reductiveness, but what is really required is the ability to distinguish, in relation to any given text, the wish to push the world in a certain direction on the one hand, and the pleasure that results from seeing the language and artfulness as what is primarily significant. These motivations are not, to say it one more time, mutually exclusive: Allen Ginsberg writing about sex with another man and to make the imagery with which he did so crisp and beautiful was at once a political poke at social conventions and an attempt to create art while doing so. Kerouac made aesthetic choices (e.g., the creating of bop aesthetics and long, freight train sentences laden with feeling) and distinctly different political choices (especially in regard to his representation of his own sexuality). Orwell insisted that there are kinds of motivation, that they coexist and sometimes contradict one another, and that we should allow each its relative value in a given text. If we apply this to writers such as Jack Kerouac, we can more precisely identify the beauty, the shortcomings, and the continued social significance of texts like *The Dharma Bums*.

Notes

1. Two texts in particular should be consulted regarding the various relationships between the Beats and the academic classroom: see *The Beats: A Teaching Companion*, ed. Nancy M. Grace (Clemson: Clemson University Press, 2021) and *The Beats and the Academy: A Renegotiation*, ed. Erik Mortenson and Tony Trigilio (Clemson: Clemson University Press, 2023).
2. William S. Burroughs in *Naked Lunch: The Restored Text* (New York: Grove Press, 2001), 111.
3. Diane di Prima, *Revolutionary Letters: 50th Anniversary Edition* (San Francisco: City Lights Books, 2021). In class I refer students to the edition of the poems published (without permission!) by theanarchistlibrary.org, requesting that they think about the form in which the poem is accessed in relation to the anarchic spirit expressed by the text itself: *Revolutionary Letters*, accessed March 1, 2024, https://theanarchistlibrary.org/mirror/d/dd/diane-di-prima-revolutionary-letters.pdf. It would be interesting to know if di Prima or City Lights ever took notice of this violation of copyright.
4. Allen Ginsberg, "Howl," Poetry Foundation, accessed March 1, 2024, https://www.poetryfoundation.org/poems/49303/howl. The line that initiated the discussion of bath culture was: "who hiccuped endlessly trying to giggle but wound up with a sob behind a partition in a Turkish Bath when the blond & naked angel came to pierce them with a sword … ."
5. Two biographies that treat the novel as if it were non-fiction are Ellis Amburn's, *Subterranean Kerouac: The Hidden Life of Jack Kerouac* (New York: St. Martin's Press, 1998) and Ann Charters' *Kerouac: A Biography* (New York: St. Martin's Press, 1987). Although I disagree with the use of "pseudo-Buddhist" to refer to the novel, Ovidiu Matiu's "*The Dharma Bums*: A (Fictional) Pseudo-Buddhist Hagiography, or a Pseudo *Ojoden*" is quite careful about the distinction between the fictional text and the parallel historical context. See Ovidiu Matiu, "*The Dharma Bums*: A (Fictional) Pseudo-Buddhist Hagiography, or a Pseudo *ojoden*," *Religions* 15 (2) (2024): 148, accessed March 1, 2024, https://doi.org/10.3390/rel15020148.
6. I have commented on the problem of writing about the novel *The Dharma Bums* as if it were biographical evidence in John Whalen-Bridge, "*The Dharma Bums*, the Four Noble Truths, and the Problem of Romantic Buddhism," *The Journal of Beat Studies* 10 (2022): 85–104.

7   John Osborne, "The Beats," in *A Companion to Twentieth-Century Poetry*, ed. Neil Roberts (Malden, MA: Wiley Blackwell, 2003), 183–96.
8   Ibid.
9   Ibid.
10 It need not be said that I am not a fan of fanfiction: sorry, not sorry.
11 Osborne, "The Beats," 184. Osborne provides an interesting list of texts that he believes are insufficiently critical or objective about the histories they relate: "Lawrence Lipton's *The Holy Barbarians* (concentrating on Venice West, Los Angeles), *The Real Bohemia* by Francis J. Rigney and L. Douglas Smith (San Francisco), Ned Polsky's *Hustlers, Beats and Others* (Greenwich Village, New York) and Iain Finlayson's *Tangier: City of the Dream*, are examples of this mode. Elsewhere, Jane Kramer's *Paterfamilias*, an account of Allen Ginsberg in the 1960s, sycophantically forebore to comment that his poetic talent was depreciating in inverse ratio to his accession to 'guru' status; Ann Charters and Dennis McNally have written biographies of Kerouac that preposterously assume his novels to be an unmediated transcription of actual events."
12 See Michael Davidson's *Guys Like Us: Citing Masculinity in Cold War Poetics* (Chicago: University of Chicago Press, 2003) for a discussion of masculinity and the politics of representation in Cold War America.
13 Osborne, "The Beats," 184.
14 Ibid. Osborne adds, "Fifty years after the events, the time has come to set a new agenda for the Beats, and one not based on any of these irresponsible meldings of the biography and the art, the lifestyle and the literature."
15 Fredric Jameson, *The Political Unconscious: Narrative as a Socially Symbolic Act* (Ithaca: Cornell University Press, 1981). "Always historicize" has been described as the 'mantra' of Fredric Jameson's *The Political Unconscious*. Kierkegaard scholar and theologian Thomas J. Millay's guides my sense of what the Jamesonian phrase means: "As Jameson practices it, historicization is the dialectical shifting back and forth between two temporal registers: the synchronic and the diachronic. These terms can be succinctly summarized: the synchronic is to be understood as all the structures that comprise a given object in the particular moment of study in which one approaches it; the diachronic is understood as how the character of that object has developed to be that way through time." See Thomas J. Millay, "Always Historicize! On Fredric Jameson, the Tea Party, and Theological Pragmatics," *The Other Journal* (22) (special issue on Marxism), accessed March 1, 2024, https://theotherjournal.com/2013/03/always-historicize-on-fredric-jameson-the-tea-party-and-theological-pragmatics/.
16 Herman Melville, *Moby-Dick; or, The Whale*, ed. Harrison Hayford, Hershel Parker, and G. Thomas Tanselle (Evanston and Chicago: Northwestern University Press and the Newberry Library, 1988), 517.
17 Eric Arthur Blair (1903–50), who wrote under the name George Orwell, was the most important political writer in English in the twentieth century. He is remembered chiefly for the dystopian works *Animal Farm* and *Nineteen Eighty-Four*, but he is also centrally important as an essayist. He is commonly discussed in relation to Burroughs, but not very often in relation to Kerouac.
18 George Orwell, "Why I Write," n.p. in the Summer 1946 issue of *Gangrel* and accessible online, accessed March 1, 2024, https://www.orwellfoundation.com/the-orwell-foundation/orwell/essays-and-other-works/why-i-write/.

19 The idea that "everything is political" has been made by speakers as unlike one another as Paul Krugman and Bob Marley. Saying so is a way to liberate attention that is constrained when we thoughtlessly segregate the political, the aesthetic, and the psychological, as if these analytic filters could be separated confidently in our phenomenological experience, but to argue that every expression is equally significant politically will quickly trivialize political activity. I made this argument in a detailed way in *Political Fiction and the American Self* in 1998, and I still think so (Urbana: University of Illinois Press, 1998).
20 See Rebecca Solnit's *Orwell's Roses* for a bio-critical review of Orwell that includes attention to his aesthetic sensibility (New York: Penguin Random House, 2021).
21 Orwell, ibid. For a basic review of Aristotle's four-way account of artistic causality, see Andrea Falcon, "Aristotle on Causality," *The Stanford Encyclopedia of Philosophy*, ed. Edward N. Zalta and Uri Nodelman, accessed March 1, 2024. https://plato.stanford.edu/archives/spr2023/entries/aristotle-causality.
22 Orwell, "Why I Write."
23 "Cancel culture" may be defined as the organized ostracism of the artist for a political purpose. See Pippa Norris, "Cancel Culture: Myth or Reality?," *Political Studies* 71 (1) (2023): 145–74. I merely want to assert that attempts to reduce an artist's impact to affirm moral solidarity, if that is the sole issue, would be highly reductive.
24 As I write this particular sentence, influencers in the Republican Party have been waging culture war on Taylor Swift because she is construed as having betrayed her "side."
25 According to the Oxford Reference online definition, literariness is the "sum of special linguistic and formal properties that distinguish literary texts from non-literary texts, according to the theories of Russian Formalism. The leading Formalist Roman Jakobson declared in 1919 that 'the object of literary science is not literature but literariness, that is, what makes a given work a literary work.'" See "Literariness," no author, accessed March 1, 2024, https://www.oxfordreference.com/display/10.1093/oi/authority.20110803100108912.
26 Douglas reviews Kerouac's attitude in her introduction to *The Dharma Bums*, which begins with this sentence: "When Gary Snyder, the Zen poet immortalized as 'Japhy Ryder' in *The Dharma Bums*, first met Jack Kerouac in San Francisco in the fall of 1955, he sensed about him 'a palpable aura of fame and death.'" See Ann Douglas, "Introduction: 'A Hoop for the Lowly,'" in *The Dharma Bums*, by Jack Kerouac (New York: Penguin Classics, 2006), vii–xxviii.
27 There is a vast and growing bibliography of articles and journalistic pieces that link "Kerouac" and "misogyny," and my point here is not to defend Kerouac at his worst, only to avoid collapsing the distinction between the life and the work. On Kerouac's response to Monroe's death, see David J. Krajicek's "Jack Kerouac, Misogynist Creep: Inside His Ugly Infatuation with Marilyn Monroe," *Salon*, October 11, 2015, accessed March 1, 2024, https://www.salon.com/2015/10/11/jack_kerouacs_unhealthy_infatuation_with_marilyn_monroe_partner/.
28 Jack Kerouac, *The Dharma Bums* (New York: Penguin Classics, 2006), 81–2.
29 Snyder's tone changes through the decades, but if one wanted to compare Japhy Ryder, and Gary Snyder, it would be best to look at the prose writings of the younger Snyder, especially, *Earth House Hold* (New York: New Directions Publishing, 1969).

30 Dana Goodyear, "Zen Master: Gary Snyder and the Art of Life," *The New Yorker*, October 20, 2008, accessed March 1, 2024, https://www.newyorker.com/magazine/2008/10/20/zen-master.
31 I discuss such details in detail in "*The Dharma Bums,* the Four Noble Truths, and the Problem of 'Romantic' Buddhism."
32 Maria Damon, "Beat Poetry: HeavenHell USA, 1946–1965," in *The Cambridge Companion to Modern American Poetry*, ed. Walter Kalaidjian (Cambridge, NY: Cambridge University Press, 2015), 173.
33 Matiu, "*The Dharma Bums,*" 148.
34 Kerouac, *The Dharma Bums*, 3.
35 See for example an article going back almost to the publication of *The Dharma Bums*: John D. Seelye's "The American Tramp: A Version of the Picaresque," *American Quarterly* 15 (4) (Winter, 1963): 535–53.
36 Citing Patrick Humphries's biography of Tom Waits, Douglas Field notes in "'Straight from the Mind to the Voice': Spectral Persistence in Jack Kerouac and Tom Waits," in *Kerouac on Record: A Literary Soundtrack*, ed. Simon Warner and Jim Sampas (New York: Bloomsbury Academic, 2019, pp. 261–78) that both Jack Kerouac and singer-songwriter Tom Waits enjoy affirming a referential reality with exact details, and the writers also share a fascination with railroads.
37 Kerouac, 4.
38 W. K. Wimsatt and M. C. Beardsley, "The Intentional Fallacy," *The Sewanee Review* 54 (3) (1946): 468–88, revised and republished in *The Verbal Icon: Studies in the Meaning of Poetry* (Lexington: University Press of Kentucky, 1954), 21.

9

Recovering Jack Kerouac's Blackface Novel *Pic*

Kurt Hemmer

Birth of Kerouac's Blackface Novel

It is nearly inconceivable today that a white author would write a novel like Jack Kerouac's *Pic*, which appropriates the voice of a Black child. Many people no longer believe that a white author can fully appreciate the complexities of the Black experience in America well enough to be able to write from the point of view of a Black character. Furthermore, Kerouac's Black dialect in *Pic* is now considered by many an offensive microaggression. If the novel is taught today it would have to be done with emphases on the different cultural climate of its production and how sensitive readers need to understand why the work could be seen as offensive considering our contemporary racial attitudes. But for scholars of Kerouac's work, *Pic* provides a clearer understanding of his complex conception of race.[1] He died shortly after finishing the novel, and the work has generally been dismissed or ignored by critics as a literary embarrassment or a confusing conclusion to his career. Like his first novel, *The Town and the City* (1950), and unlike the rest of his published novels, *Pic* does not fit effortlessly into the Duluoz Legend, the fictional retelling of Kerouac's life. Yet, *Pic* should be recovered not despite its problems but precisely because of them. Sometimes a minor work by a major writer provides insight into the motifs of that writer's oeuvre. Such is the case with *Pic*, which simultaneously discloses Kerouac's lifelong romantic primitivism and naïve perception of Blackness and his complicated grappling with his own whiteness.

Twelve years after finding himself in *The New York Times* best-sellers list with his second and most famous novel, *On the Road*, Kerouac was in financial dire straits living in St. Petersburg, Florida, with his third wife, Stella, and his ailing mother, Gabrielle. On October 12, 1969, he wrote to his agent, Sterling Lord, while sending him the conclusion to his latest novel, *Pic*, "For God's sake man, I've got to live too, that is, pay my rent."[2] With his once-prolific writing talent waning and in desperate need of money, he had given up his attempt to write a novel covering the last decade of his life, tentatively titled "Beat Spotlight," and turned to a work he had discarded before writing what would become *On the Road*. *Pic* was not a work informed by his experiences after writing *On the Road* but a return to the racial conceptions Kerouac had formulated before his fame.

Kerouac conceived of *Pic* while living with his mother, his sister, and her family in Rocky Mount, North Carolina in the summer of 1951. *Pic*, set in 1948, is a story narrated by a ten-year-old Black child, Pictorial Review Jackson, to his grandfather. The narrator is rescued by his brother, John, known as Slim, a struggling jazz musician, from being sent to a foster home. The novel depicts their travels from North Carolina to New York City and then to San Francisco to start a new life. Tim Hunt argues that *Pic* can be seen as Kerouac's third version of his "road novel," what was published as *On the Road* in 1957 being the fourth version of five different versions Hunt identifies.[3] With the public opening of the Kerouac Papers at the Berg Collection in the New York Public Library, Hassan Melehy has identified several more versions of Kerouac's "road novel" written in French.[4] Barry Gifford and Lawrence Lee point out that the original ending of *Pic* had the child narrator meet up with Sal Paradise and Dean Moriarty, the protagonists of *On the Road*, but that Kerouac's mother, an extremely religious Catholic, did not like the ending and helped her son come up with the published ending, having a Catholic priest help Pic and his brother get off the road.[5] Sal and Dean make a cameo in *Pic* as two men in a speeding car dressed in "blue choo-choo master suits" headed west who pick up Pic and Slim and drop them off in Pittsburgh.[6] The novel was dedicated to Dr. Danny De Sole, a psychiatrist who had prescribed the Dexedrine Kerouac depended on to help him complete his final work.[7] Surprisingly, considering that Kerouac's novels were notorious for generating unflattering reviews, *Pic* received a few favorable reviews when it was published posthumously in 1971, seemingly in deference for the deceased. *Playboy* said that the short novel,

> more than any other book he wrote, gives us a convincing picture of perfect, freewheeling, life-loving bliss .... The talk that pours out of Pic's breathless mouth is real, fantastic, fanciful and utterly enchanting .... It creates a world that might make many of us, hassled as we are by racial and generational conflict, dreamily nostalgic for the good old days when kids like Pic still could exist .... A lovely book.[8]

Of course, there was never a time when a kid like Pic could exist, and, in retrospect, this praise of the book is dumbfounding. Yet, it was echoed in the *Rolling Stone* review by Don Paul, calling the book "pleasurable" and "nice," and adding, "Its goodness and excitement come from Pic-Kerouac's vigorous evocation of American parts and bits of American life with words that vivify everything, magic language, words the reader hears, singing scenes."[9] Conflating Kerouac's voice with Pic's suggests that Paul saw the novel as Kerouac speaking to his readers through the child, just as Kerouac had spoken through his narrators in all his novels since *On the Road*.

Thus, *Pic* can be read as Kerouac in blackface.[10] It is a retelling of his first road experiences with an intensified naïveté, something he purposefully used to capture an emotional engagement with the world he wanted to convey to his readers. Gerald Nicosia writes, "Almost every incident in *Pic* comments on something that happened to Jack, and does so from the fresh perspective of viewing himself as a member of another race. That Kerouac should cast himself as a black boy is not so surprising considering that the Canucks were *les nègres blancs*."[11] The parallel scenes between *On the Road* and *Pic* help us discern Kerouac's attitudes about race.

Ghosts in *On the Road* and *Pic*

In *On the Road*, Sal, the narrator based on Kerouac, describes "the night of the Ghost of the Susquehanna," when he runs into a withered, little old man trying to get to Canada. The little old man convinces Sal to walk with him along the Susquehanna River in Pennsylvania looking for a bridge. Sal explains, "It is a terrifying river. It has bushy cliffs on both sides that lean like hairy ghosts over the unknown waters. Inky night covers all. Sometimes from the railyards across the river rises a great red locomotive flare that illuminates the horrid cliffs."[12] The experience is frightening for Sal, who eventually abandons the little old man when they cannot find the bridge. Sal gets a ride back to where he started from, learning that the entire time that he had thought he was going east he had been going west. He later sees the little old man again, but he is unable to convince the "ghost" that the little old man is going the wrong way. This ostensibly trivial occurrence is given symbolic weight by Sal when he says, "I thought all the wilderness of America was in the West till the Ghost of the Susquehanna showed me different. No, there is a wilderness in the East …."[13] The experience leaves Sal with a poignant understanding of the ubiquitous menace of the wilderness in America.

An episode in *Pic* is a repetition of this encounter with the "ghost," but there is a difference based on Kerouac's perception of Blackness. Walking along the Susquehanna River, which is not frightening but "most solemn and black and not makin a sound for miles," Pic and his brother run into the little old man who is going to "Canady" to meet his partner.[14] The little old man recalls that he "knew a boy three years ago on this road jess the same as" Pic and Slim—an allusion to Sal.[15] These parallel episodes elicit different reactions from Kerouac's white and Black characters. Rather than the creepy tone of Sal's encounter, there is a comic element to the scene with Pic and Slim. Pic writes, "That man was so funny, that was why Slim was followin him and talkin to him so."[16] The difference tells us that Kerouac views his Black characters as in tune with and relaxed around the supernatural, while a similar encounter by the white character, Sal, leaves him with anxiety. There is an acceptance of the mysterious by the Black characters because it adheres to their world view, whereas the white character is dislocated by the experience.

Kerouac views Blackness as fundamentally immune to what whiteness would view as uncanny. While Sal is portrayed as having the existential gloom that Kerouac associated with whiteness, Slim is portrayed as having a creative vitality that Kerouac associated with Blackness. Jon Panish argues that Kerouac uses his Black characters "as did the nineteenth-century romantic racialists," as symbolic representations of what is needed in white society.[17] Panish defines romantic primitivism as using "racial minorities as symbols of those entities" lacking in white civilization, which "desperately needs an infusion of the qualities embodied by her oppressed minorities: existential joy, wisdom, and nobility that comes from suffering and victimization."[18] The difference between "the Ghost of the Susquehanna" scenes from *On the Road* and *Pic* is striking because of the different reactions between Sal and Slim that reveal Kerouac's romantic primitivism. Sal is an existential contemplator, while Slim is admirably resolute. "The future of America lies in the Negro ...," Kerouac writes in his 1949 journal. "I know it now. It is the simplicity and raw strength, rising out of the American ground, that will save us."[19] When Kerouac writes *us*, he is talking about white America, which he sees as needing to learn from Black culture to overcome the traps of modernity—including the existential contemplation that plagues Sal.

Kerouac saw Blacks as part of the fellaheen (or fellahin), the people of the earth. Fellaheen is a term Kerouac took from Oswald Spengler's two-volume *The Decline of the West* (1918, 1922) and purposefully misappropriated. Spengler did not see the fellaheen from Kerouac's romantic perspective. The German historian saw the fellaheen as humanity's basest form surviving the death of each great culture as civilizations collapsed upon themselves. Spengler writes, "At the last, only the primitive blood remains, alive, but robbed of its strongest and most promising elements. This residue is the *Fellah type*."[20] Kerouac changed fellaheen to mean the authentic people of world whose purity was superior to the corrupted, industrialized First World "civilized" people destined to be destroyed by their own mechanization. From Spengler's perspective, "Life as experienced by primitive and by fellaheen peoples is just the zoological up-and-down, a planless happening without goal or cadenced march in time, wherein occurrences are many, but, in the last analysis, devoid of significance."[21] In conscious transfiguration of Spengler's use of *fellaheen*, Kerouac writes in *On the Road* that the fellahin (as it is spelled in *On the Road*) are "the essential strain of the basic primitive, wailing humanity that stretches in a belt around the equatorial belly of the world ... they were not fools; they were not clowns; they were great ... they were the source of mankind and the fathers of it."[22] Throughout Kerouac's oeuvre references to the fellaheen appear making it one of the foundational motifs of his writings.

The sentiment that the fellaheen were not the survivors of the decline of civilization but the saviors of it is echoed in Kerouac's novel *Desolation Angels* (1965), where he combined this idea with his enthusiasm for the invigorating power of Black jazz. The narrator, Jack Duluoz, based on Kerouac, writes of "the cool colored cats ... pouring into the Cellar to really give it some class and jazz now, the Negro people who will be the salvation of America—."[23] Kerouac positioned himself and the characters he created based on himself as adrift between Blackness and whiteness—between fellaheen and decadent civilization. In *On the Road*, Sal wishes he were "anything but what I was so drearily, a 'white man' disillusioned."[24] It is important to recognize that Kerouac places *white man* in quotation marks to emphasize that the Italian American, Sal, has an uneasy relationship with his white identity. This is a detail often ignored by critics. Sal has a similar nuanced relationship with whiteness as does the Québécois Kerouac. Identifying as white did not come easily for Kerouac. Often, the Québécois were not seen as white by Anglo Americans. At times, Kerouac identified more with the colored people of America than with whites. The Black poet Ted Joans says of Kerouac, "He was born in the United States, but to me he was still like a French Canadian. In fact, at that time I wrote a funny little bit of doggerel: 'I know a man who's neither white nor black / And his name is Jack Kerouac.'"[25] Kerouac would have appreciated Joans's recognition of the liminal space Kerouac felt he inhabited between white and Black. The characters Kerouac based on himself in his novels often struggled with their white identity. Joyce Johnson calls attention to the phenomenon of French-Canadian cultural pride, "*la survivance*," in the early twentieth century, which encouraged Québécois to view themselves as a separate race from their white neighbors in New England. This feeling of difference was entrenched by the prejudice the Québécois experienced. Johnson writes, "The French Canadians were despised by workers of other nationalities because they were willing to take the worst jobs, the ones no one else wanted, and to work for the lowest wages. The Massachusetts Department of Labor called them 'the Chinese of America'. New Englanders had other names for them—frogs, pea-soupers, dumb Canucks, white niggers."[26] Kerouac, as Johnson emphasizes, would never fully assimilate into what he considered white America.

Pic in Juxtaposition

Kerouac's romantic primitivism, which he also applied to his own Québécois identity (e.g., "a Fellaheen poolhall" in Lowell depicted in *Doctor Sax* [1959]), is easily identifiable in *On the Road* and *Pic*.[27] The romantic primitivism of *Pic* is best revealed when the novel is compared to similar works by Black authors. Gifford and Lee call *Pic* "an embarrassingly uninformed white man's version of Langston Hughes' *Not Without Laughter*."[28] Hughes's semi-autobiographical first novel, published in 1930, is based on his childhood experiences. When the child protagonist, Sandy, comes across a minstrel show, Hughes states, "Then Sambo and Rastus came out with long wooden razors and began to argue and shoot dice, but presently the lights went out and a ghost appeared and frightened the two men away, causing them to leave all the money on stage. (The audience thought it screamingly funny—and just like niggers.)"[29] Sandy suffers humiliations and indignities throughout Hughes's novel of a kind that Pic is blissfully ignorant of in Kerouac's novel. Hughes writes, "The white children across the street were frequently inclined to say 'Nigger', so [Sandy] was forbidden to play there."[30] Pic, unfazed by being called racial epithets by white children, writes, "One day two white boys came by seed me and said I was verily black as nigger chiles go. Well, I said that I knowed *that* indeedy."[31] Kerouac wanted Pic's naïveté to come across as endearing, as Sal's naïveté often does in *On the Road*, but, as the comparison to Hughes's book demonstrates, the portrayal is more readily seen as insulting to Blacks.

Another work placed in juxtaposition that effectively dramatizes *Pic*'s romantic primitivism is Richard Wright's memoir of his upbringing, *Black Boy* (1937). Both *Pic* and *Black Boy* are narrated from the perspective of a young Black child in the Jim Crow South in the first half of the twentieth century, both begin with scenes of a grandparent dying, and both depict children from families deserted by their fathers. While young Richard eventually finds himself in an orphanage, Slim rescues his brother, Pic, from being placed in a foster home. The most obvious stylistic difference between the two texts is the utter lack of Black vernacular in Wright's book, perhaps best viewed as a strategic maneuver against the racism Wright felt Black vernacular often unwittingly perpetuates. It is easy to imagine Wright dismissing *Pic* for the same reason he dismissed Zora Neale Hurston's *Their Eyes Were Watching God* (1937) of which he writes, "Miss Hurston *voluntarily* continues in her novel the tradition which was *forced* upon the Negro in the theater, that is, the minstrel technique that makes the 'white folks' laugh."[32] Certainly, Kerouac expected the white folks to laugh when he has Pic say, "They said I was the darkest, blackest boy ever come to that school. I always knowed that, cause I seen white boys come by my house, and I seed pink boys, and I seed blue boys, and I seed green boys, and I seed orange boys, then black, but never seed one so black as me."[33] While Hurston had been immersed in the Black communities of Florida from which she derived her characters' dialect, Kerouac's use of Black vernacular was uninformed and stereotypical. Though he intended to embrace what he considered the beauty of his imagined Black dialect, his ineptitude at truly reproducing an authentic vernacular could certainly lead some white readers, as Wright would fear, to self-righteous mockery.

The parallel scenes in *Pic* and *Black Boy* clash dramatically. Young Richard is not anxiety-free like Pic. "At night my sleep was filled with wild dreams," Richard says. "Sometimes I would wake up screaming in terror."[34] It is simply impossible to imagine Pic making the same statement. The source of Richard's fear is "white terror," a fear of the deadly power whites hold over Blacks, which he is acutely aware of before he is even nine years old. When approached by a white policeman after running away from an orphanage, Richard says, "His 'white' face created a new fear in me. I was remembering the tale of the 'white' man who had beaten the 'black' boy."[35] Richard's cognizance of the "white terror" is in stark contrast to Pic's obliviousness of white hatred toward Blacks. Singing for a congregation at the behest of Father McGillicuddy, an Irish priest who befriends Pic and his brother at the end of the novel, Pic writes, "Them Irish mans is so tickled they's pink as a shoat all over, but I feasable say they got troubles of their own …."[36] Rather than experiencing "white terror," Pic is amused by whites, enjoys entertaining them, and can even have empathy for *their* troubles.

Pic is oblivious to the potential violence that sometimes accompanies confrontations between white and Black children. Richard feels it is necessary to describe the fights between Black boys and white boys: "Our battles were real and bloody; we threw rocks, cinders, coal, sticks, pieces of iron, and broken bottles, and while we threw them we longed for even deadlier weapons."[37] Pic is not the least bit violent or concerned that violence may be perpetrated on him. As he waits for his brother in a park in New York City, he sees a boy with "the goldenest hair and the clearest blue eyes."[38] Pic writes of this encounter,

> I made friends with a little white boy who came into the park with his mother. He was all fine lookin in a blue suit with gold buttons, and knee high stockings, and a red huntin hat. He had a most admirable way of talkin and settin hisself on the bench. His mother read a book on the other bench and smiled at us kindly.[39]

Pic feels no anxiety about approaching the white boy and is blissfully unaware that there is anything like "white terror" in the world. He seems to recognize no categorical distinction between himself and the white boy as they bask in the white mother's smile. Pic is compassionate and intelligent well beyond his years, which plays against the dominant discourse of Kerouac's time that equated darkness with brutishness and stupidity. Yet, Kerouac made Pic painfully ignorant of the violent history perpetrated on Black bodies.

Wishing He Were Negro

Despite what seems obviously racist thinking today in Kerouac's writing, his Black contemporaries had mixed feelings about Kerouac's romantic primitivism. The Black poet LeRoi Jones (later Amiri Baraka) was the first to respond in Kerouac's defense against Norman Podhoretz's attack. In *On the Road*, Sal states, "At lilac evening I walked with every muscle aching among the lights of 27th and Welton in the Denver colored section, wishing I were a Negro, feeling that the best the white world had offered was not enough ecstasy for me, not enough life, joy, kicks, darkness, music, not enough night."[40] Podhoretz criticized Kerouac's "wishing I were Negro" passage, arguing, "It will be news to the Negroes to learn that they are so happy and ecstatic; I doubt if a more idyllic picture of Negro life has been painted since certain Southern ideologues tried to convince the world that things were just fine as fine could be for the slaves on the old plantation."[41] The next issue of the *Partisan Review*, which published Podhoretz's criticism, included a letter by Jones. Rather than taking issue with Podhoretz on a sociological level, Jones defended Kerouac's writing: "[*On the Road*] breaks new ground, and plants new seeds …."[42] Jones's rebuttal of Podhoretz shows that, at least at the time, Jones did not view Kerouac's romantic primitivism as offensive enough to cancel his novel. Jones writes, "Jack Kerouac's virtuous, mysterious, sensual black is drawn from his conscious/unconscious understanding that the white man is in evil withdrawal from the sweetest feelings in life."[43] Sal would not disagree with Jones's assessment. When walking by families sitting on their front steps in a Black section of Denver, Sal observes, "There was excitement and the air was filled with the vibration of really joyous life that knows nothing of disappointment and 'white sorrows' and all that."[44] The quotation marks around *white sorrows* signify Sal's discomfort with being too easily identified with the "withdrawal from the sweetest feelings in life" he associates with whiteness.

James Baldwin responded to the same passage from *On the Road* criticized by Podhoretz, claiming, "Now, this is absolute nonsense, of course, objectively considered, and offensive nonsense at that: I would hate to be in Kerouac's shoes if he should ever be mad enough to read this aloud from the stage of Harlem's Apollo Theater."[45] Baldwin believes that Black English, from which the word *beat* derived, existed out of the necessity for Blacks to survive in the brutal reality of white America. The Beat Generation, Baldwin feels, is mainly "composed of *uptight*, middle-class white people, imitating poverty, trying to *get down*, to get *with it*, doing their *thing*, doing their despairing best to be *funky*, which we, the blacks, never dreamed of doing—we *were* funky, baby, like *funk* was going out of style."⁴⁶ Kerouac was defended from Baldwin's assessment of the "wishing I were Negro" passage by the Black revolutionary and future Black Panther Eldridge Cleaver, who read this scene as an example of the necessary first stage in the political enlightenment of white Americans. Cleaver writes, "The howl of the beatniks and their scathing, outraged denunciation of the system ... was a serious, irrevocable declaration of war ... as clearly as in this remarkable passage from Jack Kerouac's *On the Road*."⁴⁷ Cleaver believed that the first stage in white political enlightenment was the rejection of conformity, which led to finding roles for whites to play in order to change society, which would lead to whites joining Black protestors, and then to whites taking the initiative through what they learned in the Black struggle for equality to fight against other social ills.⁴⁸

The romantic primitivism found in *On the Road* defended by Cleaver as the first baby step toward white political consciousness is also echoed in Kerouac's *The Subterraneans* (1958), where the narrator, Leo Percepied, based on Kerouac, speaks of his "old dream of wanting to be vital, alive like a Negro ...."⁴⁹ In his review of the novel, Kenneth Rexroth writes, "The story is all about jazz and Negroes. Now there are two things Jack knows nothing about—jazz and Negroes."⁵⁰ In truth, there were few white Americans who appreciated jazz more or who had spent more time in the company of Blacks than Kerouac at the time that *The Subterraneans* was written. Joans says, "Jack knew places up [in Harlem] that I didn't know, because after all, he had been in New York long before I had been .... He knew black chicks—I didn't know them, he knew them .... And he knew these places from experience ... It was really a funny bit—the white hipster showing the black around Harlem."⁵¹ Yet, the novel *Pic* makes clear that an appreciation for Black culture does not translate into a nuanced understanding of the Black experience.

In the novel, Slim takes Pic away from their aunt against the wishes of a white doctor, Mr. Otis, who feels Pic should be placed in a foster home. Slim explains to Pic that Mr. Otis's grandfather owned Pic's grandfather. Speaking like a true Southern slaveholder of the century before, Mr. Otis declares, "Well, I just got back from New York City myself and I ain't 'shamed to say it was my first time up there, and I don't think it's a fit place for folks to live whether they be white or colored."⁵² Since it appears to Pic that his grandfather was truly devoted to Mr. Otis's family, when he sees how much Slim's wife, Sheila, a Black woman from Brooklyn, loves Slim, he says, "I reckon Sheila loved Slim like she was his slave."⁵³ The naïveté of the statement may be intended to make readers smile, but it certainly makes many readers today cringe.

Pic as Blackface Minstrelsy

Pic reads like a fairy-tale reconstruction of a past when Blacks were unburdened by the history of slavery and felt no animosity toward the white world that continued to regulate their position in society. The novel dehistoricizes the Black experience and can be seen as a literary version of blackface minstrelsy with Pic, at times, standing in for attitudes Kerouac attributed to Sal in *On the Road*. Pic sounds the most like Sal when he describes Slim playing his horn: "He was pushin the horn to go ever' old way zippin here and zoopin there, he then drawed-out himself on one breath way high up, and threw it way down '*BAWP*' and again in the middle, and the drummer-man looked up from his crashing sticks yelled 'Go Slim!' jess like that."[54] Compare this passage to Sal's description of watching jazz in *On the Road*:

> The behatted tenorman was blowing at the peak of a wonderfully satisfactory free idea, a rising and falling riff that went from "EE-yah!" to a crazier "EE-de-lee-yah!" and blasted along to the rolling crash of the butt-scarred drums hammered by a big brutal Negro with a bullneck who didn't give a damn about anything but punishing his busted tubs, crash, rattle-ti-boom, crash.[55]

Pic can also be read as Kerouac reliving his experiences, just as he had with the Italian American Sal, but as a Black child in a way he thought he would have liked to convey them to his readers—full of wonder, excitement, passion, innocence, joy—and yet his characters do not have to feel the real burdens of being inside a Black body. Ralph Ellison argues that the function of blackface minstrelsy is "to veil the humanity of Negroes thus reduced to a sign, and to repress the white audience's awareness of its moral identification with its own acts and with the human ambiguities pushed behind the mask."[56] Kerouac certainly did not intend to reduce the humanity of Blacks, and he naively viewed *naiveté* itself as a positive characteristic not only for Blacks but also for white characters like Sal Paradise. Nonetheless, Ellison's critique of blackface minstrelsy can be applied to what Eric Lott would call the "racial cross-dressing" we find in Kerouac's *Pic*.[57]

Despite the blackface of his novel, Kerouac did attempt to look at racial problems through his characters Pic and Slim. Rather than characters that cause social unrest, Pic and Slim are victims of social injustice. While on the road, Pic and Slim stop to eat at a lunch wagon where a group of whites and a group of Native Americans get into a fight. As the fight goes on, a young white woman comes to the table where Pic and Slim are sitting and sits next to Slim. When the police come, Slim is nervous. Pic says, "And she smiled but Slim he was afeared of the police-men and never smiled back at her smile, besides Slim is married to Sheila, but the woman sat there actin as though she was at the same table with us and no one of the police-men offered up to bother her."[58] Pic does not recognize, though the reader does, that Slim's fear has more to do with the fact that he is a Black man at a table with a white woman than because he is married. The fact that the Native Americans are arrested and not the whites involved in the fight is also commentary by Kerouac on the racial injustice prevalent in American society. To some degree this demonstrates Kerouac's awareness of American racism. Pic recognizes his connection with the Native Americans in the social order. He writes immediately after the scene, "a whole lot of black men have Jindian blood."[59] Though it does not excuse Kerouac's romantic primitivism, it does show that Kerouac (who believed he had Native American ancestry) was aware of and capable of writing about American racism.

The Cost of Naiveté

Jack Kerouac was "murdered," claimed Gregory Corso in an aside on a panel at "The Writings of Jack Kerouac" conference at New York University on June 5, 1995.[60] The incident that Corso was referring to was described by Kerouac to his first wife, Edie Parker Kerouac, in a letter dated September 8, 1969, six weeks before his death. He had taken a friend to a Black bar called the Cactus in St. Petersburg, Florida. His white friend thought it was alright to put his arm "affectionately" around the Black band manager. Offended by this gesture from a white stranger, the band manager punched Kerouac's friend. Jack stood up. He writes,

> Another Negro came up behind me. The other five musicians got up. 25 other Negroes were watching in the door. I realized I'd have to accept a beating of some kind or wind up me and [my friend] stabbed, shot, or killed. So he mauled me …. Cops came and arrested *Me* and [my friend] for drunk. Four minutes getting stitches in the hospital…. I no more go to Negro bars.[61]

According to Jim Christy, "In a four-hour phone conversation with Edie Parker, shortly after the beating at the Cactus, Jack said he feared he might die of his injuries."[62] Corso felt the beating precipitated Kerouac's death. Whether it did or not, it seems that he had put himself in a situation where he could not accurately read the racial implications of his and his friend's actions.

Kerouac had been going to Black bars all his adult life because of his love for Black jazz. The episode in St. Petersburg was not the first time he had encountered race-based trouble. Neal Cassady's first wife, Lu Anne Henderson, recounts going to an all-Black dance in Oakland with Jack and Neal in 1949:

> We weren't that racially aware, I guess, because it came as kind of a shock when we went over there … and suddenly found ourselves in a hostile situation …. Just as I'm taking my seat, this black guy in back of us pulled the chair out, and I went *ploooof!*… Jack didn't know what to do …. The hate in people's eyes was fierce.[63]

Jack and Lu Anne were oblivious to the feelings their presence could possibly cause to the people who had experienced violent prejudice from whites all their lives. "I finally got up and went to the restroom," says Lu Anne. "Three black girls cornered me in there. I had to tell them I was a whore …. But that was the only way I could get out of that restroom without getting beaten up."[64] Lu Anne and Jack were scared and confused as they made their way out of the dance. Understanding the complexities of racial tensions takes as much work today as it did then. Kerouac would be as shocked as he was at the Oakland dance in 1949 to learn that today *Pic* can raise hostility against its author because it can be read as racist. The reasons behind racial tensions are not something he ever fully understood. It is a challenge for instructors interested in engaging with Kerouac's works to confront them with our ever-evolving discourse on race in America. The recovery of *Pic* is part of the necessary reanalysis of how Kerouac applied his racial attitudes to his texts. A better understanding of these applications will help us more accurately posit them in relation to our own contemporary racial attitudes and ultimately make us better readers of Kerouac's often race-conscious novels.

Notes

1. See Ryan Mathews, "A Beat in Blackface: Jack Kerouac and the Issue of Race" by Ryan Matthews in *Beatitude* 22 (2022): 123–44 for another discussion on this topic.
2. Jack Kerouac, *Jack Kerouac: Selected Letters, 1957–1969*, ed. Ann Charters (New York: Viking, 1999), 478.
3. Tim Hunt, *Kerouac's Crooked Road: The Development of a Fiction* (Carbondale, IL: Southern Illinois University Press, 2010), 98.
4. Hassan Melehy, *Kerouac: Language, Poetics, and Territory* (New York: Bloomsbury, 2016), 45.
5. Barry Gifford and Lawrence Lee, *Jack's Book: An Oral Biography* (New York: St. Martin's Press, 1994), 313.
6. Jack Kerouac, *Pic* (New York: Grove Press, Inc., 1971), 113–14.
7. Kerouac, *Jack Kerouac: Selected Letters, 1957–1969*, 476–7.
8. "Books," *Playboy*, February 1972, 28.
9. Don Paul, "Pic," *Rolling Stone*, May 11, 1972, 68.
10. For an enlightening discussion of blackface, see Eric Lott's *Love & Theft: Blackface Minstrelsy and the American Working Class* (New York: Oxford University Press, 2013). Charles Musser provides a nuanced reading of Al Jolson's use of blackface in the first feature-length "talkie," *The Jazz Singer* (1927), in "Why Did Negroes Love Al Jolson and *The Jazz Singer*?: Melodrama, Blackface and Cosmopolitan Theatrical Culture," *Film History* 23 (2011): 196–222.
11. Gerald Nicosia, *Memory Babe: A Critical Biography of Jack Kerouac* (Berkeley: University of California Press, 1994), 695.
12. Jack Kerouac, *On the Road* (New York: The Viking Press, 1957), 104.
13. Ibid., 105.
14. Kerouac, *Pic*, 105–6.
15. Ibid., 106–7.
16. Ibid., 107.
17. Jon Panish, "Kerouac's *The Subterraneans*: A Study of 'Romantic Primitivism,'" *MELUS* 19 (3) (Fall 1994): 107.
18. Ibid.
19. Jack Kerouac, "On the Road Again," comp. Douglas Brinkley, *New Yorker*, June 29, 1998, 54.
20. Oswald Spengler, *The Decline of the West: An Abridged Edition*, trans. Charles Francis Atkinson (New York: Oxford University Press, 1991), 251.
21. Ibid., 267.
22. Kerouac, *On the Road*, 280–1.
23. Jack Kerouac, *Desolation Angels* (New York: Coward-McGann, Inc., 1965), 123.

24. Kerouac, *On the Road*, 180.
25. Gerald Nicosia, "'Sharing the Poem of Life': An Interview with Ted Joans," *Beat Angels, the unspeakable visions of the individual* 12, ed. Arthur and Kit Knight (1982): 131.
26. Joyce Johnson, *The Voice Is All: The Lonely Victory of Jack Kerouac* (New York: Viking, 2012), 22.
27. Jack Kerouac, *Doctor Sax* (New York: Ballantine Books, 1977), 86.
28. Gifford and Lee, *Jack's Book*, 159.
29. Langston Hughes, *Not without Laughter* (New York: Collier Books, 1969), 107.
30. Ibid., 116.
31. Kerouac, *Pic*, 2.
32. Richard Wright, "Between Laughter and Tears," *New Masses*, October 5, 1937, 25.
33. Kerouac, *Pic*, 2.
34. Richard Wright, *Black Boy* (1937) (New York: Harper & Row, 1989), 98.
35. Ibid., 39.
36. Kerouac, *Pic*, 116.
37. Wright, *Black Boy*, 93.
38. Kerouac, *Pic*, 68.
39. Ibid.
40. Kerouac, *On the Road*, 180.
41. Norman Podhoretz, "The Know-Nothing Bohemians," *Partisan Review* 25 (2) (Spring 1958): 311.
42. LeRoi Jones, "The Beat Generation," *Partisan Review* 25 (3) (Summer 1958): 473.
43. LeRoi Jones, "American Sexual Reference: Black Male," in *Home: Social Essays* (New York: William Morrow & Co., Inc., 1966), 228.
44. Kerouac, *On the Road*, 181.
45. James Baldwin, *Nobody Knows My Name: More Notes of a Native Son* (New York: Dial, 1961), 231.
46. James Baldwin, "If Black English Isn't a Language, Then Tell Me, What Is?," in *Collected Essays*, ed. Toni Morrison (New York: The Library of America, 1998), 781.
47. Eldridge Cleaver, *Soul on Ice* (New York: Delta, 1968), 71–2.
48. Ibid., 71–4.
49. Jack Kerouac, *The Subterraneans* (New York: Grove Press, Inc., 1958), 70.
50. Kenneth Rexroth, "The Voice of the Beat Generation Has Some Square Delusions," in "This World," *San Francisco Chronicle*, February 16, 1958, 23.
51. Nicosia, "Sharing the Poem of Life," 130–1.
52. Kerouac, *Pic*, 26.
53. Ibid., 72.
54. Ibid., 76–7.
55. Kerouac, *On the Road*, 196–7.
56. Ralph Ellison, "Change the Joke and Slip the Yoke," in *Shadow and Act* (New York: Vintage International, 1995), 49.
57. Eric Lott, "White Like Me: Racial Cross-Dressing and the Construction of American Whiteness," in *Cultures of United States Imperialism*, ed. Amy Kaplan (Durham: Duke University Press, 1993), 474–95.
58. Kerouac, *Pic*, 112.
59. Ibid.

60 I was in the audience at this panel.
61 Kerouac, *Jack Kerouac: Selected Letters, 1957–1969*, 478.
62 Jim Christy, *The Long Slow Death of Jack Kerouac* (Toronto: ECW Press, 1998), 82.
63 Gerald Nicosia and Anne Marie Santos, *One and Only: The Untold Story of* On the Road *and Lu Anne Henderson, the Woman Who Started Jack Kerouac and Neal Cassady on Their Journey* (Berkeley, CA: Viva Editions, 2011), 136.
64 Ibid., 136–7.

10

Jack Kerouac and the Language of Populism

Nancy M. Grace

America isn't the same country anymore.... It's become a goddamn pesthole for every crummy race from the other side ... a white man can't walk down the street, or go in a restaurant, or do business, or do anything ... without having to mix up with these goddamn greasers from the other side.... Wops! ... Jews! Greeks! Niggers! Armenians, Syrians, every scummy race in the world. They've all come here, ... and they'll keep on coming by the boatload. Mark my word, you'll see the day when a real American won't have a chance to work and live decently in his own country.[1]

Thus begins Jack Kerouac's early novel *The Haunted Life*, written in 1944 and posthumously published in 2014. Featuring the young Peter Martin and his father (based on Kerouac himself and his own father), the book is an early variant of Kerouac's first published novel *The Town and The City* (1950). The introduction, spoken by the father to the son, is a populist statement, as Todd Tietchen, editor of *The Haunted Life*, pointed out, particularly in the context of what we identify as populism in the United States based on Donald Trump's presidential campaigns and presidency (2017–21). Much of that current political rhetoric has been fueled by sloganeering that is anti-immigrant, anti-media, anti-woman, anti-Black, anti-climate change, anti-LGBTQ, anti-big government, and anti-globalism—all in the name of resurrecting an imagined America that was once "Great."

If he were alive today, Kerouac's father, Leo, upon whom Mr. Martin was based and who had no use for Franklin Roosevelt's New Deal policies, may well have voted for Trump. In letters written to his son in 1942 when Jack was visiting Washington, D.C., Leo championed Republican Wendell Wilkie as a self-made man over Roosevelt, whom he derogatorily called "Roosie" and believed to be someone "born to the velvet" with dreams of becoming a dictator. He snidely signed one letter with a sexist comment: "Give my love to old Roosie, and dear! Dear! Eleanoah!—the sweet thing! Bet you get a whiff when she's in town."[2] In *Vanity of Duluoz* (1968), written years later, Kerouac recalls this same father visiting him in the hospital: "fat, puffing on cigar ... yell[ing] 'Good boy, tell that goddam Roosevelt and his ugly wife where to get off! All a bunch of Communists. The Germans should not be our enemies but our Allies. This is a war for the Marxist Communist Jews and you are a victim of the whole plot ....'" Here Kerouac uses much the same language he had employed years earlier and had taken from Leo Kerouac's letters.[3]

Leo Kerouac and his fictional avatar represent the internalization of the belief that a once-pure homeland is being destroyed by diversity, socialism, and the state. While not a mirror of Trump's unapologetic pro-dictator populism, Leo Kerouac shapes an illusionary populace composed entirely of the white working class, specifically Irish, French-Canadian, English, and Germans.[4] His is a mythic world void of pluralism and the laws and social customs necessary to provide freedom and equality for a diverse citizenry, which it quickly became as the eighteenth century gave way to the nineteenth. In the midst of such rapid expansion, it also had a profound influence, both pro- and anti-populist, on the Duluoz Legend of Jack Kerouac, whose letters, literature, and journals expose his shifts from liberal left to conservative right with numerous iterations thereof throughout his short life. As this discussion will illuminate, the process rendered Kerouac and his writing neither leftist nor rightist, but rather a torturous acrobatic feat of identity politics grounded in religious existentialism as he attempted to balance the individual good with the greater good in his quest for what he considered his authentic American self.

This mythic version of American identity and governance that Kerouac inherited can be traced back to the country's founders. In Federalist Paper No. 2, for instance, John Jay declared that divine will "had ... been pleased to give this connected country to one united people" with the same ancestors, language, religion, and social customs. James Madison, tempering Jay's position, noted in Federalist Paper No. 10 the illusionary nature of this vision, arguing that humans have a natural "propensity [to] fall into mutual animosities," leading to "violent conflicts." Madison's solution was a republican, rather than democratic, form of government, which, as he wrote in No. 51, would create a more homogenous politic, protecting "the rights of individuals, or of the minority." After almost 250 years, US history has proven Madison to be both prescient and naive, as the nation has struggled to effect the arc of moral justice for all.[5]

Despite current mainstream pronouncements on populism, it is not *solely* a de facto synonym for fascism, and it does not appear to have been so for Kerouac either. The term as political rhetoric emerged in the mid-1880s with the creation of the People's (or Populist) Party as farmers in the South and Great Plains organized for economic reforms. By the 1890s, the term became more commonplace, with Nebraskan William Jennings Bryan, the Democratic Party presidential nominee in 1896, leading a populist movement that advocated for women's suffrage, agrarian rights, free trade, labor unions, and a free press: a distinctly different animal from that ventriloquized by Kerouac's father and Mr. Martin. However, the term has become so slippery that it is now affiliated with both *economic and social* beliefs as diverse as nationalist nostalgia, the inequity of the balance of wealth, the moral and pure authority of an non-institutionalized people, and the need for a strong leader to save said people. In effect, as historian Michael Kazin contends, the term enables Americans to protest a whole host of inequalities "without calling the entire system into question."[6]

With many of these concerns, populism as a term generally stands unconnected to any systematic political philosophy, which can render it a slippery conundrum today and in Kerouac's day as well. For example, the classic American "we the people" language of populism according to Jan-Werner Müller can be used by anyone, although who "the people" are in any contested moment remains ambiguous. But when used by populists such as Leo Kerouac it claims that they and only they represent the "true" people and thus can speak for them.[7] In Leo Kerouac's case, in a letter to his son, he stated that his pay, while small, was never "stained red with the blood of the vast army of the world's underprivileged," a "we-the-people" declaration that aligned himself with them through his knowledge of their condition but unequivocally separated himself from them through his moral, non-blood-soaked superiority.[8]

However, one conceptualization that theorists seem to agree upon is that populism pits two forces against each other—a battle royale in which one group sees itself as the conveyor of the absolute truth fighting to eradicate an evil empire. This battle takes two basic forms: (1) *Exclusive* populism, which aims to shut out stigmatized groups, and (2) *Inclusive* populism, which wants the body politic open to the stigmatized.[9] In Kerouac's youth, the *exclusive* narrative emerges in histories of Leo and Jack Kerouac's New England, which after the First World War became the site for white Protestant Yankee efforts to purge the region of Catholic French Canadians. New England state legislatures were instituting "English-only" laws, the Ku Klux Klan was promoting anti-Catholic campaigns in the region, and some sociological studies found almost half of French-Canadians to be "retarded" or all French-Canadians to be barely superior to African Americans.[10]

This two-pronged umbrella concept has produced and given populist credence not only to national party politics and exclusive alt-right white supremacist movements, but it also characterized Kerouac's Beat literary movement itself, particularly the inclusive belief that the anti-academic/anti-intellectual artist is the quintessential American: the poor, every-day, and shat-upon who out of desperation or so-called "primitive" wisdom—and with the right leadership—sets out to defeat the intellectual oppressor. In some cases, the result is an opposition politics that produces a blurring of group identities. As a prime example, the Beat mantra of anti-academic/intellectualism, legitimately a characteristic of rhetoric used by many Beats themselves, erases Beat writers' actual connections to academia and their desires to be recognized by the literary establishment (and in Allen Ginsberg's case by the political establishment as well) as intelligent truthsayers. Therefore, it's common to read Beat histories and criticism that accept as uncontested fact their anti-academic posturing[11], language that also, and ironically, minimizes the significance of more mainstream academic writers/artists and institutions who mentored and supported the development of Beat poetics.

With respect to current Kerouac reception, many readers perceive him in two ways that have now virtually become accepted dogma. One, as an *inclusive* populist whose writings give voice to laborers, women, and people of color,[12] those whom he eventually came to call the fellaheen, taken from philosopher Oswald Spengler's *The Decline of the West*. Two, as a conservative, or *exclusive* populist, who was racist and sexist, despised Jews and hippies, and opposed the anti-Vietnam War movement. However, the latter, sketched in the Martin/Kerouac diatribes, should not be confused with his personal political beliefs, which were more complicated than those of his father. Jack Kerouac himself, over the course of his lifetime, wrestled uncomfortably with what it meant to be a member of the human race, first following the Christian Catholic agenda to seek the goodness of Christ, particularly through individual faith and helping the disadvantaged, and later, at a secular level, to seek as Allen Ginsberg explained, "different modalities of consciousness," that is, determining what one is as a person before the public character can be addressed.[13] The combination of these two eventually led Kerouac to the serious study of Mahayana (or big boat) Buddhist practices before he returned to Christianity. He chose to observe, think, question, and persistently measure himself against his belief in a greater—and thus in his mind authentic—spiritual good. The result was an *inclusive* balance of living with and acting for the oppressed within the *exclusive* sanctity of American individualism and nationalism, an identity that ultimately proved troubling as he shifted between believing in an authentic self and recognizing his own efforts to construct a personal identity.

Youthful Machinations

The route by which he arrived at this ontological juncture appears to have begun in his late teens with communism and socialism, a trend followed by many young people in the United States at that time and the antithesis of his father's exclusionary populism. An examination of his early as well as later literary efforts, many of which were unapologetically autobiographical and confessional as he pursued what was to become his spontaneous prose method, reveals that he was by no means a naïve youth slavishly following his father's path. The character Peter Martin, for instance, while loving his father as did Kerouac, did not share his populist bigotry and at times would tease Mr. Martin to see how far his father could string out a nasty rhetorical performance, none of which Peter took seriously. As Kerouac wrote in *Vanity of Duluoz*, he and his boyhood friends "were all pro-Lenin, pro-Communist," recalling his closest friend Sebastian ("Sabby") Sampas "in his blazing white shirtsleeves and wild black curly hair haranguing everybody about the Brotherhood of Man. It was great."[14] In an early draft of *Vanity*, he even used Sampas as the model for the character of Christopher (Alexander in *Vanity*), whom he described as "a typical Marxist" who shapes the world into a black and white division between those in the Brotherhood and those outside of it, refers to the "masses," pities their ignorance, and admires their honesty.[15]

His memories of Sampas in *Vanity* correlate with correspondence that he and Sampas conducted as members of what they called the Prometheans, a small group of Lowell, MA buddies who shared similar views of the world and wanted to be writers. During the early forties, the two carried on a copious epistolary relationship (a prelude to the confessional Kerouac/Ginsberg and Kerouac/Cassady correspondences), which included arguing about books they were reading, exchanging their own poems and fiction, calling each other "comrade," and discussing the concept of the Brotherhood of Man. Sampas is the more outspoken, reporting on his direct confrontation with white Southern racists, seeking out fellow Communist and socialist brethren, advocating for the eradication of both individual rights and "aristocratic clique[s]" in favor of "a single group" that welcomes everyone, and exposing acquaintances who out of fear and selfishness favor whatever cause *favors them*[16] (emphasis mine). Their friendship and correspondence continued until February 1944 when Sampas, who had joined the Army, was fatally wounded on Anzio Beach.

However, even more transparently inclusive is Kerouac's "The Birth of a Socialist," a short story he wrote in 1941. The story records his recognition that American workers, "[h]undreds of unquestioning fools who get up at five in the morning and rush to a huge vibrating asylum," were being cruelly exploited, their spirit and will to live eradicated by capitalist industrialists.[17] His journals at the time reveal that he based the story not on observation but on his own "we-the-people" experience working in a cookie factory: "I didn't see [the workers] coming out of the factory and sat down to write a poem about their tired faces. I went into the mill [the Megowen Educator Food Co. in Lowell] with them and worked with them. I felt what they felt."[18] But not merely satisfied to have identified a problem, he went on to proffer a solution titled "Kerouac's Socialism." His bold proclamation was that the antidote to dehumanizing work was to reduce all working hours to two to three hours per day, which in turn would create surplus hours, "the real source of surplus value." Significantly, he identified workers as both laborers *and intellectuals, and women as well,* thus cutting across race, sex, and socio-economic lines in the formation of a population much more diverse—and thus anti-populist in one sense of the term—than his father's. And it was in direct contradiction to what Leo Kerouac/Mr. Martin in *The Haunted Life* described as the "real" America: the illusion of peaceful communities in which white workers, exemplified by Mr. Martin's own father, worked eleven hours a day as laborers but remained simple, honest, quiet, and sincere folk—a classic example of populist nationalist nostalgia[19]. Perhaps thinking of his father, Kerouac added in pencil and all caps that his plan was something "ONLY SELFISH PEOPLE WILL REFUSE TO SEE ... !"[20]

But while proud to skewer capitalists, he made sure with equal fervor to condemn Communists, who might offer, he speculated, better wages and shorter hours but still engaged in slavery, and he noted that his story attacked all forms of slavery, including the Shavian concept of humans enslaved to nature.

Kerouac acknowledges that he and "Sabby" rightfully embraced "Socialism and Progress" to counter "cruelty, ugliness, bigotry,"[21] but by March 1943, he had also developed a strong mistrust of working-class movements, the members of which he saw as slavish Muscovites. He was also beginning to separate himself from Sampas's dualistic view of the world. As he wrote Sampas, "I am a Leftist ... I couldn't be otherwise, I may not be a Party-liner. ... they haven't done any good and most of them are a trifle too intolerant ... and unless the Party improves here, I'll never join it."[22] Kerouac, a fundamentally introverted and independent individual who needed to spend significant amounts of time alone, merges personal and group identification in a distinct movement away from Communism per se and institutionalized group activities in general, but without abandoning socialistic ideals.

In this same letter, Kerouac claims honorable American, almost cowboy, individualism as a form of communism and socialism brotherhood: "I would prefer branching out as a one-man Commie party, or as a solitary radical working on no platform but the simple one ... cessation of exploitation!"[23] This position—an extremely strange form of collectivism—aligns with his rejection in the same letter of the Promethean concept of living on a communal farm, which would require equal distribution of material assets and the relinquishing of his right to own property, something he was unwilling to do. He also pointed out that the boredom of such a life would counter any efforts he made to become an artist. Finally, and with a touch of elitist humor, he admits that the farm might be good for a vacation, bolstering the libertarian and capitalist position that he had outlined, while creating a lopsided alliance with non-exploitative, inclusive populism as the weaker "brother."

Practicing the Highwire Act

Clearly, the young Kerouac was experimenting with his personal identity and his greater purpose in a global world, attempting the delicate balance of friendships, personal beliefs, and larger socio-political movements. Should he, on one hand, continue to seek his identity as an individual by becoming a hermit who deceptively rejects poverty for a more comfortable life based on capitalism? He seemed enamored of this position in a 1941 journal entry entitled "If I Were Wealthy," in which he imagined himself as a wealthy writer acquiring and then hiding a lavish library in a "shack with dirty gray clapboards," a move that would trick people into believing he was poor and thus a morally pure soul.[24] Or, on the other hand, should he remain satisfied being one in a mass of other "ones," a creation of both communism and socialism, the Promethean brotherhood rhetoric to the contrary? This position, he concluded, could easily become what we now call group speak: spouting the language of opposition to oppressive forces but refusing to do anything about them. It also came to characterize his position as a writer who wanted the freedom to explore his own interests and desires but still remain cognizant of and engaging with various intellectual movements and ideas.

Toggling between both realities was a high-wire act that many in his day—and today, for that matter—engaged in, his own efforts eventually leading to his decision, supported if not encouraged by his father, to join the war effort, a more "one of the masses" alliance than a wealthy hermit.[25] Kerouac joined the United States Merchant Marines in October 1942, which was composed of civilian seamen who sailed on private as well as US-owned ships that during wartime delivered goods and personnel to support the war effort. He then briefly enlisted in the United States Navy that same year but was soon discharged as unfit to serve. While he put his life at risk in the Merchant Marines (his boat, the *Dorchester*, was sunk by German torpedoes after Kerouac had left the marines), his position relative to inclusive participation/identity eschewed military resistance and raucous protests. "The Birth of a Socialist," for instance, ends with his outright rejection of the brutal life of the factory worker when he quits his job after one day, knowing that as a man with a brain—not a "dumb animal"—his survival didn't depend on him working in slavish servitude. Instead, he decides to become a writer with the Whitmanian freedom to do whatever and go wherever he wants.[26] Later, as a result of his brief experiences in the Merchant Marines and the Navy, he declared himself a pacifist, having recognized the unfair waste of lives, including those of German youth, by laissez-faire German "Ammunitioneers."[27]

Action for Kerouac required a much more gymnastic path, an indirect and cloaked approach allowing for intellectual and economic independence, while maintaining the moral alliance with the underprivileged. As he told Sampas in a letter dated February 1943, "... my mission is to present Beauty to the Collectivists, and in turn, introduce the men of Beauty to the Collectivism .... I am ambassador, mediator, soother, host."[28] (Kerouac expanded on this idea in notes written for *The Sea Is My Brother*, identifying art as the tool by which human beings could discern Beauty and thus achieve ultimate freedom.[29]) He ended the letter with the bold declaration that "ignorance, stupidity, bigotry, brutality" can be *"repressed with slow, sullen, invincible truth*! Your comrade, Jean" (emphasis mine).[30] No matter what injustices one experiences or recognizes, the best approach to eradicating them is to remain faithful to what one knows— Truth through Art in Kerouac's case—and patiently and quietly, but persistently, present it to those in need of its guidance. These, he consistently maintained, were his compatriot Americans, a people with the unbounded ability to understand "anything and everything" if one's art, meaning his, shuns Old World European language for American forthrightness.[31] In other words, Kerouac deeply desired to be a player on a grand stage, but without becoming directly embroiled in those matters. His position signifies his engagement with art as identity politics, although he does not use that term, the efficacy of which he shapes as rhetorical optimism—his belief in an innate American optimism, still in play today, that ordinary Americans can accomplish anything they set their minds too.

This approach may explain why several years earlier he had found of interest Anne Morrow Lindbergh's *The Wave of the Future: A Confession of Faith,* which is not an overt argument for or against Hitler but a highly opaque meditation that denounces both pro-Hitler and anti-Hitler movements while invoking America's history of reformation and dreams with an inward turning (or isolationist) eye. It may also clarify Kerouac's recognition that, as in *The Sea Is My Brother*, written in the spring of 1943, the character Bill Everhart realizes that "... being simply anti-Fascist is not enough. You've got to go beyond anti-Fascism." "Anti-fascists," he contends, "believe that by destroying fascism, they will have destroyed all evil," but Bill understands that individual evil will remain, and that is what one must concentrate on remedying.[32]

At times, this tactic led to rhetoric that was so indirect as to immerse Kerouac in nationalist nostalgia, as does the conclusion of *The Haunted Life*. Peter Martin, having experienced the Second World War, agrees with his father's fatalist mantra that the people will always lose to those with more economic and political power. The fight can never be won, so get along with grace, as Leo Kerouac had once told his son regarding the draft.[33] The third-person narrator, representing Peter's perspective, explains that his father, as a member of an older generation that tended to wax nostalgic, was actually misinformed and confronts this reality with sadness, while Peter himself possesses actual knowledge of the reality: "that was the lot of the working man in this or any preceding age, to be wrong about politics. The working man produced; the politician did something else ... he was a tyrant, or else he spent his time enjoying the fruits of his office."[34] And, thus, with this knowledge, Peter's last thoughts are not about leading a Leninist revolution or living on a communal farm—or of siding in full solidarity with his father's isolationist rhetoric. Instead, he leaves the material world to imaginatively hear "screened-in voices on dark porches" [and] "the cool swishing song of the trees ... a music ... clover fresh, somehow sharp, and supremely rich."[35] An America of dreams and dreamers—what's left for him from his own "old days."[36]

At other moments, Kerouac's art explores lines of attack much more direct. Fascinatingly, for instance, the group speak that he routinely encountered troubled him so much that he included in his September 1941 letter to Sampas a fictional interlude titled "Conversation on a Street Corner," featuring a verbal skirmish in front of passers-by between an anti-Nazi named Milt Sternberger and an unnamed young man. Sternberger berates him with Nazi epithets, while the young man waits patiently for his moment to strike back. Artfully presented, his attack is the sudden declaration that he is an Army recruiter who finds Sternberger, obviously pro-war, to be an ideal recruit. Aghast, Sternberger resorts to deflated sputterings, his pro-war/anti-Nazi rhetoric brutally exposed to others.[37] The young man then bows to his audience and silently walks away. Here, Kerouac, ultimately a gentle soul his entire life, envisions through a fictional character a street theater performance of such magnitude, and likely something he himself wouldn't have done, that the enemy within is revealed for what he truly is: a cowardly blowhard.

Seeking Solid Ground

Consistent with his early inclusive populist declarations, Kerouac's Duluoz Legend focuses on the redemption of the poor and the marginalized who, as readers of *On the Road* have long known, drove his narratives. Manifestations of his resistance to exclusionary practices and beliefs emerge in many of the characters Sal Paradise encounters, such as Dean Moriarty (Neal Cassady), Old Bull Lee (William S. Burroughs), the Ghost of the Susquehanna, Slim the cowboy, and Terry the Mexican migrant worker, and various jazz musicians, Black and white. In other works, this type appears as Mardou Fox (*The Subterraneans*, 1958), Tristessa and Bill Garver (*Tristessa* and *Desolation Angels*, 1960, 1965), saxophonist Charlie brutally murdered in a Mexican bullfighting ring (*The Lonesome Traveler*, 1960), and others. Granted, Sal romanticizes the lives of these individuals to shape his own identity, a typical human action, and in the context of the political and social realities, these characterizations, as critics have discussed, fall short of transformative egalitarian representations expected by some mid-twentieth- and early-twenty-first-century readers. They also fail to forthrightly acknowledge the privilege of an economic safety net ironically provided for him by his parents, especially his mother's work as a laborer in Lowell shoe factories and his father's work as a printer. However, *On the Road*, in particular, provides subtle recognition of his awareness and perhaps ensuing guilt over his inability to fully identify with and become the excluded. Especially noteworthy are his "white man dreams" that ruin his first attempt to travel west and his later efforts to pick cotton with Terry, the Mexican migrant worker. Nonetheless, the integrity of these characters as morally pure individuals, which is how he chose to see them, within a materially based class struggle is significant in that it actualizes his unwillingness to write them off, to exclude them from his vision of a pure America.

Kerouac maintained throughout his life a fundamental awareness of the material realities of oppressive practices, which are woven throughout his art as a consistent form of resistance. A striking but unfortunately seldom referenced example appears in *Pic*, written in 1950 and posthumously published in 1971. A first-person narrative told in stereotypic Black English from the perspective of an African American boy named Pictorial Review Jackson, *Pic* fuels the argument that Kerouac was racist. And the language is decidedly uncomfortable to read. However, the novel is not a racist diatribe but rather, as Gerald Nicosia clarifies, an opportunity for Kerouac to write from the perspective of another race, to explicitly align African Americans with French Canadians who were often referred to as *les Nègres blanc* (Black Negroes), and to use some of his own experiences to tell Pic's story.[38] In the following passage, Pic's older brother Slim rescues Pic from North Carolina, and as the two ride north in a bus, they cross the Mason-Dixon line. Once the bus stops in Philadelphia, they move from the back to the front, Slim explaining that their front seat privilege is the result of them crossing "Jim Crow's line." Naïvely, Pic asks who Jim Crow is. Teasingly, Slim says that he, Pic, is Jim Crow and then proceeds to call him "Jim," a reference not only to the nineteenth-century minstrel character Jim Crow but also to the Black slave Jim in *Huckleberry Finn*. Pic replies that he didn't see any line: "[D]id we run over it or underneath?" At that point, Slim steps out of his comic role:

> But there is such a line, only thing is, it ain't on the ground, and it ain't in the air neither, it's jess in the head of Mason and Dixie, jess like all other lines, border lines, state lines, parallel thirty-lines and iron Europe curtain lines is all jess 'maginary lines in people's head and don't have nothing to do with the ground.[39]

Lines of division are human charades, Kerouac tells his readers, which, unfortunately, can be endowed with oppressive powers if both the wealthy and the impoverished succumb to either the myth of the "real" America as a homogenous state or the myth that overcoming oppression is impossible in America. In opposition, America, if not the world, should be a space in which every individual, no matter skin color or sex or economic status, should have the right to move freely, without constraint, a libertarian populism. Achieving that reality is nothing short of titanic, sometimes reaching great heights and sometimes failing catastrophically, but always beginning with the difficult task of seeing what those in power—be they inclusive or exclusive populists—fight to keep hidden—and that those without power are loathe to acknowledge. In the case of *Pic*, Kerouac makes visible an exclusionary lie—a false reality that for far too long kept too many African Americans at the back of the bus.

By the end of Kerouac's life, his populism remained fundamentally the same, a complicated balance of Christian pacifism, American socialism and individualism, Buddhist anti-egoism, and nationalist pride. Still anti-communist, he excoriated in *Satori in Paris* (1966) what he called textbook Marxist terms for the people, such as "Proletariat" and "unemployed disenchanted Ghetto-Dwelling Misfits." Kerouac's

"People" were, instead, everyday individuals standing in a cab line and named only by numbers—first, second, third, fourth, and so on—signifying the scars of oppression they bear. But through Kerouac's populist "we-the-people" language, that which he as a populist leader speaks for them, they have the power to rise up against their oppressor: "[I]f you try to bug them, you may find yourself with a blade of grass in your bladder, which cuts finest."[40] This uncharacteristic prescription for violence aimed at the oppressor is a sly Whitmanian allusion transforming a blade of grass into a scimitar of death—a threat that undermines his father's and the Martins' fatalism. But it also reaffirms, first, his own belief in his power as an artist to present Truth through Beauty and, second, his conviction that his fellow American possessed the unlimited ability to know and understand all. Action through Art would eventually lead to social and political action (violence acknowledged), and eventually to social and political change. A return, in other words, to the eclectic self-identity Kerouac had crafted for himself as a young man in his twenties.

As Kerouac aged, he remained committed to the absolute freedom of the individual, that part of himself that wanted to tell everyone he met that they should never become "ants contributing to the social body."[41] But his abilities to save the world indirectly and patiently through art had begun to desert him. In 1967, two years before his death, he admitted as much to his editor, Ellis Amburn, writing to him that he'd lost the artist's ability to concentrate on his art: "This is all over for me," he declared, seeing no silver lining to his cloud of darkness as he struggled to complete *Vanity of Duluoz*.[42] And by 1969, his distrust of US military leaders and of what appeared to him pseudo-populist leaders had become outright loathing. He wrote in "Last Words" for the *Chicago Tribune Magazine* that he couldn't figure out how he "had spawned" the likes of Jerry Rubin, Abbie Hoffman, and his once dear friend Allen Ginsberg, people who knew nothing about the real lives of Puerto Ricans in barrios and blacks in Harlem.[43] Sarcastically, he threatened to see US aggression in Viet Nam as more just than that of other nation states ("I'll try to see the difference between bombing of 'civilians' in one town and bombing of 'women and children' in another …"), and faintly echoing a John Jay/James Madison argument credited American capitalism "carved into the U.S. Constitution" for his ability to move freely across the country.[44]

The world, he concluded, had changed so much that he no longer recognized it. It was an anathema to him, which he described in a powerful Kerouacian version of Shakespearean railing, evidence that he had not yet failed as a writer:

> [E]very handshake, every smile, every gibberous applause is shiny hypocrisy, is political lust and concupiscence, a ninny's bray of melody backed by a ghastly neurological drone of money-grub accompanied by the anvil chorus of garbage can covers being banged over half-eaten filet mignons which don't even get to the dogs, let alone hungry children of the absent 'constituency'.[45]

He had held firm to his populist care for the disadvantaged, but fatalism, even when he tried to counter it, tended to overwhelm other inclinations. Had he then become a version of his father? The Leo Kerouac who acknowledged that he couldn't rhapsodize with words like his son but was a literate letter writer and continued to love and support Jack while raging against a system the complexities of which he could never fathom?[46] Yes, to some extent, especially when one considers that Kerouac had succumbed to alcoholism, viciously exposed in *Big Sur* (1962) and a condition which likely contributed to the transformation of his love of old friends such as Allen Ginsberg, a Jew, into a cacophony of disembodied slogans and sneers. Or was he simultaneously Jean Louis Levesque Kerouac, "Levesque," coming from his mother's side of the family? The Gabrielle Kerouac known as Mémere, who was a Jew-hating racist but never failed to support her son financially and emotionally as he tragically dealt with his Beat fame. Yes, perhaps he was some of this as well.

But these are easy answers. While he had held firm to his populist care for the disadvantaged, fatalism, even when he tried to counter it, as a marker of aging and exhaustion, tended to overwhelm other inclinations until he eventually concluded that the right and the left, be they "[p]olitics, gambling, hard work, drinking, patriotism, protest, pooh-poohings [were] all therapeutic shifts against the black void."[47] Neither one was good nor evil. Ultimately, he was Jack Kerouac, a learned, intuitive, and complex person, one whose language of populism and freedom began to fail him but always an artist who retained the belief that no matter one's political party, socio-economic allegiance, religion, or other activities, we all carry within us the sui generis need to validate ourselves against the darkest mystery of our existence.

Notes

1 Jack Kerouac, *The Haunted Life and Other Writings*, ed. Todd Tietchen (Philadelphia, PA: Da Capo, 2014), 30.
2 Ibid., 161, 166–7.
3 Ibid., 159.
4 Ibid., 31.
5 The Federalist Papers, *The Avalon Project: Documents in Law, History and Diplomacy*, Lillian Goldman Law Library, Yale Law School. New Haven, Ct., accessed October 16, 2023, https://avalon.law.yale.edu/18th_century/fed02.asp and https://avalon.law.yale.edu/18th_century/fed51.asp.
6 Michael Kazin, *The Populist Persuasion: An American History* (Ithaca, New York and London: Cornell UP, 2017), 5.
7 Jan-Werner Müller, *What Is Populism?* (Philadelphia, PA: University of Pennsylvania Press, 2016), 40, 68–9.
8 Kerouac, *The Haunted Life and Other Writings*, 160.
9 M. S., "What Is Populism?," *The Economist*, December 19, 2016, accessed August 3, 2023, https://www.economist.com/blogs/economist-explains2016/12/economist-explains-18.
10 For a thorough treatment of Kerouac's French roots, see Hassan Melehy, *Kerouac: Language, Poetics, and Territory* (New York: Bloomsbury, 2016).

11 Nancy M. Grace, "The Beats and Literary History: Myths and Realities," in *The Cambridge Companion to the Beats*, ed. Steven Belletto (Cambridge: Cambridge University Press, 2017), 62–76. See also, *The Beats and the Academy: A Renegotiation*, ed. Erik Mortenson and Tony Trigilio (Clemson, SC: Clemson University Press, 2023).
12 Some biographers/literary critics of Kerouac position him at other points along the spectrum. Ann Charters in *Brother Souls* saw Kerouac as a teenager who was designedly a non-pacifist if not a Hitlerite, citing a 1940 journal entry in which he endorsed Ann Morrow Lindburgh's *The Wave of the Future: A Confession of Faith* (1940) and described "Hitlerism" as providing economic freedom for the people (28). Dawn M. Ward, editor of Kerouac's *The Sea Is My Brother: The Lost Novel*, posthumously published in 2011, concluded that Kerouac "did not participate in any political parties and remained idealistically neutral" (*Sea* 213). Both positions are in some ways incorrect. Ed D'Angelo in "Anarchism and the Beats" dispels a popular sentiment that Kerouac was an anarchist.
13 Ed D'Angelo, "Anarchism and the Beats," in *The Philosophy of the Beats*, ed. Sharin Elkholy (Lexington, KY: University Press of Kentucky, 2012), 237.
14 Jack Kerouac, *Vanity of Duluoz* (New York: Penguin, 1994), 85.
15 Jack Kerouac, *The Sea Is My Brother: The Lost Novel*, ed. Dawn M. Ward (Philadelphia, PA: Da Capo, 2013), 306.
16 Ibid., 264, 317 (emphasis mine).
17 Jack Kerouac, *Atop an Underwood: Early Stories and Other Writings*, ed. Paul Marion (New York: Viking, 1999), 91.
18 Jack Kerouac, "Notes on Work, Socialism, Slavery." New York Public Library, Berg Collection, typescript, revised. B 5f.63. 1941.
19 Kerouac, *The Haunted Life and Other Writings*, 29–33.
20 Kerouac, "Notes," np.
21 Jack Kerouac, *Jack Kerouac: Selected Letters: 1940–1956*, ed. Ann Charters (New York: Viking, 1995), 51–2.
22 Ibid., 53.
23 Ibid., 52.
24 Kerouac, *Atop an Underwood*, 80.
25 Interestingly, Leo Kerouac, while against the United States entering the Second World War, wrote to his son in 1942 that since Jack was an adult, should he be drafted, he should "take it with good grace," not be a "slacker," and use the experience to make him a better person (*The Haunted Life and Other Writings*, 161).
26 Kerouac, *Atop an Underwood*, 92.
27 Kerouac, *Vanity of Duluoz*, 144.
28 Kerouac, *The Sea Is My Brother*, 349.
29 Ibid., 227.
30 Ibid., 351.
31 Kerouac, *The Haunted Life and Other Writings*, 148.
32 Kerouac, *The Sea Is My Brother*, 87.
33 Kerouac, *The Haunted Life and Other Writings*, 161.
34 Ibid., 96–7, 106.
35 Ibid., 99.
36 In notes titled "For The Haunted Life: The Odyssey of Peter Martin (1943)," Kerouac sketched a somewhat different conclusion, still focused on Peter, but who, unlike the

Peter of *Haunted Life*, had witnessed three years of war and not only experienced fatalism and fear of change, but also recognized that old worlds give birth to new worlds and that he must now go out and make his own world (*The Haunted Life and Other Writings*, 107–8).
37 Kerouac, *The Sea Is My Brother*, 277.
38 Gerald Nicosia, *Memory Babe: A Critical Biography of Jack Kerouac* (Berkeley, CA: University of California Press, 1994), 695.
39 Jack Kerouac, *Satori in Paris and Pic* (New York: Grove, 1988), 172.
40 Kerouac, *Vanity of Duluoz*, 111.
41 Ibid., 47.
42 Jack Kerouac, *Jack Kerouac: Selected Letters: 1957–1969*, ed. Ann Charters (New York: Viking, 1999), 441–2.
43 Jack Kerouac, *The Good Blonde & Others*, ed. Donald Allen, preface by Robert Creeley (San Francisco, CA: Grey Fox, 1993), 180.
44 Ibid., 187, 185s.
45 Ibid., 182.
46 Kerouac, *The Haunted Life and Other Writings*, 160.
47 Kerouac, *The Good Blonde & Others*, 188.

11

Kerouac's Fellahin Poetics: Reimagining Global Culture against Nation and Empire

Hassan Melehy

Toward the end of *On the Road*, at the wheel while Dean Moriarty and Stan Shepard sleep, Sal Paradise describes driving further into Mexico, the US border receding. The trajectory of the road in the novel has taken Sal from his home in the staid northeastern United States to the wilder West, where his new friend Dean Moriarty hails from. Not only does the road lead Sal to see the expansiveness of America but also to grasp the land as a continent: the travels that have taken him as far as "the fantastic end of America" in Hollywood,[1] across rivers and mountain ranges, among people of different national origins and ethnic communities, now reveal Mexico to him. On the trip south through the country that fascinates him and his friends for its sheer difference from what they're familiar with, Sal describes the people they see along the way. His tourist's gaze is returned: young girls in doorways "stared," in an agricultural zone men on a narrow bridge "watched us pass."[2]

Integral to Sal's experience of seeing the country, this series of steady gazes leads to the great lessons of travel, the knowledge that a world with a great variety of peoples exists beyond the borders of one's own country. Kerouac writes Sal's musings in a sentence whose length suggests the distances that various roads lead across as well as the expanse of the global culture that has started to come into view:

> Not like driving across Carolina, or Texas, or Arizona, or Illinois; but like driving across the world and into the places where we would finally learn ourselves among the Fellahin Indians of the world, the essential strain of the basic primitive, wailing humanity that stretches in a belt around the equatorial belly of the world from Malaya (the long fingernail of China) to India the great subcontinent to Arabia to Morocco to the selfsame deserts and jungles of Mexico and over the waves to Polynesia to mystic Siam of the Yellow Robe and on around, on around, so that you hear the same mournful wail by the rotted walls of Cádiz, Spain, that you hear 12,000 miles around in the depths of Benares the Capital of the World.[3]

The lesson involves seeing one's own cultural and cognitive limitations in the face of this vastness, which stretches not just across global space but also through global history: to Spain's oldest continually existing city, a site of Phoenician, Greek, Roman, Muslim, Jewish, and Christian culture; to Benares, Hinduism's most sacred city.

Though it would be easy to accuse Kerouac of primitivism simply for using the word *primitive* and apparently exoticizing a slew of non-Western populations, he makes it clear that this is Sal's imaginative understanding, his "reveries"[4] of a world he is beginning to realize is too big to be grasped all at once, and of the corollary facts of his own small stature in this world and the small stature of the United States, a country that until now has appeared vast and various. Sal can only apprehend the unfamiliar through the familiar images of geography, Western literary depictions of non-Western peoples, Hollywood movies, and related sources. As I've argued elsewhere, as a tourist his apprehension of this new place begins with what Dean MacCannel calls "markers," the cultural signs all sightseers start with, no matter what their education or intellectual disposition—in other words, stereotypes as a first phase in altering one's understanding.[5] Though Kerouac has often been accused of relying on racial and ethnic stereotypes, one of my purposes in this essay is to show that he uses them as a setup, an initial impression of intercultural contact that gives way to far greater cultural realities.

Paths of History

In the above-quoted passage, Kerouac uses one of his pet words to designate non-Western peoples as well as peoples in the United States who are outside the white Anglo-Saxon mainstream, *fellahin*. He creatively adapts the term from Oswald Spengler's *The Decline of the West*: *fellahin* is a key word in the German philosopher's theory of how all cultures decline. In the years following its publication as two hefty volumes, this book was among the most widely read in Europe and the United States. The first volume appeared in Germany toward the end of the First World War in 1918, then in revised form in 1922 alongside the second volume. The first appeared in Charles F. Atkinson's English translation in 1926, the second in 1928, simultaneously in London and New York.[6] In the wake of the recent horrors of war, Spengler offers explanations for how such carnage may occur in the midst of supposedly civilized society: he examines the West as one in a series of major civilizations in world history, viewing it as aging into decline, just as the others did. In the 1940s the book was discredited because of the German National Socialists' claiming it as an intellectual source; however, Spengler's analysis, treating the outstanding achievements of many peoples over about five millennia, refuses the idea of racial superiority, and he broke with the Nazis over this question. Nonetheless, the book remained of interest in literary and intellectual circles. It's often repeated in accounts of the early days of the Beat Generation that in 1944 William Burroughs, whose vision of humanity and civilization inclines toward pessimistic, lent *The Decline of the West* to Ginsberg and Kerouac, his two young more-or-less protégés.[7]

Kerouac first encountered the book through his boyhood friend Sebastian Sampas, whose older brother Charles, like so many other avid readers in the United States, had a copy. In the year before Kerouac met Ginsberg and Burroughs, Sampas wrote his friend a letter in which he continues conversations about art and literature that they had begun in high school. Responding to what he characterizes as Kerouac's misunderstanding of Dostoyevsky in phrasing that reads like a lively if aphoristic college philosophy paper, Sampas adeptly expounds some of Spengler's ideas. Sampas explains that the Western world, distinct among the cultures in world history for its striving for endless spatial expansion, has exhausted itself: "There are no more worlds to conquer in Western Civilization."[8] Where Spengler presents Dostoyevsky as breaking with the West and speaking for a Russian Christianity that will usher in the next great world culture,[9] Sampas rather advocates for a new art and literature in the West that builds on its remains, the result of collective effort that will leave behind the West's emphasis on individual achievement. He sees this momentous change happening in the United States: "In Eastern Europe there is little hope but in America 'a wind is rising'. [Thomas] Wolfe felt it. In 'the hills beyond', the great open spaces (remember his Northwest Pacific trip), the uncrowded places, a new soul is in conception."[10] Following this invocation of their recently deceased literary hero, Sampas paraphrases one of the most resonant lines from Shakespeare, another of their heroes and an emblem of Western literature, recommending that Kerouac play a part in the new, collective expression: "'The world's a stage and *all* men players'. Choose the last act of one play, or the first of another."[11]

Though it would be reductive to attribute epiphanic or momentous status to this letter—in his work Kerouac draws on innumerable readings and discussions—many readers will recognize that he echoes some of these ideas as he becomes an accomplished writer: a new generation and a new literary movement, drawing on monuments from the Western canon while looking to sources from around the globe, open spaces as integral to enhanced personal and artistic freedom. Moreover, from early in his work Kerouac regularly refers to Spengler. In a journal entry dated August 21, 1945, among major sources for his intellectual passion, Kerouac gives him as much weight as poets William Butler Yeats and Rainer Maria Rilke, nearly as much as Arthur Rimbaud; he places these three barely a notch below French novelist Louis-Ferdinand Céline and Thomas Wolfe, both of whom he regards as especially life-changing.[12] In his staggering amount of reading, Kerouac included many philosophers—a reading list from around 1943 names Friedrich Nietzsche, Aristotle, David Hume, and G. W. F. Hegel, among others[13]—Spengler is the only one, in the mid-1940s at least, whom he deems worthy of naming among his most beloved literary authors, an indication of the importance he places on the German philosopher's ideas for understanding culture and the world.

Spengler's word *fellaheen* or *fellahin* (alternate spellings in English, the latter more in keeping with current standard transliteration from Arabic; in German, *Fellachen*)[14] crops up in Kerouac's vocabulary no later than about 1950. The Arabic word for "peasants" (the singular is *fellah*), Spengler uses it to designate the people who, in the life cycle of cultures that he advocates understanding as analogous to the life cycle of human beings,[15] remain at its tail end and after its fall. Though he also speaks of "peasants," the people who work the earth and eventually, through organizing society and forming towns, in the long run create culture,[16] he reserves "fellaheen" for those who wander aimlessly, produce nothing, and contribute in no meaningful way to history; they embody decline. Spengler attributes his word choice to the "best-known example" of the phenomenon, the "Egyptians of post-Roman times,"[17] Egypt in his view among the first of the world's great cultures. (The German word *Kultur* also shares connotations with the English *civilization*.) He describes the life of the fellahin as "a planless happening without goal or cadenced march in time, wherein occurrences are many, but, in the last analysis, devoid of significance."[18] History is only made, in Spengler's view, by groups of people who have organized themselves into large collective bodies: "The only historical peoples, the peoples whose existence is world-history, are the nations."[19]

Just as Kerouac rewrites the work of literary authors in allusions and explicit references in his novels and poems, he reconfigures this key concept from Spengler as a way of more comprehensively grasping global culture. Though accepting the idea that Western civilization is in decline, Kerouac rather views the fellahin as entirely productive, creative people, the ones who after the fall of the West will usher in the next civilization, whatever form it will take; he sees them as a positive force rather than mere negation. This is an inversion of Spengler's meaning, something Kerouac makes explicit in an as yet unpublished essay titled "In America" (from about 1953, given the reference to John Clellon Holmes's 1952 *New York Times* article, "This is the Beat Generation").[20] Kerouac begins by characterizing African Americans as a fellahin people, taken from their African home to the United States; he then relates this population to all manner of peoples who live and have lived outside the dominant centers of various civilizations, from Asia to North Africa to the Americas, who wander yet maintain a close relationship to the earth. Though he speaks well of Holmes, Kerouac is dismissive of his friend's application of the term "Beat Generation" to a widespread youth movement in the United States: such youth, Kerouac holds, despite their claims of affinity to fellahin peoples, are far removed from the latter's experience. Nonetheless, he paints jazz as the music of late US civilization, and hence as fellahin, growing from African American life. Echoing Spengler's characterization of cosmopolitanism and global pacifism as elements of the decay of a nation and hence decline,[21] but taking it in a decidedly different direction, Kerouac sees the fellahin as a global series of peaceful nations; he adds that they actually stand outside of nations.[22]

Fellahin Movements

In *On the Road*, Kerouac extends his depiction of fellahin peoples as positive and productive forces in the world. So "the basic primitive, wailing humanity that stretches in a belt around the equatorial belly of the world," from the above-quoted passage, is a telegraphic formulation with affinity to a concept that in the last decade or so has informed the academic field of indigenous studies: a global series of populations that, though in quite varied circumstances, share the experience of living under the domination of wealthy, militarily capable nations while at the same time exceeding and resisting them.[23]

Of the creative power of the indigenous inhabitants of Mexico, along with their fellows throughout the world and through world history, he couldn't be clearer:

> These people were unmistakably Indians and were not at all like the Pedros and Panchos of silly American lore—they had high cheekbones, and slanted eyes, and soft ways; they were not fools, they were not clowns; they were great, grave Indians and they were the source of mankind and the fathers of it. The waves are Chinese, but the earth is an Indian thing. As essential as the rocks in the desert are they in the desert of "history."[24]

Kerouac grants Sal awareness of the tourist stereotypes through which he sees Mexico, which the road is urging him to move beyond. The real appearance of the people Sal sees sharply challenges the movie and cartoon images that brim in his mind. The passage dramatizes Sal's cognitive transformation as he allows the first set of images, an aggregate of what MacCannell terms "markers," to give way to another, more complicated set. As I've argued elsewhere against perennial charges of Kerouac's racism, his use of racializing clichés is the starting point in a process of challenging the limits of white, imperial cognition and pressuring it to recognize the full humanness of marginalized peoples.[25]

Sal may well embroider his observations with a few fantastical ideas about the power of the fellahin, emerging from Kerouac's critical reading of Spengler; but these observations oppose, among other things, the imperialist paternalism US tourists tend to bring wherever they go. Rather than confining to the point of caricature the identity of marginalized peoples, Kerouac stages these clichés in order to move past them. Following his poetic utterance about Indian and Chinese relationships to populations migrating across the globe, Kerouac puts the word "history" in quotation marks in order to indicate Spengler's restriction of history to the life of nations and his exclusion of all other events as (to repeat Spengler's above-quoted words) "a planless happening ... devoid of significance."[26] In characterizing the fellahin of Mexico as integral to the landscape of history, "as essential as rocks in the desert," Kerouac presents every detail of their lives as significant. In the immensity of the world of the fellahin, the conception of history as limited to or primarily involving nations—an idea shared by many besides Spengler and contested in indigenous studies[27]—becomes trivial. The nation itself, guarding its treasures with the tenuousness of borders, starts to look trifling.

Kerouac continues Sal's reveries about the indigenous people who watch him as he watches them:

> And they knew this when we passed, ostensibly self-important moneybag Americans on a lark in their land; they knew who was the father and who was the son of antique life on earth, and made no comment. For when destruction comes to the world of "history" and the Apocalypse of the Fellahin returns once more as so many times before, people will still stare with the same eyes from the caves of Mexico as from the caves of Bali, where it all began and where Adam was suckled and taught to know.[28]

The returned gaze brings Sal to awareness of himself as a petty, arrogant tourist. In the schema of history that Kerouac, and presumably Sal, has gleaned from Spengler, Western culture will fall as has each prior great culture. But in recognizing those who live outside the history of nations and empires as essential to global history much more broadly conceived, Kerouac imagines such people restarting civilization from its liminal zones.

In his mention of Adam's birth, Kerouac rewrites the myth of human origin shared by Judaism, Christianity, and Islam. If Adam was "suckled," he wasn't created by divine fiat; human time, it turns out, is much longer than that of these major world religions. And if Adam was born in Mexico, Bali, and by implication everywhere there are fellahin—in short, everywhere on earth—then human origin is dislodged from the claim these religions place on it and scattered across the globe. Wherever they live, then, human beings persist in living against the encroachment of nation and empire. In the regional history of North America, Mexico has seen the Aztec empire, which fell when the Spanish empire arrived on the scene, which in turn fell and has now been replaced by Anglo-American domination of North America—hence these "moneybag Americans" who feel free to gape as tourists.

The project of Western culture to achieve global domination is the work of what Spengler calls "Faustian man," the type of human being who strives to extend his habitat across geographical space. This being would even, as Spengler notes at the end of *The Decline of the West*, "free himself from the earth, rise into the infinite, leave the bonds of the body, and circle in the universe of space amongst the stars."[29] Spengler develops his notion of Faustian man through the thought of Johann Wolfgang von Goethe (1749–1832), whose most famous work, the colossal drama *Faust*, which he composed over sixty years until the end of his life—along with Shakespeare's oeuvre, another emblem of Western literature—has overshadowed his other writing. Spengler decries the fact that academic philosophy has given no recognition to Goethe as philosopher: granting that Goethe never presented his thought in systematic fashion, Spengler views him as one of the most important modern philosophers, alongside Nietzsche and Immanuel Kant. In his preface to the 1922 revised edition of volume one of *The Decline of the West*, Spengler says that he owes "practically everything" to Goethe and Nietzsche, the former for method and the latter for "the questioning faculty."[30] In a footnote toward the end of the first chapter, the book's introduction in which Spengler explains his conception of world history, he declares that he owes his entire philosophy to Goethe, and to a much lesser degree to Nietzsche.[31]

Though many twentieth-century thinkers draw on Nietzsche in their questioning of the capacity of reason to grasp the world and correlatively for some in their critique of Western domination (he is certainly important to Kerouac's suspicion of dominant morality),[32] Spengler views Nietzsche's critique of the West, though relentless and thoroughgoing, as fully rooted in the West and thereby as leaving it in place, not interrogating its existence and ostensible permanence, nor recognizing it as a component of world history.[33] Goethe, on the other hand, according to Spengler, conceives world history as a whole, "*Living Nature*,"[34] all things alive and interacting in a larger process of life that doesn't privilege one culture over others. Repeatedly in his work, Kerouac credits Goethe as a major literary source. For example, in "The Origins of the Beat Generation" (1959) he writes of the time during and after he first composed *On the Road*: "My hero was Goethe and I believed in art and hoped some day to write the third part of *Faust*, which I have done in *Dr. Sax*."[35] In the biographical note he provided for Donald Allen's *The New American Poetry* (1960), he states: "At the age of 24 I was groomed for the Western idealistic concept of letters from reading Goethe's *Dichtung und Wahrheit* [*Poetry and Truth*, his intellectual autobiography]."[36]

Spatial Maneuvers

In *Dr. Sax*, Goethe and Spengler turn up regularly. The first clear reference is in one of Kerouac's descriptions of the title character: "Doctor Sax had knowledge of death ... but he was a mad fool of power, a Faustian man, no true Faustian's afraid of the dark—only Fellaheen—and Gothic Stone Cathedral Catholic of Bats and Bach Organs in Blue Mid Night Mists of Skull, Blood, Dust, Iron, Rain burrowing into earth to snake antique."[37] This macabre rendition of the Faust myth links Doctor Sax to earthly and human substances as well as the dark spirits that lurk in the night in this dream version of Kerouac's hometown of Lowell, Massachusetts. Sax is a "Faustian man," striving for domination of space and matter—again, the type of human being that according to Spengler emerges with Western culture. For Faustian man, Spengler explains, "from the latter days of the Renaissance onward, the notion of God has steadily approximated, in the spirit of every man of high significance, to the idea of pure endless space."[38] He develops the close relationship between architectural space and music as integral to the development of Faustian man: in the Gothic period of the late Middle Ages, "counterpoint developed simultaneously with the flying-buttress system .... It is an architecture of human voices and ... is only conceivable in the settings of these stone vaultings."[39] In the Baroque era that followed the Gothic, "the great task was to extend the tone-corpus into the infinity, or rather *to resolve it into an infinite space of tone*." This occasions "the rebirth of counterpoint in the form of the fugal style, of which Frescobaldi was the first master and Bach the culmination."[40] Of Bach, Spengler also notes: "The free organ-playing of Bach and his time was nothing if it was not analysis—analysis of a strange and vast tone-world."[41]

In his 1943 letter to Kerouac, Sebastian Sampas neatly summarizes these elements of Faustian culture: "Your prime symbol, of course as well as all of Western mankind, is infinite space. You have had dreams of space as all Western mankind has had. Whether it be in great Gothic cathedrals, railroad stations, tunnels, the dome of heaven—whether it be received from a mountaintop or abyss, or whether it be pure infinite space."[42] Kerouac's words in *Doctor Sax*, "Gothic Stone Cathedral Catholic of Bats and Bach Organs in Blue Mid Night Mists of Skull, Blood, Dust, Iron, Rain," are a crisp echo of these statements. And the roving prose of Kerouac's novels, moving through narrative and geographic space, has everything to do with them.

Though Spengler's idea of Faustian man draws from large swaths of Goethe's philosophy, a crystal-clear formulation of the drive to spatial expansion is in one of the most famous passages from *Faust*, when the protagonist describes the urges that drive him:

> Two souls, alas, are dwelling in my breast,
> And either would be severed from its brother;
> The one holds fast with joyous earthly lust
> Onto the world of man with organs clinging;
> The other soars impassioned from the dust,
> To realms of lofty forebears winging.[43]

These words on the two souls, the one craving fixity and the other movement outward in space, strongly resonate with what I've elsewhere identified as the tension in Kerouac's writing between the drive to settle and the drive to wander.[44] He explores this theme throughout his fiction, as early as his apprentice novel *The Sea Is My Brother* (which he wrote in 1943 at age twenty-one, unpublished until 2011) through the characters of Wesley Martin and Bill Everhart,[45] and most obviously in *On the Road* through Sal and Dean.

This tension is intimately bound up with Kerouac's membership in a community in diaspora, the Québécois population whose ties to France were severed by the French defeat in the French and Indian War of 1754-63, the North American component of the Seven Years' War. This community was further unsettled by severe economic conditions resulting largely from the colonial status of Québec under British rule, leading to the migration of half the population, a total of about 900,000, to the United States, mostly to New England, between 1840 and 1930.[46] Kerouac experienced wandering and the search for settlement as integral to life in the French-speaking Québécois community he grew up in. Though he was sympathetic to the widespread expression of longing to "return" to Québec or even France—as evidenced, for example, in the idea that when his older brother Gerard died at age nine, he went to Canada,[47] as well as in the project of tracing his Breton ancestors in *Satori in Paris*[48]—he also saw it as a nostalgic fantasy, and so turned the wandering urge outward to the United States, North America, and eventually the entire world.

Goethe's tragedy presents the long story of these two souls, an allegory of the trajectory of humanity in an age of rising global domination through technology, the era we now call the Anthropocene. This theme is a major reason why Goethe's work has recently attracted attention in the academic field of the environmental humanities.[49] Toward the end of *Faust* he underscores the destructiveness of this trajectory when an elderly couple, Baucis and Philemon, who embody traditional virtues closely tied with the earth, are killed for the sake of progress.[50] Though Spengler recognizes the wonders of Faustian man's exploratory inventiveness, in the conclusion to his book he laments such callous waste: "The Western industry has diverted the ancient traditions of the other Cultures. The streams of economic life move towards the seats of King Coal and the great regions of raw material. Nature becomes exhausted, the globe sacrificed to Faustian thinking and energies."[51]

Kerouac understood *Faust* in these terms. Responding to Bernice Lemire's question of why *Faust Part Three* is the subtitle of *Dr. Sax*, he writes:

"Faust Part Three" simply means this: Goethe wrote Faust Parts one and two, ending with dull Canals, and I just wrote Part Three of the Faust Legend about the soul of the West. Faust sold his soul to the devil but Sax rushed in and called Faust a bastard. Consult Spengler on the "Faustian Western Soul" ... take a look at what Spengler said about Faust, and how Faust led up to Space Missiles because he believed in the "endlessness of the soul."[52]

Kerouac continues Goethe's story of Faustian technological violence, as Fiona Paton explains, for the era of nuclear weapons.[53] Toward the end of *Dr. Sax*, a novel blending Gothic horror, pulp fiction, and magic realism, as the Great Snake of the World stirs its way up through the earth, "The ground shuddered."[54] Of the Snake's imminent emergence, the Wizard Faustus remarks, "We will darken the very sun in our march," echoing the fact that the hydrogen bomb test of 1952 yielded a temperature well exceeding that of the sun's core.[55] The Snake is expected to bring on the type of destruction Spengler predicts, as the Wizard explains: "Hamlets will be gobbled up entire, my boy. Cities of skyscrapers will feel the weight of this scale."[56]

Taking place in Lowell but also including episodes tied to Europe, Canada, and South America, *Dr. Sax* is a story of migration and empire in global space. Again, Kerouac accepts Spengler's assessment of decline, but rather sees the fellahin as an active cultural ferment on the periphery of empire, a creative population that survives imperial collapse. The apocalypse that almost happens—averted at the last minute when the Great Black Bird snatches away the Great Snake, an image Kerouac draws from Aztec mythology—is part of the rise and fall of empires in North America. In a passage that echoes the one from *On the Road* with which this essay begins, the doleful invalid Oncle Mike recounts the fall of New France, under the command of General Louis-Joseph de Montcalm, to the British Empire during the French and Indian War: this was a major chapter in the waning of the French imperial presence in North America. The passage is the longest in French that Kerouac published in his lifetime. He writes it in the French he created partly in order to transcribe the spoken language he knew while growing up, using somewhat archaic, somewhat anglicized words and phrases in a dramatization of the removal of his people's language from the imperial center that would regulate and homogenize it. This altered French thus marks the cultural castaway status of the Francophone Québécois people in Anglophone-dominated North America, their further removal from the metropolitan center of French culture, their motion toward fellahin status.

Though elsewhere I've closely examined the French in Kerouac's writing,[57] my purpose here is different, so I'll quote only from the English translation with which Kerouac follows the French. As the passage unfolds, he translates it in segments:

Napoleon was a great man. Also the General Montcalm at Quebec even though he lost. Your ancestor, the honorable soldier, Baron Louis Alexandre Lebris de Duluoz, a grandfather—married the Indian woman, returned to Brittany, the father there, the old Baron, said, yelling at the top of his voice, "Return to that woman—be an honest man and a man of honor".[58]

The translation retains Gallicisms—for example, "the General Montcalm" for "le General Montcalm," "the father there" for "le pere la"—to indicate the persistence of a receding French in the English in which Kerouac writes. He adapts for the Duluoz family his own family's lore of a noble ancestor, a soldier who crossed the Atlantic just before the fall, a vestige of the old imperial France that for a time contended for domination of North America. Furthermore, this ancestor became fully North American by marrying a woman of the First Nations, a detail of the lore in keeping with a resonant motif of Québécois genealogy.[59] In the nineteenth century the soldier is followed by Napoleon, the archenemy of the British Empire. As for the noble ancestor's descendants, "O the poor Duluozes are all dying"[60]—in the wake of imperial fall they became peasants, fellahin, mingling with the fellahin indigenous population, and the poorest of them is sad, sick Oncle Mike.

Writing to the Future

Kerouac explicitly refers to the Duluoz family as "Fellaheen" in the genealogy he sketched in the same notebook in which he drafted *Sur le chemin*, his 1952 French-language novella (first published in 2016).[61] He thereby acknowledges his family and community's status as a population that has emerged from imperial conquest. British domination contributed heavily to remaking the French settlers and their descendants into peasants.[62] Kerouac's claims of affinity with peasant populations—here, in *On the Road*, and elsewhere—are entirely justified: both his parents immigrated to the United States from peasant communities in Québec. As survivors of the fall of the French Empire in North America and conquest by the British Empire, Québécois peasants may accurately be called fellahin according to Spengler's definition. So Kerouac's interest in and depictions of marginalized populations in the United States and throughout the world stems from his sense of shared experience; he nonetheless remains quite aware that he partakes in the bounty of nation and empire and the position it grants him to make these observations.

In "In America," the unpublished essay from about 1953 that I discuss above, Kerouac calls himself the "prophet" of the fellahin.[63] In a firm challenge to Spengler, he describes jazz, a music of fellahin origin, with some of the spatial terms that Spengler reserves for the Faustian music of Bach. Jazz, writes Kerouac, has "subterranean" possibilities, an expansion into the liminal and hidden spaces of fellahin culture. His many comparisons of his writing to jazz are a testimony to his sense of being an outsider to dominant US culture and to his idea of the creative power this position entails.[64] He will draw on the powers of jazz and more generally of the fellahin life from which he himself stems in order to undertake his creative work, writing in which he aims to participate in an emerging global literature, part of a global culture taking shape in the face of the current one's exhaustion.[65] The fellahin culture he draws on, he continually affirms, is filled with creative energy, necessitated by the perspective of those who live on the edges of dominant culture and yet must survive marginalization.[66] His fellahin poetics is not only a source of art and literature but also of a culture that may offer an alternative to the long and violent history of nations and empires.

Notes

1. Jack Kerouac, *On the Road* (1957) (London and New York: Penguin, 2003), 83.
2. Ibid., 279–80.
3. Ibid., 280.
4. Ibid., 279.
5. Hassan Melehy, "Kerouac, Multilingualism, and Global Culture," in *The Cambridge Companion to Kerouac*, ed. Steven Belletto (Cambridge, UK: Cambridge University Press, 2024), 207–22; Dean MacCannell, *The Tourist: A New Theory of the Leisure Class* (1976) (Berkeley and Los Angeles: University of California Press, 2013), 110.
6. My source on the publication information is WorldCat. The edition of Spengler's *The Decline of the West* that I have consulted is the 2021 version of both volumes from Arktos, an avowedly New Right publisher in London.
7. For example, in Ann Charters, "Introduction," in *On the Road* (1957) ed. Jack Kerouac (London and New York: Penguin, 2003), xi; Joyce Johnson, *The Voice Is All: The Lonely Victory of Jack Kerouac* (New York: Viking, 2012), 160; Paul Maher, *Kerouac: His Life and Work*, rev. ed. (Lanham, MD: Taylor Trade, 2004), 122; Gerald Nicosia, *Memory Babe: A Critical Biography of Jack Kerouac* (Berkeley and Los Angeles: University of California Press, 1994), 134.
8. Sebastian Sampas to Kerouac, in Jack Kerouac, *Selected Letters, 1940–1956*, ed. Ann Charters (New York: Viking, 1995), 68.
9. Oswald Spengler, *The Decline of the West*, vol. 2, *Perspectives of World History*, trans. Charles F. Atkinson (1928) (London: Arktos, 2021), 239–43.
10. Sampas to Kerouac, *Selected Letters, 1940–1956*, 69.
11. Ibid.
12. Jack Kerouac, "Diary (August 21–September 3)," Kerouac Papers, New York Public Library, 9.20.
13. Jack Kerouac, "Holograph notes, untitled [List of books and authors] (1943?)," Kerouac Papers, 7.71.
14. Oswald Spengler, *Der Untergang des Abendlandes*, vol. 2, *Welthistorische Perspektiven* (Munich: Beck, 1922; Google Books edition), first occurrence of the word, 125–7.
15. Oswald Spengler, *The Decline of the West*, vol. 1, *Form and Actuality*, trans. Charles F. Atkinson (1926) (London: Arktos, 2021), 1–2.
16. Spengler, *The Decline of the West*, vol. 2, 109–13.
17. Ibid., 209.
18. Ibid., 211.
19. Ibid.
20. John Clellon Holmes (credited as Clellon Holmes), "This Is the Beat Generation," *New York Times*, November 16, 1952; rpt. in *Beat Down to Your Soul*, ed. Ann Charters (New York and London: Penguin, 2001), 222–38.
21. Spengler, *The Decline of the West*, vol. 2, 229–30.

22 Jack Kerouac, "In America" (n.d.), Kerouac Papers, 15.7. Since this essay is unpublished, copyright rules prevent me from quoting from it. For a set of related ideas that Kerouac had formulated years earlier, see Jack Kerouac, "America in World History," in *The Unknown Kerouac*, ed. Todd Tietchen, trans. Jean-Christophe Cloutier (New York: Library of America, 2016), 5–10.
23 In a recent collection that contributes to defining the emerging field of global indigenous studies, the editors explain: "Our coverage reaches beyond the Anglosphere towards a global story of settler colonialism, including its ongoing legacies and its continuing practices up until the present. We have actively sought out representative historical perspectives from regions where the prominent field of 'settler colonial studies' does not always readily match up—such as in Europe, Africa, Southeast Asia, the Indian subcontinent, and South America. As various contributors to this volume demonstrate, indigenous peoples have been subjected to sustained imperial and economic, often capitalist, oppression in Southeast and North Asian nations, in the Caribbean, Africa, South America, and elsewhere." Ann McGrath and Lynette Russell, "History's Outsiders? Global Indigenous Histories," in *The Routledge Companion to Global Indigenous History*, ed. McGrath and Russell (Abingdon, UK and New York: Routledge, 2022), 9.
24 Kerouac, *On the Road*, 280.
25 Melehy, *Kerouac*, 66–81; "Kerouac, Multilingualism, and Global Culture."
26 Spengler, *The Decline of the West*, vol. 2, 211.
27 "It is important that we do not view history exclusively through the lens of imperial chronologies and histories, which is the prevailing perspective of many written histories." McGrath and Russell, "History's Outsiders? Global Indigenous Histories," 9.
28 Kerouac, *On the Road*, 280.
29 Spengler, *The Decline of the West*, vol. 2, 643.
30 Spengler, *The Decline of the West*, vol. 1, xix.
31 Ibid., 65n.
32 The first author Kerouac mentions in *On the Road* is Nietzsche: Sal says that one of the first things he heard about Dean was that he had asked Chad King "to teach him all about Nietzsche" (1). In unpublished notes from the 1940s, Kerouac quotes and comments on Nietzsche's famous aphorism "Nothing is true, everything is allowed" (from *On the Genealogy of Morality*, repeated in *Thus Spoke Zarathustra*), a statement on the hidden interests in determinations of what is right and wrong, correct and incorrect. Jack Kerouac, "Holograph Fragment of Essay" (1944), Kerouac Papers 13.43. See my *Kerouac: Language, Poetics, and Territory* (New York: Bloomsbury, 2016), 104.
33 Spengler, *The Decline of the West*, vol. 1, 31.
34 Ibid., 32; italics in the text.
35 Jack Kerouac, "The Origins of the Beat Generation" (1959), in *Good Blonde and Others*, ed. Donald Allen (San Francisco: City Lights, 1994), 62.
36 Jack Kerouac, biographical note, in *The New American Poetry, 1945–1960* (1960), ed. Donald Allen (Berkeley and Los Angeles: University of California Press, 1999), 439, doi.org/10.1525/9780520354005.
37 Jack Kerouac, *Dr. Sax* (New York: Grove, 1959), 43; ellipsis in the text.
38 Spengler, *The Decline of the West*, vol. 1, 522.
39 Ibid., 303.

40 Ibid., 305.
41 Ibid., 83.
42 Sampas to Kerouac, *Selected Letters, 1940–1956*, 66.
43 Johann Wolfgang von Goethe, *Faust*, trans. Walter Arndt, ed. Cyrus Hamlin (New York and London: W. W. Norton, 2001), 31, ll. 1112–17.
44 Melehy, *Kerouac*, 135–6.
45 Jack Kerouac, *The Sea Is My Brother* (1943), in *The Sea Is My Brother: The Lost Novel*, ed. Dawn M. Ward (London and New York: Penguin, 2011), 17–145.
46 See Melehy, *Kerouac*, 10–15. Readers will here find numerous references to sources on this history.
47 Jack Kerouac to Neal Cassady, December 28, 1950, in *Selected Letters, 1940–1956*, 260.
48 Jack Kerouac, *Satori in Paris* (1966), in *Satori in Paris and Pic: Two Novels* (New York: Grove, 1985), 5–118.
49 See Luke Fischer and Dalia Nassar, "Introduction: Goethe and Environmentalism," *Goethe Yearbook* 22 (2015), special section on "Goethe and Environmentalism": 3–22, doi.org/10.1017/9781782045298.001.
50 von Goethe, *Faust*, 313–15, ll. 11043–142; 320–22, ll. 11288–380.
51 Spengler, *The Decline of the West*, vol. 2, 646.
52 Jack Kerouac to Bernice Lemire, August 11, 1961, in *Selected Letters, 1957–1969*, ed. Ann Charters (New York: Viking, 1999), 298; ellipsis in text.
53 Fiona Paton, "Reconceiving Kerouac: Why We Should Teach Doctor Sax," in *The Beat Generation: Critical Essays*, ed. Kostas Myrsiades (New York: Peter Lang, 2002), 146.
54 Kerouac, *Dr. Sax*, 222.
55 Paton, "Reconceiving Kerouac," 146.
56 Kerouac, *Dr. Sax*, 228.
57 Here I draw on arguments I make throughout *Kerouac*. In this section of the essay I summarize parts of my commentary on *Dr. Sax*: Melehy, *Kerouac*, 119–44.
58 Kerouac, *Dr. Sax*, 119.
59 In a thoroughgoing genealogical reference, published from 1871 to 1875 and still in circulation, a source for Kerouac's own research, Cyprien Tanguay lauds the "nobility" of the French-Canadians, stemming first from their hardy, adventurous French ancestry and then from a local source: "After that, might I say that there is yet another type of nobility? Perhaps some will contemptuously reject it. But after the expressions of esteem accorded the Huron Chief Vincent, after the general satisfaction with which Abbot Vincent was elevated to the priesthood, there are those, I believe, who will learn with pleasure that aboriginal blood flows in their veins. Especially the Hurons, the faithful Hurons, so full of intelligence, and the Iroquois with their boldness hardly lag behind the tribes of Central and South America, with whom the proud Spanish did not spurn alliance." Cyprien Tanguay, *Dictionnaire généalogique des familles canadiennes*, vol. 1 (Québec: Sénécal, 1871), xii–xiii; my translation. While researching his ancestry, Kerouac photocopied two pages from volume 5 (Québec: Sénécal, 1875) of this reference: Kerouac Papers, 46.36. See Melehy, *Kerouac*, 162–3.
60 Kerouac, *Dr. Sax*, 120.
61 Jack Kerouac, *Sur le chemin* (1952), in *La Vie est d'hommage*, ed. Jean-Christophe Cloutier (Montreal: Boréal, 2016), 117–26; Cloutier translated it under Kerouac's own English title, *Old Bull in the Bowery*, in *The Unknown Kerouac*, 173–237.

62 See Leslie Choquette, *Frenchmen into Peasants: Modernity and Tradition in the Peopling of French Canada* (Cambridge, MA: Harvard University Press, 1997), especially 279–305, doi.org/10.2307/j.ctv1smjt11.
63 Kerouac, "In America."
64 For my assessment of Kerouac's relationship to jazz: Melehy, *Kerouac*, 89–94.
65 For more on this topic, see Melehy, "Kerouac, Multilingualism, and Global Culture."
66 Kerouac's critique of Spengler strikingly overlaps with that of philosopher Theodor Adorno: "In a world of brutal and oppressed life, decadence becomes the refuge of a potentially better life by renouncing allegiance to this one and to its culture, its crudeness, and its sublimity. The powerless, who at Spengler's command are to be thrown aside and annihilated by history, are the negative embodiment of the negativity of this culture of everything which promises, however feebly, to break the dictatorship of culture and put an end to the horror of pre-history. In their protest lies the only hope that fate and power will not have the last word. What can oppose the decline of the west is not a resurrected culture but the utopia that is silently contained in the image of decline." Theodor W. Adorno, "Spengler After Decline," in *Prisms*, trans. Samuel Weber and Sherry Weber (Cambridge, MA: MIT Press, 1981), 72, doi.org/10.7551/mitpress/5570.003.0006.

Part Three

Kerouac's Influence and Legacy

12

From Beat Generation to Hacker Generation: The Experimental Road Narratives *On the Road* and *1 the Road*

Peggy Pacini

The right-hand headlamp of a black Cadillac rolling past a landscape in the distance. A close-up on an electronic device on the roof and multilayered computerized voices giving a series of information. The Cadillac zooming by on the highway across the night. These are the introductory scenes of "Automatic on the Road—Gonzo AI Robot Writes Road Trip Novel."[1] The short film presents a visual depiction of Ross Goodwin's Artificial Intelligence (AI) generated novel *1 the Road* (2018) that invites immediate comparison to Jack Kerouac's 1957 iconic road novel, *On the Road*. Offering a window into Goodwin's experimental road narrative, this didactic promotional peritext largely plays on the imagery and mythology surrounding the writing of the Original Scroll of *On the Road*[2] that serves to help us re-examine Kerouac's novel and its contributions to questions of space, time, and mobility in the computer age.

The film is punctuated by close-ups on the materiality of the generated output unwinding through a thermal receipt printer, skillfully playing on the narrative mythology behind Kerouac's novel as composed on a single long sheet of paper as evidenced in Howard Cunnell's introductory essay to *The Original Scroll* edition: "the defining images of Jack Kerouac and *On the Road* in the cultural imagination remains his apparent frenzied channeling of a true-life story; the never-ending roll of paper billowing from the typewriter like the imaged road."[3] No pictures portraying Kerouac's frenzied writing over his typewriter and the unspooling teletyped paper are available, yet the readership's cultural imagination has amply been nourished by other legendary pictures of Kerouac holding a scroll—Fred DeWitt's 1958 *Time* magazine photographs of Kerouac seated at his typewriter handling *The Dharma Bums* scroll, or the c. 1960 Jerry Bauer image of a standing Kerouac holding an unrolled dangling scroll. "Automatic On the Road" repeatedly engages analogy with the *On the Road* Scroll— Goodwin is seen absorbedly reading from a scroll in his hand, holding a printed scroll, holding a printed scroll in the background of an unspooling thermal receipt paper sprawling on the backseats of the Cadillac, or, later, conclusively unrolling the scroll out of the car on a parking lot. While Goodwin's computerized writing experiment was published by French publisher Jean Boîte in 2018, eleven years after the publication of

Kerouac's *The Original Scroll* (though written in 1951), the legendary terrain on which this cultural imagination was built cannot be ignored.

These two novels, in their own styles and with the writing tools of their times, challenge the very notion of writing, offering experimental prototypes of the road trip genre. An examination of the through line from Kerouac's prototype for the road narrative to Goodwin's cutting-edge recurrent neural long short-term memories (RNN-LSTMs) experimental automation both probe for a way to write the American literary road trip as a transformative or consciousness-raising experience through the lenses of time, space, and mobility. The road narrative raises important existentialist questions.[4] Political theorist William E. Scheuerman states that "any attempt to make sense of the human condition at the start of the new century must begin with an analysis of time and space compression,"[5] adding that the horizons of human experience are determined by unprecedented possibilities for simultaneity and instantaneousness. Social theorists Paul Virilio, David Harvey, and Hartmut Rosa,[6] among others, attempted to grapple with the effects of the processes of modernization on our society and self, particularly looking into the concept of dromology (Virilio), time-space compression (Harvey), and acceleration (Rosa). This comparative study of Goodwin's *1 the Road* with Kerouac's *The Original Scroll*[7] wants to push further into how social acceleration affects the road novel on structural, thematic, and hermeneutic levels, problematizing the side-effects of (post-) modernization on self and society. If Kerouac's novel questions the accepted concept of temporality and society's use of time,[8] and if his characters claim knowledge of time, is the WordCar itself time-conscious and in what ways? Similarly, how is it space-conscious? How do both these novels offer a critical response to American culture and society?

The Culture of Speed in Creative Writing

In a letter to Neal Cassady dated May 22, 1951, Kerouac describes the Scroll to his friend as "my book about you … about your life," insisting on the experimental technique he had been using for narrating Neal Cassady's (Dean Moriarty in the novel) transformation from jailkid to saintliness, one which resorts to speed writing and innovative technique freed from conventional style and formatting. It took Kerouac twenty days to write this 125,000-word full-length novel which, he claims, is a complete departure "from previous American Lit."[9] The experimental departure precisely lies in the performative experience of writing,[10] the medium and the technique used. Letters and journals are explicit about how the issue of output is almost obsessional: how many words can he write per day on his typewriter. By defining his writing production in terms of time as output per unit time (productivity),[11] Kerouac unconsciously partakes in the logic of capitalism his novel rebels against and tries to counter. In his letter to Cassady, the writing process is translated into speedometric terms, insisting on the production rate of an average of 6,000 words a day, which he typed fast on the now iconic 120-foot-long strip of tracing paper, "because road is fast"[12]—starting with 12,000 the first day and ending with 15,000 the last day. Kerouac's word-a-day writing pace might also be interpreted as a translation of Neal's mile-an-hour driving pace in the novel. His effort to dynamize his writing, however, exemplifies the paradox of modernity which is about speeding up our life and world (Rosa), underlining the extent to which the writing process is here also subject to "acceleration" or "dromology"—the logic of speed. Quite interestingly, Kerouac's remark resonates with Rosa's interpretation of capitalism, but more generally of modernity, through dynamic stabilization, which Rosa defines as a logic of increase, acceleration, and innovation. To keep the narrative going, growing and be innovative, this "lightning typist," as John Clellon Holmes envisions Kerouac,[13] has to, physically and stylistically, yield to this escalatory logic.

This paradoxical relation to time is given significant development in the novel.[14] In fact, speedy continuum is as important to Kerouac's narrative productivity as it is for his protagonists.[15] This addictive relation to measured and controlled time imposed by concerns of productivity is coupled in the novel by concerns of surveillance and control through measurement—the speedometer.[16] If the reader is frequently reminded of Neal's exceptional speedy driving pace, the medium of controlling speed is only mentioned twice explicitly when Neal happens to break it upon leaving Denver because he "was pushing well over 110 miles an hour." Neal's conclusion to this deficiency is telling as, now, only time will tell how fast he has been driving.[17] If Neal and Jack are "freed from authoritative restraints," as Mikelli concludes, the energy that the broken speedometer translated is now only measurable by time, which cyclicity and repetitiousness eventually mirror the protagonists' cyclical and repetitive crossing and re-crossing the land, and Kerouac's perception of himself as deterritorialized.[18]

Kerouac's frenzied typing is echoed by Goodwin's data processing at the back of a Google-rented Cadillac, the WordCar. In both novels, the car is the medium of the journey and of the experience. The WordCar is also a text-generator, a computational writing experiment performance using ANNs (artificial neural networks), which challenges one of the very pillars on which fiction writing is grounded, i.e., on authorship. No one will deny Kerouac authorship of *The Original Scroll*, but serious ontological questions are raised as to whether Goodwin wrote *1 the Road*. Goodwin himself avoids solving this ambiguity, yet concedes he is the author of the machine, the "writer of writer," as stated on the book cover. More prosaically, *1 the Road* was authored by algorithms, a computer, and AI. The "Automotive AI assemblage" which gave birth to this computational writing experiment starts with a customized rotating Axis M3007 surveillance camera—a medium of controlling and recording people's actions and moves in time and space—mounted to the Cadillac trunk, capturing an image every twenty seconds. First textualized as a grayscale image with ASCII characters, the captured image is described in a sentence, which "feeds a free-associating generating neural net."[19] Three other sensors, each equipped with a script, provided the ANNs with starting points for narration: place, time, dialogues, characters. Place, or geospatial data, was given by a GPS unit—subject to "the priorities of the techno-capitalist producer and subject"[20]—fixed on the roof, connected to a Foursquare API, a location technology platform. Time was given by the clock; dialogues captured by the microphone of Goodwin's laptop. These sensors provided pictorial, locative, vocal, and temporal inputs which were then collaged with long short-term memory recurrent neural networks trained to write poetry and fiction.

The input the AI was fed with—Goodwin's favorite classics of Anglo-Saxon literature, which generated the output of *1 the Road*—partakes of the same dynamic and drive as the multiple textual references to classical literature which constitute Jack Kerouac's "input." However, contrary to Kerouac, whose literary references are mostly identifiable and partake in the writing of his own Great American novel,[21] Goodwin's references do not surface explicitly. And yet, those literary classics and American road novels are there in the uncannily concatenated "semi-sensical LSTM poetry gathered via API and surveillance camera."[22] Unlike Kerouac's text though, Goodwin's does not pretend it is a "complete departure from previous American Lit."; quite the contrary, as the machine was precisely trained on existing literature and style. The WordCar, however, departs from traditional modes of writing by resorting to the datafication of the different facets of our life while challenging literary conventions and expectations by experimenting with writing and driving simultaneously. The generated complete narrative amounts to eleven scrolls of thermal paper printed in real time by a wide format thermal printer—a printer used to such items as receipts and shipping labels, symbols of our production and consumer society—connected to Goodwin's laptop. Both published scrolls—*The Original Scroll* and *1 the Road*—result from a convergence of inputs involving word processing aggregated in the form of an open experimental narrative or perhaps as Kenric McDowell puts it of "machine poetry."[23]

Kerouac's narrative unrolls like the white line of the road on the white scroll of paper. Goodwin's scrolls also play on the analogy with that "white line on the road,"[24] which runs through the text as a central trope[25] and becomes subject to metamorphosis.[26] *1 the Road* tries to mimic the analogy. The stripe on the road is produced by the narrow column width, though it is less convincing for two reasons: first, because of page margins as the gutter margins decenter the text, and second, because each of the WordCar's unit of output, or combinatory coalescent vignette or sketch, is accompanied on the outer side of the pages by a time stamp, which dispels the illusion. *1 the Road* is divided into four parts, each one a day trip, separated by a blank page. Each part is similarly organized with one or two grayscale images and vignettes seemingly devoid of linearity, yet inscribed in a minute chronology, marked by a social construct—clock time. "Sometimes little narrative pockets or sidings emerge," Kirschenbaum almost reluctantly concedes.[27] Contrary to Goodwin's paragraphed vignettes, Kerouac's *The Original Scroll* is unparagraphed and structured into five books which are inscribed in a narrative temporal linearity stretching from the winter of 1947 to the summer of 1950.

Finally, both objects are not only experimental but mediated. The Scroll typescript is part of a composition process which challenges the genre of the road novel. Begun in 1948, it meandered through different drafts and experiments, among which *Visions of Cody*, and ended in 1957 with the iconic Viking Press version.[28] Scholarship is explicit and abundant on how the novel stands out in the genre. *1 the Road* is not only the printed version of an automotive creative project but the outcome of a lengthy process of experimental creative projects which aimed at perfecting Goodwin's research in "narrated reality"[29]—a new framework (new forms and interfaces) for writing, enabled by machine intelligence. Kerouac insisted as Tim Hunt recalls "on the writer's obligation to explore the entire range of experience whether currently fashionable or not."[30] Goodwin's experiment does fit in such exploration. Moreover, Kerouac's concern that "conscious critical mind might censor the richness of imagination"[31] does not really apply to Goodwin's novel as there is no censorship of the images produced. I would argue that Goodwin's narrative experiment with generative ANNs is a prototype that might serve as his belief and technique for AI-generated creative writing to be read as a contemporary mutation of Kerouac's essentials and beliefs. Kerouac and Goodwin exploit and explore the possibilities of language to produce their version of the road narrative, sticking to the central motifs and topoi of the genre but with the media of their times as means of composition—music and a typewriter for Kerouac, high tech and AI for Goodwin.

"Performing Our One and Noble Function of the Time: Move"

Mobility, Jack and Neal's "one and noble function of the time," is evoked as a revitalizing force that would counter cultural apathy, stasis, and conformity. By moving, they reject the concepts of time and space imposed upon them. Moreover, movement at high speeds invites new perceptive dimensions of space as acceleration of time also contracts space, which in turn also affects "its significance for orientation."[32] Both narratives are fed by mobility, but instead of acting as a revitalizing force, the WordCar acts as a narrative tool testifying of cultural apathy, conformity, and stasis, and is a narrative journey into confusion and nonsense. Due to its sensors, the WordCar is landscape and environment-sensitive and does not censor the input the sensors provide. It reads, records, translates, and concatenates the data linearly. Therefore, the realities it produces are those it is forced to read and reconfigure, in space and time. They are deprived of subjectivity. The journey is not an escapist one, but rather draws extensively on our cultures of surveillance. If "surveillance may be representative of our condition moving through (post)modernity,"[33] in *1 the Road* it also becomes a writing material which exposes not only "the fabric of our social, cultural and political lives" but surveillance capitalism, which Zuboff claims was originally invented by Google. In the AI-generated narrative,[34] mobility is not driven by the pleasures of flight, the characters will not undergo any potential transformation from their journey on the road, because there are no definite characters. The journey is the car's journey, one sponsored by Google and supervised by a group working at the Artists + Machine Intelligence program at Google Research. It is an experiment in which mobility is the vehicle that quite paradoxically captures the state of America's "cannibalistic junkspace of technocapitalism" and surveillance capitalism. Because the narrative is processed through the data received by the sensors, the road becomes a panoptic medium which offers a consumerist and productivist vision of society.

If *The Original Scroll* is concerned with "that restless desire to get up and *move*,"[35] *1 the Road* seems to rely more on fixity. The trip from New York to New Orleans records and translates a series of snapshots encapsulating fixed locations. The visions that it offers are more than often static, apathic, "monotonous," "empty," when not chaotic. In most sketches, the (non)(human) beings are described as standing, sitting, or still, echoing somehow Virilio's diagnostic of "polar inertia." "Still" counts among the words most used in *1 the Road*, its polysemy suggesting either duration or immobility, at times also an underlying expectation of movement and mobility. Very much like in *The Original Scroll*, there is an imperative to move, to take off—"I want to go away from here, the time has come."[36] This comment is supposedly made by "the painter"—one of the rare characters who makes several appearances in the text and whose voice is incarnated. "The painter," who complains about his inactivity and boredom, probably thinks like Kerouac at the beginning of *The Original Scroll* that "everything was dead." In their still-ness, characters (human and non-human) in *1 the Road* seem to be, like a black and white cat opposite the back door, "looking for little moments of the roads."[37] But to hit the road, you either need to hop on a bus, hitchhike, or drive a car—the journey is one of mobility (*The Original Scroll*), not stasis (*1 the Road*). Characters are somehow forced to stand still or be still because the car has lost its functionality as conveyance. One of the first vignettes of the novel immediately problematizes the paradox: "it was ten forty-two in the morning, and the driver had to stay alone and start back from the parking lot."[38] The car stands in streets or at the door. It is "wasted," yet "a few cars were still alive."[39] Quite strangely in a hyper-modernized and urbanized world, natural elements are given birth by the car, as if nature was taking over. The reader must wait until the penultimate vignette to infer that a journey might have actually taken place for "the boys" (perhaps Goodwin and his friends), who have reached a destination and were now standing in the doorway, while the car was on the road. Whether the car is parked on the road or moving on the road, both hypotheses are valid. In the world of *1 the Road*, everything (characters and language) is mostly anchored in stillness or repetition, yet shifting, morphing, open.

The reader in fact loses their bearing in a world that seems to have blurred its references. However, like in *The Original Scroll*, the journey is traceable. The reader can follow the WordCar's journey, as it could follow Neal and Jack's—"savoring names" of places on the road map. This provides the only landmarks—stable geographic references—allowing the reader to follow the WordCar in its journey. Besides recording place names, these stable points also expose the overwhelming presence of (chain) convenience stores, shopping malls, distribution networks, fast food franchises, toll plazas, or gas stations, which form the very layers of our consumer-capitalistic-driven surveillance society. These layers cohabit with unused, "closed," "empty," and decaying industrial and commercial infrastructures—power plants, factories, railroads, mines—punctuating the landscape with as many signs of the economic and structural remains of an industrial society, replaced by the service—and leisure-based economy of postindustrial society—hotels, restaurants, nail salons, and baseball fields. The setting of *1 the Road* is composed of what Marc Augé terms the main components of the peri-urban landscape—the topography characteristic of "supermodernity."[40] These spaces of transport, commerce, and communication, which he calls "non-places" (*non-lieux*), assign the individual to a state of loneliness and anonymity, since the peri-urban is disqualified, lost between a hypothetical past and a formless future. In *The Original Scroll*, these layers, "non-places" in the making, are primarily often intimately linked to the road trip and life on the road. They belong to the iconography of the road's poetics—lunchcarts, rooming houses, highways,[41] tunnels, crossroads stores; railroad, bus or gas stations, roadhouses; grocery stores, etc., yet also stand against huge oil tanks and refineries, housing projects, "[a] shroudy cement factory," "a Coca Cola stand," or "battered pocky storefronts." *1 the Road* then offers an updated version of American society, where the road has been contaminated by commercial transactions and has lost its purity. The road, or rather the interstate freeway in *1 the Road*, can no longer be seen with "innocent road-eyes,"[42] as it is captured by camera-surveillance eyes and carefully regulated. Moreover, Neal and Jack's automotive blurring of space as "one way of resisting capitalist consumption, since economic transactions cannot take place at 110 miles an hour"[43] is no longer possible now that economic transactions have accelerated due to a speed-up of (sub-)systemic processing.[44] The road has somehow lost this possibility of resistance though the last vignette of *1 the Road* reads rather optimistically with its opened white line on the floor and the boys standing in the doorway.

The Original Scroll presents us with characters almost always on the move, which the narrator qualifies as a ritual, a performance. On the narrative level, these moments on the road are when the action or events take place; they constitute fluid temporalities set against stasis and the fixed temporalities of clock time. Erik Mortenson suggests that "if reification congeals fluid temporality into rigid spatiality, Kerouac's insistence on the motion of travel sunders this bond by replacing stasis with flux."[45] The effect produced in *1 the Road*, I would argue, is quite the reverse, as Goodwin's narrative is entirely framed and encapsulated in rigid spatiality and fixed temporalities. The realities *1 the Road* presents the reader with are quite disturbing, a world where self is totally absent, where humans make rare appearances and are reduced to types or voices, where markers are either generic or indefinite, and are standing against very singular landscapes or among architectural fragments. The WordCar's journey tries to capture what remains of the self in a globalized market-driven society. Although the gist of the journey and narrative is movement, the snapshots generated by the AI preclude any fluidity by anchoring the journey in both rigid temporality and spatiality.

"We know time"

In his article "Beating Time: Configurations of Temporality in Jack Kerouac's *On the Road*," Mortenson contextualizes Kerouac's use of time against the backdrop of post-war America time-consciousness, which he correlates with its booming economy. He argues that *On the Road* challenges clock-generated temporality which constricts notions of time to address larger existential problems of temporality.[46] His article offers a detailed and critical analysis of temporalities in Kerouac's novel against a Lukácsian background. Kerouac's characters are not constrained by production time, and the very actions and behaviors of the novel, Mortenson argues, are set against the repetition of mechanistic rationalization. In fact, he is right when he says that the narrative is not dotted with precise dates and times but resorts to other time units such as months, and natural periodicities and cyclicities (time of the days and seasons, night, and day). *1 the Road*, on the other hand, features a world haunted by the mechanical time of industries, factories, and machines. In fact, the generated text is constantly informed by temporal markers. Time is ever present on the margin of the text in the form of a time stamp and is very often reiterated in the text by two consecrated alternating formulas—anaphoric time frames/references punctuating the narrative: "It was" and "The time was," respectively appearing seventy-four and seventy-six times. Such accumulation and reiteration of temporal markers in different forms does not so much convince the reader that, like the characters of *The Original Scroll*, they know time but rather that they are trapped into a temporal mechanical cycle, which they cannot escape. This gives the impression that time is a real concern and that production, data, and actions are constrained by time, very much like in mass-chain production. Each time stamp reveals a snapshot of the landscape zipped by. As for the conversation captured and filtered through recurrent neural networks, it is a snapshot that would then be very much like a video surveillance camera transcript, except that the transcript might sound encrypted. This is perhaps what the self-reflexive reference to Colonel Langer—head of the Polish Cipher Bureau, in charge of Polish cryptography in wartime period—in the 23:03:02 vignette of the second-day trip makes clear.[47]

Time's omnipresence in *1 the Road* finds an echo and treatment in Neal Cassady's obsession with time and scheduling. If Neal is the gist of Kerouac's novel, if he is its stamina, he is also one of the sensors of the narrative thread in many ways. He is himself many sensors in one. Central to the narrative action, he is the one who imposes rhythm to Jack's journey. As Mortenson remarks, Dean/Neal is an example of Lukácsian reification, his time is scheduled, with extreme precision, to the minute. Everything is planned out, over-rationalized even when routine is broken. Time is Neal's obsession in Book 1; he is constantly looking at his watch to make time profitable. Neal's energy is gargantuan, all-encompassing, and, in many ways, Neal is the Axis M3007 of *The Original Scroll*. I tend to think that naming the Axis "further" is all but a coincidence. It is in fact Ken Kesey's bus's name, but as Allen Ginsberg recalls, it was Cassady who, one decade after he drove Kerouac to Mexico "in prophetic automobile to see the physical body of America," drove Kesey's "Kosmos-patterned schoolbus on a Kafka-circus tour over the awakening nation."[48] Kerouac largely insists on the fact that Neal's vision, like the Axis M3007's, is panoramic. He looks in every direction and sees everything in an arc of 180 degrees around his eyeballs without moving his head. He is often described as slitting his eyes to see everywhere, to see every single face.[49] In *The First Third*, Neal Cassady develops this concept of "eyeballing," i.e., "the knowledge of action" or his principle of non-selectivity within an environment, his panoramic appreciation of time and space.[50] Hrebeniak considers that such a principle is the essence of Spontaneous Prose, "an unmediated way of seeing that collapses observation and interpretation together, a dismantling of automatic orders that schematize perception into habits of elucidation after the event."⁵¹ Perhaps one could argue that Neal is the surveillance camera of *The Original Scroll*, but the data he records in the data center which is his head are used to precisely configure time and space to his own ends; the time and space he inhabits are self-determined. The fragmentation and rationalization he imposes onto himself are used not within the framework of a capitalistic mode of production and consumption but within the framework of an economic mode of ecstasy.

Knowing time is for Neal a way to affirm his location within authentic time. Knowledge of time in *1 the Road* is rationalized and inauthentic. While the time stamps anchor the narrative to the minute and second in the present moment, the snapshots not only offer a fragmented reality but one that is mostly anchored and fixed in the past. However, what is interesting in *1 the Road* is how events are configured not so much in the moment of observation, but how the moment of observation is reconfigured to generate non-sequential and non-causal thoughts and images that need deciphering. Globalization has altered the meaning and experience of space, as the form and perception of social time are modified. Time is gradually losing its unilaterality and its orientational function as the relation between sequences and chronologies is gradually vanishing. Rosa, for instance, remarks that, on the internet, information and data recorded at different times and related to different periods of time are juxtaposed regardless of hierarchy, favoring a kaleidoscopic fragmented model. Transposed to the visual arts, Rosa argues, this phenomenon of disorientation is rendered through heterogeneous kaleidoscopic fade-outs of space-time fragments *in lieu of* the chronological and sequential order of images and narrative. This is somehow what Goodwin's WordCar-generated narrative offers the reader: discrete space-time fragments. The vignettes produced "constantly risk absurdity," to borrow Ferlinghetti's words,⁵² revealing new forms of the Real, a data-cohered and data-configured Real.

Real-world activity, Zuboff argues, "is continuously rendered from phones, cars, streets, homes, shops, bodies, trees, buildings, airports, and cities back to the digital realm, where it finds new life as data ready for transformation into predictions, all of it filling the ever-expanding pages of the shadow text."⁵³ The text, as generated by the AI and oriented by Goodwin, reveals singular environments where continuity is provided by recurring infrastructures (roads, trains, passages, stations); architectural entities (windows, doors, floors, stairs, barns, building, factories); and environmental entities (bushes, grass, wind, sun, clouds, stars, moon). As Kirschenbaum suggests, these surely shape "the possibility space of the book, an ontology of basic, navigable narrative space."⁵⁴ However, their articulation in the signifying chain of the produced statements offers more than a navigable narrative space, they challenge other ways of shaping the Real, whereby the relationship between the individual and their environment is altogether complex and floating. Proportions are altered, spaces, objects, beings are transformed/morphed to change functionality or purpose. The reconstruction of the Real produces a surrealistic vision which, in its distorted, dismembered concreteness reshapes the real to plunge it into some dystopian nowhere where human and non-human, animate and inanimate, sounds and visions are altered and displaced.

The representation of the Real is given a new dimension. While the narrative line is being paralyzed by the constant generative process of the collage montage technique used, this succession of almost mechanic snapshots reveals another vision of reality. In *1 the Road*, each sketch is a time frame, which is always descriptive and often suggestive of a possible imminent accident—i.e., an element of surprise which altogether interrupts the stillness and permanence of a reality—which can only be descriptive and fails to be performative. If we consider the painter's desire to "go away from here, the time has come,"[55] mentioned before, the character's predicament becomes symptomatic of the narrative at large. Rather than allowing the narrative to move forward, it opens small interstitial spaces out of which a new reality can be recomposed: "A white line on the side of the building was warm and small, and a floor was open when the wind blew open and the steeples were blue and pale straw. A small building appeared with the hollow barrel of the windows in the low cellar rooms, and the stars were still there."[56] Each sketch becomes a window or door opened onto this filtered version of reality where elements are recycled, looped into another sketch, another reality. On the first day, the 14:42:25 entry reads: "It was two forty-two in the afternoon. The street window was still alive, and the windows were still stacked with a shadowy spectacle."[57] The shadow text, the counter-narrative of the Real generated by the AI, cannot be seen. In *1 the Road*, windows, or doors—the most recurrent liminal architectural spaces, along with floors, open(ed)—offer interstitial spaces between the human and non-human world, the animate and inanimate world allowing the text to reorganize, compress new realities.

Coda

The Original Scroll and *1 the Road* complement one another in unsuspected ways, inviting us to rethink individual freedom in relation to our social, political, economic, and cultural environment. Goodwin's WordCar and data processing, like Kerouac's typewriting prowess, is equally an experience in pushing technology to the limits of narrativity and narrativity sense-making. Through this AI text-generated performance/experiment, the question that *1 the Road* raises is fundamentally how far are we ready to let our critical judgment affect our willingness to embrace a dehumanized production that challenges our traditional conception of prose and poetry to narrate a globalized data-controlled world which we are constantly feeding? Despite all the negative criticism that Goodwin received, what is most disturbing is the deterritorialization his narrative produces. In fact, Goodwin acknowledges his own deterritorialization as a programmer, to whom AI allows to go "further," beyond his human limits, where neural networks take over. The road narrative, be it AI-generated or human-generated, tells us of a quest to go beyond our physical capacities, needs, and natural time. The very idea of the quest is still materialized by "the car on the road," and the open "white line on the floor," but with oil price hikes and eco-responsible actions, chances are that the car might stay on the road. I then strongly disagree with Kirschenbaum when he construes that *1 the Road* is "a single, boutique exemplar of what is or soon will be the most common class of texts in the world—the progeny of what Guattari foresaw as 'machines speaking to machines before speaking to us.'"[58] On the contrary, Goodwin does speak to us, forcing us to reflect on the world we have contributed to creating and our willingness to turn on, tune in and drop out or feed on our cannibalistic techno-capitalist addictions and submissions.

Notes

1 Lewis Rapkin, dir. "Automatic on the Road–Gonzo AI Robot Writes Road Trip Novel" (Oscillator Media, 2018), https://youtu.be/TqsW0PMd8R0?si=ud27C2r6SNSkd5qj.
2 In the following pages, for practical matters and to avoid confusion, the physical original scroll will be referenced as the Scroll, and the published *On the Road. The Original Scroll* as *The Original Scroll*.
3 Howard Cunnell, "Fast This Time: Jack Kerouac and the Writing of On the Road," in *On the Road. The Original Scroll*, ed. Howard Cunnell (Modern Classics. London: Penguin Books, 2008), 2. For the legend and various misstatements about the characteristics and composition of the scroll typescript, read Matt Theado, "Revisions of Kerouac: The Long, Strange Trip of the On the Road Typescript," in *What's Your Road Man?: Critical Essays on Jack Kerouac's* On the Road, ed. Hilary Holladay and Robert Holton (Carbondale: Southern Illinois University Press, 2009), 11.
4 A study of the genre is provided in Ronald Primeau's *Romance of the Road: The Literature of the American Highway* (Bowling Green: Bowling Green State University Popular Press, 1996) and *American Road Literature* (Ipswich: Salem Press; Grey House Publishing, 2013); Rowland A. Sherrill's *A Road-Book America: Contemporary Culture and the New Picaresque* (Urbana: University of Illinois Press, 2000); Kris Lackey's *RoadFrames: The American Highway Narrative* (Lincoln: University of Nebraska Press, 1998); Ann Brigham's *American Road Narratives: Reimagining Mobility in Literature and Film* (Charlottesville; London: University of Virginia Press, 2015); and Gordon Slethaug and Stacilee Ford's *Hit the Road, Jack: Essays on the Culture of the American Road* (Montreal; New York: McGill-Queen's University Press, 2012).
5 William E. Scheuerman, "Liberal Democracy and the Empire of Speed," *Polity* 34 (1) (2001): 41–67, doi: 10.2307/3235508.
6 Paul Virilio, *Vitesse et Politique: Essai de dromologie* (Paris: Galilée, 1977); David Harvey, *The Condition of Postmodernity: An Enquiry into the Origins of Cultural Change* (Oxford [England]; Cambridge, MA, USA: Blackwell, 1989); Hartmut Rosa, "Social Acceleration: Ethical and Political Consequences of a Desynchronized High-Speed Society," *Constellations* 10 (1) (2003), doi: 10.1111/1467-8675.00309.
7 Though there is little alteration between the language of *The Original Scroll* and that of the 1957 published version of *On the Road*, the experimental turn is experienced with more intensity in the former. Consequently, the 1951 version is not only favored here because of its original formal analogy with *1 the Road* but also because reading *The Original Scroll*, one feels he is "skating on the edges of consciousness and sanity in language," argues Penny Vlagopoulos, which is what *1 the Road* also vehicles in its own way. Penny Vlagopoulos, "Rewriting America. Kerouac's Nation of 'Underground Monsters,'" in *The Original Scroll*, ed. Howard Cunnell (London: Penguin Books, 2008), 64.

8   See Erik R. Mortenson, "Beating Time: Configurations of Temporality in Jack Kerouac's 'On the Road,'" *College Literature* 28 (3) (2001): 51–67. See also Tim Cresswell, "Mobility as Resistance: A Geographical Reading of Kerouac's 'On the Road,'" *Transactions of the Institute of British Geographers* 18 (2) (1993): 249–62, doi: 10.2307/622366; Eftychia Mikelli, "'Passing Everybody and Never Halting': Dromos and Speed in Jack Kerouac's *On the Road*," *Cultural Politics* 8 (1) (2012): 139–56, doi: 10.1215/17432197-1572030; Marco Abel, "Speeding across the Rhizome: Deleuze Meets Kerouac On the Road," *Modern Fiction Studies* 48 (2) (2002): 227–56, doi: 10.1353/mfs.2002.0012.
9   Jack Kerouac, *Selected Letters, 1940–1956*, ed. Ann Charters (New York: Viking, 1995), 315.
10 Theado asserts that for Kerouac "the performance of typing was one with the act of writing." Theado, "Revisions of Kerouac," 13. For a contextualized view of Kerouac's relationship to and prowess in typing, see Theado's subchapter "A Lightning Typist" (ibid., 11–14).
11 Rosa, "Social Acceleration," 12.
12 Kerouac, *Selected Letters, 1940–1956*, 315.
13 John Clellon Holmes, "The Great Rememberer," in *Empty Phantoms. Interviews and Encounters with Jack Kerouac*, ed. Paul Maher (New York: Thunder's Mouth Press, 2005), 130.
14 See Mortenson, "Beating Time."
15 See Mikelli, "Passing Everybody and Never Halting," 147–52.
16 On surveillance capitalism, see Shoshana Zuboff, *The Age of Surveillance Capitalism: The Fight for a Human Future at the New Frontier of Power* (New York: PublicAffairs, 2019).
17 Jack Kerouac, *On the Road: The Original Scroll*, ed. Howard Cunnell (Modern Classics. London: Penguin Books, 2008), 324.
18 Mikelli, "Passing Everybody and Never Halting," 143–4.
19 Ross Goodwin, Kendric McDowell, and Hélène Planquelle, *1 the Road* (Paris: Jean Boîte éditions, 2018), 28.
20 Ibid.
21 On Kerouac's literary references, see Julien Nègre, "La ligne et la carte: visions de l'espace américain dans *Sur la route* de Jack Kerouac," in *L'espace du Nouveau Monde. Mythologies et ancrages territoriaux* (Rennes: Presses universitaires de Rennes, 2013), 73–86, doi: 10.4000/books.pur.86549.
22 Goodwin, McDowell, and Planquelle, *1 the Road*, 28, 30.
23 Ibid., 18.
24 Ibid., 49.
25 Ibid., 55, 99.
26 Through data processing, the road morphs into other architectural or spatial elements—"the white line of stairs" (ibid., 56), "the white line on the side of the building" (ibid., 63), "a white line on the ground began to begin" (ibid., 72), "a white line on the floor" (ibid., 136, 140)—or achieves complete fusion with the line—"the road is white in the back seat of the corridor" (ibid., 74), "the road is white and deserted" (ibid., 87).
27 Matthew Kirschenbaum, "Spec Acts: Reading Form in Recurrent Neural Networks," *ELH* 88 (2) (2021): 372, doi: 10.1353/elh.2021.0010.

28 Isaac Gewirtz, *Beatific Soul: Jack Kerouac on the Road* (New York: The New York Public Library, 2007); Theado, "Revisions of Kerouac"; R. J. Ellis, "'Dedicated to America, Whatever That Is': Kerouac's Versions of *On the Road*," in *What's Your Road, Man?: Critical Essays on Jack Kerouac's* On the Road, ed. Hilary Holladay and Robert Holton (Carbondale: Southern Illinois University Press, 2009), 118-38.
29 See Goodwin's "narrated reality" site section: https://rossgoodwin.com/narratedreality/ and "Adventures in Narrated Reality" (2016).
30 Tim Hunt, *Kerouac's Crooked Road: Development of a Fiction* (Berkeley: University of California Press, 1996), 2.
31 Ibid.
32 Rosa, "Social Acceleration," 6.
33 Jeff Rose, Brett Lashua, and Bonnie Pang expended on that issue in "Leisure as Surveillance, and the Surveillance of Leisure," *Leisure Sciences* 45 (2) (2023), doi: 10.1080/01490400.2023.2200153.
34 Zuboff compares AI (or machine intelligence) to a factory. This computational apparatus is fed by volumes and varieties of data (i.e., economies of scale and of scope). The products produced by this AI are computational products, which compute predictive behavioral data.
35 Hilary Holladay and Robert Holton, eds., *What's Your Road, Man? Critical Essays on Jack Kerouac's* On the Road (Carbondale: Southern Illinois University Press, 2009), ix.
36 Goodwin, McDowell, and Planquelle, *1 the Road*, 57.
37 Ibid., 89.
38 Ibid., 41.
39 Ibid., 85.
40 Marc Augé, *Non-lieux: Introduction à une anthropologie de la modernité* (Paris: Le Seuil, 1992).
41 For an in-depth exploration of Kerouac's roads, see Lars Erik Larson, "Free Ways and Straight Roads: The Interstates of Sal Paradise and 1950s America," in *What's Your Road, Man?: Critical Essays on Jack Kerouac's* On the Road, ed. Hilary Holladay and Robert Holton (Carbondale: Southern Illinois University Press, 2009), 35-59. Larson suggests that Kerouac's novel might be seen as part of a larger call for a new national circulatory system.
42 Kerouac, *The Original Scroll*, 211.
43 Larson, "Free Ways and Straight Roads," 39.
44 Rosa, "Social Acceleration," 26.
45 Mortenson, "Beating Time," 53.
46 Ibid., 52.
47 Goodwin, McDowell, and Planquelle, *1 the Road*, 106.
48 Allen Ginsberg and Bill Morgan, *Deliberate Prose: Selected Essays, 1952-1995* (New York: HarperCollins Publishers, 2000), 109.
49 Kerouac, *The Original Scroll*, 217, 231.
50 Neal Cassady, *The First Third & Other Writings*, Rev. & exp. edn. (San Francisco: City Lights, 1981), 195-6.
51 Michael Hrebeniak, *Action Writing: Jack Kerouac's Wild Form* (Carbondale: Southern Illinois University Press, 2006), 170.
52 Lawrence Ferlinghetti, *A Coney Island of the Mind: Poems*, New Directions Paperback 74 (New York: New Directions Publ. Corp., 1998), 30.

53 Zuboff, *The Age of Surveillance Capitalism*, 202.
54 Kirschenbaum, "Spec Acts," 368.
55 Goodwin, McDowell, and Planquelle, *1 the Road*, 57.
56 Ibid., 63–4.
57 Ibid., 48.
58 Kirschenbaum, "Spec Acts," 362.

13

Kerouac's Enduring Influence on Anglo-American Popular Music Composers and Performers

Simon Warner

In the spring of 1978, I arrived in the Massachusetts town of Lowell, a one time mill town of industrial importance with textile production employing significant numbers of its population. But this young Englishman in New England was then largely unaware of its blue-collar past beyond its entanglements with an author who was growing up there in the 1920s and 1930s.

Not that anyone in those anonymous afternoon streets had any real grasp or knowledge of its most famous son. My friend and I, recent college graduates who had spent the previous year laboring on construction sites to fund this transatlantic journey, were on a mission to track the trail of Jack Kerouac. But initial exchanges left us feeling despondent.

Kerouac, already dead by almost a decade as we arrived in his boyhood city, seemed to have made little impression on the ordinary men and women we met in shops or cafés or in bars as we played pool in a bid to fit in with the Main Street ambience.

Had they heard of him? Did they know members of his family, surviving or otherwise? Where was he buried? The responses were disappointingly unhelpful, even deliberately deflective. He was either already forgotten or locals were determined to blank this individual they saw as a runaway drunk, a man who had spent much of his errant life *leaving* Lowell, from their minds.

The day was gray, and we were already tired travelers having quite recently arrived in New York City and then Greyhound bussed from there to Boston and on to this relative backwater. We were, in our small way, living out the highway-hopping dream of Sal Paradise and Dean Moriarty—the fictional names of Kerouac and his great friend Neal Cassady—in the ground breaking 1957 novel *On the Road*, the figurehead account of that radical literary community known as the Beat Generation.

But I suppose we lacked the sophistication, the confidence, the persistence, to turn our literary pilgrimage into a transformative homage. As the evening fell dark, we finally discovered Nicky's Bar, the pub where the brother of Kerouac's third wife Stella Sampas held court. However, just as we arrived, we encountered a friendly reporter for the *Lowell Sun*.

He was pleased to make our acquaintance—Anglos were less familiar in the American hinterland then—yet he was more concerned about our welfare, warning us that two out-of-town longhairs were not likely to be that welcome in this brawling, bruising boozer. In short, he recommended we get out of town *toute suite* and offered us a ride to a bus depot where we could take an overnight ride into Canada. We took his tip.

The decades rolled on but my interest in Kerouac never really dipped. Early in the new millennium, I befriended his nephew Jim Sampas, one time singer-songwriter who became a successful record producer, and, in 2009, I returned to Lowell and, with this relative as my guide, finally visited the novelist's grave, not to mention the impressive commemorative garden which now proudly celebrates his connection to this reviving community.

And then, forty years after that initial, unproductive foray, I co-edited, with Sampas, by now Literary Executor of the author's Estate, a book entitled *Kerouac on Record: A Literary Soundtrack*, a celebration of the ways in which the writer and music have shared such a fertile connection: firstly, in the author's own immersion in jazz particularly and then, secondly, through the impact he has had on several generations of singers, songwriters, and bands from the 1960s onwards and well on into the new century.

In this chapter, I intend to consider again that relationship, specifically Kerouac's association with a stream of important artists, operating in the fields of rock and folk, country and blues, punk and new wave and beyond, not genres with which he had any direct association or affinity but styles that drew on his creative power, his writerly energy, his vision of individual possibility, that has inspired so many to not just read his words but to transfer the passions of the page into many realms of popular music of the last fifty and more years.

From Bob Dylan, perhaps most notably, to Tom Waits, maybe most diligently, from the Grateful Dead to the Doors and Van Morrison, David Bowie and Patti Smith to Sonic Youth, 10,000 Maniacs and Death Cab for Cutie to the Hold Steady, the Low Anthem to Fences, there is a potent, genre-vaulting genealogy of composers and groups, major and minor, keen to acknowledge a link or debt to that frenetic Kerouac consciousness, as determined traveler and voluminous documenter of his own picaresque life.

Worth noting, too, that there is an ongoing and living list of examples of Kerouac—and Cassady, too—being cited or mentioned in recordings of the later twentieth and early twenty-first centuries: an incredible 450-strong gathering to date which reflects an enduring desire in the broad rock'n'roll community to celebrate this excited, expansive, frequently exuberant, often experimental, wordsmith.

And then there are actual album-length collections paying tribute to Kerouac's pervasive presence in the creative minds of the rock community: the remarkable *Kerouac: Kicks Joy Darkness*, released in 1997, taps into the fiction and poetry of the writer and engages a cast of musicians, writers, and actors to adapt, interpret, and celebrate those words in myriad manners, while *One Fast Move or I'm Gone*, the 2009 record by Ben Gibbard and Jay Farrar, takes verbatim text from the novel *Big Sur* and sets those sections to an Americana soundtrack.

It is particularly poignant that we consider these matters now: Kerouac's Centennial has just been commemorated—he was born in Lowell in 1922—and I want here to examine his enduring influence, focusing on the reasons so many musical voices have been marked, been charged, been driven, by the novelist's passionate expressions in print—his multiple autobiographical novels, his vivid essays and travelogues, and his highly charged poetry—plus his powerful spoken word records. A century is a huge time block in the sweep of popular culture, an area of cultural practice we traditionally couple with the fleeting, the ephemeral, the swiftly forgotten, and so for this writer to be still stimulating creative responses is a potent tribute to his lasting impact.

How can we characterize this impact? For some, the power of Kerouac rests in the symbolism of the road derived crucially, of course, from the title and content of his key novel *On the Road*. Concepts of travel, movement, escape, which motivated the restless spirit of the novelist himself, can be regarded as metaphorical enactments of the arc of life itself—from birth to youth, maturity to death—but also as literal features of the live musician's experience: touring, gigging, moving on, the transient fate of the performing artist.

But there are other ways in which Kerouac's effect is imparted: the singer-songwriter, from blues through country and rock, often draws attention to the excitement but also the regrets engendered in the lure of the highway. To head for the horizon, the next adventure, is necessarily to cut ties with last night or last month, with the prospect of friendships or romances being left behind in the dust of your tires. Kerouac's odysseys are both celebrations of what is to come and nostalgia for what has probably been lost forever.

Such notions are noticeably evident in Dylan's "Tangled Up in Blue" (1975), Waits and Primus's "On the Road" (1999), the Dead's "Truckin'" (1970), Joni Mitchell's "Coyote" (1976), and Gibbard and Farrar's "California Zephyr" (2009) to name only a bare few: the theme of the journey, moving toward a new object, is a frequent feature.

Jazz, too, has something of this quality and, for Kerouac, that music was his ultimate touchstone. He tried to bring to his own descriptive craft to a spontaneous prose which echoed the extemporization of his saxophone heroes like Charlie Parker, Lester Young, and Lee Konitz.

But jazz was only one musical attraction he cited: the ballads of Hollywood and Broadway, orchestral scores, R&B and the roots sounds of America were appealing to him, too. Rock might have been outside his field of taste even if his later years coincided with the Beatles's greatest work. That said, his lifelong appreciation of the innovative, his own quest for cutting-edge art, suggests that he could have been more open-eared to the new developments in 1960s popular music than we strictly know.

Yet there is an inescapable paradox in this model of inspiration, Kerouac's transgenerational connection with a later musical scene. The new rock culture which emerged in the mid-1960s—a marked progression from the original seeds of 1950s rock 'n' roll with its teen emphasis and focus on adolescent romance—was significantly derived from a new political consciousness.

The spirit of the times, sparked by developments in race and sexual relations, the eruption of anti-war rhetoric and activism and the public debate over drugs, infiltrated not only Western youth generally but many influential musical acts who pinned their colors to the new mood of resistance. Many of the acts from Dylan to the Beatles, the Doors to the Dead and Jefferson Airplane became sonic embodiments of these waves of protest.

For Kerouac in the closing years of his life, this behavior was unforgivably antisocial. He hated the fact that his tales of wandering, his quest for individual freedom, had become a guiding light to the hippies, a subculture that would both engage with the controversial arguments of the day and turn that battalion of singers and guitarists into their galvanizing heroes.

Kerouac's innate conservatism became his critical beacon, as he railed against these rebellious forces. He emphasized his Republican tendencies, supported the military in Southeast Asia, and feared that the arrival of psychedelics—LSD was the great mind-expanding narcotic attracting most attention—was a communist plot sown to corrupt the minds of America's younger generation.

I've been in conversation with journalists and biographers, historians and commentators, who have written about Kerouac and music, too, to get a sense of why his influence persists, what it is about the author which attracts rolling phases of young musicians to pin their affiliations to his reputation.

What is it with respect to this innovative prose master, this saint of the open highway, that continues to light the blue touch paper of inspiration over five decades after his premature demise at the age of forty-seven in the early autumn of 1969? What, in Kerouac's writing, life and art, beliefs and attitudes, has managed to so capture the imagination of so many generations of popular music makers?

Marian Jago, Lecturer in Popular Music and Jazz Studies at Edinburgh University and currently preparing a book dedicated to the writer's relationship to jazz, says: "Kerouac stands as the embodiment of the American dream of freedom. A freedom which is so often expressed as freedom-in-mobility. America's sense of itself as exceptional in part rests upon the idea that if things get too bad you can always just head out and try your luck someplace new."

She adds: "This idea is at the heart of Turner's 1890s frontier thesis and is written into every American hero from Daniel Boone to John Wayne to Bruce Springsteen. Movement and second chances."

Brian Hassett, a Grateful Dead specialist and author of "the Beat Trilogy"—*The Hitchhiker's Guide to Jack Kerouac, How the Beats Begat the Pranksters* and *On the Road with Cassadys*—distils the message still further: "Kerouac is The Road. Kerouac is freedom. Kerouac is the search."

He points out:

> Even Barack Obama, when discussing his latest book in 2020, said, 'When I think about my own work, I have been shaped—just as my character has been shaped—by that quintessential Jack Kerouac open road lookin' West seeing what's next, or in the case of Frederick Douglass lookin' North to see what's next, but in either way, wanting to break the chains of whatever constraints we were born into and bound to.'

"Kerouac has sort of replaced Mark Twain as the quintessential go-to American Adventurist," Hassett believes. "And music is about adventure, and exploration, and emotion, and going furthur (as the Kesey gang spelled it). Music is about passion, and playfulness, and breaking the rules, and singing in all its meanings, and expanding on themes, and dancing in rhythms. These are all things this Beat Generation writer has in spades."

Matt Theado, Professor of American Literature and Culture at Kobe City University, Japan, who has recently overseen a major Kerouac exhibition in his adopted city, comments: "Most songwriters who know Kerouac read *On the Road* at a formative time in their lives. When they were young and aspiring performers, they got ahold of *On the Road* and saw a possible life."

"Get up off that couch, Kerouac told them. You can go out, you can meet people, you can live it up. And if you're blessed, somewhere along the way, the pearl will be handed to you. In the 1960s and '70s most rockers were young men, and like Sal Paradise, they knew they'd find 'girls, visions, everything.'"

The author's rejection of convention is also picked up by long-time music journalist Holly George-Warren, who edited *The Rolling Stone Book of the Beats* and is currently working on a major new biography of Kerouac, with the writer's Estate archives opened up for her investigative scrutiny.

She explains: "He embraced 'the other' during post-World War II America when the mainstream message was the opposite: conformity, upward mobility and materialism. His call that 'the road is life', his musical ear and literary innovations—spontaneous prose and 'sketching'—have resonated with readers and musicians since the late 1950s and in the ensuing decades as they discover his work."

Yet, for all this talk of ground breaking resistance to expectations and the norms of the day, few would disagree Kerouac descended into rambling conservatism in the 1960s. He took great exception to the counterculture and its anti-military position in Vietnam demos and was particularly affronted to be identified as a talisman by the new hippy nation. He even took the view that the mental distortions created by taking acid was part of a communist plot, hatched in the Soviet Union, to pollute the attitudes of his nation's students and adolescents.

Mark Bliesener, who organizes Denver's annual Neal Cassady "Birthday Bash," coined the band name Dead Kennedys, and is a fifty-year veteran of the music business, offers a more controversial take on the writer's perceived radicalism. "Since Kerouac's 1950s coronation as the angriest of the 'angry young men,' writers of both music and literature have been attracted to Kerouac's jazz influenced, improvisational use of language, along with the over hyped perceived cache of Kerouac's 'cool.'"

But Bliesener counters the perceived wisdom: "In reality, the heart beating inside this hedonistic 'rebel' was actually that of a classically conservative, French-Canadian Catholic 'momma's boy.'" Kerouac famously drifted back to his mother's kitchen each time his cross-country odysseys left him tired, penniless, and hungry, so the image of the freewheeling journeyman is something of a misnomer.

That said, Paul Marion, Lowell-based academic and poet, editor of Kerouac collection *Atop an Underwood* and advocate of both the writer and city, calls for more balanced understanding of these Oedipal tensions. He argues: "The rendering of

Kerouac as pathetically mother-tied is a portrait that might be touched up by now. There's no arguing with the life facts, however, a more sympathetic or even practical view might see Kerouac as single-minded in his devotion to writing, which requires making financial and even personal sacrifice."

Marion expands: "Holding on to the hearth with meals and heat and laundry service and a cat at close hand can be seen as making your own one-man writer-in-residence set up. He did his field work, took notes, and circled back to the stable domestic scene to do his focused writing. This is not consistent, of course, but there is a pattern."

Meanwhile, author Pat Thomas, the man behind acclaimed countercultural histories *Did It!*, the Jerry Rubin biography, and *Listen Whitey!*, a survey of black power and its musical soundtrack, has a simple theory why Kerouac's later life views have not deterred progressive music makers. "His classic books do not contain that kind of political conservatism," he explains, "and you'd have to read a few biographies and some essays to know that. So personally, I don't find it surprising that it's been overlooked."

Setting aside these anomalies—and which star whether literary, cinematic, or musical doesn't have contradictions in their personality—what do we think a singer or a songwriters is doing or trying to say by referencing Kerouac? What is the motivation and where is the value?

Jerry Cimino, Founder of the Beat Museum in San Francisco, remarks: "When someone references Kerouac, they're telling the world that they're hip to what he represented to so many and for so long. Whether they know his whole life or not, a casual observer likely appreciates that he was important to the culture, they have some idea of his influence, and that he had a big impact on many other people."

Brian Hassett cites a chain of influence.

> They're leaving breadcrumbs, baby. That's how I first found him. One person mentions him, and it's just some guy mentioning a book. Then you see the name again. And then again. And pretty soon it's like, 'I gotta find this book!' That's what these musicians are doing. They know their thousands or millions of fans hang on their every lyric. They're leaving clues and pointers. Just like Jack kept mentioning Charlie Parker. He was intentionally directing his readers to another great artist in a different medium.

Hassett goes on: "Jack stressed Whitman and Wolfe and Proust 'cause he knew he didn't come out of nowhere. It proves that these musicians are aware they've just taken the baton and are carrying it for their short run—and that this flame has been touched off from one to another since art began."

Ronna Johnson, long-established Beat scholar and Professor of English, Tufts University, Medford, Massachusetts, develops reasons still further, describing a number of messages that can be encoded when the Kerouac myth is summoned, including "bohemian deracination" or homelessness, the "anti-bourgeois" roots of a singer-performer, an "anti-domestic ethic," American Romanticism itself, and also the spiritual concerns often entwined with this literary territory, from Catholicism to Zen Buddhism.

But if the ideology is potent and the ideas expressed through the novels and the poetry in the songs they inspire authentically sought and powerfully wrought, isn't the actual medium—young men with guitars in amplified bands—all too gender specific and rather limited in its artistic canvas?

Pat Thomas cannot help but agree.

Come on! It can't be that surprising it's a man-thing! It's all about men! Men having sex with women, men having bromances with other men. Men leaving their women behind for kicks, thrills and what-not. I wouldn't call it homoerotic, but men often enjoy hanging out with other men—go to a bar, or a football game or on a fishing trip and tell me what you see!

Further, Bliesener argues that the Beat crowd were actually rock stars before the concept had even taken shape. "Long before the coinage of the often misused term 'rock star', Kerouac, Cassady, Burroughs, Ginsberg and others were already such forces. Via their non-conforming outsider stance, drug use, sexual liberation and rejection of the existing status quo, they conceptualized for the masses an image of the stand-alone outsider rebel or 'rock star.'"

"Like the swashbucklers and cowboy heroes predating them, the Beats, and Kerouac in particular, came to represent this manifestation of a 'pirate' or alternative lifestyle, which in the late 1940s offered a dangerously flamboyant and visionary roadmap to the more psychedelic and apocalyptic times and writers to come."

However, Brian Hassett cannot concur with the view that the music that has grown out of the Beat soil is so guitar-centered or indeed just about men expressing themselves. "I don't see it as 'guitar-centered'. Bob Dylan, Van Morrison, Donovan, Graham Parker, Ian Dury, Tom Waits, Patti Smith, David Byrne, Natalie Merchant, for instance, are all singers."

"Dizzy Gillespie, Ella Fitzgerald, David Amram, Mark Murphy, Fatboy Slim, the Beastie Boys, Lydia Lunch, Billy Joel, Medeski, Martin & Wood, Everything But the Girl, Rusted Root and so on sure as hell aren't 'guitar-centric.'"

"Nor is it just 'rock' by any stretch. Ramblin' Jack, Paul Simon, Eric Andersen, Jeff Buckley, the Waterboys, Loudon Wainwright, Richard Thompson, Aztec Two-Step—that's all singer-songwriter folk, man."

"And not fer nuthin but it ain't just 'men' either. Get this straight, man, and don't keep perpetuating the male myth. I mentioned Ella & Patti & Natalie & Lydia above—but also Julianna Hatfield & Maggie Estep & ruth weiss & Dayna Kurta, or that Gretchen Peters I just found last week."

"This is not gender specific. Don't present it as such. The striking thing is the very opposite of this question's premise. Yeah, some musicians who cite him play rock—but the beautiful thing is he inspires people in hip hop, jazz, pop, folk, alternative, fusion, you name it."

Nonetheless, despite Hassett's reassuringly upbeat reading of the current state of play, we might find some common ground in the notion that the decline of the guitar-focused rock band in the opening decades of the twenty-first century might mean that Kerouac's reputation as an inspiration will decline.

Marian Jago is not so sure. "Not necessarily," she comments.

> I also don't think the decline of the guitar-focused rock band is properly as big a deal as people sometime claim (jazz is also dead, right?). I think if Kerouac faces trouble/potential lessening of influence it will be due to the treatment of women and African Americans in his work which, while appropriate to their times, are now quite questionable to the extent that, for many, Kerouac won't be able to be read without considerable unpacking.

Jonah Raskin, leading Beat historian, poet, and the author of *American Scream* and the novel *Beat Blues, San Francisco, 1955*, puts it in more straightforward terms: "I think his influence has already declined in the Black Lives Matter era we are in. He's a white guy."

Pat Thomas surveys the bigger picture, stating that

> for so many reasons, it will decline. Some now see Kerouac as politically incorrect—and I don't mean because he voted for Richard Nixon as President! I mean because of the perceived lack of respect for women. Also, when I was growing up, we did not have cable TV or internet or video games or cell phones or social media—so reading books and/or listening to records were pretty much my only two choices growing up in rural America. Now, teens have about 50 choices of what do with their time, and sadly, rarely do many of them pick up a book!

Yet, Mark Bliesener, while acknowledging that the once predominant rock band model might well be diminished in 2021, isn't pessimistic. "The fact that the guitar-based rock band is a last century idea fast fading in our collective rear view mirror, does not necessarily diminish Kerouac's impact and importance going forward. The liberation he brought to literature strongly impacts the post hip hop world of today's more rhythmic or beat driven popular culture and music."

And Hassett, once more, remains bullish based on his own experiences on the road. "You could argue he's never been bigger. And that's with pretty much all the originals being dead. I do shows all over North America, and the audiences literally span 18 to 80 years old."

"He has crossed over some line that an artist does not fall back from. Liz Taylor, Oscar Wilde, T.S. Eliot, Baryshnikov, Mozart, Dizzy, Andy Warhol, Frank Lloyd Wright ... once an artist enters that kind of stratosphere of mass public consciousness, they never cease to be there."

But to tear open another crucial can of worms in our contemporary life. Has the image of macho bravado, linked to the author and numerous of his friends, and the bromance adventures that inhabit many of his stories alienated women from Kerouac and his homosocial world?

"No, I think some women identify with Kerouac's male characters," says Holly George-Warren.

In her new book, *The Secret to Superhuman Strength*, Alison Bechdel describes the impact that Kerouac's mountain hiking scenes in *Big Sur* inspired her. Amber Tamblin, a leader of #MeToo, is one of several women who have described Kerouac's influence in the documentary, *One Fast Move and I'm Gone* ... I think many female musicians see beyond gender when being inspired or motivated by characters in novels.

Nonetheless, Ronna Johnson faces negativity toward Kerouac in the university classroom. As she explains, "young women, generationally, even those in or now contemplating earlier generations such as Gen X and Millennial, reject Kerouac. I now have female students who take my Beat seminar who want me to argue Kerouac's relevance/importance as post-war literary artist. They are entirely offended by *On the Road* itself, alone."
Yet Brian Hassett urgently challenges this general thesis of female alienation:

That is so NOT true. I noticed it in line for the premiere of the film of *On the Road* at Somerset House in London in 2012—how two-thirds of the people were young women. And I talked to a bunch of them, and they were not there for Kristen Stewart but were citing *Lonesome Traveler* and *Dharma Bums* as well as *On the Road* as pivotal books for them. Also, "Lowell Celebrates Kerouac" year after year more than 50% of the people who come solo to the festival are women. And at my many live shows a year it's damn close to a 50-50 split. It may seem surprising, but it's true.

Also, think of all the women biographers and memoirists—Carolyn Cassady, Edie Kerouac, Joyce Johnson, Ann Charters, Ann Douglas, Brenda Knight, Joan Haverty, Jan Kerouac, Diane di Prima, Helen Weaver, Hettie Jones, Eileen Kaufman, Anne Waldman, Regina Weinreich, LuAnne Henderson, Anne Murphy, whose praising book of Neal has yet to be published, and soon Holly George-Warren doing the "official" Jack biography—and who, not incidentally, all wrote GREAT books!

Marian Jago speaks from personal experience.

I'm not sure that I want to speak for all women, but I'll say that as much as I've enjoyed Kerouac (and the other Beats), I have always had to read him knowing that I was on the outside looking into a somewhat hostile room. I think a potentially more interesting question might be formulated around the treatment of African Americans in Beat works.

Mark Bliesener attempts a more historical perspective:

The Beats, like many significant societal influencers of their era were almost exclusively and aggressively male. However, though likely under-reported, many women in the 1950s did read *On the Road* and were as equally incited by its vision of emancipation and kicks. Following the cultural upheaval of the women's movement in the 1960s and 1970s, women were no longer "shamed" for worshipping at the same altar of liberation as "the boys."

In their time the Beats were strictly a boys' club, but owing to evolution and revolution, women now openly embrace a more natural affinity with the hedonism and deliverance espoused by the Beats. The same simplicity of language and unvarnished honesty which heralded the Beat renaissance certainly appeals to contemporary female taste. The plethora of new women writers now telling their personal, unvarnished truth in song, stories and film, stand as testament to this seed change.

Jerry Cimino comments:

Some people can't get beyond the dated, even misogynistic attitudes of the Beats. Plenty of people have difficulty with that, and for good reason. On the one hand, they were products of their time, and inextricable from the circumstances and attitudes of those times. Nonetheless, in the 1940s and 1950s, Kerouac was one of the more enlightened, or at the very least open-minded people at the time.

When it came to diversity, inclusiveness, racial and gender equality, the Beats were ahead of their contemporaries, even though their language and attitudes often seem dated by modern standards. In 2021, it's easy to cancel someone because they said something 50 or 70 years ago that modern sensibilities can no longer abide. But anyone who takes that position is extremely shortsighted, in my opinion.

The debates about this literary movement and its influence on half a century of music making not to mention the critical topics of gender and race and their relation to this surging cultural flow will go on for sure, but let us close this attempt to wrestle with these intriguing, and in some ways intractable, matters with a final quote, from the Beat Museum's Cimino once more.

I don't think Kerouac's reputation will suffer, regardless of changes in styles and fads and trends. Yes, his reputation has enjoyed an enhancement by the famous people who loved him and want to make a nod to him. At the same time, his reputation is very broad and deep outside of the musical world, and outside the world of lead guitarists.

The Beats, and especially Jack, seem to recapture the energies of every new generation. The themes of the Beats are youthful, experimental, adventurous, a quest for understanding, transcending things like sexual identity, or the desire for non-traditional alternatives to the status-quo.

So, 100 years have passed since Kerouac was born; well over half a century has gone since the writer died in young middle-age. Yet the myth of this literary legend has persisted despite the multiple contradictions that characterized his relatively short life. Here was the scribe of the open road, the embodiment of an unfettered freedom, never able to disentangle himself from his beloved mother, heading back to her as often as he ran away.

Kerouac, ever associated with the exhilarating mobility of the automobile, never much liked driving and of course had Neal Cassady, the most enthusiastic motorist of them all, to often take him on those anarchic criss-crossing routes around the North American continent over many years providing him with much of the material for his finest work.

He was a radical artist who conceived a writing voice that broke molds yet he longed to commemorate values of an older America, personified by the frontier adventures of Jack London and the epic prose of Thomas Wolfe. He longed to shake off the manacles of the conventional life but remained attached, engrossed even, by the power of religion, the mysticism first of Roman Catholicism and then the philosophical disciplines of Buddhism.

His mind was often tested and extended, his art stimulated, by artificial means—marijuana, Benzedrine, and other substances—but his lasting dedication was to alcohol and the addiction would lead to his early demise. Yet he regarded the chemicals that would feed minds and souls—acid particularly—as the Summer of Love blossomed as dangers to the very fabric of his nation.

The generations of rock musicians were, I think, drawn essentially to that late 1940s version of the novelist: the still-young man pursuing his most famous escapades, the pioneer poet, the eternally handsome athlete, the dark colossus standing shoulder to shoulder with his strikingly blonde conspirator, setting out to take on America and unearth all its majestic mysteries.

The transgressions of the rockers, the folkies, the punks, the country stars, who would follow in his wake and venerate him as a template for their own searches for salvation, their individual quests for truth, might ultimately have left him disappointed, disillusioned even, that his legacy had been adopted, misinterpreted even, in this way. But that would surely have been the view of the older, more jaundiced, Kerouac gripped by the tortures of a declining drunk.

Today, anyway, the guitar and its amplified gospel might seem a somewhat dated and tame combination. In the realm of popular music, the rule breakers, the headline grabbers, are the rappers on record or the DJs in the festival marquee. The spoken vocals of African-America, the dance beats of electronica, the rhythms of the world, are at the cutting edge of this dynamic culture. The open air rock festival is more heritage than state of the art.

So, can we still draw a line from the Kerouac inheritance to the present musical playing field? Well, we might argue that as long as Dylan's never-ending tour goes on, as long as Beat fans like Thurston Moore and Lee Ranaldo from Sonic Youth continue to make intriguing experimental sounds, as long as Patti Smith performs her hypnotic poetry, and as long as singer-songwriters generally forge identities and pen original songs based on creative autobiography, the spirit of Jack will survive, no longer a raging flame perhaps but still a potent flicker in our collective listening imaginations.

Note: Beat specialists Dave Moore and Horst Spandler have compiled a remarkable list of popular songs which reference Jack Kerouac and Neal Cassady. "Jack & Neal on Record" can be found here: http://www.beatbookcovers.com/music/

14

Jack Kerouac American Avatar

Ronna C. Johnson

Jack Kerouac's centennial in 2022 occasioned many tributes, evaluations, and renewed judgments. He has never been a writer who has evoked neutral responses, from the glamorization of his first review of *On the Road* in September 1957, in which Gilbert Millstein proclaimed it *The Sun Also Rises* of its postwar generation, to Norman Podhoretz's 1958 denunciation of the novel's alleged anti-intellectualism, to the academy's widespread dismissal and scholarly neglect.[1] As literary art was defenestrated by factious critical theory in the 1990s, Kerouac's great artistic creativity was devalued by anti-art nonliterary dogma, on one hand and, on the other, by indifference to and avoidance of the rigors of interpreting literary representations in favor of facile face value meanings that even in praising him underestimate the author as artist, as in the profusion of writings by amateur critics and fan-enthusiasts, and by scholars not trained in American writing and literary heritage but who revere Kerouac. Even the wayward youth initially exhilarated by *On the Road* has withdrawn its corroboration in the twenty-first century, conforming to contemporaneous cancel culture norms with regard to gender, race, and identity, and censuring Kerouac.[2] Over time, Kerouac has become less a literary figure than an idol and ideological target.

Outside the United States, however, the opposite obtains, as Kerouac has been claimed and celebrated as a "natural" inheritor of non-Anglophone literature, an heir to Rimbaud and Baudelaire rather than to his obvious American predecessors Walt Whitman and William Carlos Williams, and, as Tim Hunt saliently argues in his ground breaking 1981 study *Kerouac's Crooked Road*, to Herman Melville, Mark Twain, and F. Scott Fitzgerald.[3] The non-Anglophone, European genealogy imposed on Kerouac depends on a dubious transnationalism. This concept, popular in late-twentieth- and early-twenty-first-century literary and cultural studies for its postmodern emphasis on the local, misleadingly abets arguments about Kerouac's literary lineage and aesthetic inventions having origins in European cultures that may admire him, but that did not—and could not—have actuated his artistic emergence and character. The critical embrace of Kerouac as transnational writer has had the effect of effacing his distinguishing Americanness, misconceiving the artist's huge, hubristic literary sprawl and geographic grasp as transnational border-crossing rather than as an expression of the "manifest destiny" of the American character that Kerouac's distinctive art venerates. The transnationalist appropriation lends support to a European descent in place of, or over, Kerouac's American origins and heritage, a muscular imperialism that seizes and innovates its national influences.

It is against European presumptions to the writer as a native son, and to his concomitant, and unpersuasive, appropriation as an exponent of European "beat" literature and cultural expressions, that this essay theorizes and elaborates Jack Kerouac as American avatar in his centenary. While "avatar" personification is a trope more frequent in digital media contexts than in literary critical ones, for a centennial reclamation of an artist who has been lost to media exaggerations and mediazed fantasies of "beatdom," it suits; "avatar" tallies with the impacts and achievements of a writer of the US postmodern high-low cultural visibility and intellectual controversy of Jack Kerouac. His works' narrative formations and symbologies, far-flung geographies, and multiplicitous Whitmanic subjectivities comprise his designation as American literary avatar, and cement the appellation. In some precincts, this is doubtless a controversial gambit, but Americanists—students of the country's literary history and experts on the intricacies of its literary sensibilities—might reckon that after over fifty years of Kerouac's disavowal in his home keep, and his attempted capture abroad, his centennial provides the opportune occasion for deliberating and effectuating his return.

Many of his works attest that Kerouac is, rather than a border-crossing transnational writer, a "global" acolyte of the great "railroad earth" of the Americas—literally via the Southern Pacific Railroad, and by continental horizontal and vertical roads and routes. He is a writer in the "classic" American New World imago and its binary lineages of quest and conquest, of liberties natural and civil, and of moralities individual and communal, discourses expounded by Kerouac's American literary precursors such as Henry David Thoreau, Whitman, Melville, Nathaniel Hawthorne, Williams, and others. Kerouac's existential and geographic dynamism is an American vibration—a pulsing energy on the threshold of the discovery that F. Scott Fitzgerald mythologizes in *The Great Gatsby*: "the old island here that flowered once for Dutch sailors' eyes—a fresh, green breast of the new world" primed by wonder for the taking.[4] Kerouac celebrates such New World origins. His American vibration in *On the Road* is a cumbrous yet frenetic locomotion: looking east "before me was the great raw bulge and bulk of my American continent, somewhere far across, [was] gloomy, crazy New York" and, more illustriously lyrical, looking west "in America when the sun goes down and I sit on the old broken-down river pier watching the long, long skies over New Jersey and sense all that raw land that rolls in one unbelievable huge bulge over to the West Coast," in which a fatigued postlapsarian wonder is beatified.[5] Movement between these coastal bookends and beyond is preeminently prized. Kerouac's "Author's Introduction" to *Lonesome Traveler* lists immense "travels [that] cover the United States from the south to the east coast to the west coast to the far northwest, cover Mexico, Morocco, Africa, Paris, London";[6] this "American" scope imperialistically "covers" the world; the "railroad earth." A road-making apotheosis of a white male working-class hero, Kerouac "wrote [while] on the road, as hobo, railroader, Mexican exile";[7] he is an innovation on the American writer in the Herman Melville-Woody Guthrie-Jack London tradition of journeyman explorer/recorder.

The Kerouac American avatar configures a panoptic subjectivity, the individual as autonomous agent of wide-ranging locales. This white male subject is a postwar personification and dilation of a familiar American trope of the hobo storyteller, one who refashions the modernist artist-hero into the hybrid postmodern character-narrator, transmuting a writer-inventor into a teller who invents from immediate "life." This American subjectivity is particularly available to a Western white man of Kerouac's unique mid-twentieth-century generation, one that is balanced on a brink defined by a pivotal before-and-after interval, the advent and then deployment of the atomic bomb. Kerouac was born in 1922 into an existential security that was undermined by the Great Depression, then devastated by Hiroshima and Nagasaki, and, in a different key, by Auschwitz-Birkenau. Kerouac's American birth date marks a liminal point between an innocence that was spoiled for him when he was four years old by the death of his older brother Gerard in 1926 (see *Visions of Gerard*, 1963) and an atomic catastrophe in the antique postlapsarian apocalyptic sense that spoiled the innocence of the world in 1945. Kerouac was of the last generation to know pre-Bomb insularity from global annihilation, and then to know from that vantage the annihilation itself: the American "wild self-believing individuality" that "had begun to disappear around the end of World War II with so many great guys dead"; "so many were killed—from Lowell—for nothing."[8] In this he is a paramount twentieth-century avatar of American containment. But that was transient, and even if it chimes too well with a now-discredited, implausible American exceptionalism, it augured a rebirth with the emergence of the American postmodern in arts and culture anticipated and embodied by the compelling, propulsive writings of Jack Kerouac.

An American avatar, Jack Kerouac, whose life began in 1922 in Lowell, Massachusetts and was extinguished in 1969 in St. Petersburg, Florida is a personification of America and of being American; perhaps he is the final such twentieth-century American writer, as expatriation and the postmodern blurring of cultural and national boundaries relocated and reoriented many of his peers and successors. His pivotal generational position ensured a complicated literary subjectivity reflected in his art. Kerouac is a latest embodiment of a classic trope of the national litterateur, R. W. B. Lewis's American writer as American Adam,[9] a writer created and creating himself from an historic past and a present moment of composition—an Adamic artist who names the (postwar) New World. His self-generating vision established the multi-volume Duluoz Legend, an heroic—epic—American literary poetics and consciousness that encompasses a pre- and post-Second World War life, and at the same time persists as a challenge to it in the postmodern playfulness, genre swapping, and technical hybridity of its masterpiece volume, *Visions of Cody* (written 1952; published 1972). His legacy is complicated and antipodean in what becomes a hallmark of postmodern malleability—the contingency and uncertainty enshrined in his mind by mortal termination. A self-contradictory "America" as discourse, ideology, and nation coexists in Kerouac's work with a simultaneous questioning of classic literary forms as codified in the writer's 1953 manifesto, "Essentials of Spontaneous Prose," which anticipates other radical shifts of the post-Bomb era, such as Abstract Expressionism and Pop in the visual arts.[10] An incongruity with, even a negation of, his romanticization of the artist—he "[a]lways considered writing my duty on earth"[11]—dovetails with Kerouac's intimation of the postmodern turn that came with the atomic disaster, and that found later expression in the install-and-subvert double move that Linda Hutcheon theorized as postmodern, a turn that was quantified in Kerouac before it was named "postmodern."[12] By his liminal position on the existential divide of the invention and deployment of the atomic bomb, Kerouac was born a forerunner of postwar artistic evolutions; he was culturally, genetically, a pre-postmodern artist.[13]

Texts Kerouac wrote contemporaneously with his 1951 scroll typescript of *On the Road*, and before the 1957 Viking Press publication that brought him blinding notoriety, furnish a context for appraising his centenary legacy. With the preliminary novel *The Town and the City* published finally in 1950, the stories "Mexico Fellaheen" and "The Railroad Earth" written in 1952 and collected in *Lonesome Traveler*, and the novel *The Subterraneans* written in 1953 stand out to offer cosmogonies of the Kerouac idiom that host and inscribe the distinctive narrative tropes and symbologies, the geographies, and the multiplicitous Whitmanic subjectivities that comprise his designation as American avatar. Later texts such as *Satori in Paris* (1966), as well as *Maggie Cassidy* (1959) and *Visions of Gerard* (1963), contribute to this American expression. The "American" Kerouac exemplifies consists in and is characterized by: hybridity of languages, of cultural competencies, and of kinetic identities; indigenous descent; immigrant lineage and national origins; and quest and conquest goals and designs, such as Kerouac's great writer/great athlete ambitions. Narrative tropes populating the Kerouac idiom are exemplified in "Mexico Fellaheen" in border geopolitics and cannabis, in a bull fight and a rabbit's foot, in the Crucifixion and the actor Robert Mitchum that Americanize Mexico; are found in "The Railroad Earth" in football plays and jazz riffs, railroad lingoes, and Buddhist aphorisms, and in San Francisco disguising New York City redbrick byways. Poetry and prose conflated in pre-postmodern modes that reflect postwar American shifts are discursivized in *The Subterraneans* in displays of white obliviousness to race and devotion to jazz styles, writing and street spectacles, misogynous love and loss, solitude and community that hipsterize America. Such jagged binaries recombine in Kerouac's representation of narrating subjects, quantums of his identity as American avatar. They bear witness to the fact that Kerouac is foremost an artist, not a philosopher or thinker, nor an ideologue.

Satori in Paris attests to a further essential Americanness manifested by its narrative telling of the classic national incapacity, enshrined by Thomas Wolfe, an important model for writing *The Town and the City*, in his 1934 novel published posthumously in 1940, *You Can't Go Home Again*, that commemorates the thwarted return "home."[14] For Kerouac as American avatar, the failures of the search in France for his European identity origins and roots, and the confusion about the illumination or satori he seeks and maybe experiences, attest to the writer's inescapable Americanness; they are measures of his American Dream. With the exception of indigenes, "Americans"— most—are born of immigrants to America, and of the persistent nostalgic wish, the obsessive though futile desire, to connect to cultures, languages, and countries of origins. This nostalgia for *temps perdu* especially plagues the first American-born generation. Kerouac's claims to indigeneity, his concerns with his Bretonesque origins and his noble ancestor, his pastiche of first spoken languages (European French and Québécois French), all attest to a classic American identification.[15] Kerouac is an avatar of the desire to be America and all that that entails for him—the all-American athlete, the ambivalent Merchant Marine, the great American literary rememberer redeeming life from darkness.

Kerouac aspired to write the Great American Novel; that was also of his American Dream. He gave his life to that aspirational "duty," literally refusing all connections or commitments—paternity, friendships, marriages—when they became obstacles more than means to realizing that ambition.[16] His juvenilia, his letters, his writing journals, his novels, poetry, and confessions to others, all attest to two central aspects of his genius: the absolute and cardinal importance of writing, and the complexity of being American.[17] He conceived of himself as an American multivocal artist—"The modern young writer [is] ... faced with the problem of many voices in America"[18]—who must respond to its specific obligations. Kerouac's consciousness of being American dominates his writing, both published and unpublished. "I have begun a huge study of the face of America itself ... My subject as a writer is of course America ... I must know everything about it."[19] He did not conceive of himself as an American writer in an antipodal relation to America, in the sense that Allen Ginsberg inhabited in his poem "America." There the poet-speaker is a subject to an object America, as in this apostrophe addressed to a second person "America" ("you"), which is variously structured as an object-entity, a lover, even a separate but inferior subject, as, for example:

America I've given you all and now I'm nothing ....
Go fuck yourself with your atom bomb.
I don't feel good don't bother me ....
America when will you be angelic? ...
I'm sick of your insane demands.[20]

Kerouac's America is not an addressee in binary opposition to the writer-poet-declaimer, as in Ginsberg's iconic poem, but the one and same self as the artist that elevates his personal national vision to an inalienable national signifier, "America." In *The Town and the City* Kerouac "wanted a universal American story .... [the novel] was an American story."[21] The American neo-beat punk rock poet and musician Patti Smith deconstructed this bid for universalism a generation later in her manifesto, "Babelogue," which breaks it down to composites: "in heart i am an american. in heart i am moslem. in heart i am an american artist and i have no guilt .... i have not sold myself to god" ("Babelogue");[22] Smith inveighs that she has not bartered her agency for transubstantiation; her national- for pan-identity. She stands *sui generis*, unbeholden to any authority, even her early biblical education as Jehovah Witness, as Kerouac could not do, raised in a devout Catholicism that he later seasoned—or mitigated—with Buddhist beliefs and practices.[23] Yet unlike Smith, Kerouac is not severable from America; not a *sui generis* artist but one intrinsically attached to the groundings of his life-art. Kerouac's narrators celebrate what is found and seen—in Dean Moriarty or Mardou Fox or Maggie Cassidy; in Des Moines or Central City or San Francisco—and what is attached to these as opposed to the later postmodern artist, *pace* Smith, who is defiantly (and guiltlessly) stationed apart from such sources and contexts. Kerouac figures as the American soul and spirit, naming himself such and acquitting himself as American writer on the road, in jazz clubs, in bohemian enclaves. In Kerouac the American body is rendered with and through the mind of the artist's literary productions and performances.

What kind of America—and American—did Kerouac exemplify, and devote his writing to (self-)confessing? Like the canonical literatures his work descends from, he was a "classic" American, comprising ethnic and national mixed origins, foundational tropes of the storied historical "American." Kerouac descends from both the indigenous and the immigrant, combining in his figure a self that is always already there and one that is always already arriving. Kerouac specifically claimed French aristocratic blood as well as indigenous heritage. He was of the First Nations of the Americas, the French Canadian Caughnawaga, whose territory lay in southern Québec, and the Mohawk, whose lands straddled the border between New York and Canada; he was also of immigrant naturalized peoples of European and Québécois descent. In the "Author's Introduction" to *Lonesome Traveler* he writes, "My people go back to Breton France, first North American ancestor Baron Alexander Louis Lebris de Kerouac of Cornwall, Brittany, 1750 or so, was granted land along the Riviere du Loup after victory of Wolfe over Montcalm; his descendants married Indians (Mohawk and Caughnawaga) and became potato farmers."[24] With a descent from the New World quest that concluded in its conquest and colonization, Kerouac was of the class that committed the genocide of indigenous peoples and colonized their lands, a galling and common New World dual phenomenon, to be of both the oppressor and the oppressed classes. Which brings to mind origins of African Americans who may descend from both the slaver and the enslaved.

Kerouac frequently claims or alludes to his indigenous heritage. His persona Jacky Duluoz was a "kid ... with just a touch of the Canuck half-Indian doubt and suspicion of all things non-Canuck, non-half-Indian."[25] Kerouac devotes *Satori in Paris* to the unsuccessful search for his Breton roots that posit noble Old World ancestry: "As in an earlier autobiographical book I'll use my real name here, full name in this case, Jean-Louis Lebris de Kerouac, because this story is about my search for this name in France."[26] His entwined North American indigenous and European immigrant ancestry is fundamentally, foundationally New World American, and Kerouac makes a granular parsing of this descent. He derives from Québécois peoples and culture directly through his parents, both of whom were born in Québec and emigrated from there to Nashua, New Hampshire, and from there to Lowell, Massachusetts. This descent fills stories. In "Search by Night" (circa 1962), men "lustily greet each other in a vulgar & ugly jargon called New England French-Canadian ... prattling incoherently, half the time in coarse & obscene N.E. French-Canadian, half of the time in rowdy, faulty English."[27] Kerouac's first language was *joual* or "French-Canadian French ... definitely a dialect of its own" according to the scholar of folklore and the oral tradition, Brigitte Lane, who notes the "languagey language" used in the Québec community in Lowell.[28] As the narrator of *The Subterraneans* tells it, "I am a Canuck, I could not speak English till I was 5 or 6, at 16 I spoke with a halting accent";[29] in a 1950 letter Kerouac writes that "(I never spoke

English before I was six or seven). At 21 I was still somewhat awkward and illiterate-sounding in my speech and writing."[30] And even without speaking a tribal language, or coming up in the tribes of his descent, Kerouac perceives a mixture of multiple ethnic origins he cannot quite square: "I'm not American, nor West European, somehow I feel like an Indian, a North American Exile in North America ... maybe because I have an Indian great-great-grandmother—or have strong Quebec Plain Peasant feeling."[31] He could identify specific European ancestries and named as his "first United States descendant [sic., ancestor] my grandfather Jean-Baptiste, [a] carpenter [in] Nashua N.H.—my father's mother a Bernier related to explorer Bernier—all Bretons on father's side—My mother has a Norman name, L'Evesque,"[32] providing micro-specificity to his French Québécois descent. His assiduous accounting of his several ethnic, regional, and national origins emphasizes his Americanness and establishes its classic multiplicities of identity and their vintage; it is not an abstract or generic identity, nor a recent one, but a variegated and individualized set of genotypic departure points that combine in the writer born in Lowell, Massachusetts in 1922.

Kerouac's bilingualism as well as his concomitant biculturalism are coming into study[33] and are significantly implicated in his Americanness and literary commitment to writing the "American" novel. Kerouac had three languages, at least—*joual* French-Canadian French; northeastern New England Lowell, Massachusetts English; American hipster—and at least three cultures—French-Canadian; northeastern American; bohemian hipster—that combined, conflating into a personal expression of Kerouac as American avatar. Paul Marion notes that "[i]n naming the language of his household, Kerouac used the terms Canadian French, New England French- Canadian, patois, and even 'Canuckian Child Patois Probably Medieval.'"[34] A bilingual prodigy, Kerouac wrote full texts in Québécois *joual* and in many instances interspersed that language in stories (see *Atop*) as well as using it in full passages in his novels (*Visions of Cody; Visions of Gerard; Vanity of Duluoz*) and in two novellas he composed entirely in *joual*, "Old Bull in the Bowery" (*Sur le chemin*, 1952) and "The Night Is My Woman" (*La nuit est ma femme*, 1951).[35] His work is also formally studied by academic scholars of European French languages and literatures.[36] The triple aspects of Kerouac's American ethnic origins—indigenous, Bretonesque, Québécois—attest to his canonical "classic" American identity; he embodies the multiplicities of the American national, ethnic composition. Intermingled, they contribute to making a personal literary language and speaker, Jack Kerouac, avatar of a new, postwar America; Jack Kerouac, "American" lingual mediator.

Kerouac reconfigures the terrain of postwar "America" and renews its linguistic expression. His American idiom is not only of his language(s)—Northeast American English, Québécois *joual*, Breton French, hipster langue—but also of his compositions' free-ranging dictions and linguistic inventions which amalgamate in American archetypes. His idiomatic speech is a hegemonic notation that effects a new American, mixed-language lyric, a mid-century, postwar, post-atomic (Whitmanic) song. In "The Railroad Earth" he writes, "Visitation Tower that by old Okie railroad men of now-California ain't at all mexicanized in pronunciation, Vi Zi Tah Sioh, but is simply called Visitation."[37] Or "the long freight train you see snaking down the track with a puff puff en jyne pulling."[38] In the "Author's Introduction" he decrees *Lonesome Traveler* "a mishmosh of life as lived by an independent educated penniless rake going anywhere."[39] The pieces comprising *Lonesome Traveler* that Kerouac—self-identified as the actual narrator throughout the collection—described as a "mishmosh," a melange or ragbag of literary expressions, accord with the vagabondage of its eight episodes and the Whitmanic multiplicity of subjectivities in play in them.

This American avatar contains multitudes. He is a graduate of a "certain madcap prep school" (Horace Mann) who is "a victim ... of his own I ma JHI Na Tion;"[40] a Catholic repentant nauseated by witnessing and painfully recounting a Mexican bullfight from the bull's perspective—an "animal murder"—that, in postmodern literary terms, is a filial homage to that is also a revolt from, *The Sun Also Rises*;[41] a "Columbia halfback"[42] football hero apprenticing as a "crazy student" railroad brakeman[43] persistently and comically miscalled "Kerouayyy"[44] rushing to catch his train for a "deadhead" assignment; "a big adventurer of the American night"[45] who speaks in football jargon, a vernacular poetics of his free run after the train—"cut into track fast as off-tackle where you carry the ball ... and feint ... buried in the hole in tackle ... flying into the [football] hole ... flying into the [train] track;"[46] a hung over "messman" on a Merchant Marine ship "washing galley pots and pans all afternoon;"[47] a "fire lookout [on Desolation Peak] ... in the High Cascades of the Great Northwest;"[48] an American hobo of "a definite special idea of footwalking freedom"[49] and more. But who is this "rake" of a narrator-protagonist, the hard-working apprentice brakeman of "The Railroad Earth"? A narrator-voyeur who fantasizes about Carmelita and Jose having sex in the fields that they work,[50] he relishes strong Mexican marijuana on bus travels that end reverentially in a little Catholic church in Redondas, Mexico "contemplating the void" where the effigy of the crucified Christ evokes "young Robert Mitchum."[51] This inspires Buddhist associations of "realizing that it is all a great strange dream"[52] in which a Hollywood actor known to enjoy smoking marijuana himself is cast as Jesus on the Cross. The football player as railroad brakeman is an especially brilliant convergence of tropes, languages, poetics, and narrative approaches to play-by-play and action-play, a kaleidoscope of conflated subjectivities, selves, narrative roles; avatar identities.

This galvanic narrative energy finds apotheosis in *The Subterraneans,* the 1953 novel that brandishes a much harder physical word play than the sweet evocations of "Mexico Fellaheen," performing a dark side of the American avatar. *The Subterraneans*'s exposition of an infamous mixed-race love affair propels the novel's prose and its idiomatic, often offensive vitality. The story moves along a meta color-line that the novel's idioms trace between the 1903 warning of the renowned American-Ghanian intellectual W. E. B. DuBois in *The Souls of Black Folk* that "The Problem of the twentieth century is the problem of the color-line"[53] and the 1967 Supreme Court case *Loving v. Virginia*, which ruled state bans on interracial marriage to be unconstitutional. The novel's narrative reproduces the unstable, divided America of the mid-century classic Civil Rights movement era through Leo Percepied, writer, narrator, and "American" protagonist of a tale Kerouac produced at the apex of his development of spontaneous prose poetics. Leo Percepied introduces this tale of bohemian life and love as "the story of an unself-confident man, at the same time, of an egomaniac,"[54] a central narrative contradiction that replicates the multiplicities of the author's competing ethnic origins. Similarly, Leo calls himself by a slur, a "Canuck,"[55] but also an all-American athlete; and a Merchant Marine. The literary expression of Kerouac's Americanness is in its idioms, language that underwrites his identity as a postwar American avatar of diverse ethnic and hence lingual origins that figure his representations of both protagonists and auxiliary figures in his tales, and who resemble the multiplicities and bilingualities of his own descent. Multiple linguistic inventions that are sometimes merely syntactical play incarnate his American language amalgams, as in *Maggie Cassidy*, "a moment's drowned in thinking and kissing in it and I praying and hoping in the mouth of life when life is young to burn cool and eye-blinking joy."[56] Leo notes this phenomenon in Mardou Fox, the antagonist of *The Subterraneans*, a woman of mixed-race, historically relevant, materially charged lineage: she is descended from a "Negro mother dead for birth of her [and an]—unknown Cherokee-halfbreed father a hobo."[57] She speaks a complex argot of American languages and linguistic innovations, its slangs and langues and non-standard forms making a spoken-word patois poetics: Leo recognizes in her talk the "cultured funny tones of part [North] Beach, part I. Magnin model, part Berkeley, part Negro highclass, something, a mixture of *langue* and style of talking and use of words I'd never heard before" (italics in original).[58] She's a hipster, a high fashion model, student, Black socialite—or so her various accents, speaking styles, and linguistic patterns sound as heard and rendered by the Kerouac narrator. Kerouac formulated his insight into the meta-implications of language, "My important recent discovery and revelation is that the voice is all,"[59] and his work pays assiduous attention to that recognition. His American voices manifest an unsettling micro- and macro-linguistic heterogeneity, exemplified by Mardou's finely parsed langues on the one hand and Leo's combative declamations on the other.

 A storyteller of libidinal literary drive, a quantum of Kerouac's post-Second World War American invention, Leo Percepied also aspires to write the Great American Novel. The story told in this narrative is largely about race and sex, but Leo conceptualizes writing as strangely devoid of erotic charge: he cherishes "the asexuality of the WORK," its visceral non-consummating (cerebral) kick, "the sudden gut joy ... when the visions of great words in rhythmic order all in one archangel book go roaring through my brain"[60] in an undivided unitary textuality, an alternative Americanness to Whitmanic multiplicity; a "humping" of the American dream, as Fitzgerald devotee and Kerouac legatee Hunter S. Thompson puts it.[61] Indeed, this narrative is obsessed with writers and writing. Filling the narrative frame, numerous well-known writers make pseudonymous but barely concealed appearances. This trick of cataloging bohemia's literary crew is not a matter of writing autofiction, or even autobiographical confession, though both elements obtain. Rather, it has the effect of putting the writing life or the profession itself, and the literary languages the vocation enlists and invents, front and center in this novel and in its narrative; these writers are the ur-subterreans of the title. Among the discussions of writing values ("selectivity," "details are the life of it")[62] and techniques ("start at the beginning and let the truth seep out")[63] there is a paean to literary integrity that Mardou inspires: "I had never heard such a story from such a soul except from the great men I had known in my youth," Leo's sources who are "great heroes of America ... with whom I'd adventured" and "boys [who] beat on curbstones seeing symbols in the saturated gutter," ironically "the Rimbauds and Verlaines of America on Times Square."[64] For Kerouac, the archetypal American story resides in the "heroes of America," who themselves are Americans impersonating Rimbauds and Verlaines for kicks, slouching over phantom congas on the concrete sides of New York's then-slummy theatre district, Times Square, where everything could be bought or traded, even a masquerade of European heritage. But that is only Kerouac's tossed-off masquerade of a couple of symbolist poets, not the real Jack Kerouac American thing. That would be American bebop.

The postmodern bebop literary style which refuses distinctions between verse and prose is also introduced into the manifest narrative in Leo's quarrel with a younger poet: "it's poetry, poetry, all of it is poetry, great prose is poetry, great verse is poetry."[65] But the validated aesthetic-poetics is given to the younger poet to argue, not to the Kerouac avatar Leo, which puts this central narrative explorer in the eclipse of the era's literary experimentalism. Yet this marginalizing consignment is redeemed when the affair falters in a petty and contrived denouement, and Leo decisively terminates the story with this famous reversal by which he is transmuted from beleaguered lover to master litterateur: "And I go home having lost her love. / And write this book."[66] This elevation of the product over its inspiration, this veneration of the tale over its existential source, is a natural-born American conclusion, fitting for an avatar of the American cosmos. In the American conclusion, outcomes matter, though Kerouac was a process writer at heart. In the American avatar, outcomes and processes are combined.

As American avatar, Kerouac expresses the American will to consume, to inhale, to re-enumerate America itself, embodying a discursive force for making the world an "America" of his poetics. Emerging in the era after the Second World War, Kerouac may be a final voice for the American paean expressed by the literature of that cosmos, even if only as a bass-line reverberation beneath the grievous lead story of the evisceration of the postwar twentieth century. His multiple languages and multiple cultures combining, conflating, make one new, unprecedented postwar personal expression of an old idea—the American avatar now revived and embodied by Jack Kerouac. Given the resistance abroad to understanding Kerouac's writings and the writer himself as American—indeed given a demonstrated a lack of clarity abroad about what is an American writer—it may be necessary especially in his centennial year, to be American to understand Jack Kerouac, to "get" his work and the postwar American avatar he truly and well personifies.

Notes

1   See Gilbert Millstein, "Books of the Times," rev. of *On the Road*, *New York Times*, September 5, 1957, 27. Also Norman Podhoretz, "The Know-Nothing Bohemians," *Partisan Review* XXV (2) (Spring 1958): 307, 308, 317; rpt. in 2001, Ann Charters, ed., *Beat Down to Your Soul* (New York: Viking), 481–93.

2 See Ronna C. Johnson, "Gender, Sexuality, and Race in *On the Road*," in *The Beats: A Teaching Companion*, ed. Nancy M. Grace (Clemson, SC: Clemson University Press, 2021), 87–104. Also Ronna C. Johnson, "Kerouac's Representations of Women," in *The Cambridge Companion to Kerouac*, ed. Steven Belletto (Cambridge, UK: Cambridge University Press, 2024), 178–91.
3 For relevant discussions of Kerouac, see Tim Hunt, *Kerouac's Crooked Road: The Development of a Fiction* (Carbondale, IL: Southern Illinois University Press, 2010). Also the understudied George Dardess, "The Delicate Dynamics of Friendship: A Reconsideration of Kerouac's *On the Road*," *American Literature* 46 (1974): 200–6, rpt. 1979, Donaldson, 411–18. For claims of European appropriations of Kerouac for European aggrandizement that are disguised by blaming the writer as the appropriator of European art, see Veronique Lane, *The French Genealogy of the Beat Generation: Burroughs, Ginsberg, and Kerouac's Appropriations of Modern Literature, from Rimbaud to Michaux* (New York: Bloomsbury Academic, 2019).
4 F. Scott Fitzgerald, *The Great Gatsby* (New York: Scribners, 1926), 182.
5 Jack Kerouac, *On the Road* (1957) (London and New York: Penguin, 2003), 105, 309.
6 Jack Kerouac, "Author's Introduction," in *Lonesome Traveler* (New York: Grove Press, 1960), viii.
7 Kerouac, *Lonesome Traveler*, vii.
8 Jack Kerouac, "The Origins of the Beat Generation" (1959), in Kerouac, *Good Blonde and Others*, ed. Donald Allen, 55–65 (San Francisco: City Lights, 1994), 57, 59.
9 See R. W. B. Lewis, *The American Adam: Innocence, Tragedy and Tradition in the Nineteenth Century* (Chicago and London: University of Chicago Press, 1955).
10 Jack Kerouac, "Essentials of Spontaneous Prose," in *The Portable Beat Reader*, ed. Ann Charters (New York: Viking Press, 1992), 57–8.
11 Kerouac, *Lonesome Traveler*, viii.
12 See Linda Hutcheon, *A Poetics of Postmodernism: History, Theory, Fiction* (New York: Routledge, 1988); Andreas Huyssen, *After the Great Divide* (Bloomington, IN: University of Indiana Press, 1986); Ronna C. Johnson, "'You're Putting Me On': Jack Kerouac and the Postmodern Emergence," *College Literature* Special Issue 27, 1 (2000): Teaching Beat Literature, ed. Jennie Skerl, Winter (2000): 22–38, rpt. in *The Beat Generation: Critical Essays*, ed. Kostas Myrsiades (New York: Peter Lang, 2002); Tim Hunt, *The Textuality of Soulwork* (Ann Arbor: University of Michigan Press, 2014). Though Charles Olson first used the signifier in a 1950 letter to Robert Creeley, the earliest US postmodern novel is *The Crying of Lot 49* in 1965 by Thomas Pynchon (an acknowledged heir to Kerouac, specifically *On the Road* in this novel), and European critics did not theorize the postmodern until the late 1960s (e.g., Foucault, Barthes). See also Jack Kerouac, *Visions of Cody* (New York: McGraw-Hill, 1972) written in 1952; and William Gaddis, *The Recognitions* (1955) (New York: Dalkey Archive, 2012).
13 Ronna C. Johnson, "'You're Putting Me On': Jack Kerouac and the Postmodern Emergence."
14 See Thomas Wolfe, *You Can't Go Home Again* (New York: Scribner, 1934) for what is remembered about a home of origin that vanishes in the belated return.
15 Annie de Saussure, "Ancestral Uprooting and Literary Homecomings: Kerouac's 'Return' to Brittany," *Journal of Beat Studies* Volume 11 (2023): 5–21.
16 Kerouac, *Lonesome Traveler*, 104: the one exception was Kerouac's mother, who housed him with his vocation till his death: "It was another of the many opportunities she's given me all her life just to stay at home and write."

17 See Jack Kerouac, *Atop An Underwood*, ed. Paul Marion (New York: Viking, 1999); *The Sea Is My Brother: The Lost Novel*, ed. Dawn Ward (London and New York: Penguin, 2011); *Windblown World: The Journals of Jack Kerouac 1947–1954*, ed. Douglas Brinkley (New York: Viking, 2004); and his published and unpublished correspondence, for evidence of Kerouac's preoccupations with writing and with being American.
18 Jack Kerouac, *Selected Letters, 1957–1969*, ed. Ann Charters (New York: Viking, 1999), 232.
19 Ibid., 107.
20 Allen Ginsberg, "America," in *Howl and Other Poems* (San Francisco, CA: City Lights Press, 1956).
21 Kerouac, *Selected Letters, 1957–1969*, 229.
22 Patti Smith, *Patti Smith Collected Lyrics* (New York: HarperCollins, 2015). Smith is a devotee of Rimbaud and Europe in an American way of worshipful internationalism; she recently purchased Rimbaud's house in the village of Roche, on the French-Belgium border, a rehabbed version of the poet's childhood home, where he is said to have written *A Season in Hell* (*Architectural Digest*, March 23, 2017, accessed March 17, 2024).
23 See Jack Kerouac, *Visions of Gerard* (New York: McGraw Hill, 1958) and *Dr. Sax* (New York: Grove Press, 1959) for depictions of Kerouac's early Catholicism; for Kerouac's admixtures of Catholicism and Buddhism.
24 Kerouac, *Lonesome Traveler*, vii.
25 Jack Kerouac, *Maggie Cassidy* (New York: McGraw-Hill, 1959), 30.
26 Jack Kerouac, *Satori in Paris* (New York: Grove Press, 1966), 8.
27 Kerouac, *Atop an Underwood*, 173.
28 Brigitte Lane, qtd. in *Atop an Underwood*, 150, writes that the regional French features "extreme modernisms (acquired through the borrowing and reshaping of American linguistic forms)" and "ancient" terms. "Franco-American French is indeed a language of its own: an incredibly direct, concrete and flexible language whose linguistic features are frequently discussed with passion by the more educated Franco-Americans." See Brigitte Marie Lane, *Franco-American Folk Traditions and Popular Culture in a Former Milltown: Aspects of Ethnic Urban Folklore and the Dynamics of Folklore Change in Lowell, Massachusetts* (New York: Garland Publishing, 1990).
29 Jack Kerouac, *The Subterraneans* (New York: Grove Press, 1958), 5.
30 Kerouac, *Selected Letters, 1957–1969*, 228–9.
31 Ibid., 381–2.
32 Kerouac, *Lonesome Traveler*, vii.
33 See de Saussure, "Ancestral Uprooting and Literary Homecomings." See also Hassan Melehy, *Kerouac: Language, Poetics, and Territory* (New York: Bloomsbury, 2016); and Jean-Christophe Cloutier in Jack Kerouac's *The Unknown Kerouac*, ed. Todd Tietchen, trans. Jean-Christophe Cloutier (New York: Library of America, 2016).
34 Kerouac, *Atop an Underwood*, 150.
35 Both *Sur le chemin* and *La nuit est ma femme* were published in 2016 by the Library of America in *The Unknown Kerouac*, translated into English by Jean-Christophe Cloutier.
36 See Melehy, *Kerouac*, and de Saussure, "Ancestral Uprooting and Literary Homecomings."

37 Kerouac, *Lonesome Traveler*, 61.
38 Ibid., 67.
39 Ibid., viii.
40 Ibid., 7.
41 Ibid., 30–3.
42 Ibid., 51.
43 Ibid., 73.
44 Ibid., 45, 68, 70.
45 Ibid., 81.
46 Ibid., 51.
47 Ibid., 99.
48 Ibid., 118.
49 Ibid., 173.
50 Ibid., 78–80, 83.
51 Ibid., 33.
52 Ibid., 33, 36.
53 W. E. B. DuBois, *The Souls of Black Folk* (New York: Penguin, 1903), 1–2. "The Problem of the twentieth century is the problem of the color-line,—the relation of the darker to the lighter races of men [sic] in Asia and Africa, in America and the islands of the sea."
54 Kerouac, *The Subterraneans*, 1.
55 Ibid., 5.
56 Kerouac, *Maggie Cassidy*, 36.
57 Kerouac, *The Subterraneans*, 22.
58 Ibid., 10; italics in the original.
59 Kerouac, *Selected Letters, 1957–1969*, 233.
60 Kerouac, *The Subterraneans*, 57.
61 Hunter S. Thompson, *Fear and Loathing in Las Vegas: A Savage Journey to the Heart of the American Dream* (New York: Random House, 1971), 54. A signature trope of the novel links gambling to the American Dream: "… big crowds … like caricatures of used-car dealers from Dallas … .—still screaming around these desert-city crap tables at four-thirty on a Sunday morning. Still humping the American Dream, that vision of the Big Winner somehow emerging from the last-minute pre-dawn chaos of a stale Vegas casino."
62 Kerouac, *The Subterraneans*, 80.
63 Ibid., 1.
64 Ibid., 49–50.
65 Ibid., 114.
66 Ibid., 152.

15

The Futures of Kerouac's Past: Public Humanities and the Kerouac Archive at 100

Michael Millner

The Centennial Question

Because I teach English at a university in Kerouac's hometown—Lowell, Massachusetts—and because I have curated museum exhibits about Kerouac and worked with Kerouac's archive for many years, I am sometimes asked by the press, and sometimes by my colleagues and friends, often on Kerouac's birthday or deathday each year, and especially during the centennial anniversary of his birth, the following question: What does Kerouac mean to us today? Or sometimes the question comes in a slightly different form: What does the future hold for Kerouac?

It's a difficult question for me, one that I never know exactly how to answer. It's a question that wants an answer that neatly sums up a complex and conflicted author and his complex and conflicted legacy. It's nearly impossible to answer in a soundbite without falling into cliché. For this reason, it is the kind of question that scholars like me dislike, especially when we are put on the spot by a reporter or a fan. But it is also a necessary question, I think, that has a value to a broad public that feels the need to situate Kerouac's complexities in relationship to their own lives and also in relationship to the larger scheme of American culture.

There are, of course, many answers to this question, and my answer, which I will outline below (thankfully not in soundbite brevity), develops out of my experience with the Kerouac archive at my university. For me, the future of Kerouac is in this archive. In many ways, Kerouac's archive is his greatest unpublished work, and I want here to speak about its potential future uses. Those uses will surely include the well-established scholarly uses that any significant author's archive makes possible, but I am more interested in what might be thought of as the "public" uses of the Kerouac archive or, put slightly differently, the public's engagement with his archive. There are a number of complications which travel with the kind of "public humanities" orientation I will propose for Kerouac's archive, but I think Kerouac and his extraordinary archive can present an occasion for thinking through these complications. Ultimately, I will suggest that Kerouac's archive can be a model of how an author's archive might become a powerful opportunity for a more publicly engaged humanities—and in a world where the humanities is endangered and must think creatively about its future, this seems essential.

"All My Molecules": The Kerouac Archive

First let me describe the archive of Kerouac material that I oversee, with the help of many colleagues, at the University of Massachusetts in Lowell.[1] I often refer to this collection as the most comprehensive archive of Kerouac materials in the world. It really is an extraordinary collection! It includes the papers of some of the seminal biographies of Kerouac—of particular significance are Dennis McNally's papers for his biography *Desolate Angel* (1979), as well as Gerald Nicosia's research collection for his biography *Memory Babe* (1983). A priceless portion of the Nicosia collection contains tapes and transcripts of the interviews Nicosia did not only with Kerouac's Beat literary cohorts and professional associates but also with his family members and childhood friends from Lowell and other periods in his life. The Kerouac Archive also holds significant runs of rare Beat- and Kerouac-related journals and zines as well as the papers of the non-profit community organization Lowell Celebrates Kerouac!—compendiums that offer a picture of Kerouac's reception and celebration since his death in 1969. Other Kerouac and Beat scholars and collectors have also donated their compilations of books, photographs, periodicals, and ephemera to the university's collection.

But the crown jewel of the University of Massachusetts Lowell's Kerouac Archive are the papers of John Sampas, who oversaw the author's estate from 1991 until Sampas' death in 2017. The Sampas part of the Kerouac Archive comprises over 7,000 items amounting to tens of thousands of pieces of paper that cover all aspects of Kerouac's life and career. John Sampas oversaw the Kerouac estate from the Sampas family home about two blocks from my English Department office in Lowell. Kerouac's wife at the time of his death was Stella Sampas, the sister of one of Kerouac's best friends growing up in Lowell, Sebastian Sampas. After Kerouac's death, his estate—his papers, belongings, copyrights, and even the rights to his likeness—traveled through the Sampas family and eventually ended up under John Sampas's oversight in 1991. For a quarter-century, Sampas collected, managed, published, and generally masterminded the legacy of Jack Kerouac. When Sampas died in 2017 at age eighty-four, he left his Kerouac papers to my university. The material bequeathed by John Sampas became the foundation for the most comprehensive collection of Kerouac papers in the world.[2]

At the center of the Sampas collection are Xerox copies of most of Kerouac's manuscripts, notebooks, drawings, and other written materials. Sampas also compiled copies of letters sent to and from Kerouac—letters between friends, publishers, and fans. When Sampas came to oversee the estate in 1991, the estate still possessed a very large number of Kerouac's original manuscripts, notebooks, paintings, and other works. Sampas made facsimiles of most of these originals, and the original manuscripts are now held in the Berg Collection at the New York Public Library and other major libraries and private collections around the world. Yet, everything has been brought together in Lowell. It is an extraordinary boon to researchers to have all these items in one place and so easily accessible.

These copies of the Kerouac manuscripts, however, constitute only a portion of the Sampas collection, which stretches to over 110 banker boxes. The John Sampas bequest also included two major series of publishing artifacts: Kerouac's own correspondences with editors, galley proofs, contracts, and other publication related documents as well as all the records of the Kerouac estate. The estate records not only chart Kerouac's publication history but also his pop-culture history—they include deals, realized and unrealized, with advertising agencies, clothing companies, and automobile manufacturers, for instance—in addition to records of legal suits to protect copyrights and litigate other issues. This means that in the archive contains the foundations for a history of Kerouac's publishing career, as well as a history of Kerouac as an important figure in pop culture. These papers also reveal the workings of a modern literary estate—one of the most active and determinative of its author's fortunes that emerged during the late twentieth century. Indeed, the Sampas collection will help scholars chart how literary estates began to play a crucial role in the development of the literary canon and notions of authorship over the past fifty years.

And then there is still everything else in the Sampas collection—the otherwise unavailable sound recordings, ephemera, photographs, and other biographically related artifacts. The wood-and-chicken-wire cat carriers that Jack used to carry his beloved cats Pitou, Dobie, and Timmy (Kerouac wrote each cat's name above the doorway of each handmade carrier) from temporary home to home. The full-color 120-foot copy of the *On the Road* scroll. The memorabilia, fan letters, and other articles left on Kerouac's grave in Lowell that John Sampas collected over the years. The copies of all of Kerouac's paintings and drawings. The old reel-to-reels of Kerouac riffing and rapping. The Kerouac bobbleheads. And, rather spectacularly, the foreign-language editions of Kerouac's many, many works published around the globe—from China to the Czech Republic to the Basque region of Spain.

I have come to love this collection, and I love in particular the fact that it is in Lowell. But when I first came to Lowell eighteen years ago to interview for my current job (as a specialist in nineteenth-century American culture), I remember being surprised when one of my future colleagues told me that Kerouac had grown up in the city. Lowell, with its hulking (but now abandoned and neglected) factory buildings shadowing its narrow nineteenth-century streets, didn't seem to have much connection to the Kerouac of the open road, the Cascades, and Big Sur.

But in certain ways Kerouac had been important to me in the past. I had read *On the Road* when I was in high school in the mid-1980s, and I remember being charged by it. I think I was more taken with what the book and Kerouac stood for—the free road, a philosophy of experience, and a specific kind of masculinity—than I was by its prose style or plotline. I did go, if I remember correctly, from *On the Road* to *The Dharma Bums* and *Big Sur*, and then to Allen Ginsberg's *Howl* and William S. Burroughs' *Naked Lunch*.

When I say I read them in high school, I should clarify that I read them while I was in high school, not in my high school classes. I went to a conservative, Southern, all-boys

Episcopalian school where we were well versed in a catechistic New Criticism. Kerouac didn't fit in well with this pedagogy, and my high school teachers told me not to bother with him. With that, of course, the die was cast. I kept reading these authors as an act of rebellion, but also because they seemed to live in a world that I could at least partially recognize. You see, neither my high school nor my general day-to-day life taught me that writers lived in a recognizable world. I didn't know any writers. Or the writers that I had been introduced to—Shakespeare, Melville, T. S. Eliot—were long dead, and on top of that, didn't live in any world I knew. They lived only in books, and I wrote five-paragraph essays about them. Kerouac and the Beats changed all of that. And I followed them to other writers from the 1960s, 1970s, and 1980s, and my world was changed.

But by the time I arrived for my job interview in Lowell eighteen years ago, all of this had changed again. When my future colleague told me Kerouac was from Lowell, I had pretty much forgotten about him and the Beats more generally. Kerouac wasn't part of any research agenda I had imagined for myself. I was focused on deeply archival work of the American nineteenth century. But more than that, I felt that my youthful infatuation was a little too youthful and naïve. What Kerouac had been to me—an incitement to experience, a way of being male and an artist—had begun to seem too easy. This was especially true when I considered the role people of color played in his work as exoticized and idealized avatars of freedom, and also true when I thought of the parts women often occupied in his novels as dupes of either domesticity or desire. For me, Kerouac had become someone to leave behind.

So, how did I find my way to my work with the Kerouac archive? There are two answers, really. The first is Lowell: Kerouac wrote five novels that were set in large part in Lowell, and his work and life were deeply shaped by his experiences growing up in the city and especially in its French-Canadian community. This is a fact well known by Kerouac scholars, but often only barely recognized by Kerouac's general readers. Most readers—and I had been one of them—paid little attention to his less-popular Lowell novels or his early biography. But my understanding of Kerouac was deepened by my experience of Lowell, and my experience in Lowell was deepened by reading Kerouac's Lowell novels. For instance, after reading *Doctor Sax*, it's difficult to cross one of Lowell high bridges over the swift Merrimac River without thinking of the "watermelon man," who dies late one night while "staring at the waves below with shining eyes."[3]

The second explanation for my return to Kerouac is John Sampas. As I got to know John, he began to open my eyes to the many ways one could work with a great author. I would visit John occasionally at his home office a few blocks from my university office to discuss various Kerouac projects he was working on and that the university might be involved in, and in each visit I was struck by the broadness of his vision for Kerouac. Most notably, he wanted Kerouac to be both an object of serious scholarly study and a pop icon. He understood Kerouac's connection to the city of Lowell, but he also understood how people around the world looked to Kerouac for inspiration. Sampas's many projects as head of the Kerouac estate—from the publication of Kerouac's lost writings and Kerouac's entrée into the esteemed and canonizing Library of America series to the selling of Kerouac as a coverboy for Gap khakis—shaped Kerouac for new audiences with both erudite seriousness and sharp business acumen. John could be difficult to work with at times, and, for some Kerouac scholars, he became a controversial figure. But in a world where the humanities struggled more and more for public relevance with each passing year, John Sampas's work was innovative and even inspiring.[4]

In the above personal remarks, I wanted to briefly touch on what motivated me to spend considerable time with the Kerouac Archive in order to make the point that archives can be places of powerful personal resonance. Kerouac himself felt powerfully about his own archive. He sometimes boasted about how highly organized he was in keeping his papers, and he sometimes carried his notebooks, manuscripts, and letters from place to place in big, tattered suitcases during his peripatetic life.[5] His personal archive was important to him not simply as a collection of notes and drafts of projects, but as—and I don't think it's too grand a phrase—a reservoir of his own being. He understood all those notebooks and drafts as providing a sense of his own self, his conscious and unconscious experience. One way of understanding Kerouac's writing is as an attempt to find a form for this messy accrual of his memories and experiences that he couldn't quite find a bridge back to or fit together.

When I began working in Lowell and read Kerouac's Lowell novels, I suddenly understood this point. I came across the following rather tortuous but stunning sentence from *Visions of Gerard*, a book that recounts Kerouac's relationship with and the death of his beloved older brother Gerard in Lowell. Gerard's death is one of Kerouac's primal scenes. Here Gerard kneels to stroke a cat, like a child saint recognizing God's lowliest being, sparking in Kerouac the narrator the following reflection:

> Would I could remember the huddling and the love of these forlorn two brothers [Gerard and the cat] in a past so distant from my sick aim now I couldnt [sic] gain its healing virtues if I had the bridge, having lost all my molecules of then without their taste of enlightenment.[6]

Perhaps, Kerouac seems to think, the archive of memories recovered through writing can provide "healing virtues" and "enlightenment," that its recovery could help fit back together the "molecules" of his past self, although he doubts his prospects of success.

My vision for Kerouac's archive is different from this vision, of course. Mine has been shaped by what I learned from John Sampas, and it has been colored by my interest in the city of Lowell. It developed from my background in the humanities and my desire for a more publicly engaged humanities. And it is created out of my own distant memories of reading Kerouac as a young person, as well as my conflicts with him. But like Kerouac, I hope the archive will bring users a "taste of enlightenment."

Between Hope and Critique

What would a publicly engaged Kerouac archive look like? What would it mean to think about the Kerouac Archive at my university through the lens of the "public humanities"? In short, those of us who are concerned with creating a more public humanities—a more publicly engaged humanities—seek to bridge the gap between the academy and the wider public, promoting dialogue, collaboration, and mutual understanding by making scholarly insights in the humanities accessible and relevant to everyday life. This goal comes with some dilemmas. Let me take a moment to further outline some of the difficulties because they are instructive of how to better think about Kerouac as part of an engaged humanities. I will turn to a specific experience I had more than a decade ago.

"Jack Kerouac at 90: A Discussion of His Life and Influences," held at the National Park in Lowell in 2012, was a three-person panel designed for a general, non-academic audience as part of the celebration of Kerouac's ninetieth birthday. What I found interesting about this panel was that two of the three panelists explicitly envisioned Kerouac as a kind of saint. Not an actual saint, but someone whom audience members might emulate or at least learn from because he offered us knowledge of universal truths. For one of these speakers, Kerouac was a Catholic holy figure who suffered for our sins, and for the other, he was a kind of Protestant minister who guided us in questions of faith. The third speaker wasn't as religiously specific as the first two, but he did make Kerouac into a sort of Wandering Jew, associated with Allen Ginsberg and Bob Dylan and other subterraneans. All of this—this deeply religious identification with Kerouac—was brought home to me when one of the first questions from the audience for the panel involved whether or not Kerouac's body should be exhumed from his grave in Lowell and "returned" to the Kerouac family plot in nearby Nashua, NH. This question was part of a long local dispute over Kerouac's burial, but the general point was clear: the relics of a saint were at stake.

The panel was both a strange and enlightening experience. The audience seemed to love it, and in terms of audience engagement and pleasure, it succeeded as a public humanities event. As I recall, not only did many questions follow the panel, but also many attestations to the importance of Kerouac's life and work to audience members' lives.

But what the panel brought on for me was a complicated set of responses about Kerouac and what people do with him. Most academics like me are suspicious of what I took to be a large dose of hagiography from the panel. We academics resist seeing Kerouac or any author as a guru, guide, or saint to be celebrated without critique. We tend to resist identification with the author or the work. Indeed, it was difficult to figure out how to bridge the gap between the panel conversation and the kinds of conversations that might circulate around Kerouac in the academy. Those academic conversations might focus on Kerouac's use of various religions in his work, his background and experience with these various religions, the connections between his prose style and specific religious texts, and nearly endless additional possibilities, but academics don't typically celebrate Kerouac as a model for spiritual life in the ways that the panel did. For many of us, our first inclination is to find such celebrations a little naïve. We might well be interested in the work this celebratory identification is doing—perhaps it helps establish community, or in psychoanalytic terms, perhaps it is part of turning Kerouac into an object of attachment—but this kind of critical inquiry was not part of the discussion at the panel. For the non-academic public—many of whom might be positively and importantly engaged by Kerouac and the humanities more generally—such celebration and identification, without any concern for critique, are extremely powerful. That general public tends to be a little mistrustful of academics like me, sensing that we sometimes act as gatekeepers to special knowledge, or that we want to transform them into an object of our anthropologic gaze. They wouldn't be wrong. The two groups often operate with two different sets of values and goals.

This divide is common in public humanities projects, but it frequently goes unresolved and even unrecognized, as Carin Berkowitz and Matthew Gibson, two executive directors of state humanities councils, have recently noted. Berkowitz and Gibson, who both hold PhDs in the humanities, often find their professional positions on humanities councils as "very much those of two people occupying the liminal spaces" between the public and the academy.[7] Most of the time, they point out, "when scholars have talked about public versions of disciplines, they have meant merely that their wisdom would be understood by or distributed within a public."[8] They encourage a different approach:

> We need to find the bridges between academic institutions, nonprofit humanities organizations, and broader communities. Together, we need a humanities that is rooted in disciplines and methods drawn from the academy but that is also rooted in our communities, that is supported by the academy without being appropriated by it.[9]

As we've seen, Kerouac often comes to exemplify the polarization that Berkowitz and Gibson discuss. He frequently becomes an exemplar of the tension between the academy and the community, between scholars and enthusiasts that so often challengingly structures the public humanities. What is surprising, I think, is that many of my fellow academics would agree with Berkowitz and Gibson about the need to find ways to ameliorate the conflict. It strikes me that Berkowitz and Gibson's directive is aligned with one of the most influential calls for transformation *from within* the discipline of literary studies over the last quarter-century—Eve Kosofsky Sedgwick's "Paranoid Reading and Reparative Reading, or, You're So Paranoid, You Probably Think This Essay Is About You" (1997). In that essay, Sedgwick calls out the field of literary studies for being obsessed with critique—so obsessed that we often act like a bunch of paranoiacs, convinced that there is a corrupting ideology hidden within every text. (I fear that Sedgwick may have been talking about me at the 2012 panel.) Instead, Sedgwick suggests we academics at least sometimes turn to other modes of interpretation that don't first and foremost take critique as their goal. The public humanities might provide a space for different modes of interpretation, what Sedgwick calls "reparative reading." English professor Julie Ellison goes so far as to suggest that the public humanities can be a site for the reconciliation of "paranoid reading" and "reparative reading" in her lecture "Between Hope and Critique." I find this passage especially inspiring:

> One of the most important outcomes of public scholarship in the arts and humanities, therefore, can be the reconciliation of hope and critique. Hope is a

practice, just as critique is a practice. We can become skilled in hope, without abandoning the necessary energy of skepticism.[10]

What Ellison calls "hope," I have been calling celebration and identification, both of which seem to me like relations of hope in that they can present pathways to a different, perhaps better, future. As I said, many in my discipline agree with this—hope for this amalgamation—but we don't know how to achieve it.

Reading Ellison, Sedgwick, Berkowitz, and Gibson, and many others in the field of public humanities[11] inspired me to think of my university's Kerouac collection as an opportunity for public engagement. I wanted this archive to live in the city—as part of its bloodstream and consciousness—and not only in acid-free folders and archival boxes. At first it may seem counterintuitive to think of an archive as public. Archives can be scary places; I'm sometimes anxious and sweaty when I'm working in them. There is a lot of signing in and a lot of rules. You feel a little like you've stepped into the panopticon. They are really one of the last places in most libraries that are not wonderfully welcoming to the general public.

It might also seem strange to fly the flag of Kerouac over a public humanities project. He is doubtlessly a problematic character for the reasons that I have already pointed out. But I also think Kerouac presents a rare opportunity. He is a world-renowned artist, perhaps even the first pop author,[12] who is also the greatest chronicler of Lowell, Massachusetts, one of those mid-size factory cities that speckle the map of America but have been generally forgotten. Lowell inspired Kerouac, let Kerouac inspire Lowell.

Experiments in the Archive

About two years before the Kerouac centennial in 2022, several groups in Lowell—scholars from the university, curators and staff from the National Park in Lowell,[13] members of the community group Lowell Celebrates Kerouac!, staff from the city's cultural office, and representatives of the Kerouac estate—started to plan for the celebration. Central to this commemoration would be an expansive exhibit at the National Park that would include the *On the Road* scroll manuscript, which had previously visited Lowell in 2007, but many of the objects on display would be from the university's Kerouac Archive. The exhibit was our first opportunity since the archive had arrived at the university to engage a broad public with its holdings.

One of the immediate issues I encountered as my team began to develop the exhibit was the old sense of straddling two very different domains. Any exhibit would need to be pitched to a wide public, that is, to a public that probably didn't know much about Kerouac. We wanted this public to be charged up by what they learned about Kerouac and to understand his important place in and contributions to American and even global culture. We wanted to celebrate him and allow him to inspire. But how to balance the practice of celebration with the practice of critique? We were not going to create an exhibit that ignored Kerouac's racial and gender biases (or overlook the environmental consequences of an obsession with internal combustion engines).

Indeed, we wanted to engage visitors with these difficult parts of Kerouac and invite them to consider the consequences.

We settled on an approach that felt capacious—it presented Kerouac through several lenses: as an experimental writer, as a Lowell writer, as someone connected to an arts movement, and as a global icon. Within these overarching categories, we incorporated several small stations in the museum space where people might respond to specific pieces of writing and sound recordings. The purpose of these stations was to provide an opportunity for critique by placing parts of Kerouac's life and writing in juxtaposition. We called these opportunities for critique and exchange "juxtaposition stations."

The most interesting of the stations used a series of letters to Kerouac from Beatrice Franco Kozera (1920–2013), who was the model for the "Mexican Girl" in *On the Road*, whom Kerouac fictionalized as "Terry." The letters were in Xeroxed form in our archive, and they had not been published widely (we used them in the exhibit with permission from and compensation to her estate). The fictionalized "Terry," living in a tight community of family and friends, works as an agricultural laborer in California, and in the novel, Sal Paradise joins her laboring in the fields for about two weeks before leaving her with some reluctance to return East. Sal's relationship with Terry constitutes one of his most intense bonds in *On the Road* beyond those with his male friends. In a well-known passage, in which Sal briefly becomes part of the laboring community, he blissfully declares himself "a man of the earth" who works in the fields with the migrants, and he even refers to himself and the others as "we Mexicans."[14] He takes pride that the whites who own the trailer camp they all live in thought he was one of the migrants: "They thought I was a Mexican, of course; and in a way I am."[15]

Kozera's letters to Kerouac once he has returned East are wonderful. Writing in English and with meticulous care and penmanship, Kozera expresses a longing to visit with Kerouac. Her longing is more sweet and maternal than libidinal. She imagines Kerouac eating ice cream any time he wants from the new Frigidaire that he and his mother have bought, and she imagines the Christmas tree in Kerouac's window. Yet, she reiterates that any trip East will require her to make more money in the fields picking grapes for a winery, and her letters often return to this labor.[16] In other words, Kozera's letters offer a much more complex picture than Kerouac's fictionalized account of Terry. In fact, she isn't a Mexican national, as readers are led to believe, but an American citizen born in California,[17] and she doesn't yearn to be an outsider but rather dreams of a familiar kind of domestic American good life, complete with a modern appliance filled with ice cream and a Christmas tree in the parlor.

At our juxtaposition station, we asked visitors to compare the Kozera letter to the Kerouac passage about his being a man of the earth and "in a way" a Mexican. My exhibit team and I felt that this comparison raised a number of questions that were at once critical of Kerouac's representation of Kozera and people of color more generally, but also celebrated the interracial connections important to Kerouac's work as well as Kerouac's attention, however knotty, to labor. There were similar juxtaposition stations in the exhibit, including a comparison of the "Forward" to *The Negro Travelers' Green Book* with a passage from *On the Road* (both published in the same year). The Green Book offered a listing of hotels and restaurants that welcomed

African Americans as they traveled across a segregated nation. "The White traveler has had no difficulty in getting accommodations, but with the Negro it has been different" the Greenbook's "Forward" explains.[18] In the passage from Kerouac, we find him "zooming across the Arizona desert." "I had a book with me," Sal Paradise tells the reader, "but I preferred reading the American landscape as we went along. Every bump, rise, and stretch in it mystified my longing."[19] Two very different experiences of the open road.

In the end, we felt that these juxtaposition stations never quite reached their potential, especially in terms of engagement. We wanted to create a genuine opportunity to participate in an ongoing conversation between members of the public about these dilemmas in Kerouac's work. But much of the commentary we received from visitors seemed fairly superficial. Perhaps we didn't provide the best media (web comment boxes) for this kind of participatory engagement? Or perhaps we didn't know enough about our audience? Who were they and what was their background with Kerouac? Or perhaps we didn't produce enough guidance for visitors, asking them to compare passages without asking them specific questions? Or perhaps the opposite was true: We were being too directive, and visitors began to feel we had an axe to grind about race, gender, and labor? These were the kinds of juxtapositions that work well in the classroom, where students expect teachers to shape the discussion in large part. But they didn't work very well in a museum setting, and they especially didn't work well in creating a sense of participation in the critique and celebration of Kerouac's work. I wanted our visitors to be creators, but most remained spectators.

As soon as the centennial exhibit at the National Park closed, I began to imagine future projects that might better engage participants, allowing them to be creators and critics. I found inspiration in a collection of art projects that riffed off *On the Road*. In 1967, the visual artist Ed Ruscha self-published 1,000 copies of a spiral notebook he called *Royal Road Test* that provided a kind of crime-scene, forensic report (mostly using black-and-white photographs) documenting the tossing of a pre-war, Model 10 Royal typewriter out the window of 1963 Buick Le Sabre while racing at 90mph through the desert one hundred miles from Las Vegas. (*On the Road* isn't mentioned in the short text, but the novel is central to Ruscha's art, from his *Twentysix Gasoline Stations* in 1963 to his own photographic version of *On the Road* from 2009.) *Royal Road Test* seems to me both a homage to and a sly deconstruction of Kerouac's art and Beat aesthetics more generally: the holy typewriter done in by the forensic photograph; the declaration of the finale of road writing; the dumping of the Beat body just beyond Pop Vegas. Turning to a more recent project, I also love Ross Goodwin's *1 the Road*, which is sometimes referred to as the first AI novel. Goodwin created a "wordcar" with mounted surveillance cameras to capture roadside images as the car sped along, feeding those images through AI technology which translated them into "semi-sensical" words—a kind of Dadaist, often hilarious, frequently banal poetry—that printed out on receipt paper in the back of the wordcar.[20] Goodwin drove the autowriter from Brooklyn to New Orleans, roughly along a route taken by Sal Paradise in *On the Road*, thus producing a new iteration of the novel, written by a machine, at least in part, because that is one of the big questions for Goodwin—who is the author?—the AI, the car, the environment itself, Goodwin himself, all of the above? *1 the Road* uses Kerouac's original as an incitement, an inspiration, an updating of Kerouac's "Spontaneous Prose." It critiques and celebrates our technologized interactions with the world and challenges our standard ideas of creativity.

These are brilliant conceptual projects that quickly exceed the level of complexity typical of an engaged humanities project offered to the public. But they are also wonderful exemplars of interactions with a core text that allow participants to be creators and not just spectators or commentators and that encourage participants to both experiment and critique. Which is to say those participants are encouraged to hope and critique through their engagement. Doris Sommer, a scholar of Latin American literature, has never written about Kerouac, but she helpfully offers some basic templates for public humanities projects focused on the literary that approximate in many ways the work of Ruscha and Goodwin. One such template she calls "Pre-Texts," and she uses "Pre-Texts" assignments with students ranging from elementary school to graduate school.[21] Here a core text—the "pre-text"—serves as a jumping-off point for creating a new work of art. That new work might be an additional chapter of novel, a photograph, a short film, a painting, a collage, a remix, a rap—really anything. In making the new work in relation to the core text, the maker has the opportunity to research, interpret, problem solve, and design. I like this idea because moving from one medium to another tends to challenge participants to move beyond simply replicating Kerouac's subject matter and style. They have an opportunity to transform and critique, like Ruscha and Goodwin, but the outcome need not be especially complex (involving AI or Buick Le Sabres). Sommer also presents a related kind of project she calls "tangential texts."[22] Again, there is a core text, and participants choose a new text—it might be any kind of text: an article, short story, essay, film, advertisement, photograph—that has some kind of connection to the core text. The tangential text comments on, celebrates, critiques, updates, demonstrates the agelessness of, or suggests some other kind of relation to the core text.

The Kerouac Archive offers many opportunities for tangential text and pre-text experiments. These experiments can be simple: they might simply ask people to read a passage about the city of Lowell—maybe a passage written in Kerouac's own hand—and use it as a starting point for creating a pre-text or researching and presenting a tangential text. Scholars will, of course, continue to use the Kerouac Archive at my university in the ways that they have long used literary archives. They will use it to investigate Kerouac's Franco-American background and to ask when and why Kerouac turned to writing in French. They will use it to investigate Kerouac's early life in Lowell and the connection between the city and his work. They will use it to investigate the reception of Kerouac and the way he has been used by others. They will use it to discover Kerouac's own relationship to archiving, and they will use it to better understand the connections between a literary estate and the legacy of an author. They'll use it to better know Kerouac as a pop artist, not only a literary artist. This is the work of scholars. But I also believe that literary archives like Kerouac's can serve an even broader function as places of intense public humanities engagement, which offers opportunities of both hope and critique.

When I think back on my first encounter with Kerouac, I've come to understand better why I was drawn to him. It wasn't because of some sense of freedom he offered. It wasn't a sense of the vastness and possibility of the North America continent he captured. It wasn't the kind of masculinity he embodied. Rather it was his model of a scene—a collection of friends who were artists, who were creating things together. Through his archive, we might again create this kind of engaged, participatory scene. I hope this will be at least one of his meanings in the future.

Notes

1. For more information on the University of Massachusetts Lowell Kerouac Archive, visit "The Jack Kerouac Archive at UMass Lowell," The Jack and Stella Kerouac Center at University of Massachusetts Lowell, accessed October 18, 2023, https://jackkerouac.org/jack-kerouac-archive-at-umass-lowell.
2. I recount my relationship with John Sampas and his relationship to the Kerouac archive in Michael Millner, "Kerouac's Archive Fever at One Hundred," *The Missouri Review* 45 (1) (2022): 166–83.
3. Jack Kerouac, *Doctor Sax: Faust Part Three* (1959) (New York: Grove Press/Atlantic, 2023 ebook), 128.
4. On John as a difficult figure and my relationship with him, see Michael Millner, "Kerouac's Archive Fever at One Hundred," *The Missouri Review* 45 (1) (2022): 166–83.
5. Ann Charters notes how organized Kerouac's letters were in her introduction to his *Selected Letters*. See Jack Kerouac, *Jack Kerouac: Selected Letters, 1940–1956*, ed. Ann Charters (New York: Viking, 1995), vii and xxi.
6. Jack Kerouac, *Visions of Gerard* (1963) (New York: Penguin Publishing Group, 1991), 4.
7. Carin Berkowitz and Matthew Gibson, "Reframing the Public Humanities," *Daedalus* 151 (3) (2022): 69, doi.org/10.1162/daed_a_01929.
8. Ibid., 73.
9. Ibid., 78.
10. Julie Ellison, "Between Hope and Critique," Engaged Scholar Speaker Series, Michigan State University, April 27, 2006, accessed August 15, 2023, https://engagedscholar.msu.edu/Speaker/ellison.aspx.
11. Also, of great influence on my thinking about engaged curation, Nina Simon, *The Participatory Museum* (Santa Cruz, California: Museum 2.0, 2010).
12. There were, of course, popular, famous, legendary, best-selling authors before Kerouac—Jack London even designed his own trademark!—but were there pop authors? Kerouac stumbled into the confluence of radio, recording devices, film, photography, and television that became possible for the first time in the 1950s and would by the 1960s become the foundation for what we have ever since referred to as "pop." For the most part, he hated being a popstar.
13. Located at the center of the city is the Lowell National Historical Park, part of the National Park system. The Lowell National Park focuses on the city's important contributions to the history of American industrialization and immigration.
14. Jack Kerouac, *On the Road* (1957) (New York: Penguin Publishing Group, 1976), 90.

15 Ibid.
16 Beatrice Franco Kozera, Letter to Jack Kerouac, October 25, 1947, Jack Kerouac Archive, University of Massachusetts Lowell.
17 For a fuller account of Kozera, see Tim Z. Hernandez, *Mañana Means Heaven* (Tucson: University of Arizona Press, 2013).
18 Green, Victor H. Green, *The Negro Travelers' Green Book: 1957* (New York: Victor H. Green & Co., 1957), 2.
19 Kerouac, *On the Road*, 95.
20 Ross Goodwin, Kenric McDowell, and Hélène Planquelle, *1 the Road* (Paris: Jean Boîte Éditions, 2018), 28.
21 Doris Sommer, *The Work of Art in the World: Civic Agency and Public Humanities* (Durham: Duke University Press, 2014), 107–34.
22 Ibid., 114–15.

16

Kerouac in Translation: A Conversation with Farid Ghadami, Minami Aoyama, and Maciej Świerkocki

Erik Mortenson and Tomasz Sawczuk

Erik Mortenson, Tomasz Sawczuk: Let's start with an obvious question. Can you talk a bit about the rationale behind choosing to translate Kerouac? Can you go first, Farid? Why did you choose to translate *The Dharma Bums* and *Big Sur* in particular?

Farid Ghadami: I can express it in a simpler and clearer manner: in my opinion, *The Dharma Bums* represents the pinnacle of Kerouac's unique writing style, which he refers to as jazz improvisational and spontaneity. The novel captivates readers with its long, breathy phrases that resemble a passionate storyteller in a cafe. On the other hand, the novel *Big Sur* showcases a different style, characterized by its poetic language and long dashes reminiscent of Louis-Ferdinand Céline's three dots. The awe-inspiring and fascinating nature depicted in *The Dharma Bums* turns terrifying in *Big Sur*, leading Kerouac to escape from the nature's voice, from "Sea Sounds of the Pacific Ocean at Big Sur." The vagaries, adventures, and orgies that pervade *The Dharma Bums* or *On the Road* become abruptly absurd and painful in the context of *Big Sur*.

In other words, *Big Sur* supplements Kerouac's body of work from a Derridean perspective. According to Jacques Derrida, a supplement is not simply an addition or enhancement; it reveals a fundamental lack or insufficiency in the original work while simultaneously completing and undermining it. In this sense, *Big Sur* serves as a supplement to Kerouac's other works. I firmly believe that reading Kerouac's works should always be accompanied by this supplement, the antidote of *Big Sur*. The novel stands as Kerouac's rebellion against himself, his style, his optimism, and his passionate romantic spirit. While in *The Dharma Bums*, even the tragic suicide of Rosie Buchanan is overshadowed by Kerouac's Buddhist optimism, overlooking the profound tragedy of a woman losing her life in a horrific manner due to fear of the police, *Big Sur* unveils a contrasting perspective. In this novel, even the death of a mouse instills terror within Kerouac.

Let me admit that *Big Sur* is my favorite novel of Kerouac. We know that Pier Paolo Pasolini considered casting Jack Kerouac in the role of Jesus Christ. Pasolini started working on the movie *The Gospel According to St. Matthew* at the same time that Kerouac wrote the novel *Big Sur* in the early 1960s. But Kerouac was no longer the handsome young man whom Salvador Dalí called the most beautiful man in America, more beautiful than Marlon Brando. He had been worn down by alcohol and grief. Kerouac himself suggests that Dalí might have been attracted to him due to their shared blue eyes and black hair. For me, it is impossible to ignore the connection between an author's physical presence and their writing. I hope that one day I can explore this topic further in an essay. Anyway, Pasolini had aptly chosen Kerouac for the role of Christ, but unfortunately, before he could begin his work, his Messiah had succumbed to the cross of alcohol and sorrow, leaving him buried before his time. In my opinion, *Big Sur* is *The Gospel According to St. Kerouac* which supplements, completes, and undermines his *Old Testament* of *On the Road*, *The Dharma Bums*, *The Subterraneans*, *Tristessa*, and *Desolation Angels*.

EM, TS: Minami, how about you and your decision to translate *On the Road* and *Tristessa* into Japanese?

Minami Aoyama: *On the Road* is my favorite book since I first read it in English when I was an undergraduate. So, when I was asked to translate *On the Road* by my reliable editor, I jumped to his proposal. It is my regret that my translation was published after he had passed away.

After I translated *On the Road* and *On the Road: The Original Scroll*, I went to Mexico and stayed there for a year. I was so enthralled by the Mexican scene, and I remembered that *Tristessa* is Kerouac's Mexico novel. So, when I came back to Japan, I told an editor my hope to translate *Tristessa*. Of course, I want to translate *Mexico City Blues*, but it seems too difficult to translate because of its many wordplays.

EM, TS: When your translation of *On the Road* came out in 2007, it was not entirely a new text for Japanese readers—it was first translated into Japanese as early as 1959 by Minoru Fukuda. What was the reception of a retranslated work that already existed in Japanese?

MA: The first Japanese text of *On the Road* was published only two years after the original text was published. *On the Road* is full of many American things. But then Japan was so poor that people weren't familiar with them. The late editor told me that the first Japanese text of *On the Road* was a collaboration of many newspaper reporters who knew about American things a little bit better than ordinary Japanese people. Above all, the notion of driving around the continent was too difficult to imagine for many Japanese people, because having a car was almost an impossible dream for them then. But "the Beat Generation" was a topic as an American youth phenomenon in Japan, too. That's why *On the Road* was an appeal to many Japanese youth. They didn't care about many American things, they wanted to know just about what's happening in America. It was received as a topical book.

The late editor, who knew the backstory of making the first Japanese text, believed that it should be translated anew. There are some flaws because of the lack of knowledge on American things. Many new readers have noticed that. For they are familiar with American things and know the joy of driving a car. *On the Road* is not a topical book any more for them.

EM, TS: Maciej, what about your decision to translate *Maggie Cassidy*, *Big Sur* and *Wake Up: A Life of the Buddha*?

Maciej Świerkocki: I didn't choose these three works by Kerouac, they were commissioned by my publisher. I could accept or refuse. I decided to accept because I respect the author and feel there exists a kind of a personal bond between us. Let's say I owed it to him as well as to myself.

EM, TS: Did the process of translating Kerouac's works reveal any new aspects of his writing?

MA: Whenever I ran into songs while translating *On the Road*, I did listen to songs that were mentioned. In this age it is quite easy to get to old songs, and I enjoyed listening to many songs through *On the Road*. But these old songs didn't necessarily help me to translate *On the Road*'s fast style. Even Charlie Parker didn't. Then I found that The Doors are the best help for translating *On the Road*'s fast style. So, I always translated *On the Road* while listening to The Doors' songs. Eventually it turned out that Jim Morrison was a fan of Kerouac. Listening to The Doors' music, I recognized clearly Kerouac played *On the Road* more than wrote it.

EM, TS: Did it change your understanding of his life?

MŚ: I'd known quite a bit about Kerouac, his life and work before I started working on *Big Sur* which was the first of his novels that I translated. However, I think it was only then that I realized how deep his depression was at the time of his writing *Big Sur* and how devastating his nervous breakdown and alcoholism were.

EM, TS: Did any of you feel that working on Kerouac challenged your conception of the nature of translation?

FG: To be candid, for me, translation serves as a method of deep comprehension. In essence, when I strive to fully grasp a text, I embark on the journey of translating it. While reading a text, it's possible to remain indifferent to certain nuances, overlook certain gaps, and be primarily impacted by the original impact of the work. However, when engaging in translation, disregarding even the tiniest details becomes impossible. Hence, translation demands an intensified form of reading, where every aspect must be carefully considered.

In Benjaminian terms, translation strips away the aura of a work, allowing the translator to approach it with a critical perspective, detached from its rhetorical impacts. The experience of translating *Big Sur* was truly peculiar for me. Upon my initial reading, I was captivated and immediately decided to undertake its translation. However, when I eventually started the translation process two or three years later, I encountered a sense of fear and frustration that hindered my progress. Despite having a contract with my publisher for the translation, I found myself unable to proceed beyond one or two pages at a time. While the literary intricacies of Kerouac's narrative style fascinated me during my first reading, the act of translating evoked a profound sense of terror within me. Just as Kerouac was frightened by the sound of the sea in the novel, his voice in *Big Sur* intimidated me. It took approximately five or six years, with persistent urging from my publisher, for me to finally complete the translation. If I had solely read the novel without attempting its translation, my perception of it would undoubtedly be different. To this day, the mere recollection of Kerouac's words, "as far as I can see the world is too old for us to talk about it with our new words," sends shivers down my spine.

EM, TS: Kerouac is a writer known for innovative writing that relies heavily on the aural tones of spoken language, as well as on the improvisational jazz music that he loved and emulated. What were the challenges of capturing his "spontaneous bop prosody" style? What were the payoffs?

MŚ: Those challenges were actually fun because I've always been a jazz fan myself. In fact, I often listened to Charlie Parker and other musicians of "the Kerouac period" while working especially on *Big Sur*, but also *Maggie Cassidy*, in order to capture and recapture all the improvisations, beats, broken notes and so on and try to find good Polish equivalents for them in the realm of words which of course are also vehicles of sound. I frequently read the most musical fragments of Kerouac's works aloud in Polish to establish whether their musical qualities at least resemble bebop or other jazz subgenres. The only payoff was the mostly sympathetic reaction of the readers. *Maggie Cassidy*, if my memory serves me right, was broadcast on one of the Polish national radio stations.

FG: I found conveying the unique auditory qualities of spoken language in Kerouac's writings to be my most challenging task as a translator. I had to ensure that his breathtaking sentences and paragraphs were translated in a manner that preserved their innate beauty and passion while effectively conveying their intended meaning. Luckily, the Persian language possesses a highly flexible structure, allowing for easy rearrangement of verbs, subjects, adverbs, etc. within sentences to achieve the desired tone. This characteristic owes much to the influence of Persian poetry, which has played a significant role in shaping the language. Persian, as it stands today, is a testament to the remarkable contributions of Iranian poets who kept the language alive during the Arab rule over Iran. Consequently, the poetic heritage of Persian has softened its linguistic structure.

In traditional Iranian schools, Persian was taught through the works of Sa'di Shirazi, a renowned Iranian poet from the thirteenth century. The poetic and adaptable nature of the Persian language greatly facilitates the translator's work. However, it is important to note that Persian traditionally favors shorter sentences compared to English. Additionally, there exists a substantial distinction between the written and spoken forms of Persian. Unlike English, where the written and spoken forms of most words are similar, Persian exhibits the opposite pattern. In spoken Persian, the written form of words often undergoes significant changes. Consequently, translating *The Dharma Bums* required considerable creativity in order to capture the essence of the original text.

Furthermore, Kerouac's writing style mirrors the fluidity and spontaneity of jazz improvisation, untouched by editing. Conversely, the translation process necessitates meticulous editing. This inherent contradiction arises because translation, being an artificial endeavor, must also strive to convey the naturalness and unedited quality of the language found in Kerouac's works.

EM, TS: Can you comment on any unique characteristics of your native tongues that either worked against or in favor of your efforts to produce a successful translation? What was gained, and what was lost, in the translation of Kerouac's work? Is there something about Kerouac's work that is untranslatable, in your opinion?

MŚ: One thing that usually helps a translation from English into Polish is the fact that Polish in an inflectional language and that using specific morphemes may compensate for the mood or style achieved in the original by way of other, for instance lexical, means. But this is true in the case of any English-language writer, not just Kerouac. I can't really say what was lost and what was gained in my translation of Kerouac's work. Certainly, something was lost and something gained, it always is, but one would have to pinpoint such losses and gains, analyze both texts in detail, which I'm unable to do off the top of my head after so many years.

On the other hand, I hope that the general atmosphere, style, message etc., the general characteristics of the original(s) have been preserved in the Polish translation. And no, I don't believe there is anything untranslatable in Kerouac's work. I think that in translation—which for me is a creative process—it's always a question of close reading the text first and then of finding the proper form in one's own language to convey the form of the original. Those forms differ, of course; they have to differ being expressed in a different language/culture, just as certain other elements of a translation which is never, thank God, "a copy" of the original.

FG: The open structure and vast vocabulary of the Persian language provide ample room for a skilled translator to employ their creativity and execute the translation work effectively. What I refer to as the "hospitality" of the Persian language allows both the author and translator to explore new structures within Persian, thereby enhancing its richness in terms of syntax and vocabulary. I believe that my translations of Kerouac's works have accomplished this to a significant degree by contributing to the depth and diversity of the Persian language.

To illustrate, let's consider an example from *The Dharma Bums* where Japhy Ryder (Gary Snyder) and a character named Princess transform a Tibetan Buddhist ritual called *Yab Yum* into an Americanized, sensual Buddhist ritual. In my translation of the novel, I opted to retain the original term while integrating it into the Persian text. Remarkably, after almost a decade, this word has now entered Persian slang to describe a specific erotic position. This exemplifies how a well-crafted translation can introduce new linguistic elements and contribute to the evolving nature of a language.

Additionally, I've noticed among some contemporary writers a tendency to improvise and create long uninterrupted sentences that capture a breathless quality, similar to Kerouac's style. This experimentation with sentence structure and a preference for unedited prose can be seen as a reflection of the influence Kerouac has had on the new generation of Persian writers.

EM, TS: Let's talk a bit about the cultural context for these translations. What do we need to know about Iran, Poland and Japan in order to understand how Kerouac's work is received in those countries?

FG: Iran, as a country, holds a deep appreciation for literature and reading. The Iranian people, in general, have a profound connection to literature, making it an integral part of their cultural identity. An interesting fact is that Enghelab (Revolution) square and street in Tehran, which serve as Iran's most significant political and commercial center, are also the hub for bookstores. This means that the heart of the city and the country is dedicated to literature, comparable to the significance of Champs Élysées in Paris. Can you imagine if the entire Champs Élysées was dedicated to bookstores, instead of clothing brands?

As I mentioned earlier, literature, particularly poetry, plays a paramount role in Persian culture. It is not an exaggeration to say that at least one out of every ten Iranians writes poetry, of course mostly for personal expression rather than publication.

In the last four decades, particularly since the Islamic Revolution, Iran's political relationship with the Western world has become significantly restricted. Consequently, people have sought to compensate for this limitation by delving into Western literature and cinema, with a strong preference for American, French, and German works. Almost every significant literary piece published in Europe or America is swiftly translated into Persian, with few exceptions. This is particularly true for the literature of the Beat Generation, which was relatively unknown in Iran before my translations.

In general, I want to emphasize that Iranians have a deep fascination with literature, including Western literature. When it comes to the Beat Generation, and specifically Kerouac's works, their literature resonates strongly with the Iranian spirit. Iranian readers have been able to recognize the modern face of the Iranian spirit in works such as *The Dharma Bums* and *On the Road*. These works embody a spirit that values freedom, happiness, tolerance, and living in the present moment. This spirit finds echoes in the poetry of renowned Persian poets like Khayyam (1048–1131) and Hafez (1315–1390).

Interestingly, sexual repression in Iran is a more recent phenomenon. Classical Persian literature, ranging from the works of Hafez and Saadi (1210–1291) in poetry to Obeyd Zakani (1370–1371) in prose, illustrates that Iranian poets and writers historically viewed a natural sex life as encompassing both heterosexual and homosexual encounters. Celebrating life through poetry, wine, and music has long been an integral part of Iranian culture, as reflected in the works of Khayyam and Obeyd Zakani. Obeyd's humorous short stories, which depict real-life situations, reveal a tolerant approach to sexual life in Iran. For instance, in one of his stories, a couple engages in oral sex on their porch, and when a beggar approaches asking for food, the woman jokingly offers him a choice between the food she is consuming (her husband's genitalia) or the slaps she gives her husband out of excitement. This kind of scene, reminiscent of a Beat writer's text, showcases the open-mindedness of past Iranian culture.

The Beat Generation can be seen as a contemporary revival of the spirit of Khayyam and Obeyd, embodying sexual tolerance, a celebration of life, and an appreciation for the passion of existence. These themes are presented in a modernized form in the works of the Beat Generation, and for many Iranians, reading their works is a discovery of their own repressed cultural heritage. The emergence of modernity in Iran was accompanied by sexual repression and the curbing of various freedoms. Later, modernism became intertwined with religion, resulting in a unique situation where modernism and religion in contemporary Iran, from the early twentieth century or mid-nineteenth century onward, have influenced each other and imposed significant restrictions on individual and societal freedoms. In contrast, in the West and most other parts of the world, modernism and religion have been perceived as opposing forces. This divergence adds to the allure of figures like Jack Kerouac, Allen Ginsberg and William Burroughs for Iranians, as they challenge the prevailing norms and ideologies in Iran.

The works of the Beat Generation continue to hold a significant counter-cultural meaning for us, even though they have to some extent integrated into mainstream Western society. Within the late capitalist system, literature has largely been depoliticized and neutered. It has been manipulated to promote authors and books that align with the existing culture, the status quo. These books are often amusing and devoid of any potential to impact the minds and lives of readers; they merely provide temporary entertainment for a few hours.

Fortunately, I can confidently state that literature in Iran has not yet succumbed to complete apoliticalness. It still maintains a somewhat radical character. This is why writers like Kerouac, Burroughs and Ginsberg can be incredibly popular and influential in Iran. Despite being influenced by universal culture, Iranian readers continue to seek literature that challenges norms and assumptions. Iranian literature possesses a resilience that has not been entirely subdued by the commercialized mainstream culture prevalent in late capitalism. This allows works of the Beat Generation and other countercultural voices to resonate deeply within Iranian society and leave a lasting impact.

MŚ: I suppose the most important factor here is that Poland has been mentally a part of the Western world for decades, if not centuries, at least among the educated public. Geopolitically speaking, it rejoined the West at least in 1989, so it is a part of the global market, prone to the same fads, vogues and trends as any other European country. When translating *Big Sur* in 2010–11 I used a French and a Czech translation of the novel to see how my colleagues from France and the Czech Republic coped with the problems I also had to solve. It was interesting and helpful, but what struck me first and foremost was the fact that *Big Sur* and Kerouac were in print in those countries, and I had no trouble with obtaining the book. In my opinion for some reason those years—let's say the last decade of the previous century and the first decade of the twenty-first—might even be called the Kerouac revival (there was also a *Big Sur* movie around, as well as new editions of other Beat and subversive writers like Ginsberg and Burroughs). As far as I know, Kerouac was then widely published, translated and retranslated. For a while Poland was a part of that movement—but Kerouac's works didn't sell as well as the publishers hoped so they called it quits, at least for the time being. But he did have and still has a pretty strong following, especially among those readers who somehow identify themselves with the beatniks, hippies and other representatives of what one might call contestation culture and/or the neo-avantgarde.

MA: When the first Japanese edition was published, it was received like a report about an American youth phenomenon, "the Beat Generation." But when my new translation was published, it was received as a road novel. When the first one was published, Japanese readers didn't know the word "road novel" itself. This is a big difference between the first one and mine as to receiving *On the Road*.

EM, TS: How did you deal with translating Beat lingo and slang? Some Turkish translations, for example, offer various translations for the term "Beat" itself, while others prefer not to translate it at all. Are there any "underground" or rebellious groups or communities from either contemporary society, the mid-twentieth century or perhaps even earlier that provided a correlative to Beat terms or conceptions?

MA: When the first one was published, there were some young groups called "Taiyo Zoku" (Sunshine Tribe) here in Japan. The name came from the novel, *Taiyo no Kisetsu* (*The Sunshine Season*) written by Shintaro Ishihara. The book was published in 1956 one year before the publication of *On the Road*. It is a novel about rich unruly rebellious young people in Tokyo. It got the prestigious literary prize and became a best seller. "Taiyo Zoku" tried to follow the novel's characters' fashion and behavior. But it was a fad.

The word "Beat Generation" is mentioned in a 1961 movie called *Buta to Gunkan* (*Pigs and Battleships*) directed by Shohei Imamura. It is a movie about young hooligans around the port of Yokosuka, where the American naval base is located. The main character is a wild fraud who does business with American sailors. Someone asks him, "Do you know there is the Beat Generation in America?" in the movie. He reminds me of Dean Moriarty a little. Kerouac, a fanatic movie goer, would have loved this movie. It is a masterpiece.

MŚ: I used dictionaries and Polish slang—and asked around if I had to, mostly native speakers. We don't have a problem with terms like "Beat" or "beatnik" because we've included them in our vocabulary and we're familiar with them. In other words, they don't need translation. As to the underground or rebellious groups—yes, we've had a few of those. Some appeared as early as the fifties. We also must remember how important jazz (and later rock music) was in the slow process of the cultural and political liberation of Poland after 1945 and Yalta. Jazz was a symbol of freedom and a carefree lifestyle. Especially young people (who belonged to the next generation which reached adulthood in the sixties) looked up to figures like Kerouac, lived "on the road," wanted to be like him, drink like him (nothing surprising or difficult in Poland) and write like him. Sometimes they formed official groups and wrote manifestoes, while sometimes they were just odd individuals, living on the margins of the "socialist" society, on the edge, like *poètes maudits*, often in trouble with the law and morality, outsiders. The funny thing is, writers like Kerouac, Ginsberg, Corso or Burroughs weren't published in Poland at the time (the first novel by Kerouac, *On the Road*, came out in 1993!) except for some literary magazines or poetry collections. This means that if they were read, it must have been seldom and in the original, and that they were known in Poland rather indirectly than directly. Kerouac's life was more hearsay and gossip than valid information you could get from books or local mass-media.

FG: Regarding the term *Beat*, I have chosen not to translate it in my translations of works from the Beat Generation. Instead, I explain its meaning in the introductions I wrote, referring to the post-Second World War American situation. In the case of slang and argot words, I attempt to translate them into their contemporary Persian equivalents, or coin them in Persian, sometimes including footnotes to assist unfamiliar readers. In my opinion, a crucial aspect of a translator's role is to provide introductions and footnotes. This approach is well-received by most Iranian readers as well, whereas in France, the preference is typically the opposite, with readers disliking footnotes in books. I believe this preference reflects our fundamental attitude towards novels and literature: whether we read literature for entertainment or to be influenced by it. Is a novel a round-trip ticket that temporarily transports us somewhere before returning us to our starting point, or is it a one-way ticket that forever changes our perspective? I consider literature to be a one-way ticket, somehow aligning with the views of Roland Barthes, who distinguishes between the "pleasure" of the text and the "jouissance" of the text.

In his book *Le Plaisir du Texte*, Roland Barthes discusses two types of texts based on the enjoyment they bring to readers: *plaisir* (pleasure) and *jouissance*, translated into English as "bliss," but encompassing the meaning of "orgasm" or "ejaculation" in French. Pleasure primarily arises from texts that form part of our cultural heritage, seemingly connecting readers with shared social values. On the other hand, reading jouissance is a radically anti-social experience, akin to a sexual orgasm. Those who read for amusement gain mere pleasure from the text, whereas those seeking more than entertainment, even beyond knowledge, can find jouissance within the novel. Consequently, I consistently provide my translations with numerous introductions, afterwords, and footnotes to enable readers to readily engage with the text, understand its historical and political context, and more. For instance, if someone reads Russian poet Ossip Mandelstam's poems in English without any knowledge of the Soviet situation during his time, they will fail to grasp the essence of his poetry.

I often emphasize that our cultural situation in Iran shares many similarities with the cultural climate of the United States and perhaps Europe in the 1950s and 1960s. It's not surprising that the May 1968 movement was highly appealing to me and many of my contemporaries in Iran. The first article I published in the Iranian press, at the age of fifteen, was a tribute to the May 1968 movement. Maybe due to my introductions, Iranian readers often associate Beat Generation writers with the counterculture movement and everything that led up to May 1968. However, I cannot claim that there has ever been a specific movement in Iran equivalent to the Beat Generation, to the extent that their slang or argot could be used in translation. Even if such a movement existed, I believe that the uniqueness of each author or a particular movement cannot be reduced to something purely indigenous.

The essence of translation lies in encountering something entirely new. Even though we can observe similarities, for example, between the literature of the Beat Generation and a portion of classical Persian literature, it would be overly simplistic to suggest that the Beat Generation literature had nothing new to offer us. This is the task of translation: to disrupt the complacency of local culture with the dagger of a foreign language and literature. In other words, I consider translation to be fundamentally a counter-cultural endeavor, aiming to bring forth something fresh and radical that challenges the existing local culture.

EM, TS: How have your readers responded to these translations?

MŚ: The readers' reception was rather positive but not very wide. Someone told me they understood Kerouac in Polish for the first time and that especially *Big Sur* seems very moving. I was happy to hear that, of course.

There was a company that wanted to publish that novel as an audio-book, about a year ago (2022), but they never called again to sign the contract. A few people borrowed Kerouac's works from me to read because they went quickly out of print. And they caused a slight stir on the web—the public was talking about the Beats again for a while.

FG: The answer to this question is quite intricate. The reactions to my translations from the Beat Generation are often intertwined with my own identity as a writer in Iranian literature. Similarly, the impact of my translations also influences the reception of my own works, including those from the Beat Generation. For instance, I once came across an article in a Persian media outlet that criticized the "communist" Kerouac! The author of the article clearly lacked knowledge about Kerouac, but due to the frequent attacks from right-wing media labeling me as a "communist," they automatically extended the same accusation to Kerouac. Since the publication of Burroughs' *Naked Lunch*, and Kerouac's *Big Sur*, I have faced numerous critiques. Some individuals believe that these works promote immorality, while others wrongly associate my translations with support for the Islamic State of Iran. Because they believe that by publishing these works in Iran, the government can make a fake gesture of freedom of expression.

However, despite these challenges, I have observed through my interactions with readers on Instagram that the enthusiasts of Beat literature in Iran are among the most passionate readers of literature. Whenever news about Beat works is released, they reach out to me, eager to know how they can obtain the books sooner. They also share their feelings and impressions about the books with me. This direct connection with my audience has allowed me to witness the profound impact of Kerouac's writing on his readers. Allow me to share an interesting memory: in a surprising turn of events, even employees at the censorship office displayed an interest in Kerouac's work. On one occasion, one of my own novels was banned from publication in Iran for two years. When I visited the Ministry of Culture, an employee from the censorship office recognized me and expressed how *The Dharma Bums* had transformed and saved his life. A decade ago, Kerouac was relatively unknown in Iran, but today he is one of the most beloved authors among Iranians. The audience of the Beat Generation in Iran is incredibly diverse, although it might be true that the majority consists of students and young people. In general, the subversive nature of Beat works and their exploration of societal control and power dynamics make them relevant to individuals interested in critical theory and alternative perspectives on social structures.

Following the publication of *The Dharma Bums*, a backpacking movement emerged in Iran, inspiring many people to embark on journeys under the influence of this novel. The striking similarities between the natural landscapes of Iran and America have also played a significant role in this fascination.

Moreover, the proliferation of the Internet over the past two decades has significantly expanded access to films and archives for readers. As an example, a majority of Beat literature enthusiasts in Iran have likely watched film adaptations of novels like *On the Road* and *Big Sur*, as well as documentaries featuring Burroughs. It's important to mention that Iran lacks a copyright law specific to foreign works. Consequently, accessing free and unauthorized versions of movies and books in Iran is both simple and widespread. However, I genuinely hope that acknowledging this reality won't lead to the arrest of myself or other Iranian citizens in Europe.

EM, TS: Is there anything that your readers have a hard time understanding about Kerouac or his work? On the other hand, what is universal in Kerouac's writing?

FG: When considering the universality of Kerouac's work, I hold the belief that literature, at its core, possesses a universal nature. It transcends national boundaries and exhibits an intercultural essence. This perspective may contrast with Heidegger's view on poetry and modern art, as he argued that art and literature are inherently tied to a specific historical people or nation (*volk*), akin to an architectural structure shaping the existence of a particular people. However, in my view, even in pre-modern literature, a universal character can be discerned. The primary obstacle in the pre-modern era stemmed from the lack of knowledge between nations regarding each other's history and literature, which resulted from limited communication technologies. Nonetheless, this limitation did not negate the universal potential inherent in literature itself.

MŚ: It's hard for me to say, it's rather a question you should put to the readers. When I was still an academic teacher I had to explain to my students the cultural context in which to place Kerouac, so we spoke a lot about counterculture, the social and economic situation in America of the 1940s, 1950s, and 1960s, the music of the times and so on. And about the beatniks, naturally, where they came from and where they ended up. But like I said before, American culture and literature was always present in the mind of an average Polish reader and was never considered too exotic or cryptic to understand, even when we were still behind the Iron Curtain. A universal factor in Kerouac's writing? I think it's most of all the human factor—the author's fragility, sensitivity and feeling of isolation, as well as the inability to deal with practical, "normal" life. Poland had writers, especially in the '60s, who intentionally or unintentionally emulated Kerouac and the Beats; who dedicated themselves to something they called "life-writing," composing spontaneous prose and verse devoted mainly to their lives and travels (Edward Stachura, for instance, Andrzej Bursa or Rafał Wojaczek).

EM, TS: In the US context, Kerouac, along with the Beats in general, has come under closer scrutiny for his depiction of women and minority groups. While Kerouac's works are certainly being read, there seems to be an increased criticism of many of his books. Here in the west, we have also heard quite a bit recently about the protests of Iranian women frustrated with misogyny and social repression. Are readers of your translations voicing similar concerns, or do they see Kerouac as a liberating force? What do you see as the future for Kerouac in Iran, Poland and Japan?

FG: Let's start with the recent movement that emerged in Iran in early September 2022. The central slogan of this movement is "Woman Life Freedom." During this time, Iranian women and men united against political and governmental discrimination targeting women, as well as other issues such as the lack of social and political liberties, systemic discrimination against women and ethnic groups, and widespread government corruption. Notably, a significant demand of this movement is the repeal of the mandatory hijab law, which is a political imposition by the State rather than a reflection of the will of the people or the culture. It is important to highlight that over eighty percent of Iranians oppose mandatory hijab. However, it is worth noting that the majority of those killed, executed, or imprisoned during these protests were Iranian men.

Regarding the recent criticism of the representation of women and minorities in Kerouac's works, I believe three key points are significant. Firstly, these critiques should be acknowledged and respected as they enable multiple interpretations of Kerouac's writings and foster dialogue surrounding his texts. Anything that enhances the possibility of dialogue deserves appreciation. Secondly, it is essential to recognize that applying certain contemporary discourses to Kerouac's texts can sometimes be entirely anachronistic. Every writer is inevitably influenced to some extent by the prevailing ideologies and discourses of their era. Louis Althusser taught us that, despite their radicality, writers and intellectuals cannot entirely free themselves from the ideologies and discourses of their time.

Thirdly, it is important to understand that literature is not a sacred text that must be devoid of any flaws or strive for absolute perfection, loftiness, and sublimity. This applies to Kerouac as well. In the words of William Burroughs, Kerouac was like a bullfighter who confronted real bulls. Burroughs says that many individuals who label themselves as writers and have their names on book jackets are not writers and lack the ability to write. The distinction lies in the fact that a "bullfighter" engages with a real bull, whereas a "bullshitter" makes empty gestures without any substance. A writer has truly experienced something, or they couldn't write about it. Kerouac was neither a prophet nor a holy man expected to possess omniscience or foresight. He was a writer, a bullfighter. Nothing more. This perception has become a common American attitude that elevates writers and poets to the status of prophets. Consider Whitman's image among Americans—he has been transformed into a prophet, and prophets are presumed to possess all-encompassing knowledge, including about the future, making them immune to criticism. Whitman was undoubtedly a great poet, just as Kerouac was a remarkable writer. Any form of criticism can lead to further engagement and dialogue with their works.

Given that in Iran, the oppression of women has always been intertwined with broader social repression, which is itself a component of political repression and the curtailment of fundamental freedoms, it is challenging for the Iranian audience to specifically single out the representation of women in Kerouac's work or label him as anti-feminist or misogynistic. Kerouac explores the freedom of diverse forms of life, pushing the boundaries as radically as possible within his own era. It is this fervor for freedom that resonates with the Iranian audience when engaging with his works.

MŚ: It depends who is talking and voicing those or any other concerns. Certainly there are people who criticize and even censor everything (Roald Dahl in Britain comes to mind) that does not comply or agree with the world-image created by political correctness, radical feminism and other Leftist social and intellectual movements. But Kerouac is also still perceived as a herald of personal freedom and escape from "the system," from the establishment. And he is read as the product of his times, not only unfavorably as a "dead white male."

I have no idea about his future in Poland but I do believe he will be read at least by a minor group of followers. He is a literary legend and as such he'll survive, at least in my view. He might get forgotten but he'll get rediscovered soon enough. His place in the history of American literature is, I think, secure, regardless of what some people might think about his—sometimes undoubtedly unfair—treatment of women or minority groups. But the writer's task is not necessarily to be fair, it's rather to speak the truth about himself and the world, and truth cannot be "fair."

MA: Sal is a mama's boy, Dean is macho. Some say it like that and that is correct. There used to be no opinions like that. Sal is passive, Dean is active. Some say it like that. That is correct, too. Kerouac is of French-Canadian descent. He is of a minority group. He will be read in this context in future.

EM, TS: Finally, do you have additional Kerouac projects in the works? What would you like to see translated going forward?

MA: He wrote many Sketches and Haikus. I am very interested in translating these if possible. Nobel Laureate Kenzaburo Oe translated one of Kerouac's Haikus.

MŚ: No, not at the moment. He was not a financial success, so he's not published any more, at least for the time being.

Actually I'd like to see the lot; or at least all of his prose works in Polish. There are still a few left, like *Satori in Paris* or *Visions of Cody*. Kerouac's letters would be interesting, too. I'm sure sooner or later somebody's going to do them.

FG: Yes, I began the translation of the short novel *Tristessa*, almost three years ago, but I had to set it aside temporarily as I started working on my PhD thesis focusing on Walt Whitman. Additionally, the completion of my co-authored book with Oliver Harris, titled *Two Assassins: William Burroughs and Hassan Sabbah*, also took priority, causing a pause in the translation process. Nevertheless, I am determined to resume the translation soon. On another note, I have also translated the short story "cityCityCITY" and intend to publish it as a pocket-sized book after completing the final editing. These projects are dear to me, and I'm excited to bring them to fruition and share them with readers.

Afterword
Tim Hunt

When I was writing my doctoral dissertation on Jack Kerouac in the early spring of 1974, I duly presented on my research at a graduate student forum. In those days, writing one's dissertation on a non-canonical figure (and in 1974 Kerouac was not in the least canonical) wasn't good form. Still, my fellow grad students with their careers smartly committed to Beowulf, Wordsworth, and even Melville along with the faculty who were piously guiding them in the ways of academic righteousness listened respectfully as I rehearsed the evidence that Kerouac had made a series of attempts at *On the Road* before the so-called *scroll* draft of April 1951, and they even listened as I tried to suggest that these experiments in style and point of view meant that this famous/infamous spate of typing had aesthetic purpose and thematic depth. When it came time for the ritual of Q&A, the first—and only—question came from a senior Faulkner scholar, who asked, with a kind of pained earnestness, *But ... but ... but ... Is he any* ***good****?*

In 1974 as New Criticism and Historicism were jousting for control of literary studies without a clue that THEORY was about to storm the Ivory Tower and lock them in the dungeon, the first question was, indeed, the aesthetic one—and the only one. If a writer's work had somehow come to be deemed *good*, then the work could be seriously engaged and even the work's author, as distinct from its writer, might be considered—but only if doing so helped in appreciating the work. In 1974 *On the Road* was a piece of pop product that had somehow been typed (but not written) by an unreflective joy riding adolescent with a penchant for Benzedrine inhalers and illicit smokes. Hitching a ride with Sal and Dean was an illicit lark—the academic equivalent to undergrad spring break high jinks before signing on to the Pequod to go whaling or river rafting with Huck and Jim. In 1974, the issue was *what* to make of the work, and with *On the Road* (the primary emblem for Kerouac at the time) the answer was less than *not much* because *On the Road* wasn't a *work*. It wasn't literature. It wasn't *aesthetic*. The myth of its *composition* proved it couldn't be *any good*. Case dismissed. Court adjourned.

A half-century later, how and why we talk about literature have changed. If the challenge was once to confront the (implicitly New Critical) question of *Is he* (i.e., the work) *any good*, the question is now *Is he* (i.e., the corpus of work, the person, and the figure, even *brand* we've collectively constructed from the actual figure) *productively and/or problematically significant for our social and cultural and historical interrogations*. The essays gathered in *Rethinking Kerouac: Afterlives, Continuities, and Reappraisals* reflect this change, and from their varied angles, occasions, and methodologies they demonstrate that Kerouac, as person, as writer, and as body of work, is *significant*. The Kerouac variously constructed in these pieces is at the center of the problematics of mid-century culture, and they reframe the study of Kerouac in ways that parallel changes over the past half-century in how and why we talk about literature and writers. They demonstrate that what now matters is how Kerouac—as work or person or cultural emblem or some amalgam of all three—provides a significant occasion for engaging an array of problematics, including race, gender, and myths of national identity. Instead of the writer's work mattering for aesthetic reasons, the work and the writer matter for the cultural work they enable and can sustain. And as such it matters less that Kerouac failed to resolve such crucial problematics as race and more that his attempts to engage race (from the perspective of his own conflicted experiences of ethnicity sexuality, and class—his awareness of *Americanness* as a problematic) require and repay close attention.

Among the values these articles offer, both individually and collectively, is that they move decisively beyond *On the Road* and the once prevailing assumption that one work distils Kerouac's career and encompasses its significance. Instead, they broaden the field to include not only his other novels but also his non-fiction, his poetry, his perhaps uncategorizable texts, and his visual art. The Kerouac who matters now might be said to be *genre fluid*, and this brings to the fore the question of whether he is best understood as a symptom of his era, a kind of cultural seismograph acutely registering its fault lines and shiftings, or a capacious observer/analyst mapping his era. Truman Capote's snide quip, *That's not writing, that's typewriting*, has become a false, and thereby irrelevant, binary. However we each answer this question in the present and however we may collectively answer it in the years to come, Kerouac has become a figure who occasions and repays explorations—and will continue to do so.

The essays in *Rethinking Kerouac* demonstrate the value of focusing on the writer as cultural actor rather than the author as *il miglior fabbro*—as T.S. Eliot once celebrated Ezra Pound for his role in shaping *The Waste Land*. But even as our recognition of Kerouac as cultural symptom embodying his era's contradictions, as cultural observer, as pop culture figure, and as the brand *Kerouac* have come to the fore and helped lead to the recognition of Kerouac as a significant figure, the old question of whether his writing, the books, are literarily *good* still matters—not because the cultural elitism of the New Critics still matters but because the question mattered to Kerouac and is yet another of the contradictions that make him such a protean figure. And yet another value of this collection is the way it points to the need to engage Kerouac's literary ambitions as necessary to, but not sufficient for, exploring his personal and cultural ambitions and why they might matter going forward.

Kerouac's work journals for the months following the April 1951 scroll draft of *On the Road* show him caught between his desire for commercial success as a writer and his desire for literary significance. He toyed with revising *On the Road* to make it more commercial but also longed to write without regard for the narrative conventions and stylistic norms of the market, even though doing so would mean abandoning any hope for publication. And he imagined having his cake and eating it, too, by cranking out a "potboiler" to make enough money to buy the time to write what he wanted to write as he wanted to write it. Kerouac's attempts to resolve this conflict are part of the back story to his experimental magnum opus, the book we now know as *Visions of Cody* but which was, when he finished it in the spring of 1952, titled *On Road*.[1] But even as he finished this *Cody* version of *Road*, Kerouac was still searching for ways to be both a success in the market and literarily significant. In his April 7, 1952 letter to Carl Solomon, who was then working for his uncle A. A. Wyn at Ace Books, Kerouac urges Solomon to have Ace "publish full ROAD in hardcover" because this "full ROAD (i.e., *Visions of Cody*) will make Wyn a first-rate reputation" (i.e., bring Ace Books renown as a publisher of literature rather than just a publisher of titillating mass market paperbacks). But at the same time he imagines Ace publishing a "papercover" of what he terms the "sexy narrative stretch" of this version of *On the Road* (pages 338–98 of *Visions of Cody*). This, Kerouac insists, "is no dope idea, this is real money idea." The whole of *On the Road* (i.e., *Visions of Cody*) as a "hardcover" for the bookstores with the concluding narrative unit as "papercover" for the drugstores and dime stores book racks and rail station kiosks would, Kerouac wanted to believe, yield literary significance coupled with market success.[2] But if Kerouac had to choose between these two, his letter to Allen Ginsberg just over a month later shows the choice he would make:

> I know you will love *On the Road* [i.e. *Visions of Cody*]—please read it all, no one has read it all yet …. *On the Road* is inspired in its entirety … I can tell now as I look back on the flood of language. It is like *Ulyssees* and should be treated with the same gravity. If Wyn or Carl insist on cutting it up to make the "story" more intelligible I'll refuse.[3]

The art of the *Cody* version of *On Road* is, Kerouac insists here, in its "flood of language," which is to say the writing itself and not its narrative or "story."

Kerouac's insistence that the *Cody* version of *On the Road* is high art in the same sense as Joyce's *Ulysses* brings us back to the question of whether Kerouac's writing is actually *good* and what conceptual or historical framing might enable us to determine that. But the social, cultural, and institutional reframings presented in *Rethinking Kerouac* make this a different question than it was in 1974, a half-century ago, and it points us to the question of what it meant to Kerouac to set aside the *Cody* version of *On Road*, return to the April 1951 scroll *On the Road*, and undertake the process of working it into the version that Viking Books finally published in 1957. At the very least this entailed, for Kerouac (and Ginsberg and Malcolm Cowley as they variously participated in the process) negotiating the conflict between market and art, between "story" and "flood of language." Examining this is one way to probe Kerouac's conflicted relationship to publishing and readership as those options were actually structured and practiced at mid-century and to recognize, as well, that those structures and practices were changing. *On the Road* might be, as Cowley proposed, *The Sun Also Rises* for the Beat Generation, but in the 1950s it was no longer possible for a book to be critically hailed for its literary value and to dominate the market as reflected in the best seller lists. Writing intended as literature and writing intended as commercial entertainment were diverging. For Hemingway in The Roaring Twenties, the possibility existed, if perhaps only briefly, to be an artist and a celebrity, indeed a celebrity artist. For Kerouac, partly because of who he was but also because the cultural moment and the cultural market had both shifted creating a gap between the work as commodity and the work as art, it was an either/or matter: to be a celebrity threatened to erase one's identity, at least in the public sphere, as an artist. It was both Kerouac's good fortune and his tragedy that the content of the book that made his reputation and his own biography could so be seen as one and the artistry of *On the Road*, Kerouac's intricate dialectic of "story" and "word flow" either missed entirely or misconstrued and dismissed as merely *typewriting*.

The work collected in *Rethinking Kerouac* deepens and problematizes our understanding of Kerouac as a creator, broadens and enriches our awareness of his career, and offers a new mapping of his cultural engagements. The Kerouac in these articles is not the Kerouac I earnestly offered my fellow graduate students in 1974. It is instead a Kerouac informed by and in dialogue with the current configuration of literary and cultural studies. And that is as it should be. Moreover, these rethinkings demonstrate that Kerouac and his work will continue to repay our thinking and rethinking in the years ahead. And such sustained engagement with a writer and his work is a sign that the writer is, in fact, a major figure. And major figures are by definition *good*.

Notes

1   See Chapter 4 of my Tim Hunt, *The Textuality of Soulwork: Jack Kerouac's Quest for Spontaneous Prose* (Ann Arbor: Michigan University Press, 2014) for a discussion of this material.
2   Jack Kerouac, *Selected Letters 1940–1956*, ed. Ann Charters (New York: Viking, 1995), 342–3.
3   Kerouac, *Selected Letters 1940–1956*, 355.

Notes on Contributors

Minami Aoyama has translated Philip Roth (*The Ghost Writer*), Joan Didion (*Slouching Towards Bethlehem*), Bernard Malamud (*The Tenants*), and more than twenty writers' voices from *The Paris Review Interviews*. He is also an author of many books of essays. He lives in Tokyo.

Steven Belletto, professor of English at Lafayette College, is author of *The Beats: A Literary History* (Cambridge UP, 2020) and *No Accident, Comrade: Chance and Design in Cold War American Narratives* (Oxford UP, 2012). His edited books include *The Cambridge Companion to Jack Kerouac* (Cambridge UP, 2024), *American Literature in Transition, 1950–1960* (Cambridge UP, 2018), *The Cambridge Companion to the Beats* (Cambridge UP, 2017), and, as co-editor, *Neocolonial Fictions of the Global Cold War* (U of Iowa P, 2019), and *American Literature and Culture in an Age of Cold War: A Critical Reassessment* (U of Iowa P, 2012). He is currently completing a critical biography of Ted Joans.

Frida Forsgren is Associate Professor in art history at the Department of Visual Arts and Drama at the University of Agder, Norway. She has published extensively in Early Modern Studies, Modernism, Feminism, and Beat Studies. She teaches an interdisciplinary course in Beat Studies at the University of Agder. She also works as a critic and a curator.

Deborah R. Geis is Professor of English at DePauw University in Greencastle, Indiana, where she specializes in twentieth- and twenty-first-century literature, especially drama/performance poetry, African American literature, Beat Studies, and culinary literature. She is the author of *Postmodern Theatric(k)s* (Univ. of Michigan), *Suzan-Lori Parks* (Univ. of Michigan), *Read My Plate: The Literature of Food* (Lexington Books), and the forthcoming *Culinary Cinema*. She has also edited three anthologies: *Approaching the Millennium: Essays on Angels in America* (co-ed. Steven F. Kruger; Univ. of Michigan); *Considering MAUS* (Univ. of Alabama); and *Beat Drama: Playwrights and Performances of the "Howl" Generation* (Bloomsbury Methuen).

Farid Ghadami is an Iranian writer and literary translator, who has to date published more than fifty books in the fields of literature, art, philosophy, engineering sciences and mathematics. He is best known in Iran for his humorous and critical novels with a radical counterculture outlook, as well as his translations of controversial literature, including that of the Beat Generation. He is the first translator of many major literary works into Persian, including *Ulysses* by James Joyce, *Naked Lunch* by William Burroughs, *Howl* by Allen Ginsberg, *Big Sur* and *The Dharma Bums* by Jack Kerouac.

His first Beat Generation translations were published in 2008, and since then he has continuously introduced Beat Generation literature to Persian speakers. In 2021, after years of teaching in Iranian engineering faculties, he came to Paris to write his doctoral thesis in American literature on "Walt Whitman and the literary community" at Université Paris-Est Créteil. In 2023, he co-authored the book *Two Assassins* with Oliver Harris, exploring the portrayal of Hassan Sabbah in the writings of William Burroughs.

Nancy M. Grace is the Virginia Myers Professor of English (emerita) at The College of Wooster. She is the author of *Jack Kerouac and the Literary Imagination* (winner of the Choice 100 top book awards), editor of *The Beats: A Teaching Companion*, and co-editor with Ronna C. Johnson of *Girls Who Wore Black: Women Writing the Beat Generation* and *Breaking the Rule of Cool: Interviewing and Reading Women Beat Writers* (winner of the Choice 100 top book awards), and with Jennie Skerl of *The Transnational Beat Generation*. She has written numerous articles on Beat writers, including Diane di Prima, ruth weiss, William S. Burroughs, and Ed Sanders. She is a founding member of the Beat Studies Association, founding editor of the *Journal of Beat Studies*, and founding editor of the Clemson University Press Beat Studies book series.

Kurt Hemmer is the editor of the *Encyclopedia of Beat Literature* and a Professor at Harper College. With filmmaker Tom Knoff, he produced several award-winning films. His essays have appeared in *Naked Lunch@50: Anniversary Essays*; *A History of California Literature*; *Beat Drama*; *The Cambridge Companion to the Beats*; *Approaches to Teaching Baraka's Dutchman*; *William S. Burroughs: Cutting Up the Century*; *The Beats, Black Mountain, and New Modes in American Poetry*; and *Harold Norse: Poet Maverick, Gay Laureate*. He organized The Jack Kerouac Centenary Conference. Currently the Secretary of the Beat Studies Association, he is working on a Gregory Corso biography.

Tim Hunt's critical work includes two studies of Kerouac, *Kerouac's Crooked Road: Development of a Fiction* and *The Textuality of Soulwork: Kerouac's Quest for Spontaneous Prose*, and *The Collected Poetry of Robinson Jeffers*. His six collections of poetry include *Voice to Voice in the Dark* and *Western Where*. Originally from the hill country of northern California, he was educated at Cornell University. He concluded his teaching career at Illinois State University where he was University Professor of English. He and his wife, Susan, live in Normal, Illinois.

Ronna C. Johnson, Ph.D., is Lecturer in English at Tufts University. She is writing *Inventing Jack Kerouac: Reception and Reputation 1957–2007* (Camden House Press). She is co-author of *Breaking the Rule of Cool: Interviewing and Reading Women Beat Writers* (UP Mississippi, 2004), and she co-edited *Girls Who Wore Black: Women Writing the Beat Generation* (Rutgers UP, 2002). Johnson is founder and coeditor of the *Journal of Beat Studies* and founder and series coeditor of the Beat Studies Book Series. Recent essays include "From Beat Bop Prosody to Punk Rock Poetry: Patti Smith and Jack Kerouac; Literature, Lineage, Legacy" and "Gender, Race, and Narrative in *On the Road*."

A. Robert Lee, formerly of the University of Kent UK where he taught American Studies, was Professor at Nihon University and Waseda University, Tokyo, 1997–2011. His full-length book publications include *Designs of Blackness: Mappings in the Literature and Culture of Afro-America* (1998, 25th anniversary edition 2020), *Multicultural American Literature: Comparative Black, Native, Latino/a and Asian American Fictions* (2003), which won the American Book Award in 2004, *Gothic to Multicultural: Idioms of Imagining in American Literary Fiction* (2008), *Modern American Counter Writing: Beats, Outriders, Ethnics* (2010), *The Beats: Authorships, Legacies* (2022), *Native North American Authorship: Text. Breath, Modernity* (2022), and *Moderns: Chaucer to Contemporary Fiction* (2025). He also has a varied portfolio of creative writing.

Hassan Melehy teaches French, English, and comparative literature at the University of North Carolina at Chapel Hill. His 2016 book, *Kerouac: Language, Poetics, and Territory*, is the first full-length study of the author's French-language heritage and its immense role in his writing. Melehy also writes about the European Renaissance, critical theory, and cinema; he is a contributor to *The Many Worlds of David Amram: Renaissance Man of American Music* (Routledge, 2023). He has translated several works of philosophy and social science from French. Melehy is also a poet: his first collection, *A Modest Apocalypse*, came out in 2017.

Michael Millner is Associate Professor of English and American Studies at the University of Massachusetts Lowell, where he also serves as the Director of the Jack and Stella Kerouac Center in the Public Humanities. The Center oversees the university's extensive Kerouac archive. From 2020 to 2022, he held the appointment of the Nancy Donahue Professor in the Arts.

Aldon Lynn Nielsen currently serves as the Kelly Professor of American Literature at Penn State University. He has also taught at Howard University, San Jose State, UCLA, Loyola Marymount, and Central China Normal University. He was the first recipient of the Larry Neal Award for poetry, and has also been honored with the Kayden Prize, the Darwin Turner Award, and others. His books include *Reading Race, Black Chant, Integral Music, The Inside Songs of Amiri Baraka, Back Pages: Selected Poems*, and *Spider Cone*.

Peggy Pacini is Associate Professor at CY Cergy Paris University where she teaches American literature and translation. In her PhD and in various articles she addressed the issue of language, identity, cultural heritage, and ethnicity in Kerouac's Duluoz Legend. Among these: "*Satori in Paris*: Deconstructing the French Connection or the Legend's Satori," "Roots Always Precede Routes: On the Road, through a Glass Darkly," "Les romans de Lowell: des romans géographes." She translated *The Letters of Allen Ginsberg* (Gallimard, 2008), and also published articles on other members of the Beat Generation (Allen Ginsberg, ruth weiss) and the French reception of the Beats.

Pierre-Antoine Pellerin is Associate Professor of American literature at the University of Lyon where he teaches twentieth-century American fiction, gender studies, and translation. His research deals with the experience and representation of masculinity in American culture, with a particular focus on Jack Kerouac and other Beat Generation writers. He has published several articles on those topics in journals like *Angles, Transatlantica, Leaves, Interfaces, Transtext*(e)s, and *Theatre Topics* and was the recent guest-editor of an issue of the *French Review of American Studies* devoted to "The Art of Failure."

Brett Sigurdson recently completed his PhD in English Literature at the University of Minnesota. There, he completed a dissertation on Jack Kerouac's posthumous reputation, *We Know Jack: On the Road with the Influencers Shaping the Legacy of America's Most Iconic Author*. He is currently revising the project for a book. He has also taught courses on the Beats in Minnesota, Utah, and Vermont.

Maciej Świerkocki is a former academic teacher with a PhD in comparative literature, as well as an award-winning freelance translator, critic, screenwriter, and novelist. He's translated more than eighty books from English into Polish, including works by John Barth, Angela Carter, Cormac McCarthy, Robert Graves, Richard Hughes, Jack Kerouac, Henry Miller, John Irving, Eleanor Catton, John Updike, Richard Flanagan, Joseph Conrad, and James Joyce. His prose was published in English in *The Tampa Review* and *The Yellow Nib*. His latest translation into Polish is James Joyce's *Ulysses* (2021), which received an important "Gdynia" literary prize (2022). Author of *Łódź Ulissesa* (2021), an essay/diary of translating *Ulysses*, which was honored with the Tadeusz Kotarbiński Award for the best Polish book on arts/humanities in 2023. Member of the Polish Writers' Association and the Polish Film Academy. He lives and works in Łódź, Poland.

Matt Theado is Professor of American Cultural Studies at Kobe City University of Foreign Studies, Japan. He is the author of *Understanding Jack Kerouac* (University of South Carolina Press, 2000) and editor of *The Beats: A Literary Reference* (Carroll & Graf, 2003) and *The Beats, Black Mountain, and New Modes in American Poetry* (Clemson University Press, 2021). He serves as president of the Beat Studies Association and co-editor of the *Journal of Beat Studies*. He is a member of the editorial board of *The Journal of the American Literature Society of Japan*.

Simon Warner is Visiting Research Fellow in Popular Music at the University of Leeds in the UK. He was awarded his PhD in 2010. Warner is the author of *Text and Drugs and Rock 'n' Roll: The Beats and Rock Culture* (2013) and co-editor of *Kerouac on Record: A Literary Soundtrack* (2018). He has been the director/producer of various live Beat events, including *Howl for Now* (2005), *Still Howling* (2015), and *Kerouac on Screen* (2019) and a co-creator of the live centenary show *Kerouac Lives!* (2022). He is also founding editor of the website *Rock and the Beat Generation* (simonwarner.substack.com), established in 2021, which explores the interface between Beat writing and popular music.

John Whalen-Bridge is the author of *Political Fiction and the American Self* (1998) and *Tibet on Fire: Buddhism, Rhetoric, and Self-Immolation* (Palgrave, 2015). "Buddhism and the Beats" appeared in *The Cambridge Companion to the Beats* (2017). He is currently working on a book about engaged Buddhism and postwar American writers, as well as literary biography of Maxine Hong Kingston. Together with Maxine Hong and Earll Kingston, Joe Lamb, David Johnson, Joanne Palamountain, and Katherine Taylor, he performed selections of *Lincoln in the Bardo* for the 2018 American Literature Association, which was fun.

Index

Abbott, Craig S., *An Introduction to Bibliographical & Textual Studies* 18
addiction to drugs, Kerouac's 197
Adler, Ed 56, 57 n.6
  Departed Angels: The Lost Paintings 9, 45
Adorno, Theodor W., "Spengler After Decline", *Prisms* 170 n.66
affordances, Kerouac's art 56–7
African Americans 37–9, 132, 134–7, 207, 222
Alexander, Thomas M., *John Dewey's Theory of Art, Experience and Nature: The Horizons of Feeling* 57 n.8
Alfred Knopf publishing company 23
Allen, Donald 33
  The New American Poetry 1945–1960 31, 163
Allen, Steve 33–4, 37–8
  "Charlie Parker" 32–3
  "Deadbelly" 38–9
  Poetry for the Beat Generation 32–4, 38
  The Tonight Show ix, 34, 36
Althusser, Louis 238
American Adam. *See* Lewis, R. W. B.
Americanness, Kerouac's 199–208, 241
Amitabha Buddha 77
ancestry of Kerouac 137, 169 n.59, 204–5
ANNs (artificial neural networks) 175, 177
Aoyama, Minami (on translation of Kerouac's works) 228, 233–4, 239
archives, Kerouac's ix, 6, 12–13, 213–17
  Berg Collection, New York Public Library 214
  experiments in 220–4
  Kerouac Archive, University of Massachusetts 214, 220, 223
  Kozera's letters to Kerouac 221
  public humanities 213–14, 217–20, 223
  Sampas collection 214–15

Aristotle 117, 122
Armstrong, Louis, "Old Man Mose" 38–9
Artificial Intelligence (AI) technology 12, 175–7, 181–2, 185 n.34, 222–3
"Automatic on The Road-Gonzo AI Robot Writes Road Trip Novel" short film 173
avant-garde 9, 62, 66–7, 99, 114

Baldwin, James 135–6
Bandera, Sandrina, *Kerouac Beat Painting* 9, 45
Baraka, Amiri 31, 39, 41, 135
Barthes, Roland, *Le Plaisir du Texte* 235
Bay Area Figuration art movement 49–51, 56
Beardsley, M. C., "The Intentional Fallacy" 123
Beat art 46–7
Beat Culture and the New America 1950–1965 exhibition (1996) 58 n.10
Beat Studies Association 4, 10, 13
Bebop 34, 208
Belletto, Steven, *Cambridge Companion to Jack Kerouac* 4
Berkowitz, Carin 219
biculturalism, Kerouac's 205
Big Sur (Kerouac) 3, 68, 71 n.44, 80, 88–90, 153, 188
  Ghadami on translation of 227–9
  Lorenzo Monsanto (fictional character) 88
  Świerkocki on translation of 229, 233
bilingualism, Kerouac's ix, 205
Blair, Eric Arthur 125 n.17
Bliesener, Mark 191, 193–6
Bloch, Bertram 66–7
Boîte, Jean 173
bookmovies/mindmovies 66–7
Bowen, Michael, *Dream-Figure Moves Outside Cave* 54

Brakhage, Stan 67
Brando, Marlon 62, 228
Bremser, Ray, *Black Is Black Blues* 41
Brown, Joan 50
Bryan, William Jennings 144
Buddhism, Kerouac's interest in viii, 9, 74–83, 83 n.8, 84 n.10, 120, 123, 197, 206
   absolute reality 77, 81
   ālayavijñāna (storehouse consciousness) 81–2
   Bodhisattva 77, 80
   Fellaheen with 76–8
   Mahayana Buddhism 77, 146
   mandalas, Buddhist 54–5
   Pure Land 76–8
Burroughs, William S. 5–6, 63–4, 70 n.27, 94, 114, 158–9, 238
   And the Hippos Were Boiled in Their Tanks 64
Buta to Gunkan (*Pigs and Battleships*) film (Shohei Imamura) 234

California School of Fine Arts 46, 50
cancel culture 126 n.23, 199
Capote, Truman 68
Carr, Lucien 40, 63–4, 69 n.20, 93
Carus, Paul, *The Gospel of Buddha* 84 n.10
Cassady, Carolyn 40
Cassady, Neal viii, 2, 17, 36, 40, 68 n.13, 138, 174–5, 180, 188, 197
   The First Third & Other Writings 180
   letter from Kerouac (1951) 174
Catholicism 53–5, 87, 90, 93, 130, 145, 197, 203, 206, 210 n.23, 218
Céline, Louis-Ferdinand 159
Charters, Ann 89, 91, 125 n.11
   Brother Souls 154 n.12
Christianity 145–6, 159, 162
Cimino, Jerry 192, 196
Cleaver, Eldridge 136
Communism 100, 146–8
confession/confessional narrative 10, 87, 90, 93–4
Corso, Gregory 138
   "The Roaming Beatniks" 80
Count Basie Band 32
Cru, Henri 65

Damon, Maria, "Beat Poetry: HeavenHell USA, 1946–1965" 122
Davidson, Michael, *Guys Like Us: Masculinity in Cold War Poetics* 100
Davis, Miles 32, 39
Dead Kennedys band 191
DeFeo, Jay
   The Eyes 46
   The Rose 55
   Wise and Foolish Virgins 55
Dempsey, David, review on *On the Road* 3
Derrida, Jacques 227
   Archive Fever: A Freudian Impression 6
Desolation Angels (Kerouac) viii, 79–80, 82, 91, 100, 132
   Jack Duluoz (fictional character) 79, 82–3, 132
Dewey, John 55–6, 57 n.8
   Art as Experience 45
DeWitt, Fred 173
The Dharma Bums (Kerouac) 8, 11, 44, 53, 75–6, 79, 91, 113–14, 118–24, 173, 232
   Alvah Goldbook (fictional character) 121
   Avalokitesvara the Bear 80–3
   confusion of history and biography 114–16
   depolarization 116–17
   Ghadami on translation of 227–8, 230–1, 236
   Japhy Ryder (fictional character) 79–80, 114, 120–1, 123, 126 n.29, 231
   Ray Smith (fictional character) 75–6, 79–80, 114, 119–20, 122–3
Dickens, Charles, *A Christmas Carol* 65
The Dilexi Gallery 47
di Prima, Diane 41, 114
   Revolutionary Letters: 50th Anniversary Edition 124 n.3
Dostoevsky, Fyodor 2
Douglas, Ann 92, 120, 126 n.26
DuBois, W. E. B., *The Souls of Black Folk* 206, 211 n.53
Duchin, Eddie 38
Duke Ellington Orchestra 32

Duluoz Legend (Kerouac) 8–9, 73–5, 81–3, 88, 129, 144, 150, 201
  Atop an Underwood: Early Stories and Other Writings 191, 210 n.28
  Big Sur (*see Big Sur* (Kerouac))
  Desolation Angels (*see Desolation Angels* (Kerouac))
  The Dharma Bums (*see The Dharma Bums* (Kerouac))
  Doctor Sax 2, 6, 66–7, 133, 163, 165, 216
  Maggie Cassidy 207, 229–30
  On the Road (*see On the Road* (Kerouac))
  Satori in Paris 88, 90–2, 151, 202, 204, 239
  The Subterraneans (*see The Subterraneans* (Kerouac))
  The Town and the City (*see The Town and the City* (Kerouac))
  Tristessa 228, 239
  Vanity of Duluoz: An Adventurous Education viii, 63, 83, 87, 92–4, 100, 143, 146, 152
  Visions of Cody (*see Visions of Cody* (Kerouac))
  Visions of Gerard 217
Dylan, Bob 5, 197, 218

Elliot, Helen 57 n.6
Ellison, Julie 219–20
Ellison, Ralph 137
Europe/European 149, 208, 209 n.3, 232, 235
  The Decline of the West in (Spenglers's) 158
  Kerouac's European ancestry/genealogy 199–200, 202–5
  liberal progressive values 113
  exclusive populism 145, 151. See also inclusive populism

Fallout 4 video game 14 n.16
Farrar, Jay, *One Fast Move or I'm Gone* 188
fellaheen/fellahin 11–12, 76–8, 132, 158–63, 166–7
Ferlinghetti, Lawrence viii, 44, 88, 115

Fields, W. C. 68 n.13
  The Dentist 63
Fitzgerald, F. Scott 207
  The Great Gatsby 18–19, 70 n.27, 200
Fleming, Dean 51–2, 58 n.21
Foursquare API platform 175
Fox, Joseph M. 23
Frank, Robert, *Pull My Daisy* 62
Freud, Sigmund 52, 55, 111 n.53

gender, Kerouac's treatment of 10–11, 109
Genter, Robert 90
George-Warren, Holly 5, 191, 195
  "Can a Feminist Still Love Jack Kerouac?" 4
Gewirtz, Isaac 21
Ghadami, Farid (on translation of Kerouac's works) 227–39
Gibbard, Ben, *One Fast Move or I'm Gone* 188
Gibson, James J. 56
Gibson, Matthew 219
Gifford, Barry 130, 133
Ginsberg, Allen 5–6, 10, 33, 38, 40, 62–4, 68, 73, 99–100, 103, 105, 114, 119, 121, 123, 125 n.11, 145–6, 152, 153, 158–9, 180, 203, 218, 242
  "America" 203
  "The Bloodsong" 64
  "Howl" 33, 114, 124 n.4
  "In Back of the Real" 37
  "The Roaming Beatniks" 80
  The Village Voice 20
Giroux, Robert 21
Goddard, Dwight, *A Buddhist Bible* 74, 84 n.10
Goethe, Johann Wolfgang von 11
  Faust 162–5
Gold, Herbert, *The Nation* 3
Goodwin, Ross
  1 the Road 7, 11, 173–83, 222–3
  narrated reality 177
  recurrent neural long short-term memories (RNN-LSTMs) 174, 176
  The WordCar 174–9, 182, 222
Grace, Nancy M. 66–7
Green, Victor H., *The Negro Travelers' Green Book: 1957* 221–2

Index

handwriting method (composition process) 19
Harvey, David, time-space compression 174
Hassett, Brian 190–5
The Haunted Life (Kerouac) 143, 147, 149, 155 n.36
    Peter Martin (fictional character) 149
Haverty, Joan 24
Henderson, Lu Anne 138
Hinduism 53
Hoffman, Abbie 152
Holladay, Hilary, *What's Your Road, Man?: Critical Essays on Jack Kerouac's On the Road* 13 n.7
Holmes, John Clellon 100, 175
    "The Philosophy of the Beat Generation" 3
    "This is the Beat Generation" 160
homophobia/homophobic 100, 105, 109
homosexuality 100–7, 109, 232
Hughes, Langston, *Not Without Laughter* 133
Huncke, Herbert viii, 115, 121
Hunt, Elle 4
Hurston, Zora Neale, *Their Eyes Were Watching God* 134
Hutcheon, Linda, postmodern 202

inclusive populism 145, 151. *See also* exclusive populism
Iran
    cultural context for Kerouac's work in 232–3, 235, 237–8
    Woman Life Freedom movement 237–8
Ishihara, Shintaro, *Taiyo no Kisetsu (The Sunshine Season)* 234
It's a Wonderful Life film 64

"Jack Kerouac at 90: A Discussion of His Life and Influences" 218
"Jack Kerouac Centenary Conference," Beat Studies Association's 4
Jacquet, Illinois, "Flying Home" 32
Jago, Marian 190, 194–5
Jakobson, Roman 126 n.25
Jameson, Fredric, *The Political Unconscious: Narrative as a Socially Symbolic Act* 125 n.15

Japan, cultural context for Kerouac's work in 228, 233–4
Jay, John 144, 152
jazz music viii–ix, 8, 34, 39–41, 46, 166, 188–90, 230
Joans, Ted 132–3
Johnson, Joyce 133
Johnson, Ronna 93–4, 192, 195
Jones, James 80, 111 n.53
Jones, LeRoi. *See* Baraka, Amiri
Joyce, James, *Ulysses* 2, 242, 247

Kamstra, Jerry, *The Frisco Kid* 49
Kaufman, Bob 41
Kazin, Michael 144
Kengor, Paul G. 14 n.17
Kerouac Archive, University of Massachusetts 214, 220, 223
Kerouac, Edie Parker 138
Kerouac, Gabrielle 129, 153
Kerouac, Jean Louis Levesque 153
Kerouac: Kicks Joy Darkness (1997) album 188
Kerouac, Leo 143–5, 149, 153, 154 n.25
Kingston, Maxine Hong, *The Woman Warrior* 120
Kinsey report (1947) 100
Kirschenbaum, Matthew 176, 181–2
Kozera, Beatrice Franco 221
Krajicek, David J., *Salon* 120–1
Kristiansand Cathedral School 47

Lamantia, Philip 46
Lane, Brigitte 204, 210 n.28
Leadbelly 39
Ledbetter, Huddie. *See* Leadbelly
Lee, Lawrence 130, 133
Leslie, Alfred, *Pull My Daisy* 62
les Nègres blanc (Black Negroes) 151
Lewis, R. W. B. 201
LGBTQ 113–14
Life Is Strange video game (Square Enix) 14 n.16
Lindberg, Anne Morrow, *The Wave of the Future: A Confession of Faith* 149, 154 n.12
literariness 126 n.25
Lomax, John 39

Index

Lonesome Traveler (Kerouac) 9, 73, 76, 79–83, 209 n.16
  "Author's Introduction" 73, 200, 204, 206
  "Mexico Fellaheen" 76, 202
  "The Railroad Earth" 202, 205
Lopez, Vincent, "Swinging with the Goon" 38
Lord, Sterling 62, 100, 129
Lowell Celebrates Kerouac! organization 214, 220
Lowell National Historical Park, Lowell, Massachusetts 224 n.13

Madison, James 144, 152
Mailer, Norman, "The White Negro" 3
mandalas, Buddhist 54–5
manuscripts 19, 21
Marion, Paul 191–2
Martin, Fred 52
Mbembe, Achille 38–9
McClure, Michael viii
McCracken, Michael, *Portrait* 47
McLuhan, Marshall 67
McNally, Dennis, *Desolate Angel* 214
Melville, Herman ix, 1–2
  "The Needle", *Moby-Dick* 116
Mémere. *See* Kerouac, Gabrielle
Merleau-Ponty, Maurice 55
  Phenomenology of Perception 60 n.46
Millay, Thomas J. 125 n.15
Miller, Henry 117
Miller, Mitch 34
Millstein, Gilbert 2, 199
Milton, John, *Paradise Lost* 116
misogyny 4–5, 10, 100, 196, 237–8
Monroe, Arthur 49, 51–2
Moore, Dave 198
Mortenson, Erik, "Beating Time: Configurations of Temporality in Jack Kerouac's *On the Road*" 179–80
Mulvey, Laura 109
musical attraction of Kerouac 188–97
  association with artists 188 (*see also specific artists*)
  conservatism 190
  decline of guitar-focused rock band 193–4
  jazz 188–9
  rock'n'roll community 188–9

Nagar, Richa 88, 92
Najarian, James 84 n.10
Neal Hefti Orchestra 34
New Yorker Theater 63
Nicosia, Gerald 99, 130, 151
  Memory Babe 214
Nietzsche, Friedrich ix, 162, 168 n.32

Obeyd Zakani 232
Olson, Charles 39, 209 n.12
On the Road (Kerouac) viii, 1–2, 4–5, 33, 36, 38, 44, 55, 61, 68, 76–9, 88, 91, 101, 104, 106, 129–33, 135–7, 150, 160, 163, 165–6, 173, 179, 183, 189, 191, 195, 199, 215, 222–2, 229, 232–3, 240–3
  Aoyama on translation of 228
  audiobook version of 17, 27
  "Ben Boncoeur excerpt (written January Jan. 1951 in Richmond Hill)" 21–2
  changes in publications (versions) 17–18, 26–7
  changes in storyline 21–6
  composition process/typescripts 19–27
  Dean Moriarty (fictional character) 25–6, 33, 36, 62, 64, 100, 130, 157, 174, 187, 240
  Dempsey's review on 3
  digitized versions of 28
  Ghost of the Susquehanna 131–2
  Gold's review on 3
  Laura (fictional character) 21–4
  Sal Paradise (fictional character) 21–6, 62, 64, 71 n.44, 76, 78, 130–3, 135, 137, 150, 157–8, 161–2, 168 n.32, 187, 191, 221–2, 240
  Stan Shepard (fictional character) 157
  Terry (fictional character) 221
  Wald's review on 61–2, 64–5
On the Road: The Original Scroll (Kerouac) 21–2, 77, 173–81, 183, 202
Orlovsky, Peter 40, 63, 115
Orwell, George 120, 122, 124
  "Why I Write" 11, 116–18, 120
Osborne, John 114–15, 125 n.14
  "The Beats" 125 n.11

paintings of Kerouac 8–9, 43–6, 48. *See also* works of Kerouac
  Blonde in the Grass 50–1
  The Gary Buddha The Gary Buddha 53
  Heart and Handgun 43
  painting manifesto (1959) 49
  The Slouch Hat 48
  Truman Capote 44–5
  Woman (Joan Rawshanks) in Blue with Black Hat 50
Panish, Jon 131
Park, David 49, 56
Parker, Charlie 33–5, 38, 40
  Charlie Parker With Strings 34
Pasolini, Pier Paolo, *The Gospel According to Matthew* 227–8
Paton, Fiona 5, 165
Penguin Modern Classics publication 27, 120
Perry, David, *The Jack Kerouac Collection* 33
Pic (Kerouac) viii, 1, 11, 129–39, 151
  as blackface minstrelsy 136–7
  Blacks/Blackness 129–36
  Father McGillicuddy (fictional character) 134
  Mr. Otis (fictional character) 136
  Pic/Pictorial Review Jackson (fictional character) 130–7, 151
  romantic primitivism of 129, 131–3, 135
  Sheila (fictional character) 136–7
  Slim/John (fictional character) 130–4, 136–7, 151
Podhoretz, Norman 135, 199
poetry, Kerouac's viii, 8–9, 33–4, 37–9
Poland, cultural context for Kerouac's work in 233–4, 236–7, 239
Pollock, Jackson 52
  paintings of 55
popular music. *See* musical attraction of Kerouac
populism 11, 143–53
posthumous publishing of Kerouac 5, 130, 143, 151, 202
postmodernism 12, 99, 199–202, 208, 209 n.12

Pound, Ezra 13 n.3
  Cantos 31
primitivism 11, 39, 158. *See also* romantic primitivism
The Princeton Dictionary of Buddhism 77
Prometheans 146, 148
public humanities 213–14, 217–20, 223

Québécois community 132–3, 164–6, 204–5

race/racism viii, 5, 10–11, 129–39, 151, 161, 206–7, 241
radical vulnerability 10, 87–94
Randolph, Zilner, "Old Man Mose" 38–9
Raskin, Jonah 194
Reich, Wilhelm 52, 55
religious belief (syncretistic) of Kerouac 53–4, 197, 218. *See also* Buddhism; Catholicism
religious imagery/paintings 54–5
Rimbaud, Arthur 159, 199, 210 n.22
romantic primitivism 129, 131–3, 135–7. *See also* primitivism
Roosevelt, Franklin 143
Rosa, Hartmut 174–5, 181
Rothko, Mark 55, 59 n.43
Ruscha, Ed 223
  Royal Road Test 222

Saltz, Jerry 87–8
Sampas, Jim 188
Sampas, John 13, 44, 214, 216–17
  Sampas collection (Kerouac's archive) 214–15
Sampas, Sebastian (Sabby) 6, 146–7, 149–50, 158–9, 214
  letter to Kerouac (1943) 163
Sampas, Stella 2, 92, 187, 214
sand painting 55
Schapiro, Meyer 44
Scheuerman, William E. 174
screenwriting (screenplay), Kerouac's 9, 61–8
  America 61
  Christmas in New York 65, 70 n.29
  Doctor Sax 66–7

The French Night 66
  from real-life events 63–4
  "Rebel Without a Clue", *Quantum Leap* 68
  "The Wild Galoots" 66
Sedgwick, Eve Kosofsky, "Paranoid Reading and Reparative Reading, or, You're So Paranoid, You Probably Think This Essay Is About You" 219
Seward, Tom 70 n.27
sexuality, Kerouac's treatment of 10–11, 109, 124
Signet publication 26–7
Sinclair, Upton, *The Jungle* 123
Singapore 113–14, 118–20
The Six Gallery 47, 51, 113, 118, 121
sketching methods of Kerouac 49, 52, 55–6, 99
  Catholic religious imageries 54
Slam and Spoken Word poetry 33
Smith, Patti 197–8, 204
  "Babelogue" manifesto 203
  Patti Smith Collected Lyrics 210 n.22
Snyder, Gary 119, 121, 126 n.29, 231
socialism 118, 148
social media accounts of Kerouac 5
Solnit, Rebecca
  Orwell's Roses 126 n.20
  Secret Exhibition: Six Artists of the Cold War Era 10 n.58
Solomon, Carl, letter from Kerouac (1952) 115, 242
Some of the Dharma (Kerouac) 77–8, 82, 84 n.10
  deep form 75
  Mind Essence 74–5, 77
Sommer, Doris, "Pre-Texts" 223
Spandler, Horst 198
Spengler, Oswald 6, 11, 159–66, 170 n.66
  The Decline of the West 76, 132, 145, 158, 162
  Faustian man 162–4
  view on Egypt 160
Spicer, Jack 46, 58 n.12
Spivak, Gayatri, radical vulnerability 10, 87

spontaneity viii, 6–7, 41, 100, 106, 227, 230
Stern, Milton R., *The Fine Hammered Steel of Melville* 116
Sterritt, David 62–3
"Still Outside: Kerouac@100", City Lights's 4
The Subterraneans (Kerouac) viii, 36, 38, 44, 64, 136, 202, 204, 206
  Leo Percepied (fictional character) 206–8
  Mardou Fox (fictional character) 207–8
Surrealists 52
Świerkocki, Maciej (on translation of Kerouac's works) 229–31, 233–4, 236–9
syncretistic religious view of Kerouac 53–4, 76

Tanguay, Cyprien 169 n.59
Tanselle, G. Thomas 27
  "Reproducing the Texts of Documents" 28
texts, composition 18–21
  defined 18
  handwritten text (manuscripts) 19, 21
  initial stage of 19
  original scroll typescript of *On the Road* 21–2
  typescripts 19–27
Thomas, Pat 192–4
Thompson, Hunter S., *Fear and Loathing in Las Vegas: A Savage Journey to the Heart of the American Dream* 211 n.61
The Tonight Show (Steve Allen) ix, 34, 36
Tourneur, Jacques, *Out of the Past* 64
The Town and the City (Kerouac) 2, 21, 64, 65, 129, 143, 202–3
  Judie (fictional character) 69 n.22
transnational/transnationalism 6, 199–200
tribute (commemoration) to Kerouac 188–9, 220
Trump, Donald 143–4
Twain, Mark 18, 191, 199

The United States 146, 166, 200, 235
   The Decline of the West in (Spenglers's) 158
   fellahin 158–60
   homosexuality 100
   religious painting in 55
   populism 143
   Québécois population, migration to 164
The United States Merchant Marines 148
University of Agder (Norway), art collection at 44, 47–9, 56

Viking Press publication 17, 21, 23–7, 176, 202, 242
Virilio, Paul 174, 178
vision 73–6, 81–3, 83 n.8
Visions of Cody (Kerouac) viii, 2, 10, 75, 89, 99–100, 176, 201, 239, 241–2
   anti-homosexual paranoia 105, 109
   Cody Pomeray (fictional character) 66, 100–3, 106–8, 111 n.46
   heterosexuality 4, 10, 100, 103, 105–7
   homosexuality/homoerotic 10, 100–9
   Josephine (fictional character) 101, 103
   masculinity 100–1, 105–9
   pornography 107–8, 111 n.46
   Swenson (fictional character) 104
visual affordances of Kerouac's art 56–7
Vlagopoulos, Penny 183 n.7
vulnerability. *See* radical vulnerability

Wald, Jerry 63, 68
   review on *On the Road* 61–2, 64–5
Walsh, Raoul, *White Heat* 64
Weinreich, Regina 3, 99
weiss, ruth viii, 44, 46, 193
Welch, Lew 89, 122
Wennesland Collection 47, 54
Wennesland, Reidar 44, 47
Western culture 12, 38, 40, 76, 159–60, 162–3, 233
Whalen, Philip 122

Whitman, Walt 238–9
Wideman, John Edgar, *Writing to Save a Life: The Louis Till File* 31
Williams, William Carlos, "Ol' Bunk's Band" 38
Williams, William Proctor, *An Introduction to Bibliographical & Textual Studies* 18
Wimsatt, W. K., "The Intentional Fallacy" 123
Wolfe, Thomas 197, 202
   You Can't Go Home Again 202
women biographers 195
works of Kerouac. *See also* paintings of Kerouac
   "Alone on a Mountaintop" 79–82
   The Beat Generation 62
   "Beat Spotlight" 129
   "The Birth of a Socialist" 147–8
   Book of Blues 37, 41
   "Bop Prosody" 32, 41, 48
   "Cerrada Medellin Blues" 41
   "Charlie Parker" 32–3
   Collected Poems 8, 33, 37, 39, 41
   comparisons of Kerouac's works (with fellow writers) 2, 13 n.3
   "Deadbelly" 38–9
   Desolation Peak 79–81
   Duluoz Legend (*see* Duluoz Legend (Kerouac))
   "Essentials of Spontaneous Prose" 2, 31–2, 49, 52, 99, 201
   The Haunted Life (*see The Haunted Life* (Kerouac))
   "Heaven" 39–40
   And the Hippos Were Boiled in Their Tanks 64
   "In America" 160, 166, 168 n.22
   "Lead killed Leadbelly" 39
   Lonesome Traveler (*see Lonesome Traveler* (Kerouac))
   Mexico City Blues viii–ix, 32–5, 37–8, 40, 53
   "Mexico City Blues 239–241" 33
   "October in the Railroad Earth" 37
   "Old Angel Midnight" 41

"Origins of the Beat Generation" 3, 163
Pic (*see Pic* (Kerouac))
Playboy 130
Poetry for the Beat Generation 32–4, 37–8
"The Roaming Beatniks" 80
Scattered Poems 37
The Scripture of the Golden Eternity viii, 74–6

The Sea is My Brother 149, 164
Some of the Dharma (*see Some of the Dharma* (Kerouac))
Wake Up: A Life of the Buddha 75, 78, 229
Wright, Richard, *Black Boy* 133–4

Zuboff, Shoshana 181, 185 n.34
  surveillance capitalism 177
Zwaska, Erin, *On the Open Road* 6